THIS VOLUME IS DEDICATED TO EARL W. STEVICK, PH.D., PIONEER IN THE FIELD OF LANGUAGE TEACHING.

Contents

Language acquisition: Learning and the learner

Language variation

Linguistics and teacher education

Introduction to the volume

James E. Alatis, *Chair, GURT '96*
Carolyn A. Straehle, *Coordinator, GURT '96*
Maggie Ronkin, *GURT Associate*
and Brent Gallenberger, *GURT Associate*

This volume contains the published version of papers from the 1996 Georgetown University Round Table on Language and Linguistics, also known as the Round Table, or GURT, for short. The theme of the 1996 conference, held March 14 through March 16, 1996, was "Linguistics, language acquisition, and language variation: Current trends and future prospects."

The 1996 conference, which was the forty-seventh annual Round Table, was sponsored by Georgetown University's Center for International Language Programs and Research. Each year, the Round Table brings together college and university professors, program administrators, researchers, Government professional staff, elementary- and secondary-school teachers, authors, and students of languages and linguistics. Scholars and students from the United States and other countries—Australia, Germany, Italy and Japan, to name a few—gathered to listen, discuss, and learn from one another.

The conference was opened by the Chair, James E. Alatis, the evening of Thursday, March 14. Dr. Alatis dedicated the proceedings of the 1996 Round Table to Earl W. Stevick, Professor Emeritus of Linguistics at the Foreign Service Institute, a pioneer in the field of language teaching. In recognition of his distinguished achievements in the field of linguistics and faithful friendship to the Round Table Conference, Dr. Stevick was awarded a distinguished achievement medal. The podium was then turned over to David Crystal, from the University of Wales, Bangor, who delivered the opening plenary address. The dedication to Earl Stevick and the plenary by David Crystal form the first section of this volume.

The rest of the conference featured seventeen other speakers in two full days of plenary sessions; an all-day, preconference tutorial by Stephen Krashen preceded the main conference. The broad theme of the 1996 Round Table conference allowed presenters the opportunity to examine language education and teacher education from a wide variety of perspectives. The articles in this volume are grouped into sections according to shared themes or approaches; within sections, they are organized alphabetically by the authors' last names.

A majority of the papers consider issues in second-language acquisition. The papers in "Language acquisition: Politics and policies" concentrate on the larger social and societal context in which language learning and acquisition occur. Among the topics highlighted is the current, often controversial, discourse on bilingual and multilingual education. In "Language acquisition: Learning and the learner," the articles deal more specifically with the roles of learners and instructors in language acquisition and learning.

In the section on "Language variation" are several contributions that examine language variation in creoles, endangered dialects, and languages of wider communication. This group of studies also addresses the implications of language variation on second-language-acquisition research and for language and community education.

Rounding out the volume is the section on "Linguistics and teacher education." The article in this section builds on the discussion of issues raised in earlier Round Table volumes, including the past, present, and future role of linguistics in language pedagogy. The closing and opening articles of this volume complement each other well, and to a great extent encapsulate the spirit of the 1996 conference.

In closing, we the editors wish to thank the other members of the Round Table staff who were instrumental in the organization of the conference: Wirote Aroonmanakun, Sarah Fearnow, Stefan Kaufmann, Hyouk-Keun Kim, and C. Ping Wei.

Dedication of Round Table Proceedings to Earl W. Stevick

James E. Alatis
Georgetown University

It has become a Round Table tradition to recognize important scholars in the field of languages and linguistics—scholars whose achievements have been many and distinguished, and whose association with this conference has been vital and significant—by dedicating the published *Proceedings* in their honor. Recent honorees have included Kenneth Pike, Robert J. Di Pietro, the Reverend Francis P. Dinneen, John B. Carroll, and Charles A. Ferguson.

To the roster of distinguished scholars whom the Round Table has recently recognized, we now add the name of Earl W. Stevick. Professor Emeritus of Linguistics at the Foreign Service Institute, U.S. Department of State, Earl Stevick is one of the most widely respected writers on the theory and practice of language teaching. He received his M.A. in Teaching English as a Foreign Language from Teachers College, Columbia University, in 1950, and his Ph.D. in Linguistics from Cornell University in 1955.

Ever since he tutored a fellow high-school student in Latin in 1940, Earl Stevick has dedicated his life to learning and teaching languages. During his long and illustrious career he has taught, supervised instructors, conducted teacher-training, and developed materials in English as a second language and a variety of uncommonly taught languages, such as Greek, Hebrew, Turkish, and Swahili and other African languages.

Professor Stevick has always been generous with his time and talents. In addition to the Foreign Service Institute, his employers have included the Methodist Church, the Peace Corps, and the University of Maryland. For over twenty-five years he has regularly conducted full-day seminars on language teaching for the School for International Training in Vermont. He has also offered courses on linguistics and language-teaching methodology at Linguistic Society of America and TESOL Summer Institutes, and for numerous institutions including Georgetown University and the Mediterranean Institute in Barcelona.

A scholar of extraordinary range and depth, Professor Stevick has integrated theoretical and applied concerns, demonstrating the intrinsic unity of scholarship. He is the author of more than a dozen books and textbooks and numerous articles. Among his more recent publications are *Memory, Meaning and Method*

(1976, 1996), *Teaching Languages: A Way and Ways* (1980), *Images and Options in the Language Classroom* (1986)—for which he received the Duke of Edinburgh Award, English Speaking Union (1987)—and *Humanism in Language Teaching*. So valued are his numerous accomplishments to the field of linguistics that he has also received the Mildenberger Medal from the Modern Language Association and the Lifetime Achievement Award from Heinle and Heinle Publishers.

The papers which Professor Stevick has delivered at Round Table conferences in the past constitute some of this meeting's most important contributions to the field of linguistics. Over the years he has also been a close personal advisor and source of advice about Round Table matters. I often refer to him as the philosopher of the language-teaching profession. It is, therefore, with great pleasure that, in recognition of his distinguished achievements in the field of linguistics, and in recognition of his faithful friendship to this Round Table Conference, we hereby dedicate the *Proceedings* of the 1996 conference in honor of Earl W. Stevick; and, as a token of our admiration, I present to him the GURT Distinguished Achievement Medal.

Playing with linguistic problems: From Orwell to Plato and back again

David Crystal
University of Wales, Bangor

Introduction. According to tradition, King Arthur devised the round table so that, when his knights were seated around it, none of them could claim precedence over the others. This has always seemed to me to provide an excellent precedent for those who have found their happiness levels circumscribed because they are unable to determine priorities among levels of linguistic representation. There is something intuitively satisfying about circles, and I have always found it helpful to work with a circular model in which different levels of language rest side by side, with none constituting a beginning or end, and all patently equal. I am very comfortable with this—apart from one thing: that the segments of the circle which identify each level all narrow inexorably towards a single, shared central point. This of course (models being the way they are) makes the naive linguist ask, What might be there? Is this where the linguistic equivalent of the Holy Grail lies? Is there a function which informs all linguistic levels—or at least, the three main ones (if you will allow me to state succinctly, or minimally, a contemporary—albeit déjà vu—formulation) of a phonetic component and a semantic component linked by some sort of computational procedure—or, as my alliterative module prefers to say: the levels of sound, syntax, and sense?

We all know that you see further when you stand on the shoulders of others. Chomsky's shoulders must be especially strong, given the numbers who have stood on them in recent decades, so they will hold my few pounds also. *Knowledge of Language* (Chomsky 1986: xxv) begins by drawing a distinction between two problems concerning human knowledge, which have passed into linguistic metalanguage under the headings of "Plato's problem" and "Orwell's problem." Plato's problem is defined as "the problem of explaining how we can know so much given that we have such limited evidence"—the obvious area of illustration being the existence of language acquisition in children. Orwell's is defined as "the problem of explaining how we can know so little, given that we have so much evidence"—the obvious area of illustration being the existence of institutionalized mind-sets which block our understanding (Chomsky's examples include various kinds of totalitarian systems). "To solve Orwell's problem we must discover the institutional and other factors that block insight and understanding in crucial areas of our lives and ask why they are effective" (1996: xxvii). Chomsky had originally intended to investigate Orwell's problem in his book, alongside Plato's, but decided not to do so, because "the character of inquiry into these two problems is so different" (1996: xxviii). The former, he asserts, is a question of scientific investigation; the latter one of socio-political inquiry, and, as a consequence, much less intellectually challenging. And he concludes his preface with the observation that, unless we can get to grips with Orwell's problem, and overcome it, the human race may not be around long enough to discover the answer to Plato's.

All of this makes an ideal frame of reference for the theme of this year's Round Table. The study of language acquisition, insofar as it helps to illuminate the nature of the language faculty, is of direct relevance to the solution of Plato's problem. The study of language variation, insofar as it draws attention to the distinctive way in which sociopolitical institutions use (or abuse) language, is of direct relevance to the solution of Orwell's. Linguistics sits in the middle, looking in both directions at once. The question for the linguist, it seems to me, is How do we relate these two perspectives? Let us call this "Crystal's problem"—for the next few pages, at any rate.

I'm not sure about the extent to which Orwell's problem is less of an intellectual challenge than Plato's, actually; but I do agree that unless we make some progress towards solving Orwell's problem we cannot fully solve Plato's. My impression is that the contrast between the two positions, as introduced by Chomsky, is there for rhetorical reasons. Indeed, after introducing it, Chomsky dispenses with it. There is no further reference to Orwell as he expounds Plato, and when he adds an appendix on Orwell, there is no reference to Plato within it. We are presented with two different worlds. These worlds can of course be related at an ideological, sociopolitical level, as people have recognized for some time: It is evident that a being with a language faculty of the kind which presents us with Plato's problem ought not to be treated in ways which are part of the characterization of Orwell's problem. But to be truly interesting as a linguistic (or sociolinguistic and psycholinguistic) issue, it ought to be possible to find an apolitical, purely linguistic account of the relationship between these two worlds. So, we arrive at Crystal's problem: How does our language ideology relate to the nature, development, and use of our language faculty? To answer this question, we need to move from Orwell to Plato, and back again.

From Orwell: Language as a regime. My starting-point is the nature of language as an institution in its own right. Language is not merely an exponent of the conceptualization of a regime; language is itself a regime. If Orwell's problem has to deal with "the institutional and other factors that block insight and understanding" (ibid.), then we must ask what factors in the way we study language block our understanding of language—and then move on to ask how these factors might be eliminated. But first, a simple example of the way in which Plato relates to Orwell, in the popular mind.

In Britain at the moment there is considerable debate about the way in which the new National Curriculum on English language, which has brought a fresh focus on language analysis, should best be implemented. There are two sources of tension, one internal to the school, one external. Internal tension arises between teachers who have been trained in different linguistic descriptive methodologies (those of traditional grammar versus one or other of the linguistics-inspired approaches) or who have received no training in analytical terminology at all. External tension arises between teachers who understand and are trying to implement the egalitarian and realistic principles of the new curriculum (which recognizes, for example, the importance of local dialect alongside the notion of national standard, and the inevitability of language change) and parents, school governors, and other commentators (who are invariably schooled in the prescriptive tradition, and for whom any recognition of dialect use and language change is an attack on standards, and another nail in the coffin that "trendy lefties" are preparing for the eventual demise of the English language).

Feelings run high in such circumstances, and when one finds oneself (as I do from time to time) having to run a workshop on language for a group of teachers, the situation can become volatile. And on one occasion it came to pass that the group was discussing a point of usage in students' written work—whether a serial comma (as in *tall*, *dark*, *and handsome*) should appear before the *and*. One teacher felt strongly that it should be there, and said he would correct a student's work which did not have it; another felt that it should not be there, and would cross it out, if a student used it. Neither person would yield, as they talked (correction: shouted) their way around the point. Eventually, one of them reacted to the other by saying: "That's just what I would expect from someone who wears a tie like yours!" The other person responded spiritedly, and within a minute the basis of the entire debate had shifted from the linguistic to the couturiological.

As linguists, we should not be surprised at the notion that linguistic argumentation should introduce nonlinguistic considerations. When we ourselves routinely invoke such enticing notions as elegance and simplicity when evaluating linguistic models and analyses (as in the modern application of Occam's razor in the minimalist program), we should not be too shocked to find linguistic arguments being routinely reduced to sociological ones. Linguistic discussion about usage leads inevitably to a discussion of linguistic standards and, just as inevitably, to a discussion of standards in general. It is a short jump from linguistic behaviour to social behaviour—and people are very ready to make it. In February 1996, in Britain, we heard the BBC Reith lectures, an annual series of intellectual enquiries held in honour of Lord Reith, who founded the BBC. This year, they were being given by a linguist, Jean Aitchison, who holds a chair at Oxford. (You will perceive that these lectures are very much an establishment domain.) In her first lecture, she addressed, in terms which have been familiar to linguists for over 50 years, the question of popular attitudes to language, and in particular the view that language is sick and deteriorating. She quoted Lord Tebbit, a senior government minister in 1985, who said: "If you allow standards to slip to the stage where good English is no better than bad English, where people turn up filthy ... at school ... all those things tend to cause people to have no standards at all, and once you lose standards then there's no imperative to stay out of crime." In a ferocious counterblast to what he perceived to be Aitchison's dismissive approach to standards, Paul Johnson, writing in *The Daily Mail* of 8 February 1996 (under the headline, "A woman wot hates English as it is writ"), comments: "Norman Tebbit is almost certainly right to assume that the decline of English standards in the school and the increase in crime are connected." In other words, split an infinitive today and you will be splitting heads tomorrow. End a sentence with a preposition, and you will end up with your own lengthy sentence. Indeed, it is enough to make you think of suicide, but that "the dread of something after death ... puzzles the will, And makes us rather bear those ills we have Than fly to others that we know not of" (*Hamlet*, III.i).

But you cannot win an argument through ridicule, or by quoting Shakespeare. If that were so, the Paul Johnsons of this world would have won two centuries ago, for their stock-in-trade is ridicule not reason. The matter was already being debated in precisely these ways not long after the publication of the grammars of Lindley Murray and Robert Lowth, in the eighteenth century, when such rules as "Never end a sentence with a preposition" were being promulgated. "It is no defence," these grammarians argued (though this is my paraphrase), "to cite Shakespeare as authority for such a usage (as in the *Hamlet* quotation). Even Shakespeare can commit grammatical error. He is only human. None of us is immune. That is why we must always be on our guard." The usage versus standards issue has been debated regularly and frequently over the past 250 years, on both sides of the Atlantic. Whether we look at the differences of opinion between Robert Lowth and Joseph Priestley in the 1760's, or the criticism of William Cullen Bryant by Fitzedward Hall a century later (Bolton and Crystal 1969: 41–53), or the arguments about usage in the great Webster dictionary debate a century later, the same points are being made on both sides. The points have often been made dispassionately, but the fact of the matter is that the vast majority of people remain unconvinced—or, perhaps more accurately, seem incapable of being convinced. Dissident linguists are pilloried in the press (and not only the conservative press). Any comment about being fair to divided usage is immediately construed as an attack on standards. The metaphors we are forced to live by are those of aggressive political radicalism.

The Paul Johnson article uses such phrases as "frontal assault on the rules" and "frivolous linguistic sabotage." We are close here to Orwell's world.

Indeed, the last 250 years has seen the largest and most successful exercise in popular brainwashing that I know of—largest, because it crosses linguistic and cultural boundaries with ease, and because within a language it affects everyone. Certainly questions of norms, deviations from norms, standards, acceptability, and related matters are in place long before children encounter formal education. We know that parents routinely draw their children's attention to matters of social linguistic etiquette from around age three, and often their comments reflect a linguistic orthodoxy which sees children as prone to error from the outset. "Don't talk with your mouth full." "Don't say that, it's rude." "You'll have nothing until I hear that little word" (e.g. *please*, or *ta*). "I won't hear any bloody swearing in this house." If there is a language acquisition device (LAD), for these parents it is a BAD LAD—a functional linguistic manifestation of original sin. And once in school, the institution takes over, and the "don'ts" continue, proliferating as the child gets to grips with written language. We now find a more formal manifestation of original syn(tax), both in speech—"Don't say ain't, Johnny." "That sort of language may be all right for the playground..."—and in writing, notably in the myriad corrections which appear in the margins of early essays, several of which (such as the opposition to sentence-initial *and*) are structurally unmotivated. The regime proves to be highly successful in instilling feelings of linguistic inferiority in most of us by the time we have learned to read and write.

Searching for explanations. BADLAD, of course, stands for "Blind And Deaf to Linguists' Arguments and Data." In a piece I wrote by way of commentary on the opening Reith lecture (*The Independent on Sunday*, 11 February, to be published in *English Today*), I expressed the view that the more interesting questions to address are to do with explanations rather than justifications: Why are people so reluctant to listen to linguistic reason? Why do they persist in believing that spoken language is sloppy, or that language is like a crumbling castle of former excellence, or that language change is a disease? Why do people continue to value written language over the spoken? Why is it so difficult to replace the view (only some two centuries old) that "we need eternal vigilance to keep the language intact" by a view of "eternal tolerance?" Indeed, why is it so difficult to be tolerant of other people's speech? Why do people ridicule accents, and are themselves so hurt when others attack the way they speak—even (there are several attested cases; for a report of one, see Crystal 1995: 298) referring to this as a factor in their suicide? The really interesting question is not Is our language sick? but Why do we want to think that our language is sick? Or, Why is language sickness thought to be so serious a disease anyway? and Why is it chronic? It is not enough to say, as linguists tend to say, that there is no disease—to point out that language change is the normal state of health. Why do people think that there is a disease in the first place? We don't need the linguistic equivalent of a physician, to help us: We need a psychiatrist.

Ten "why" questions is enough for one lecture, especially if the lecturer is not going to be able to answer any of them. But I am not alone: Linguists on the whole (the much missed Dwight Bolinger is one of the few exceptions; see Bolinger 1980) do not ask why, and even less often look for solutions. It is not enough for us to adopt a modern perspective, which would incorporate the prescriptive tradition into a sociolinguistic model, handling it seriously and not dismissively, and recognizing it as an important element in the history of language attitudes. If we have any applied linguist in us at all—and deep within all theoretical linguists I do believe there is an applied linguist trying to get out (not even Chomsky is immune, as Orwell's problem illustrates)—we need to go further, and aim for a more explanatorily adequate view.

One problem is that people have gone for educational solutions without spending enough time finding out about social explanations. In particular, there is a widely held view that increasing a person's (and specifically a child's) awareness of language, through sensitively devised and linguistically informed educational programs, will be enough to change deep-rooted language attitudes. Although I have been much involved in writing such materials myself in the U.K., in collaboration with teachers, I am not convinced that this is the answer. Materials of this kind have now been around since the 1960's. Several generations of school children have been exposed to linguistic ideas. But I see no sign that the latest generations of university students are any less insecure about their language, or less intolerant of other accents, than those of a generation before. They may be more able to understand the rational basis of the linguistic situation, but emotionally they are no nearer applying it to themselves. Why is this? Perhaps they are being unconsciously influenced by their parents, who lack schooling in the modern perspective, or by the pundits whose words are prominent in the papers and magazines they read. Certainly these days I frequently encounter the "external tension" I referred to above, in which teachers are taken to task by parents (or even grandparents) for not correcting a grammatical shibboleth in a pupil's usage, or for conveying the message (by permitting such projects as the study of slang or local dialects) that "anything goes." And when employers, politicians, and the Prince of Wales are on very public record complaining about falling standards of grammar, and illustrating these by such matters as split infinitives, what is an ordinary parent, let alone student, to believe? And what chance has an informed teacher, let alone a linguist, of altering the situation?

That there can be a major gap between intellectual and emotional acquiescence to beliefs about language is often unrecognized. We teach a class about linguistic equality and language attitudes, set assignments, and are satisfied if we find a fair number of A's and B's. We believe we have taught a point of view. We have not. We may have provided a mind with some intellectual content, but it does not therefore follow that we have reached a heart. I recall a fascinating discussion with an Arabic student who had attended such a course of mine, and who had got an A for his assignment. At an end-of-course departmental party, he took me on one side, and spent some time trying to persuade me that, although my views about languages being equal were largely correct, they needed to be qualified in one major respect, for I had not yet taken into account the underlying truth that Arabic has special status, among all languages, because of its role as the language of the Koran. He understood why I had not mentioned this, but left me in no doubt that the fault was mine. I looked again at his assignment. There was nothing in his written work to suggest that he held anything other than the orthodox linguistic view. He had conceptually accommodated to this linguist's mind-set, and he got an A for it. I do not yet know how to incorporate ideological perspectives of this kind (they are by no means unique to Islam, or even to religion) into my bread-and-butter linguistics. This I hope will be one of the topics which that branch of our subject sometimes called institutional linguistics will one day investigate.

So I am under no illusions about the difficulty of persuading people to change their attitudes about language, which may relate to deeply held feelings or beliefs about religion, ethnicity, history, and society in general. But before linguists talk of change, they should first attempt to explain where these attitudes come from. And perhaps it is easier to find explanations by reversing the "why" questions I asked above: Instead of asking Why do so many people have an inferiority complex about their own language?, let us instead ask Why do some people manage *not* to develop such a complex? I have carried out no survey, except on me, so I ask: Why do *I* not have one? What follows is a psychiatrically uninformed answer, and I am quite prepared for reanalysis later, in which it might transpire that, as the child of a Catholic mother and a Jewish father, growing up in a world in which the Irish optimism which forms one strand of my DNA is mixed with the Welsh gloom that forms the other, I was forced into a spiritual and ethnic confrontation which has given me no complexes at all. (I should explain the issue of Celtic mood: It is said that an Irishman, faced with a field of dancing daffodils, is likely to say "Praise be to God for those lovely flowers." A Welshman, faced with the same field, is likely to say "Duw [God], they'll be dead soon!" [Only a mixed-race Celt like myself dare tell this joke, by the way.])

I do believe, in all seriousness, that mixed backgrounds of this kind provide a fertile soil for the development of a linguistically secure state of mind. A largely neglected benefit of a bilingual environment—Welsh and English, in my case, with the occasional piece of Irish Gaelic thrown in—is the way in which the young learner is led, wide-eyed, into situations where the juxtaposition of different languages inevitably shapes a dynamic relativism—and the more volatile the culture (where one language is under threat, as in the case of

Welsh), the more likely is this dynamic to be emotionally foregrounded. Nor is it simply a matter of bilingualism. Holyhead, where I live, is a port town where Irish, Welsh, and English populations coexist, all using very different varieties of English. One of my earliest memories is of having my attention drawn to the fact that I was so accommodating—in the sociolinguistic sense, I hasten to add (not that the other sense was ever in question either). My accent changed as often as the high and low tides, but (unlike the tides) I do not recall ever feeling, diglossically, that one accent was high and the other low. I would be Irish with the Irish at church, Welsh with the Welsh at school, and English with the English in the streets. Then, at age ten, my family moved to Liverpool, where I spent the whole of my secondary school career carrying the nickname of "taffy," despite the broad Scouse (Liverpool) accent which grew within months. A degree course in London brought me into close contact with Received Pronunciation (RP, which I studied at length as part of my phonetics course), and marriage to an RP-speaking speech therapist would, some might expect, finally give me the chance to take on board God's own accent which had been missing all my life. RP did indeed have an influence on my public speaking voice—though, unlike the public-school boys of old, for me it is an extra accent, not a substitute accent—and the kind of modified RP I use in lectures lacks the consistency and character of that still spoken by the news-readers of the BBC. My equally accommodating wife, in the meantime, claims that my Scouse-Welsh mix has destroyed her own pure RP forever.

This biographical excursus is intended to make more than the point that my personal accent and dialect is, technically speaking, a Mess. It is to suggest that early close encounters with language and dialect variation, and an early history of social mobility might have been factors in explaining my present equanimity with regard to usage. It might even explain why I became a linguist. But we shall not find out until, both for the exceptions as well as the norms, we obtain case studies. The analogy with the early history of medicine is not misplaced: Before people could arrive at confident diagnoses, there were decades of single-subject case studies. If we take seriously the metaphors of sickness and disease which imbue popular attitudes to language, then before we can arrive at confident linguistic diagnoses we need to look into people's backgrounds. Yet a paradigm of sociolinguistic case studies, analogous to those which can be found in psycholinguistics or clinical linguistics, seems to be lacking—or when it appears it tends to be dismissed as anecdotal. But we should not miss out on the chance to use the techniques of oral history to accumulate information about language attitudes. The information is there, if we only take the trouble to listen. After a radio program on split infinitives I did once, a listener wrote to tell me: "The reason why the older generation feel so strongly about English grammar is that we were severely punished if we didn't obey the rules! One split infinitive, one whack; two split infinitives, two whacks; and so on." And he went on to make it clear that he didn't want all that suffering to be in vain, which is why he continued to complain whenever he heard a BBC presenter use one.

One thing we do not know is how representative such people are. A popular method of researching language attitudes is to collect corpora of data derived from newspaper letter columns, talkback radio programmes, and the like; but this produces a wildly unrepresentative sample—for the simple reason that the only people who write in about language are those who wish to complain about it. In 1986 I did a program for BBC Radio 4 in which I played people a piece of text in which various shibboleths had been hidden, and asked listeners to write and say what they thought of the language—I stressed I wanted good points as well as bad points. I got nearly a thousand letters, but only three said something positive. One other (from a 25-year-old housewife) said she did not know what the fuss was about. The generally negative nature of these communications is reflected in the BBC's mail bags every week, and in the press. When did you last read a letter to an editor praising someone for an elegant use of word order or an appropriate use of inflections?

It might be that error detection (i.e. perceived errors) is simply easier to do than strength detection (witness the history of error analysis, but not of strength analysis, in foreign language teaching). More likely, the negativism lies in the personal background of the writers. BBC research into the nature of their audiences can be illuminating, in this respect. In the case of my 1986 program, for example, it transpired that most of the listeners were in the upper age bands—mostly over 50. This means they went through school in the 1940's, long before any new language-teaching attitudes were being promulgated. (My solitary 25-year-old does not necessarily reflect a broadening of language attitudes. Admittedly, she would have been at high school in the early 1970's, when very little formal grammar teaching was taking place in British schools; on the other hand, she couldn't see any errors or strengths in the text I played—which rather suggests the need for some kind of formal language awareness teaching.) But in the absence of proper case studies, in which personality traits as well as personal educational histories are taken into account, it is difficult to say anything for certain.

I say "personality" advisedly. Two hundred fifty years of inferiority complexes and variety intolerance has led to a curiously schizoid public, where on the one hand people are ready to say they hate the dropping of *-ng* (in words like *fishin'*) as lazy and ugly when they hear it in the mouth of a schoolboy in inner-city Birmingham, then praise exactly the same effect as rustic and beautiful when they hear it in the rural speech of a Devonshire farmer. It is an overreacting public, too, well illustrated by the letter published in *The Listener* in 1981 during the week that the Pope was shot. The letter began: "Dear Sir, I was appalled ..." You would expect this letter to be about the assassination attempt; in fact, it was about a BBC presenter's use of grammar. If words like *appalled* are to be used with reference to grammar, one might wonder, what language is there left to express our feelings when people like popes get shot? Most letters, I also noticed, when doing these radio series, carried first- not second-class stamps—as if there was an urgency about the language observation. The impression was strongly conveyed: The bad news must reach the BBC as quickly as possible, otherwise it may be too late! I sometimes wonder what research programs into, say, language handicap in children might have been funded if all those second-class pence had been saved. And what political energies might have been rechannelled into the promotion of worthier causes if the attention of senior politicians had been directed less towards split infinitives and other such shibboleths, and more towards the genuine strengths and attractions of World Standard English, seen in relation to the difficulties of linguistic minorities and the plight of endangered languages. That is where the real issues are—as a U.S. audience, in these days of official English controversy, does not need to be told.

Searching for solutions. The search for explanations highlights what I believe is a neglected area of socio-psycho-linguistic research into the origins of language attitudes. If we were practitioners of scientific method, according to the theory, we would wait now until that research were complete before moving to a discussion of solutions. But no scientist I know is so scrupulous about method. Indeed, by investigating possible solutions, there may even be a chance that we shed some light on the nature of the explanations. The medics actually have a name for this way of proceeding, when carrying out a differential diagnosis: They call it "diagnosis by treatment" (Crystal 1988: 20).

The aim of the exercise is to engage people's interest in language in a positive way, so that the world of Plato (as illustrated in this talk by the notion of naturally emerging language acquisition) is brought into connection with that of Orwell (as illustrated here by the negative language attitudes imposed by a prescriptive linguistic regime). I do not believe it is possible to do this by a frontal assault on these established language attitudes: Notions such as the belief in language sickness, the fear of language change, the opposition to language deviance, and the intolerance of language variety, I am suggesting, are immune to linguists' tinkering. Rather, I think it is necessary to try out an alternative strategy, in which we focus on aspects of language which people value positively, and use these to demonstrate that such matters as change and deviance are not only normal, but are indeed widely practised and appreciated in contexts by exactly the same people who in a socio-educational context perceive them to be threatening.

There are of course many linguistic topics which do seem to attract positive interest. For example, most people seem to be fascinated by etymology, whether it be the history of personal names, place names, or vocabulary in general. There is also a genuine interest in language history—in such questions as the origins of language, or the links between human and animal communication. But these issues are all somewhat removed from present-day realities: They do not engage the emotions, because they are often so speculative. They also make us look back in time, whereas the worries we have been talking about are worries about the future. If we wish to establish an ethos of positive language attitudes, we need to look elsewhere. The ideal topic will be one which is as emotionally deep-rooted as the attitudes which we are trying to confront. It needs to be one which people perceive to be widely relevant to their lives. And because prescriptivism is based on a "bottom-up" approach—focusing on the identification of low-level, individual solecisms, drawing attention to forms at the expense of functions—any fresh approach ought ideally to be "top-down," giving centrality to texts as wholes, and where the end of achieving a particular functional effect is seen to justify the means.

My contention is that there is such an ideal topic: namely, language play. Of all areas of language use, I see language play as the one which is most capable of altering popular linguistic perceptions—powerful enough to "take on" prescriptive attitudes and provide an alternative, positive view of language. It has this power, I believe, because it is grounded in some of our earliest behavior in infancy, and is highly developed long before negative attitudes to language arise. It is a natural behavior—something which people do without conscious reflection. It is also pervasive—a democratic behavior, in the sense that everyone plays language games, without regard to educational background or social class; once a language has been learned as a mother tongue, no further special intellectual or physical skills are required. Because play is often incorporated within the educational process, there is a natural link with the development of early institutionalized linguistic thinking. And playing with language also presupposes the first step in metalinguistic awareness—the ability to step back and use (reflect on) language as an entity in itself. I conclude from these preliminary observations that, if we can promote people's awareness of what is going on in language play, it may well be that we are in a better position to draw their attention to the more serious "games" which can be played with language, such as those which are characterized by Orwell's problem, and perhaps provide a means of placing the games found under the prescriptive language regime in perspective.

In view of these claims, then, it is all the more surprising that language play has never attracted much attention within our subject. Ludic linguistics, as we may call it, has been curiously neglected. For example, we have journals on pretty well everything these days—over 130 routinely covered by *Linguistics Abstracts*—but none of them yet on language play. In a well-known collection, Kirshenblatt-Gimblett (1976) brought together a contemporary statement of research into the genre, but it did not lead to an explosion of interest. Perhaps the intellectual climate of the 1970's was too sombre to take the subject seriously. Or maybe the fact that speech play was routinely referred to as a "genre" kept it marginalized. For this paper, all I can do is argue that language play is much more than a genre. It is more than a ritual behaviour occasionally indulged in by secretive cliques, street gangs, children in the playground, and other groups beloved of anthropologists and ethnographers. It is more than a limited range of fixed-format structures, such as the riddle and the joke. It is more than the deviations from norms plotted by stylisticians or the interactive strategies lauded by discourse analysts. It is more important than to act as a piece of extra evidence to bolster up a phonological theory (as in the quaintly named "ludlings" much admired by non-linear phonologists). Language play, in my view, is—or should be—at the centre of our Round Table concerns as linguists.

Towards Plato: Adults at linguistic play. Everyone, regardless of cognitive level, plays with language or responds to language play. The responses range from the primitive pleasure experienced by severely mentally handicapped children when they hear dramatically contrasting tones of voice (in such interactive games as "peekaboo") to the cerebral bliss experienced by highly sophisticated connoisseurs as they explore the patterns of sound-play in, for example, James Joyce's *Finnegans Wake*. Between these extremes, there are the hundreds of books with titles such as *1000 Jokes for Kids* and, I'm afraid, *Another 1000 Jokes for Kids*, which are packed full of linguistically-based exchanges, read avidly (though with surprisingly unsmiling mien) by children—and not a few adults—all over the English-speaking world. Most of the jokes involve plays on words of all kinds, as in these examples from Katie Wales's *The Lights Out Joke Book* (1991). *Where does a vampire keep his money? In a blood bank* is a straightforward lexical pun. Most involve more than this, such as those which depend on phonological play (*What's a ghoul's favourite soup? Scream of tomato*), phonetic play (*Doctor, doctor, I've just swallowed a sheep! How do you feel? Very baaad*), graphological play (as in the book-title *Witch-hunting for Beginners by Denise R. Nockin*), or a fixed grammatical construction in the question stimulus (*What do you get if you cross a sheep with a kangaroo? A woolly jumper*).

Language play involves far more than jokes, however. I once counted all game shows on British radio and television, and found that two-thirds were language based. They included games in which the aim was to guess a word in a well-known phrase (*Blankety Blank*), to distinguish between real and false etymologies (*Call My Bluff*), to talk for a minute without hesitations or repetitions (*Just a Minute*), and several which built up words using randomly generated sequences of letters. Open the published broadcasting guides, and you would see such programme titles as *My Word*, *Catch Phrase*, and *Chain Letters*. The names will differ in the U.S.A., but the games will be broadly the same. Why are there so many such games? My own view is that language-based games are so popular because everyone can play them without training. Once you have learned to talk (or, for the writing-based games, to spell), you need no other special skill. It is not like *Mastermind*, a quiz game where you need to acquire a highly specialized area of knowledge, or *The Krypton Factor*, where you need above-average strength and athleticism. To participate in, say, *Blankety Blank*, all you need is your linguistic intuition about what word is most likely to fill the blank in such a phrase as, say, *life and* _____ (*limb, soul, death*). In such games we are all equal.

Media word games are only the tip of the iceberg of language games. There are hundreds of word games recorded in Gyles Brandreth's *The Joy of Lex* (1987), Tony Augarde's *The Oxford Guide to Word Games* (1984), or Ross Eckler's *Making the Alphabet Dance* (1996), for example, ranging from the familiar crossword puzzle and *Scrabble* to linguistic pastimes which are bizarre in the extreme. *Scrabble*, for example, is now thought to be the most widely played game in the English-speaking world, with a formal competitive dimension, a world championship, and associated books of commentary, just like chess. But think, for a moment, about what we are doing when we play *Scrabble*. It is a game where we set ourselves a physical limit (a grid on a board), assign numerical values to letters (based on our intuitions of frequency), and then hunt out and use the most obscure (because highly scoring) words in the language. This is not rational linguistic behaviour. Words don't normally 'score' anything. We do not listen to a sentence, then hold up score cards, as in an ice skating competition (even though some psycholinguists have hinted that something like this may go on when we have intuitions about grammaticality). Moreover, in *Scrabble* it is not even necessary to know what the words mean: All we need to know is that they exist. There are many publications which list all the words in English consisting of two letters, of three letters, and so on, or those which are most useful because they are highest scoring (such as *xebec*, *qaid*, and *haji*). None of them say what the words mean. If challenged, we look them up in a dictionary—and if we are playing "professionally," in the game's official dictionary (*Chambers*). In a market survey of dictionary use a few years ago, most people said they used their dictionaries most often when they were playing *Scrabble*.

The impulse to play with words makes us behave in a truly bizarre way. What could be stranger than deliberately constructing sentences which are difficult or impossible to pronounce, as in the popular tongue twister? Perhaps deliberately constructing a written sentence which only makes use of one vowel (a *univocalic*). A Victorian wordsmith, C. C. Bombaugh, constructed several poems based on this principle: "No cool monsoons blow soft on Oxford dons/ Orthodox, jog-trot, bookworm Solomons ...". Another game is to avoid the use of a particular letter of the alphabet (a *lipogram*)—not difficult with, say, Q or Z, but very difficult with the most frequent letters, such as E or T. Ernest

Wright wrote a 50,000-word novel, *Gadsby*, which made no use of letter *e*: "Upon this basis I am going to show you how a bunch of bright young folks did find a champion; a man with boys and girls of his own ..." Another is to find a word or a sentence which reads the same way in both directions (a *palindrome*), as in *madam* and *Draw o coward*—the longest reputedly over 65,000 words. Or constructing anagrams which make sense: You can, if you try long enough, take the letters of *total abstainers* and make up *sit not at ale bars*; *astronomers* produces *moon-starers*. There are competitions you can enter if you want to do this kind of thing. And, as a final example, there is the *pangram*, the target being to construct a meaningful sentence containing every letter of the alphabet, with every letter appearing just once. The typist's *The quick brown fox jumped over the lazy dog*, is a very poor pangram containing 36 letters. *Veldt jynx grimps Waqf zho buck* is a 1984 prize-winner, though you need recourse to a major dictionary to determine its meaning.

The long history of word play has some strange episodes. *Gematria* is probably the strangest—a medieval mystical practice in which secret messages were thought to be hidden in the letters of words. If we use modern English, and assign numerical values from 1 to 26, in serial order, to the letters of the alphabet, Gematria texts will show you some remarkable correspondences—identical totals, or adjacent totals, or totals separated by 100. If you add the numerical value for *arm* to that for *bend*, you get the total for *elbow*. *King* + *Chair* = *Throne*. *Keep* + *Off* = *Grass*. More significantly, according to its practitioners, *Jesus, Messiah, cross, gospel*, and *son God* each totals 74. Let me show you how it works, from the present conference. Why did Alatis end up a Dean? Because ALATIS is 62 and UNIVERSITY is 162. Why is Crystal at GURT? Because CRYSTAL totals 98 and GURT totals 66 (x3 = 198). Why are ALATIS and CRYSTAL sharing the same podium today? The numbers tell it all: 6x JAMES E. ALATIS is 690; 5x DAVID CRYSTAL = 690. People who know me well usually call me DAVE (32); people who know James E Alatis well call him JIM (32). We ought to get on famously, especially in WASHINGTON (130), the same as DAVE CRYSTAL (130). And where else could ROUND TABLES (131) develop but in WASHINGTON (130) and in GEORGETOWN (129), thus completing a series? Still, let's not get too cocky: That series can be capped by the combination of CLINTON and GORE (who together total 132). Is it especially significant that LANGUAGES = 87, and so does CLINTON? But I am not a political animal; therefore, let me say straight away that GEORGETOWN (129) also equals LAMAR ALEXANDER, and LINGUISTICS (142) equals PATRICK BUCHANAN.

What a waste of time! Or is it? I enjoyed the half-hour I spent seeing what would work out, and most people find the results amusing. I don't suppose we will try and live our lives by these numerical coincidences, as did happen in medieval times—only travelling on days whose value was felt to be auspicious, or arranging marriages on the basis of numerical identity. Some people get very serious about word games. For instance, you don't mess with crossword enthusiasts. I know a man who gets very nasty if he can't complete his *Times* crossword in an hour. And it is perhaps no coincidence that so many crossword compilers, such as Ximenes and Torquemada, chose as their pseudonym the name of a practitioner of the Spanish Inquisition. But most of us appreciate the fun involved in playing with our language, manipulating letters, searching for coincidences, looking for the unexpected links between words. It is all around us. Look on the walls of many a subway and you will find thousands of examples of linguistic ingenuity—the apparently unending set of variations on *—rules OK*, for example. Begun as a soccer fan's slogan, *Arsenal Rules OK?*, it has generated thousands of variants, and continues to do so. (Recent ingenious cases include *Archimedes rules—Eurekay*! and *Mallet rules croquet?*)

Some professions rely greatly on verbal play. Newspaper sub-editors all over the English-speaking world devise headlines or subheadlines with great ingenuity. From the *Sydney Morning Herald*, for example: *A shedentary life* (an article on men's garden sheds), *A roo awakening* (an article on gourmet kangaroo meat). Advertising agencies make their living by it. One of the most successful sequences in advertising history, still going after 20 years in the UK, is the word-play of the Heineken lager series, which began in 1974 with *Heineken refreshes the **parts** other beers cannot reach*, and which later included such word substitutions as *pilots, parrots, pirates, poets*, and *partings*, each accompanied by a failed visual situation (such as a poet unable to compose verse) which was then turned into an immediate success after ingesting quantities of the appropriate lager (Crystal 1995: 389). But this is not just a professional matter. Listen to any informal conversation, especially among young people (which is most of us) and there is evidence of language play: the mock regional tone of voice adopted when someone is telling a funny story ("There was this Irishman ... ") or the twisting of each other's words to score or make a silly point, as in the repartee which followed the arrival of someone whose arm was in plaster, in which various participants said such things as *No 'arm in it, Got to hand it to you, Put my finger on it, did I?* (Chiaro 1992: 115). Literature aside, everyday conversation is the most creative of language varieties.

Lastly, nonsense. It would be wrong to conclude this brief review of adult ludic language without some reference to the occurrence of controlled unintelligibilityas a feature of language play. At least all the above examples are meaningful. But literal nonsense also exists, in a range of everyday contexts from euphemistic swearing (where a nonsense word is used to avoid a blasphemy or obscenity) to the conversational use of such memory-fillers as *thingummy* and *watchamacallit*. Language play makes use of nonsense, too, as in the case of scat singing and, at a literary level, in such creations as Lewis Carroll's "Jabberwocky," many of the neologisms of James Joyce, or the crazy verbal concoctions of Ogden Nash. Malapropisms and spoonerisms are other famous examples. And while we are in the literary world, we should not forget the use of abnormal spelling as a source of language play, seen at its best in the oeuvres of Josh Billings and Artemus Ward, which so dominated the American social scene in the late nineteenth century (Crystal 1990; 1995: 84).

These examples are brought together to substantiate the view that verbal play is natural, spontaneous, and universal. It is practised in some shape or form by everyone, whether they are born jokers, or people who would never receive an Oscar for their sense of humour. It is not solely a matter of humour, after all, but involves notions of enjoyment, entertainment, intellectual satisfaction, and social rapport. Although patterns and preferences vary greatly, the phenomenon seems to cut across regional, social, and professional background, age, sex, ethnicity, personality, intelligence, and culture. (See the review by Kirshenblatt-Gimblett 1976.) Whether the motivation which drives it is innate or learned, I do not know; but when we examine the classic example of Plato's problem, child language acquisition, we see it there from the outset. From Scrabble, we therefore turn to babble.

Children at linguistic play. Language play is at the core of early parent-child interaction. We see it in the deviant linguistic behavior which characterizes much parental speech to babies—such features as higher and wider pitch range, marked lip rounding, rhythmical vocalizations, tongue clicking, mock threats, and simple, repetitive sentence patterns (Snow 1986). We see it in the words and rhythms of the songs parents sing—their lullabies and nursery rhymes. We see it in the early play routines parents use, in which considerable pleasure is taken by all participants in developing a dynamic language that complements the patterns of visual and tactile contact. Nuzzling and tickling routines, finger-walking, peeping sequences, bouncing games, build-and-bash games, and many other interactions are not carried on in silence: On the contrary, they are accompanied by highly marked forms of utterance (which people, incidentally, are often quite embarrassed to hear later out of context). Moreover, as Bruner and others have often pointed out (e.g. Ratner and Bruner 1978), these interactions have a clear-cut task structure, with a limited number of semantic components, considerable repetitiveness, and high predictability, and this promotes the emergence of a "play within the play": Having established in the child, through repeated occurrences, an expectation that a game is to develop in a particular way, parents are then very ready to disrupt this expectation, in the hope that it will elicit an even stronger response. For example, a game such as "round and round the garden," which has a rapid and highly tactile climax, is deliberately varied by introducing a pause before the climax—making the child "wait for it," in effect—and thus eliciting extra enjoyment. Given the remarkable emphasis placed upon language play in child-directed speech during the first months of life, one would expect it to be a central element in subsequent language development.

What is extraordinary is that the development of language play in the young child has been so little studied. Kirshenblatt-Gimblett provided an anthropological, cross-cultural perspective in 1976, but speech play seemed to fall out of fashion in the increasingly serious tone of academic linguistic discourse of the following years. In a general review, Ferguson and Macken commented (1983: 249): "In the sizeable literature on play languages which has come to our attention, we have not found a single study in which children's use of a particular play language is followed developmentally." And in a review of all issues of the leading journal in the field, *Journal of Child Language*, now over 20 years old, there is no paper on the general phenomenon, and only half a dozen on specific games, mainly from just one researcher. The domain is not mentioned at all in the standard child language anthology of the 1980's (Fletcher and Garman 1986) nor in the latest child-language anthology to appear, *The Handbook of Child Language* (Fletcher and MacWhinney 1995). However, from the limited literature which exists, some hints about developmental progress, at least for production, can be established. (See further Sanches and Kirshenblatt-Gimblett 1976.)

Phonetic play seems to be the first step. From around age one, children have been recorded in which long sequences of vocal modulation occur, with no one else around, which have been interpreted as a primitive form of vocal play (Garvey 1977). Vocalizations accompanying motor activities become noticeable between one and two—melodic strings of syllables, humming, chanting, singing. Symbolic noises increase, and sounds are brought in to represent actions, such as noises to represent ambulances, police cars, telephones, motor horns, and things falling down, and these may be lexicalized (*ding ling, pow pow, beep beep*). Children, often in pairs, begin to "talk funny," deviating from normal articulation: Everyone in the group talks in a squeaky or gruff way, for example, and the sounds themselves seem to be the main focus of the play (a contrast with the adoption of special tones of voice in games of pretend role play, later). They also begin to associate tones of voice with entities: In one babbling monologue, from a child aged 1;3, the babble accompanying play with a toy rabbit was uttered in a high pitch range, and that with a panda in a low pitch range.

Phonetic play is followed by more structured phonological play, from around age one introducing prosodic variations, producing language-specific, conversation-like utterance which is often referred to as "jargon" (Crystal 1986). From around age two, variations are introduced into syllable structure, using reduplication, sound swapping, and the addition of pause within a word. Bryant and Bradley affirm: "The two-and-a-half-year-old child recognize[s] rhyme and produce[s] rhyming sentences with ease: she also changes the very form of words which she knows to suit the rules of rhyme" (1985: 48). Garvey reports one girl of 3;0 who spent nearly 15 minutes engaged in taking apart and varying the syllabic structure of the word *yesterday*—the versions being mostly whispered in a soliloquy as she played with various objects in the room. This kind of play is typically a solitary behaviour, often heard in pre-sleep monologues, as reported in detail by Weir (1962): Her Anthony at around 2;6 produced many such sequences of the kind *bink ... let Bobo bink ... bink ben bink ... blue kink* ... Some were also meaning-related: *berries ... not barries ... barries ... barries ... not barries ... berries* ... We should not be surprised at this: When you are alone in the dark, at this age, there is not much else you can do but play with language. Delight in the sound of words is also reported by James Britton (1970), who tells the story of a small boy, brought to collect his father from a psychology conference, who went dancing through the hall chanting repeatedly the phrase "maximum capacity." "Words are voices" said one 2-year-old, when asked.

Within a year, these monologues can become very complex—Britton calls them "spiels" (1970: 83). They may be spoken alone or to an audience. An example from Clare, nearly three: "There was a little girl called May ... and she had some dollies ... and the weeds were growing in the ground ... and they made a little nest out of sticks ... for another little birdie up in the trees ... and they climbed up in the trees ... and they climbed up the tree ... and the weeds were growing in the ground ..." This is not communicative language: The tone of voice is sing-song, meditative, and there is no logic to the sequence of ideas. It is associative freedom, what Britton calls "a kind of celebration" of past experience—recall for its own sake, with repetition of favourite strings ("the weeds were growing in the ground" is repeated three more times in the next 10 clauses). It is a primitive poetry. Such speech may be dialogic in form, but the one child performs both parts in the dialogue. If there are other children in the room, they tend to ignore such vocalizations, not treating them as communicative. Sharing of language play seems to follow later. (An exception is the twin situation, where the twins do play with each other's vocalizations, as seen in the report on the Keenan twins (Keenan 1974).)

Between three and four, children start using each other's play language as a trigger for further variations. They may add rhymes: A says *Go up high*, B says *High in the sky*. They may alter initial sounds, sometimes to make real words, sometimes nonsense words: In one of Garvey's examples, A says *Mother mear (laugh), mother smear*, then *I said mother smear mother near mother tear mother dear*, B responds with *peer* and A adds *fear* (1977: 37). Bryant and Bradley report several examples of rhyme-play by 3- and 4-year-old children (1985: 47), such as *The red house / Made of strouss, I'm a flamingo / Look at my wingo*, and use this as evidence to support their hypothesis about the importance of rhyming and reading ability. By five, this dialogue play can be very sophisticated. There might also be morphological play, an ending being added to various nouns: *teddy* leads to *fishy, snakey*, and others. Here is another Garvey example, this time between children aged 5;2 and 5;7:

A: Cause it's fishy too. Cause it has fishes.
B: And it's snakey too cause it has snakes and its beary too because it has bears.
A: And it's ... it's hatty cause it has hats.

This is the first sign of children trying to outdo each other in verbal play, trying to score over the previous speaker, or maybe just trying to keep the game going, as in the adult *'armless* sequence (i.e. *No 'arm in it*) quoted above.

Original sin manifests itself in young children very early on. Once they learn a way of behaving, or are told how to behave, they seem to experience particular delight in doing the opposite, with consequential problems of discipline for the parent. This is obvious at the nonverbal behavioral level. What is less obvious is that exactly the same process goes on at the linguistic level. Being naughty with language seems innately attractive—the BADLAD notion again. From as early as three, children can be heard to home in on an inadvertently dropped adult obscenity with unerring instinct. Within hours of arriving at school they learn their own rude words, such as *bum* and *knickers*, which will keep them surreptitiously giggling throughout kindergarten. They will be rude at adults or other children by altering the sounds of words: *Dad Pad* said one 5-year old to me in a real fury, as he was stopped playing in order to have a bath. His whole demeanour showed that it was the worst insult he could imagine saying, to express his disapproval. And name-changing is done for fun, too. Nonsense names might be *Mrs. Poop, Mr. Ding, Mr. Moggly Boggly*, all coming from 4-year-olds. Nicknames appear soon after, and certainly after arrival in school. Older children often deliberately misname for fun, calling a cup a saucer, or mislabelling the objects in a picture. They break pragmatic rules, e.g. saying *good morning* when it is night time. I think all parents have encountered the "silly hour" when they seem unable to get their child to talk sense.

Verbal play exists in many forms by six, both serious and humorous, and rapidly increases in sophistication over the next few years. They demonstrate sophisticated concatenation games, in which one rhyme is joined to another in a list (Sanches and Kirshenblatt-Gimblett 1976: 88). Verbal games such as "Knock-knock" and "Doctor doctor" become fashionable after age seven. Riddle comprehension grows (Fowles and Glanz 1977), and the type of riddle used increases in sophistication (Sutton-Smith 1976). Wolfenstein's classic study (1954) shows how joke preferences and performances vary with age (from four to seventeen): She found an important transition at around age six, from the improvised and original joking fantasy to the learning and telling of ready-made jokes (typically the riddle): "With striking punctuality children seem to acquire a store of joking riddles at the age of six. As one six-year-old girl remarked: 'We didn't know any of these jokes last year'. Then later, at around 11, the formulaic structure of riddles gives way to a freer and more elaborate narrative." Metaphor studies also show a growth in awareness well into the teenage years (Gardner, Kircher, Winner and Perkins 1975). More "intellectual" language games, often of great intricacy, begin to be used. Cowan (1989) monitored a boy's acquisition of Pig Latin (where the onset of the first syllable is shifted to the end of the word, and followed by [ei], e.g. *please* becomes *izplei*) throughout the year preceding first grade (5;3–6;5). At the beginning of the period, the boy seemed unable to transform any words, after an explanation of the game, but performance improved over time. Cowan and his colleagues have also studied backwards speech in some detail, indicating some developmental changes in the ability of children aged eight/nine to talk back-to-front (Cowan and Leavitt 1982; 1987). Finally, there are the pseudo-intellectual games played by children of around ten ("If you insinuate that I tolerate such biological insolence from an inferior person like you, you are under a misapprehended delusion": See Sanches and Kirshenblatt-Gimblett 1976: 101) which continues into the early years of high school (as nicely portrayed in the adolescent use of group solidarity nonsense which is the title of Jack Rosenthal's television play *P'tang yang kipperbang*, 1982).

Statistics on verbal play are few. In several studies on metaphor development, the frequency of figurative language in the language children hear around them is strongly stressed: Nearly 40% of teachers' utterances to students in Grades 1–8 contain nonliteral uses (Lazar, Warr-Leeper, Nicholson and Johnson 1989), and its frequency in reading materials for older children is regularly stressed (Milosky 1994). Wolfenstein makes some useful comments on joking preferences: "At six or seven about three times as many joking riddles are told as jokes in any other form. In the following three years the percentage of riddles is little over half. At eleven or twelve it is reduced to a third; riddles are being discarded in favor of anecdotes" (1954: 94). In an informal collection, Sanches and Kirshenblatt-Gimblett (1976: 101) found that Opie-type rhymes varied from an average of one per child at age five to a peak of six per child at age eight, thereafter decreasing until about the age of eleven "at which point interest in many of these kinds of productions drops off sharply and other kinds of verbal art ... appear to be of greater interest" (1976: 102). Esposito (1980) found that word and sound play occurred in 13% of the experimentally elicited utterances of 3- to 5-year olds, though a third of the subjects showed none at all at that age. Ely and McCabe (1994) looked at several categories of language play in children between 5;5 and 6;8, and found instances in 23% of the utterances—almost one in four. Their context was natural discourse, where it is evidently much more common than in experimentally controlled settings or those where a teacher or other adult is present. Language play here was defined broadly: It included distinctive sound play (repetitive, rhythmic or melodic phonation, onomatopoeic sound effects), word play (e.g. rhyming, neologisms, metaphor), role play (adopting another voice), and verbal humor (including riddles, jokes, teases, nonsense remarks, and jokey allusions, such as *What's up doc?*). Sound play represented nearly a third of all language play, showing the persistence of this modality from the first years of life.

It is difficult to escape the conclusion that language play is an important element in language development. The point is nowhere more strongly stressed than in Chukovsky's book, where he refers to

> the inexhaustible need of every healthy child of every era and of every nation to introduce nonsense into his small but ordered world, with which he has only recently become acquainted. Hardly has the child comprehended with certainty which objects go together and which do not, when he begins to listen happily to verses of absurdity. For some mysterious reason the child is attracted to that topsy-turvy world where legless men run, water burns, horses gallop astride their riders, and cows nibble on peas on top of birch trees. (1963: 96)

The various collections of children's play make this point empirically—the vast amount of rhyming material in Opie and Opie (1959), for example, in such domains as counting out, jumping rope, or bouncing ball, much of which is so nonsensical that the only possible explanation can be delight in the sound as such. As the Opies say, at the very beginning of their book, "Rhyme seems to appeal to a child as something funny and remarkable in itself, there need be neither wit nor reason to support it" (p.17). The "tumbling and rhyming" (a description by Dylan Thomas) of children as they spill out of school is universal. And if one asks why they do it, there is no better account of the various factors than that provided by the Opies who, commenting on the jingle "Oh my finger, oh my thumb, oh my belly, oh my bum," remark that this "is repeated for no more reason than that they heard someone else say it, that they like the sound of the rhyme *thumb* and *bum*, that it is a bit naughty, and that for the time being, in the playground or in the gang, it is considered the latest and smartest thing to say—for they are not to know that the couplet was already old when their parents were youngsters" (p.17).

Piaget and Vygotsky, among others, had already drawn attention to the notion of "play as practice": Children are most likely to play with the skills which they are in the process of acquiring. And Bruner comments that language is "most daring and most advanced when it is used in a playful setting" (1984: 196). The persisting absence of language play is likely to be an important (though hitherto little remarked upon) diagnostic feature of language pathology.

Chukovsky (1963) suggests as much, with reference to rhyme: "Rhyme-making during the second year of life is an inescapable stage of our linguistic development. Children who do not perform such linguistic exercises are abnormal or ill." And indeed, children with language delay or disorder are known to have very poor ability even to imitate simple patterns of language play (copying rhythmic beats, for instance), and tend not to use it spontaneously.

But which aspects of language development is verbal play related to? It would seem: all of them. The play as practice model suggests that it makes a major contribution to phonological development through its focus on the properties of sounds and sound contrasts; there are examples of morphological play in the literature, and the riddle is a genre which heavily depends on syntax for its effects; playing with words and names, and the notion of nonsense, suggests a link with semantic development; and the kinds of dialogic interaction illustrated above suggests that there are important consequences for pragmatic development. Sanches and Kirshenblatt-Ginblett (1976: 102) suggest there may be a developmental progress in the child's interests, moving from phonological to grammatical to semantic to sociolinguistic, but the situation is undoubtedly much more complex. Above all, it is suggested that language play, by its nature, contributes massively to what in recent years has been called metalinguistic awareness, which in turn is a major element in language awareness.

It is important, at this point, to stress that language play is not the same as language awareness. In recent years, a great deal of attention has been paid to language awareness in general: There is now a whole journal devoted to the topic (*Language Awareness*, from 1992). But this topic is a very broad one: It includes, for example, adult awareness of the functions of different languages within a community as well as issues to do with the learning of foreign languages. Language play is just one piece of the evidence to show that children are developing their linguistic awareness. Similarly, language play is not the same as metalinguistic awareness. The latter is also a much broader notion, including all reflective activity relating to language. Metalinguistic awareness is the ability to understand and use words and terms for talking about language (from the most primitive, such as describing a tone of voice as "high" or "loud," to the most complex, such as describing the syntactic structure of a subordinate clause). Much of the above discussion is only indirectly related to metalinguistic skills, and conversely, a great deal of what goes on under the heading of metalanguage is nothing to do with language play. Ability to name the letters of the alphabet is part of metalanguage, but is not language play. The same applies to a child's ability to say that certain words begin or end with the same sound, or to describe words as nouns and verbs: This is not part of language play. On the other hand, language play and metalinguistic skills have one thing in common: They both involve the person "stepping back" from language—in the case of language play, by intuiting the norm and manipulating it; in the case of metalinguistic skills, by talking about what is normal or abnormal.

The relevance of all this to later language skills should be apparent. Sanches and Kirshenblatt-Gimblett(1976: 105) conclude that "speech play is instrumental to the acquisition of verbal art" (by which they mean eloquence, rhetoric, poetry, etc.). And there is an equally apparent link with reading: Several authors have concluded that the ability to manipulate language is associated with success in learning to read. We know that early awareness of nursery rhymes can predict later literacy skills (Bryant and Bradley 1985), and ability to understand riddles seems to have some relationship to reading ability, both according to teacher report (Hirsh-Pasek, Gleitman and Gleitman 1978) and in relation to a reading ability test (Ely and McCabe 1994). Phonological awareness has been isolated as "a major determinant of the early acquisition of reading skill and one of the keys to the prevention of reading disability" (Stanovich 1987: 22). Play with language is a direct contributor to metalinguistic awareness (Cazden 1976), and as reading and writing are first and foremost metalinguistic tasks—they are both one remove away from the natural state of speech, and in almost all cases are interpreted through the medium of speech—it is obvious that language play is likely to relate to later literacy achievement (though it is conspicuous by its absence from most reading materials: See Crystal 1996).

And back again. The aim of my paper has been to find a way in which two very different kinds of linguistic concern—characterized as Plato's problem and Orwell's problem—can be interrelated. I believe that the task of forging such a relationship is important, in order to develop a conception of theoretical linguistics which applies equally plausibly to phonological, syntactic and semantic domains, on the one hand, and to sociolinguistic, psycholinguistic, pragmatic, and applied linguistic domains, on the other. Language play is of direct relevance to both: Because it is based on the notion of formal manipulation—of sounds, structures, sense—it bears directly on the nature of deviance, which is a critical element in our sense of the grammatical. And because it is chiefly motivated by the desire to create an effect in others, it bears directly on fundamental issues in pragmatics, acquisition, and variation, as well as on our judgments about what counts as creativity. If anything should be proposed as a Grail at the centre of the 1996 Round Table, therefore, given its theme, it ought to be language play.

Apart from this general motivation for a renewed focus on ludic linguistics, I have also argued that it could be a promising means of getting to grips with the negative language attitudes associated with the prescriptive tradition which linguists routinely encounter. I hope it is not too much to suggest that, if some progress can be made with this regime, we may learn something about how to tackle the more dangerous games that people are known to play with language, and which motivated Chomsky's original characterization. But that is for the future. All I have done today is begin with a manifestation of Orwell's problem, propose a way forward in the form of language play, and turn to Plato for a helpful perspective. By getting Plato talking back to Orwell, I think I have solved Crystal's problem—though, admittedly, I may have to use James Joyce as a translator.

REFERENCES

Augarde, Tony. 1984. *The Oxford guide to word games*. Oxford: Oxford University Press.

Bolinger, Dwight. 1980. *Language: The loaded weapon*. New York: Longman.

Bolton, Whitney and David Crystal (eds.). 1969. *The English language, Volume 2*. Cambridge, U.K.: Cambridge University Press.

Britton, James. 1970. *Language and learning*. London: Allen Lane.

Brandreth, Gyles. 1987. *The joy of lex*. London: Guild Publishing.

Bruner, Jerome. 1984. "Language, mind, and reading." In H. Goelman, A. Oberg, and F. Smith (eds.), *Awakening to literacy*. Exeter, New Hampshire: Heinemann.

Bryant, Peter and Lynette Bradley. 1985. *Children's reading problems*. Oxford: Blackwell.

Cazden, Courtney B. 1976. "Play with language and metalinguistic awareness: one dimension of language experience." *Urban Review* 7: 28–39.

Chiaro, Delia. 1992. *The language of jokes: Analysing verbal play*. London: Routledge.

Chomsky, Noam. 1986. *Knowledge of language*. New York: Praeger.

Chukovsky, K. 1963. *From two to five*. Berkeley, California: University of California Press.

Cowan, Nelson. 1989. "Acquisition of Pig Latin: A case study." *Journal of Child Language* 16(2): 365–386.

Cowan, Nelson and Lewis A. Leavitt. 1982. "Talking backward: exceptional speech play in late childhood." *Journal of Child Language* 9(2): 481–495.

Cowan, Nelson and Lewis A. Leavitt. 1987. "The developmental course of two children who could talk backward five years ago." *Journal of Child Language* 14(2): 393–395.

Crystal, David. 1986. "Prosodic development." In Paul Fletcher and Michael Garman (eds.), *Language acquisition, Second edition*. Cambridge, U.K.: Cambridge University Press. 174–197.

Crystal, David. 1988. *Introduction to language pathology*. London: Whurr.

Crystal, David. 1990. "Linguistic strangeness." In Margaret Bridges (ed.), *On strangeness*. Swiss Papers in English Language and Literature, 5. Tübingen: Gunter Narr Verlag. 13–24.

Crystal, David. 1995. *The Cambridge encyclopedia of the English language*. Cambridge: Cambridge University Press.

Eckler, Ross. 1996. *Making the Alphabet Dance*. New York: St. Martin's Press.

Ely, Richard and Alyssa McCabe. 1994. "The language play of kindergarten children." *First Language* 14(1): 19–35.

Esposito, A. 1980. "Children's play with language." *Child Study Journal* 10: 207–216.

Ferguson, Charles A. and Marlys Macken. 1983. "The role of play in phonological development." In Keith E. Nelson (ed.), *Children's language, Volume 4*. Hillsdale, N.J.: Erlbaum.

Fletcher, Paul and Michael Garman (eds.). 1986. *Language acquisition, Second edition*. Cambridge: Cambridge University Press.

Fletcher, Paul and Brian MacWhinney (eds.). 1995. *The handbook of child language*. Oxford: Blackwell.

Fowles, Barbara and Marcia E. Glanz. 1977. "Competence and talent in verbal riddle comprehension." *Journal of Child Language* 4(3): 433–452.

Gardner, Howard, Mary Kircher, Ellen Winner, and David Perkins. 1975. "Children's metaphoric productions and preferences." *Journal of Child Language* 2(1): 125–141.

Garvey, Catherine. 1977. "Play with language and speech." In Susan Ervin-Tripp and Claudia Mitchell-Kernan (eds.), *Child discourse*. New York: Academic Press, 27–47.

Hirsh-Pasek, Kathryn, Lila R. Gleitman, and Henry Gleitman. 1978. "What did the brain say to the mind? A study of the detection and report of ambiguity by young children." In W. J. M. Levelt , A. Sinclair, and R. J. Jarvella (eds.), *The child's conception of language*. New York: Springer Verlag.

Keenan, Elinor Ochs. 1974. "Conversational competence in children." *Journal of Child Language* 1(2): 163–183.

Kirshenblatt-Gimblett, Barbara (ed.) 1976. *Speech play: Research and resources for studying linguistic creativity*. Philadelphia: University of Pennsylvania Press.

Lazar, Rhea Tregabov, Genese A. Warr-Leeper, Cynthia Beel Nicholson, and Suzanne Johnson. 1989. "Elementary school teachers' use of multiple meaning expressions." *Language Speech and Hearing Services in the Schools* 20(4): 420–429.

Milosky, Linda M. 1994. "Nonliteral language abilities: Seeing the forest for the trees." In Geraldine P. Wallach and Katharine G. Butler (eds.), *Language learning disabilities in school-age children and adolescents*. New York: Merrill. 275–303.

Opie, Iona and Peter Opie. 1959. *The language and lore of schoolchildren*. Oxford: Oxford University Press.

Ratner, Nancy and Jerome Bruner. 1978. "Games, social exchange and the acquisition of language." *Journal of Child Language* 5(3): 391–401.

Sanches, Mary and Barbara Kirshenblatt-Gimblett. 1976. "Children's traditional speech play and child language." In Barbara Kirshenblatt-Gimblett (ed.), *Speech play: Research and resources for studying linguistic creativity*. Philadelphia: University of Pennsylvania Press. 65–110.

Snow, Catherine. 1986. "Conversations with children." In Paul Fletcher and Michael Garman (eds.), *Language acquisition, Second edition*. Cambridge: Cambridge University Press. 69–89.

Sutton-Smith, Brian. 1976. "A developmental structural account of riddles." In Barbara Kirshenblatt-Gimblett (ed.), *Speech play: Research and resources for studying linguistic creativity*. Philadelphia: University of Pennsylvania Press. 111–119.

Stanovich, K.E. 1987. "Introduction: Children's reading and the development of phonological awareness." *Merrill-Palmer Quarterly* 33 (3): 175–190.

Stanovich, K.E. 1991. "Changing models of reading and reading acquisition." In L. Rieben and C.A. Perfetti (eds.), *Learning to read: Basic research and its implications*. Hillsdale, N.J.: Erlbaum. 19–31.

Weir, Ruth H. 1962. *Language in the crib*. The Hague: Mouton.

Wolfenstein, Martha. 1954. *Children's humor: A psychological analysis*. Glencoe, U.K.: Free Press.

Language development in two-way immersion: Trends and prospects

Donna Christian
Center for Applied Linguistics

Introduction. Two-way bilingual immersion (or two-way bilingual education) blends the goals and methodologies of language immersion for majority language speakers (in the United States, English language speakers) with maintenance bilingual education for minority language speakers. In these programs, students from two language backgrounds (the majority language and one minority language) receive academic instruction together in both languages. The students are integrated for most, if not all, of their instruction. Typical goals for such programs include: high academic achievement; high levels of proficiency in the native language and a second language; and positive cross-cultural attitudes and understanding.

Differences between two- and one-way immersion stem primarily from the presence of native speakers of the target language in significant numbers in the classes. In one-way immersion, all (or nearly all) of the students are immersed in a language that they do not speak natively. (For example, in a French total immersion program in the United States, English-background first graders learn 80% to 90% of their academic content in French-medium instruction.) The primary model for the new language being learned is the teacher, and the language may not be used widely in the local community or the society at large. In two-way immersion, half of the students are native speakers of the target language, so they can be models and resources for English speakers during instruction through the target language. (For example, in Spanish-English two-way programs, fluent Spanish speakers are integrated with English-background students during Spanish-medium instruction, and vice versa.) One consideration for programs, then, is how to maximize the use of peer resources for language learning.

A similar comparison can be made with bilingual education. As they have evolved in the United States, bilingual programs do not typically include native speakers of English, while two-way programs do, making available peer language models and resources during English-medium instruction for language minority students. The fact that classes are heterogeneous also addresses the concern that bilingual programs may isolate language minority students from others in their school and community. Most bilingual programs today do not foster maintenance of the students' native language; instead, they generally aim to move students into all-English instruction as soon as possible.[1] Two-way programs, on the other hand, continue to provide substantial amounts of instruction in the native language, even after proficiency in English has developed, and thus facilitate maintenance and development of the native language for language minority students along with high levels of English. Bilingual programs often suffer from social and political controversy surrounding them, as well as from frequent characterization as remedial programs for disadvantaged students. Depending on the orientation of the school and the community, two-way programs may inherit some of these negative attitudinal features, or they may escape them.

Thus, two-way programs bring potential advantages for language learning when compared with other language instruction contexts. This paper will examine the promise of language development in these programs and how the promise is being realized (bearing in mind that this is just one of several important goals in these classrooms[2]). After a brief discussion of two-way immersion in practice, I review some findings of ongoing research and consider some factors that may affect the development of proficiency, including individual student characteristics, instructional and program characteristics, school features, and the sociolinguistic context of the local community and beyond. Finally, I summarize by commenting on prospects for the future and issues that deserve further attention.

Language development in two-way immersion: The promise. Although two-way immersion is by no means uniformly implemented across sites, some generally shared features promise to promote dual language development for students in these programs. All students receive substantive, meaningful content instruction in their native language (L1) and in a second language (L2) and interact with peers who, as native speakers, are expert resources in the second language their fellow students are learning. In addition to the assistance in understanding content instruction that may be provided, recent research indicates that interaction with native speakers may provide better input and feedback for language learners than interaction with other L2 learners (Pica et al. 1996).

Thus, two-way immersion appears to offer conditions conducive to second language development. For native speakers of English, immersion in another

---

[1]This goal is widespread, despite evidence that sustained cognitive development in the native language is a key factor in promoting academic success for language minority students (Collier 1995).

[2]Academic and social outcomes of two-way immersion programs must be recognized and valued. There is evidence of positive results in both domains, including in the study reported on here. See Collier (1995), Lambert and Cazabon (1994), Barfield (1995), and Lindholm (1996), among others.

language is a proven approach and the availability of peer models would be expected to enhance the experience. For language minority students, access to sustained academic development in the native language while adding English in meaningful ways, along with the ability to turn to peers as resources, would similarly be expected to lead to high levels of bilingual proficiency. The environment in two-way schools and classrooms is by definition an additive one, where both languages are highly valued and supported. Thus, the two-way model holds great promise for building dual language proficiency among students in both groups.

Two-way immersion in the United States. Two-way immersion appears to be gaining in popularity in the United States, and we are beginning to develop a knowledge base (and a growing list of questions) about the approach. In a 1995 study, 182 schools reported operating some form of two-way immersion (compared with 30 schools located by Lindholm (1987)). These schools are located in 18 states and the District of Columbia, and the programs include more than 25,000 students (Christian and Whitcher 1995). The vast majority of programs offer instruction in Spanish and English and are found in elementary schools. Target languages other than Spanish include Korean, French, Navajo, Cantonese, Japanese, Arabic, Portuguese, and Russian. Many programs are relatively new; about two-thirds of the schools have offered two-way immersion for five years or fewer.

For those who have not been in a two-way immersion classroom, it may be helpful to describe this educational setting. Brief profiles of three schools covered in the study reported on here can serve as illustrations. (For a fuller discussion of the case studies, see Christian et al. 1996). They exemplify the most common type of program: elementary schools with Spanish and English as the languages of instruction. Unlike most programs, however, they have all been in operation eight or more years.

Site A. Located in the eastern United States, this program extends from kindergarten through fifth grade at an elementary school site (with extensions at a middle and a high school). Students from Spanish- and English-speaking backgrounds learn together in a modified magnet arrangement (about half of the students live in the school's neighborhood district). The program was established in 1986 with a single first grade class, and in 1994–1995, 318 students participated out of 600 total in the school; in 1995–1996, the school became entirely two-way. Throughout the program, all students receive half of their instruction in Spanish and half in English on a daily basis. The language switch occurs at lunch time, when classes move from one language medium to the other. For example, a second grade class may learn language arts, reading, and mathematics in the morning in English, and then deal with language arts, social studies, and science in the afternoon in Spanish. Since much of the subject matter instruction is organized thematically, there is opportunity to treat all disciplines in both languages on a regular basis.

Site B. This program, in the western U.S., operates school-wide for 380 students in preschool through Grade 6. It serves as a magnet school in the district's desegregation plan. Like Site A, the program was founded in 1986, bringing together Spanish and English language background students. The school is currently about two-thirds Latino. Site B follows the "90/10" model: in kindergarten and first grade, all students have 90% of their instruction in Spanish, with 10% of the time devoted to oral English language development. All students learn initial literacy in Spanish. During English time, students develop oral English skills through literature, poetry, and music. In second grade, the amount of English time is increased to 15%, and in third grade, to 20%, when English literacy is introduced. Fourth and fifth grades are 60% Spanish/40% English, and in sixth grade, instruction is evenly divided between the two languages.

Site C. Site C is a magnet school for Grades K through 8 in a large city in the midwestern United States. It currently serves 630 students, 60% from low income families; when they enter, about 40% of the students are limited English proficient, 20% are bilingual, and 40% are monolingual English speakers. The school-wide two-way program was established in 1975 using a "50/50" model, but the instructional plan was later changed because it was felt that students were not gaining enough Spanish proficiency. As a result, the program now operates on an "80/20" basis, as follows: In kindergarten through third grade, 80% of instruction is given in Spanish. Students are grouped by language background for language arts instruction (the only time they are separated), and all students learn to read in their native language. In fourth through sixth grades, Spanish is the language of instruction 60% of the time and, in seventh and eighth grades, instruction is evenly divided by language.

Language development in two-way immersion. Although this paper focuses on language development, it is important to remember that this is not the only goal of two-way immersion. These are comprehensive educational programs with strong academic and social growth dimensions, and they respond to and reflect all the advantages and constraints of the local context and resources. My review of language development findings deals briefly with oral language proficiency and literacy in two languages and then turns to some observations about language use and language choice.

Language proficiency. All three sites report impressive levels of oral proficiency in both Spanish and English among all students. In general, on tests like the Language Assessment Scales, students score as fully fluent in both languages by fourth or fifth grade. Spanish speakers tend to reach the highest scores in oral English somewhat before English speakers reach the same level in Spanish. Site A administers the Language Assessment Scales-Oral (LAS-O) to measure English language development, for example. This program reported that, by third grade, 78 percent of students scored at the highest level (5) and the other 22 percent were at level 4, with both native speakers of English and Spanish performing comparably. At the end of the school year, Spanish oral proficiency was recorded on a teacher rating scale, assessing comprehension, fluency, vocabulary, pronunciation, and grammar. With 25 as the maximum, average scores moved from 16.85 in kindergarten, through 20.23 in second grade, to 22.50 in fifth grade.

LAS-O results for Site B were reported for both English and Spanish, with students identified by language background. All native speakers, not surprisingly, were rated as fully proficient in their L1 at all grade levels. Non-native speakers were for the most part rated fully proficient in their L2 by third or fourth grade. Among Spanish speakers, 50% were fully English proficient at the end of first grade, and 100% were fully proficient by fourth grade. For English speakers, 47% scored as fully Spanish proficient at the end of first grade, and by fifth grade, 100% were fully proficient.

Thus, our picture of oral proficiency, at least in these programs, indicates strong skills in both languages by third or fourth grade.

Proficiency is also a factor in other standardized test scores that were reported. Site A administers the Iowa Test of Basic Skills (in English) to all fourth graders. The average percentiles for two-way immersion students on the language and reading subtests can be compared to those for other fourth graders in the school district and the state. In the 1995 administration, the program average (for both Spanish L1 and English L1 students) exceeded both district and state levels. (See Table 1.)

Table 1. Site A: Average percentiles on Iowa Test of Basic Skills, 1995 (Grade 4)

	Subtest: Language	Subtest: Reading	Subtest: Math
Site A	79	89	93
District-wide	71	74	81
State-wide	64	61	66

Site B administers the Comprehensive Test of Basic Skills (CTBS) each year to assess reading and mathematics in both Spanish and English. The percentile averages for this test for Grades 1, 3, and 6 appear in Table 2. When reviewing the percentiles, it is important to remember that students are not introduced to reading in English until the third grade in this program. Although some fluctuation occurs, these results suggest strong performance in the native language and growth in second language achievement.

Table 2. Site B: Average percentiles on Comprehensive Test of Basic Skills (Grades 1, 3, 6)

		Spanish		English	
Grade	L1	Reading	Math	Reading	Math
1	Spanish	76	72	15	48
1	English	73	64	27	68
3	Spanish	67	69	29	83
3	English	44	68	49	49
6	Spanish	63	62	36	59
6	English	45	58	79	87

Site C shows similar results when assessing achievement through Spanish (using La Prueba Riverside de Realización en Español) and English (using a state-wide assessment). The Spanish achievement averages by grade level for Grades 3 through 8 are shown in Table 3.

Table 3. Site C: Average percentile scores for reading and writing achievement in Spanish

Grade	Reading	Writing	Grade	Reading	Writing
3	69.1	67.0	6	61.3	53.2
4	64.5	70.0	7	58.9	66.8
5	60.6	62.2	8	61.9	57.0

On the English state-wide assessment, 79% of third graders and 71% of eighth graders met and exceeded the state goals in reading (compared to 45% and 49%, respectively, district-wide). For writing, the performance of these students was even higher.

These selected assessment results are not intended to give a detailed picture of language development and growth, but rather to serve as indicators confirming the reports of teachers and administrators that dual language proficiency is being developed, including the ability to use a second language to demonstrate subject matter mastery.

Language use and language choice. Observations at all three sites complemented and extended the picture of language development available from the measures mentioned above. Throughout grade levels, in their L1, both Spanish and English speakers maintained their fluency and expanded the complexity of their grammar, vocabulary, and other language skills. As mentioned above, students progressed steadily in their second language as well. By fourth or fifth grade, it was generally reported that English L1 and Spanish L1 students could not be distinguished when they spoke English.

The findings for English L1 students learning Spanish also showed high proficiency, but some minor issues surfaced. Comprehension skills developed throughout the program, as did fluency. By fifth grade, English L1 students were able to express themselves with ease in Spanish, although their grammatical constructions and vocabulary were more limited than those of the Spanish L1 students. There was also evidence of occasional, but recurring inappropriate grammar and word choices, such as those in (1) through (3) below:

(1) subject-verb agreement
Yo necesita (vs. *necesito*) *más*. (Grade 2)
I need more.
Yo dice (vs. *yo digo*) (Grade 6)
I say ...

(2) noun/article or noun/adjective gender agreement
un persona (vs. *una persona*) (Grade 6)
a person
mi pequeño hermana (vs. *mi pequeña hermana*) (Grade 4)
my little sister
nuestro tierra (vs. *nuestra tierra*) (Grade 5)
our land

(3) word choice
una sugestión (vs. *una sugerencia*) (Grade 5)
a suggestion
hizo la iqual célula (vs. ... *la misma célula*) (Grade 5)
... the same cell
no estaba justo (vs. *no era justo*) (Grade 6)
it wasn't fair

In addition, some infelicities of use were noted, such as using *tú* with the teacher, when she had been addressed as *Señora*. These structural and pragmatic characteristics are reminiscent of the "immersion" dialect noted for one-way immersion, where certain non-standard grammatical constructions may become fossilized in the speech of language learners in the classrooms (Genesee 1987).

Looking at patterns of language use as they relate to language choice and code-switching, there was a marked preference for using English as much as possible at all sites, particularly among the older students. At Site A, observers noted that students adhered to using Spanish during the designated time "almost always when speaking directly to the teacher and most of the time when performing academic tasks ... [however] when speaking among themselves, English was the predominant language in classrooms where the students did not fear being punished for using English during Spanish time ... English use for social purposes during Spanish time seemed the same at all grade levels ... Use of Spanish during English time was infrequent and usually limited to an occasional word or phrase" by both Spanish and English L1 students (Christian et al. 1996: 33).

At Site B, English was also used more often than Spanish when students had a choice, particularly at the upper grade levels. Observers in classrooms noted some code-switching from Spanish to English when students were uncertain of the language forms. (This rarely happened from English to Spanish.) Teachers and administrators commented that perhaps the fifth and sixth grade English-speaking students had reached a plateau in their Spanish.

Observers at Site C concluded that "it is clear that the language of preference among students is English. Most of the talk in and out of the classroom is English. English is the preferred language for social purposes for those students who have achieved a certain level of fluency in it" (Christian et al. 1996: 90). Spanish is heard primarily among younger students or more recent immigrants. Program administrators noted that moving the Spanish proficiency of both groups to the level of their English proficiency has been a challenge; Spanish-dominant students are so drawn to English that they are less motivated to improve their Spanish skills (beyond the oral proficiency that is useful outside the school). As mentioned earlier, to counter this tendency, the school has already taken steps to increase Spanish instruction in the early grades from 50% to 80%, and they are considering even further moves to support the Spanish language.

Tarone and Swain (1995) recently discussed the diglossic situation that may occur in (one-way) immersion situations, where target language proficiency is restricted to academic contexts because students seldom choose to use their L2 when not required. In those cases, a functional distribution of native and target language often emerges because the target language is rarely used in non-academic conversations in or out of the classroom. Students' language preferences stem from both ease of use and influences of broader societal attitudes toward languages other than English. Such a trend may characterize two-way immersion as well.

Factors influencing language development. From this very brief overview of three programs, the following summary of language development in two-way programs might be fair. First, all students appear to be moving toward high levels of proficiency in English, including both oral language and literacy, as well as the ability to use English to demonstrate mastery of subject matter. Second, all students appear to develop high proficiency in Spanish as well, but the evidence suggests that language-choice preferences may intervene for some students. While there appears to be promising bilingual development in the early years of programs, that rate of development seems to be harder to sustain at higher grade levels. It is important to recognize that our sights are set very high. There has not been any comparison of the Spanish language skills of the two-way program students with those of students in traditional foreign language classes, or with those of native speakers of Spanish in other types of educational programs.

What are some factors that influence language development in these classrooms and schools? Factors related to the participating students, features of the programs, and the school/community context may all play a role.

Students. Two-way classrooms contain diverse sets of students, and many of the background characteristics they carry with them may affect language development, including their sociocultural background, home communities, and existing levels of proficiency in both L1 and L2 when they enter the program. On the one hand, language minority students have some English proficiency when they begin schooling; some may be quite bilingual by that time. On the other hand, English speakers are typically monolingual when they enter school. If most students can communicate in English, this may favor greater use of that language. The composition of each class may also matter, in terms of the relative proportions and proficiencies of native Spanish and English speakers.

Program features. As mentioned above, programs vary along a number of dimensions, and the consequences of these differences for language development are not yet well understood. In particular, the amount of target language instruction, especially in the early grades, varies widely (a major distinction between the "90/10" and "50/50" models). Anecdotal evidence suggests that the target language (here, Spanish) would be stronger in programs that use it most, but this study does not find the level of Spanish to be an important consequence of model choice.

There are, however, important issues to be confronted in the implementation of any model. As anyone who has worked in schools can attest, the biggest challenge for research-based innovations lies in applying their principles to real schools in ways that create conditions that lead to desired outcomes (in this case, the implementation of two-way immersion to achieve the goals that have been set, including the development of bilingual proficiency). This observation raises many more issues than can be addressed, but it is worth mentioning one as an illustration. All schools experience mobility and transiency among students to a greater or lesser extent. Two-way programs are developmental; to make them work optimally, students should remain in them so that language development takes place over adequate time. (One suggestion is a minimum of four to six years for full benefit (Lindholm 1990).) When students leave, it may be impossible to replace them, since newcomers will not be likely to have bilingual skills, especially in academic domains, comparable to those of their grade-level peers in the program. In some schools, this means upper grades have fewer, smaller, or combined-grade classes. Some schools admit newcomers to the program, particularly L1 speakers of the target language, at any grade level. Any of these alternatives may create a less than ideal context for students to realize the benefits of two-way immersion, but they may be unavoidable, given the realities of population mobility and schooling today.

School and community. As noted earlier, two-way programs report that students in the upper elementary grades have a strong preference for English and use the target language only when required in the classroom. Minority as well as majority students tend to participate in this shift, even at the expense of their native language.

McCollum (1993) investigated the impact of the "cultural capital" carried by English in a middle school two-way program and the role it might play in the power exerted by English. In the school, where English was preferred by all students, McCollum found ways in which Spanish carried less cultural capital, despite strong expressions of support for bilingualism. Some routine school practices conveyed the message that English was the language of power. (The daily vocabulary word for the school was always an English word, for example.) Although both English and Spanish achievement tests were given, the English test was signalled in many ways as more important—The English test was heavily prepared for and administered to all students at the same time; the Spanish test was given in class whenever it could fit in. McCollum found that subtle cues like these influenced students to use English rather than Spanish.

The presence of native speakers of the target language in two-way programs raises the matter of dialect differences. McCollum (1993) found that the variety of Spanish used by the native speakers was not generally accepted in the school, so that their language was devalued rather than taken as a foundation on which to to build. Programs need to look at varieties of both English and the target language brought to school by the students in order to determine how they can be built on and used as resources. These sorts of school factors can impact significantly on target language development.

Community and school administration support and understanding also influence schools and classrooms. Two-way programs are voluntary, and parents must support them by enrolling their children. Community support is often enthusiastic, however, especially after the programs demonstrate effectiveness over several years, and demand for access may be high.

Support from all levels in the education hierarchy can be crucial. Dolson and Lindholm (1994) cite the case of a school district with a two-way program option in its magnet school plan to promote racial integration. Student enrollment and school assignment were done in the district central office. Because racial integration was the highest priority, Latino students were assigned to the immersion school based on ethnic group membership rather than language background, and the school ended up with primarily English-speaking Latino and Anglo students. Spanish-speaking Latinos were underrepresented because of the random assignment. Such an imbalance of students by native language has a potential negative effect on dual language development in a two-way context.

Further, two-way programs exist in an environment of increasingly negative attitudes toward immigrant and minority groups and their languages. Although there is a long history of indifference toward learning languages other than English in the United States, there remains a significant difference between attitudes toward English speakers learning other languages and language minorities continuing to develop their native languages while they learn English (and after). Two-way programs experience ambivalent policies about foreign language learning, as well as potentially threatening ones stemming from attitudes toward minority languages and bilingual education.

Many examples of possible influences—direct and indirect—on language development could be listed, but the issues described above are indicative of the range of concerns to be dealt with.

Prospects. Two-way immersion is an exciting and effective approach to educating our diverse student population. The results reported here, along with those of other researchers, including Collier (1995) and Lindholm (1996), support the effectiveness of this educational approach when implemented in ways consistent with program goals.

This is a good point at which to caution against basing conclusions on program labels and also to comment on the prospects for the model. There is a great deal of variability in two-way programs around the country (Christian 1996), and some programs use the label, but do not implement designs consistent with the principles or goals set out earlier. Thus, it is important to look beneath the label at what is happening inside school buildings, or "two-way" could become meaningless. Specifically in terms of language development, high levels of dual language proficiency should only be expected when conditions are optimal for this to occur.

Second, programs need to decide how important high target language development goals are. The shift toward English in language preference and use during elementary school is pervasive. In order to promote target language maintenance and development, greater attention—and action—may be needed. Actions to combat the development of an "immersion dialect" may be called for; longer periods of content instruction through the target language may be needed; and more motivation to read widely in the target language would be desirable. In addition, thought needs to be given to these programs' articulation with those at the secondary level in order to sustain and further develop language skills after elementary school.

It would be possible, of course, to accord less priority to language development goals and accept the level of language skills that emerges, as long as academic and other goals were met. It would be unfortunate if programs take that course, however, because two-way programs have the prospect, and potential, for creating better language resources in the United States, with speakers of other languages maintaining and developing their native language proficiency and English speakers having the opportunity to learn other languages. Two-way immersion provides a model for effectively educating all students in schools where conditions, like composition of the population, allow it. Effective implementation of the approach could contribute to our country's language resources by helping students develop high levels of native and second language proficiency. The prospects are somewhat fragile, but exciting.

REFERENCES

Barfield, Susan. 1995. *Review of the ninth year of the partial immersion program at Key Elementary School.* Washington, D.C.: Center for Applied Linguistics.

Christian, Donna. 1996. "Two-way immersion education: Students learning through two languages." *The Modern Language Journal* 80(1): 66–76.

Christian, Donna, Chris Montone, Isolda Carranza, Kathryn Lindholm, and Patrick Proctor. 1996. *Two-way bilingual education: Students learning through two languages.* Final report. Santa

Cruz, California and Washington, D.C.: National Center for Research on Cultural Diversity and Second Language Learning.

Christian, Donna and Anna Whitcher. 1995. *Directory of two-way bilingual programs in the United States, revised.* Santa Cruz, California and Washington, D.C.: National Center for Research on Cultural Diversity and Second Language Learning.

Collier, Virginia. 1995. *Promoting academic success for ESL students: Understanding second language acquisition for school.* Trenton, New Jersey: New Jersey TESOL/BE.

Dolson, David and Kathryn Lindholm. 1994. "World class education for children in California: A comparison of the bilingual immersion and European schools models." In Tove Skutnabb-Kangas (ed.), *Multilingualism for all.* The Netherlands: Swets and Zeitlinger Publishers.

Genesee, Fred. 1987. *Learning through two languages: Studies of immersion and bilingual education.* Cambridge, Massachusetts: Newbury House Publishers.

Lambert, Wallace and Mary Cazabon. 1994. *Students' views of the Amigos program.* Research report No. 11. Santa Cruz, California and Washington, D.C.: National Center for Research on Cultural Diversity and Second Language Learning.

Lindholm, Kathryn. 1987. *Directory of bilingual immersion programs.* Los Angeles, California: UCLA/Center for Language Education and Research.

Lindholm, Kathryn. 1990. "Bilingual immersion education: Criteria for program development." In Amado Padilla, Halford Fairchild, and Concepcion Valadez (eds.), *Bilingual education: Issues and strategies.* Newbury Park, California: Sage. 91–105.

Lindholm, Kathryn. 1996. "Evaluation of academic achievement in two-way bilingual immersion programs." American Educational Research Association, New York City, April 12, 1996.

McCollum, Pamela. 1993. "Learning to value English: Cultural capital in a two-way bilingual program." American Educational Research Association, Atlanta, Georgia, April 16, 1993.

Pica, Teresa, Felicia Lincoln-Porter, Diana Paninos, and Julian Linnell. 1996. "Language learners' interaction: How does it address the input, output, and feedback needs of L2 learners?" *TESOL Quarterly* 30(1): 59–84.

Tarone, Elaine and Merrill Swain. 1995. "A sociolinguistic perspective on second language use in immersion classrooms." *The Modern Language Journal* 79: 166–178.

Foreign-language teaching after the year 2000

Reinhold Freudenstein
Philipps-Universität, Marburg

Imagine having met one hundred years ago, on March 16, 1896, for a conference like the Georgetown Round Table on Languages and Linguistics. The conference would probably have been organized by an association of teachers of modern languages in higher education—had it existed at that time—primarily interested in philological problems and in the teaching of grammar, translation, and literature. Most foreign-language teachers at that time were very skeptical about ideas to introduce new methods into the foreign-language classroom. A few years earlier a German professor of English, Wilhelm Viëtor, had written a book entitled *Der Sprachunterricht muß umkehren*, i.e. "Foreign-language teaching has to turn around," or "Foreign-language teaching must find a new orientation" (Viëtor 1882). He could not understand why modern living languages were taught in the same way as the ancient languages, Latin and Greek, i.e. on the basis of grammar and translation. He wanted to see the Grammar-Translation Method replaced by direct contact with the foreign language in meaningful situations. He had started a movement which resulted in a variety of individual methods with various names, such as *New Method, Reform Method, Natural Method, Oral Method*—in short, it was the era of direct methods which were supported internationally by linguists like Jespersen, Palmer, and others. To this day, the statements by the leaders of this movement make stimulating reading. I'll give you a few examples. Viëtor (1902: 30) observed that "Durch Wörterlisten und Regeln kann man nicht sprechen und verstehen lernen," i.e. "On the basis of word lists and rules you cannot learn how to speak and to understand." Otto Jespersen (1904: 96) notes the following: "The disadvantage of dictation, as of all written class work, is that it consumes more time than oral exercises." Or, take Palmer (1917: 116): "A certain number of regular sentences should be thoroughly assimilated in the early stages as primary matter in order to serve as model sentences to be developed by the student in the form of substitution tables." But not very many language teachers at the end of the last century were convinced that new directions in language teaching should be sought. At that time, the main languages taught in European higher education were—besides Latin and Greek—English, French and German, and the main media of instruction were the blackboard, textbook, and chalk. In other words, teachers were using the same items that had been used by Comenius in the seventeenth century.

If you look at the foreign-language scene today, not very much has changed. In my country, Germany, and in many other European states as well, English, French, or German, and Latin are still the leading school languages, as they were at the end of the last century. A few years ago, Viëtor's book was republished after one hundred years, and most of his statements, proposals and recommendations are still valid today (Schröder 1984). Of course, there have been changes since the time that popularized direct methods. Textbooks look very different from a century ago. Many more young people—and specifically girls—now have the opportunity to learn foreign languages. Foreign-language learning in school is no longer a privilege of the social elite. And the objectives in the foreign-language curriculum have changed considerably, particularly since the middle of this century when American scholars like Fries and Lado re-introduced the Oral Approach as the "Audiolingual Method" on a sound scientific basis (Fries 1952, Lado 1964). Since then, "communicative competence" has replaced goals like "learning about masterpieces of great writers" or "gaining insight into the spirit of other cultures."

But the teaching and learning of foreign languages at the school level has not really changed as far as the results of the teaching process are concerned. In spite of modern objectives like teaching communicative skills, very few students are in a position to use the foreign languages they have learned in school for communicative purposes. If they can use English, French, or German freely—effectively and without hesitation—in addition to their mother tongue, they have learned so outside of school: as an exchange student, for instance, in a foreign country. Most of our students have no practical command of the languages they learned at school. A survey conducted in Germany (before reunification in 1989) revealed that only 58% of the population can use English as a foreign language in everyday situations, 22% French, 7% Italian, 5% Spanish, and 1.6% Russian. In other words, fewer students speak these languages than those who have learned Latin. Other languages spoken in the European Union (E.U.), such as Portuguese, Danish or Greek, do not play any role at all. In a more recent study which included the new "Länder" (federal states) in Germany, only 35% of the population confessed that they knew a foreign language well enough to negotiate in that language or write a letter in English or French. Language needs for business and social purposes are therefore covered by other institutions: by private language schools, adult language centers, or the in-service training programs of industrial firms.

In Germany, all the major industrial companies teach foreign languages for their employees in in-service training programs. They do not offer foreign languages for special purposes. English for Specific Purposes (ESP), for example, is not normally very problematic as long as students have a basic knowledge of English; instead, these companies offer courses in general language use for beginners and intermediate learners. The people responsible for in-company language training come together at conferences twice a year to exchange their experiences and talk about their problems and needs (Freudenstein et al. 1981; Freudenstein and Beneke 1994). They have been doing so for more than twenty-five years now. When they first met in the late 1960s, they hoped that their mission to fill the language gaps of their employees would be temporary, because there was hope that language teaching at the school level would change under the influence of the new objective called "communication." But the conferences still take place regularly, and the need to teach foreign languages *for* the job and *on* the job is still very much felt. In these centers—as in other adult learning institutions—English and French are the most commonly taught languages; in other words, these are the same languages taught in our schools. Obviously, there must be something wrong with the foreign-language teaching at the school level. One of the main problems is that 40 to 60% of the time available for language instruction is devoted to the teaching of formal grammar. This is a finding of empirical research conducted in Germany (Zimmermann 1984: 31), and I think that the situation in other European countries and in other parts of the world is not very much different.

This is the background of my plea for a new language policy, not only in Europe, but perhaps for the rest of the world as well. In the E.U., eleven languages have been officially recognized so far (in alphabetical order): Danish, Dutch, English, Finnish, French, German, Greek, Italian, Portuguese, Spanish, and Swedish; others will follow in due course. The E.U. is a multicultural society, and this necessarily means that it is a multilingual society. Not every European can learn all the languages spoken in the Union. But multilingualism can be practised effectively if European, American, African, Australian, and all the other citizens of the world are bilingual. In order to achieve this goal, we must start today, not only by thinking about a new language policy, but also by doing something about it.

If we want the situation to change during the next ten, twenty or thirty years, then—in my view—six guidelines should be observed. I will present them to you, and share a few ideas with you about the teaching of English after the turn of the century. It goes without saying that my guidelines are open for discussion. They offer a great number of advantages, but they are certainly not entirely free of disadvantages. But I think the time has come to try, at least, to move the language-learning situation forward. So far, in the history of European foreign-language teaching and learning during the past century, we have done nothing else but correct details here and there and from time to time modify only slightly what has traditionally been normal procedure in the foreign-language classroom. This is why—in regular intervals—we repeatedly hear the same complaints about ineffective language teaching. This cannot be the solution for language teaching and learning after the year 2000.

I now present you my six guidelines, commenting on the context of each of them.

1. The first foreign language is taught at the primary level. In only a few countries in Europe is this already common practice. For example, there is early foreign-language teaching in Austria, Finland, Luxembourg, and Italy. In Germany, three of the sixteen federal states started obligatory early foreign-language teaching for all pupils in 1993: In Saarland it is French, in Hamburg it is English, and in Saxony there is a choice between English, French, Russian, and Polish, the language of a neighbouring state. But in most E.U. countries, foreign-language learning starts much later, normally at the beginning of secondary education when children are ten or eleven years old. What are the advantages of an early start? There is sufficient evidence from research and personal experience that young children can achieve success unsurpassed by any other age group (Freudenstein 1979). In pronunciation they can establish a sound basis for life-long foreign-language use. But not only linguistic considerations speak in favour of an early start. We know that bilingual children can be superior to their monolingual peers in verbal and non-verbal behaviour. This shows that early bilingualism might affect the very structure of the intellect. Intellectually, children's experience with two language systems seems to give them greater mental flexibility, superiority in concept formation, and a more diversified set of mental abilities. Early language experience may be the factor that determines the language aptitude which stabilises around puberty and continues without much change throughout adult life. But these are not the only advantages. Children who start a foreign language early in life can better understand their native language as they become conscious of the existence of language as a phenomenon. Their cultural outlook is wider than that of monolingual children, who often believe that their own culture, language, and customs are the only ones that matter in the world. The introduction of a foreign idiom into the child's world helps develop tolerance towards people who are different, and in the long run contributes towards international understanding. In the context of global education, international understanding is most certainly an aspect of peace education, which has become even more important after the breakdown of the historical East–West conflict, as can be witnessed in many parts of the world today, including Europe. Teaching foreign languages at the primary level, therefore, not only paves a way towards bilingualism, but also makes a contribution towards the support of general educational objectives.

In most of these early language programs, language learning starts in the third year of primary school. In the future, it should begin when children start their formal education, that is, in the first year of primary school. It is well-known that this is possible, because there are many successful foreign-language projects even at the pre-school or kindergarten level. In the Waldorf school system,[1] foreign-language teaching beginning at Form 1 has been long-established. The results are encouraging, not only in one language, but in two taught simultaneously. In Germany, Waldorf school parents can choose among three languages for their children: English, French, and Russian. I strongly support this very early start, particularly in view of my second guideline which deals with bilingual education.

The question of which languages to teach at the primary level can only be answered under special consideration of a particular local situation. It could be the language of a neighbouring country, such as Polish in Saxony, French in the German Saarland, Dutch in Northrhine-Westphalia, Italian in Bavaria, Portuguese in Spain, or German in Denmark. It could also be the language of children from other countries sharing the same classroom with local children, for instance Portuguese in a German city with a large Portuguese community, such as Dortmund. In this context, the role of English should be reconsidered. We all know that English is an important world language, and in many respects it already serves as a lingua franca. This might have been the reason why a former president of the *Fédération Internationale des Professeurs de Langues Vivantes*, the International Federation of Modern Language Teachers Associations (FIPLV), has suggested taking English out of the school curriculum altogether. Because of the importance of English, one can assume—this was his line of thinking—that it will be learned by most people later in their lives anyway, and therefore early language acquisition should be reserved for less commonly taught languages. For many parents, educators and teachers, this is most certainly not a very popular idea, but in the framework of a new language policy for the world of tomorrow it should at least be considered relevant. If early foreign-language learning is a contribution towards general education, it really does not matter—more or less—which language is chosen for that purpose.

2. All schools should become bilingual institutions. Why should it not be possible in a multicultural and multilingual society to introduce bilingual education as the standard form of schooling? Wherever schools offer bilingual schemes, even in a mother-tongue environment, only good reports and positive results about their work have been published. Fortunately, the number of bilingual schools in Germany is increasing rapidly, specifically in Northrhine-Westphalia, and not only in institutions of higher education, i.e. in "Gymnasien," but also in "Realschulen," and even in schools for less gifted

[1]The educational policy of the Waldorf school system is based on the anthroposophical philosophy of Rudolf Steiner (1861–1925). The first school was founded in 1919, financed by the Waldorf-Astoria cigarette company (thus the name) for children of their employees in Stuttgart, Germany. Today, there are more than one hundred Waldorf schools worldwide, most of them in Germany. They are private schools fully recognised by the state educational authorities.

children. In the past, the learning of foreign languages has always been regarded as a difficult task, and that is why it was excluded from many curricula. In the meantime, it has become common knowledge that language learning does not need to be more difficult than the teaching of any other subject area; it is the methods we use that makes it difficult. If, however, foreign-language instruction starts at the primary level—where language learning cannot be based on cognitive insights but is focussed on children's interests and is rather play-oriented—there is hope that after four years of instruction in a foreign language, various school subjects could then be taught in that language. This means that each school could become an institution of bilingual education. Such a school system would be open to all children, not only the highly talented. The advantages of using a second language for regular instruction are obvious. When history, geography, or mathematics is offered in Spanish, English, French, or Italian, children learn to use and accept different languages for their general education and not purely for the sake of learning another language—or, as I said before, in many cases the grammar of another language. I think this could be a model for the United States as well.

If this guideline is accepted, basic changes are foreseeable in two areas. First, the initial training of teachers has to be reconsidered and most probably reorganised. Today, not very many foreign-language teachers can teach another school subject besides the foreign language they have studied. In-service training programs should therefore prepare teachers for the job of teaching various subject matters as long as teachers for bilingual instruction are not yet available. In the long run, this problem could be solved in another way which I will present later under guideline 6: foreign- and second-language instruction by native speakers only.

Second, we need entirely new teaching materials for bilingual types of schools. Authentic textbooks from other countries could be used, and new materials, specifically designed for bilingual classrooms, must be published. One finds a very encouraging beginning in Germany with the publication of a textbook for the teaching of geography and history in English in Forms 7 and 8, i.e. after two and three years of learning English. It is called *There and Then*, and it covers topics like "Farming in Great Britain," "The weather," "Food and harvests," and "The Olympic Games—Ancient and modern." These materials are supposed to be used not only in situations where bilingual schools already exist, but also in regular schools which support the idea of teaching subject matter in languages other than the mother tongue. I hope that more materials of this kind will be offered in coming years, not only in Germany. Such help can introduce a new dimension in foreign-language teaching: It can transform foreign languages into second languages.

3. All children should learn two languages at school. The Commission of the E.U. and the Council of Europe favour this policy, and most educators also agree: All children should have the opportunity to learn at least two languages during their school years. And "all" children really means not only the gifted ones. I know that teachers very often think that language learning is an additional burden which should not be imposed upon children with learning difficulties. In Hessen, for instance, the German federal state where I come from, children —if they are not good at German and mathematics—need not learn a foreign language at the "Hauptschul" niveau, the school type for the less gifted.What is the logic behind such a decision? The mastery of one's mother tongue or knowledge in mathematics has nothing to do whatsoever with the learning of a foreign language. In Northrhine-Westphalia, the same student population can choose between learning English or learning how to drive a motor bike. At the age of thirteen or fourteen, language learning, of course, is no alternative at all to the offer of motor-biking. But I would also like to stress that by "learning another language," I mean "learning to communicate" in that language. For more than a century now, language teaching in Europe has been regarded as a gateway to a so-called higher culture, to "great" literature and to "foreign" civilisation. It was therefore restricted to an elite segment of the population, and many Europeans still believe that language learning should remain the privilege of a few. Or—even worse—they feel that the knowledge of foreign languages is not necessary at all, even in a multilingual society.

Let me give you an example. There is a story that the German Chancellor, Helmut Kohl, at a press conference, was asked why he never learned English. He had been educated in a humanistic school environment and his main school languages had been Latin and Greek. Journalists told him that former foreign minister Hans-Dietrich Genscher, who also had learned Latin and Greek at school, could communicate in English without interpreters and without problems after having studied English later in life. Kohl's answer was: "The German people have elected me as Chancellor of the Republic, not as an interpreter." I don't know if the exchange between Kohl and the reporter really happened like this, but the spirit behind the story is certainly true. If such an attitude prevails, there is politically and practically no room for a new and progressive language policy. In Bonn, at least—or I had better say—in Berlin—there is no politician who would favour multilingualism in Germany; there is no sign that would encourage bilingual programs on the educational scene. There are no national foreign-language weeks as is the case in the United States in March every year. It is my firm belief that this total neglect of the language problems by politicians in the E.U. will be fatal. We can only hope for a vital and functioning E.U. if its citizens can communicate with each other in many languages. This message must reach not only Berlin, but the other European capitals and perhaps other continents as well.

The knowledge of other languages besides one's mother tongue is—in spite of a wide-spread belief—not the exception to the rule; the reality is that bilingualism is the rule. Mario Wandruszka, a German language expert, claims that each individual in this world is multilingual anyway. His book entitled *Die Mehrsprachigkeit des Menschen*—"The multilingualism of humanity" (Wandruszka 1979)—reflects this view. In the E.U. of the twenty-first century, learning and using several languages should therefore not be regarded as a luxury for a few, but a prerequisite for all who live and work in a multicultural society. A German educator, Picht, has said: "We all should become Luxembourgers." What does he mean by that? If you want to sell flowers at Luxembourg's main railway station and be successful, you have to know at least three foreign languages, English, French and German. For people in Luxembourg this is the rule. They speak their dialect as they are growing up, learn German when they begin school at the age of six, and study French from the age of nine. For most of them, a fourth language, English, follows in secondary school. Thus two languages—next to their mother tongues—for all pupils in Europe during their school time is a realistic goal. The first language could be learned at primary school, the second language in secondary school. Requirements for university students must necessarily be higher. Four foreign languages should be the minimum for those who wish to study at a university. Given the Luxembourger precedent, guideline 3, that all children learn two languages at school, is a realistic objective.

4. The number of languages at school has to be increased. As mentioned above, the standard number of languages offered at the school level is three; there are exceptions to this rule, I know, but very often languages other than those traditionally taught are offered on a voluntary basis only. In the E.U., however, all languages of its member states have equal status, and this is why they all must become part of the curriculum in the European educational system. It goes without saying that not all of the offical languages of the Union—eleven so far, but not far now from twelve or fifteen—can be offered in every school. But it could easily be arranged, I think, to offer these languages within a reasonable distance from each citizen's home. Cooperative programs could be set up within school districts so that public and private schools, commercial language centers, and evening and adult schools together could cover the language needs of language learners. One of the ideas of the German "Volkshochschul-Verband," the German adult-education association, is to convince all adult language centers in Germany to offer, by the year 2000, courses in all the languages spoken in the E.U. Programs like this are necessary to prepare people for their future lives: A French teacher working in Greece, a German doctor practising in Portugal, an Italian baker working in Denmark—these scenarios will not be exceptions twenty or thirty years from now, but they will only succeed if the language problems that are inevitably involved have been solved by then. I hope that in the future, people in the United States of Europe will think of their neighbours in the same way in which Americans in the United States of America think of their fellow citizens today. They all belong to one nation, whether from Indiana, Florida, California or Texas. Americans have one great advantage, however: Their main common medium of communication is English. This will not and should never happen in Europe. The E.U. will remain multilingual, but I hope that Europeans will soon share a common feeling of belonging together. Ideally, there should not be Italians, Germans, French and other nationalities any longer, but Italian Europeans, German Europeans, French Europeans, and so on. And these Europeans should be bi- or multilingual so that the Union can function.

In addition to the languages of the E.U., other important languages cannot be excluded from being offered in and outside of schools. Eastern and Northern European, Asian, and Arabic languages must have an equal place in local language programs so that they too can be learned for private or business purposes.

In sum, with English, French, German and Latin, the European future can never be mastered. Many more languages have to be added to the curriculum in order to prepare for effective communication in the twenty-first century—not only in Europe, but in the rest of the world as well.

5. The length of instruction must be shortened. One of the shortcomings of traditional foreign-language teaching at the school level has been the length of time needed to study. Let's face it: It is demotivating to spend five, seven or even nine years on the same subject, and this is still the rule in many countries. I therefore propose that a foreign language should not be offered more than four years in any school curriculum. This is enough time to enable individual learners to acquire the basic knowledge of a language, upon which they can build should it become necessary later. So far, in my country at least, pupils in advanced foreign-language classes study literature, analyse philological problems, and deal with complex grammatical problems. In our school system and in many other European school systems as well—in the tradition of the nineteenth century —pupils are prepared for futures as language teachers, professors of philology at universities and the like. But most of our students have entirely different foreign-language needs. They want to become business people, work in commerce and industry, and therefore do not need to know too much about Shakespeare or French classics. Those who are interested in studies like this should be given the opportunity to do so; but the majority of language learners are better served by short, communicative courses in several languages than by long-term language classes of the traditional type.

New forms of language instruction must therefore be introduced. I have mentioned bilingual education already. Let me name a few more. There are compact courses which could shorten the time for language learning and at the same time guarantee better results. More than fifteen years ago the International Federation of Modern Language Associations, FIPLV, promoted a project of multilingual education through compact courses (Freudenstein 1989). It showed that by rearranging traditional forms of language instruction, more languages could be offered and learned by pupils than ever before. In a London comprehensive high school pupils were introduced to four languages which they could learn to various degrees of competence. There are the so-called alternative methods—from Community Language Learning to Suggestopedia, Superlearning, and the Silent Way, as well as other commercialized concepts. Their methods and strategies seem to work, because institutions offering this kind of instruction have no problems recruiting language learners for their (often very expensive) programs.

In Germany many years ago, a teacher introduced a new form of learning French: He taught one year's worth of traditional French instruction in three weeks—two weeks at the beginning of the school year and one week at the end—with remarkable results in comparison to classes taught the ordinary way, i.e. four hours a week of textbook instruction; the intensive course students were simply better (Preisendörfer 1974). In Switzerland, a teacher of French did away with the textbook altogether and proclaimed a concept of "learning in freedom." His students could do whatever they liked to during the four hours of French per week, as long as it had to do with the French language. So some read newspapers, others played cards, listened to records, or talked about things they were interested in. At the end of the school year, these students showed better communicative results than those who had been taught during the same period of time in the traditional way (Kaufmann 1977). Many more examples could be mentioned, and they all show similar results: There are many ways in which foreign-language learning can be improved by introducing new ways of instruction. Unfortunately, not very many teachers—not to mention the administrators—believe in them. Whenever I report about the project "learning in freedom" at teacher-training courses, the normal reaction is: "Impossible—that can't be true!" So a great deal of work remains to be done to convince teachers that there are other and better ways of instruction than those they themselves have experienced and which they practise in their own classrooms.

Offering more languages in school does not, by the way, mean that more time is required in the curriculum. The time available for language teaching must only be reorganised and used in a different way. If you have, for example nine years allotted to the teaching of English, four years to French, and three years to another foreign language, the time available could easily be used to teach four languages with the general objective of communicative competence.

6. The regular language teacher should be a native speaker. Whenever I propose this idea in my country, many teachers do not agree at all. They claim that a teacher should know the language of their students very well, that they themselves should have been educated in the school system in which they teach, and that they should be accepted by the students as one of "theirs," not as a foreigner. I do not believe in this ideology. In the E.U., native speakers cannot be regarded as "foreigners" anymore, as was the case in the past. If they leave their home country and move to another state within the Union, they are still live and work in the E.U. Thus, there are French Europeans, Spanish Europeans, German Europeans and so on available for teaching purposes, wherever and whenever they are needed—theoretically, that is. I know that, here again, many practical problems are involved, for instance, the question of payment, which is still varies considerably in the different E.U. member states. But I also think that these are questions which can and will be solved in the years to come. Native speakers are the best language teachers—provided they have completed a study program for that purpose—because they know best what it is all about: a total command of the language which they use and teach. They speak the language better than any foreign-language teacher who has learned the language as a foreign language, and they can react spontaneously and realistically to unforeseen communicative situations. Native speakers are the rule in situations where languages are taught in order to train communicative skills for everyday situations, for instance, in private language schools or in industrial firms. In adult education courses you also often find native speakers—despite never having had any formal teacher training—who are preferred to well-trained university language instructors. Of course, in order to qualify native speakers to teach their mother tongues, new programs of study have to be introduced in teacher education programs at university level.

I have a vision: By the middle of the next century, all French language classes all over the world should be taught by native speakers of French, all Italian classes by native speakers of Italian, and all German classes by native speakers of German who have been trained to teach their mother tongue as a foreign language. This would move us forward to a truly multilingual, multicultural society.

Conclusion. Let me add a final consideration. The six guidelines which I have mentioned could well become—in my view—the basis for a new language policy, not only in Europe, but worldwide. I do not know if they constitute the best possible framework for the needs of tomorrow, but they are, at least, a framework, and many more people should start thinking about them so that a suitable model can be transformed from theory into practice. The earlier this happens, the better, because the next generation expects us to prepare its way for a future worth living—a future in many languages.

REFERENCES

Fries, Charles C. 1952. *The structure of English. An introduction to the construction of English sentences*. New York: Harcourt, Brace and World.

Freudenstein, Reinhold (ed.) 1979. *Teaching foreign languages to the very young*. Oxford: Pergamon.

Freudenstein, Reinhold, et al. (eds.) 1981. *Language incorporated: Teaching foreign languages in industry*. Oxford and München: Pergamon and Hueber.

Freudenstein, Reinhold (ed.) 1989. *Multilingual education through compact courses*. Tübingen: Narr.

Freudenstein, Reinhold and Jürgen Beneke (eds.) 1994. *Die Sprache des Kunden: Fremdsprachenlernen für Wirtschaft und Beruf*. Bonn: Dümmler.

Jespersen, Otto. 1904. *How to teach a foreign language*. London: Allen and Unwin.

Kaufmann, Franz. 1977. "Lernen in Freiheit—im Fremdsprachenuntderricht." *Praxis des neusprachlichen Unterrichts* 3: 227–236.

Lado, Robert. 1964. *Language teaching. A scientific approach*. New York: McGraw-Hill.

Palmer, Harold E. 1917. *The scientific study and teaching of languages*. New York: World Book.

Preisendörfer, Hans. 1974. "Ein Jahrespensum Französisch in zwanzig Tagen?" *Praxis des neusprachlichen Unterrichts* 3: 283–293.

Schröder, Konrad (ed.). 1984. *Wilhelm Viëtor: Der Sprachunterricht muß umkehren. Ein Pamphlet aus dem 19. Jahrhundert neu gelesen*. München: Hueber.

Viëtor, Wilhelm. 1882. *Der Sprachunterricht muß umkehren*. Heilbronn: Henninger.

Viëtor, Wilhelm. 1902. *Die Methodik des neusprachlichen Unterrichts*. Leipzig: Teubner.

Zimmermann, Günther. 1984. *Erkundungen zur Praxis des Grammatikunterrichts*. Frankfurt: Diesterweg.

The case against bilingual education

Stephen Krashen
University of Southern California

The case for bilingual education. Before presenting the case against bilingual education, it will be helpful to present the case for bilingual education. When we give children quality education in their primary language, we give them two things:

(1) Knowledge, both general knowledge of the world and subject matter knowledge. The knowledge that children get through their first language helps make the English they hear and read more comprehensible.

Consider the case of two limited English proficient children. One has had a good education in the primary language, and is well-prepared in math, while the other has not had a good foundation in math. They enter a fourth grade class in which math is taught only in English. Clearly, the child with a good background in math will understand more, and will thus learn more math, and acquire more English, because she is getting more comprehensible input. The child with a poor math background will learn less math and acquire less English.

(2) Literacy, which transfers across languages.

Here is a simple, three-step argument supporting the transfer of literacy from the first to the second language:

(1) As Frank Smith and Kenneth Goodman have argued, we learn to read by reading, by making sense of what we see on the page. (See, e.g., Smith 1994.) This hypothesis is very similar to the input hypothesis (Krashen 1994);
(2) If we learn to read by reading, it will be much easier to learn to read in a language we already understand; and
(3) Once you can read, you can read. The ability to read transfers across languages.

Another aspect of literacy transfers as well: the ability to use language to solve problems and thereby grow intellectually. Once someone can use the composing process in one language, it can be used in any other: Once we are educated, we are educated.

Rossell and Baker complain that "it is impossible to say why" native language development will help second language development: "There is no underlying psychological mechanism that accounts for the facilitation effect" (1996: 31). According to my understanding, knowledge and literacy together make up what Cummins refers to as "academic language" (formerly CALP). This characterization helps us understand what the advantages are in providing first language support: Knowledge gained through the first language makes English input more comprehensible, and literacy gained through the first language transfers to the second.

The three components. If the arguments given here are correct, they predict that good bilingual programs will have the following components:

(1) Comprehensible input in English, through high quality English as a Second Language (ESL) and sheltered subject matter teaching;
(2) Subject matter teaching in the primary language, without translation. This provides children with knowledge that will make the English they hear more comprehensible; and
(3) Literacy development in the first language, which transfers to the second.

A gradual exit, variable threshold plan. It is quite possible to organize programs that meet these characteristics, combining ESL, sheltered subject matter teaching, and instruction in the first language. In these programs (e.g., the "Eastman plan," used in California), all core instruction is initially in the primary language for the monolingual non-English speaking child, and ESL is provided as well. As the child grows more proficient in English, subjects using more contextualized language (math and science) are done in sheltered classes, and eventually in the mainstream. In this way, the sheltered classes function as a bridge between instruction in the first language and the mainstream. In advanced levels, the only subjects done in the first language are those demanding the most abstract use of language (social studies and language arts). Once full "mainstreaming" is complete, advanced first language development is available as an option. Table 1 presents this kind of plan.

Thus, the plan is a "gradual exit" plan, which avoids problems associated with exiting children too early, that is, before the English they encounter is comprehensible. It also avoids problems associated with keeping children in full first language programs too long, past the point where they can handle classes taught in English. At the same time, however, it allows children to have the advantages of advanced first language development.

Table 1. A gradual exit-variable threshold plan.

INSTRUCTION TYPE / STAGE	First Language	ESL/Sheltered	Mainstream
Beginning	all core subjects	ESL	art, music, PE
Intermediate	language arts, social studies	ESL, math, science	art, music, PE
Advanced	continuing L1 development	ESL, social studies, language arts	art, music, PE, math, science
Mainstream	continuing L1 development		all subjects

This is also a "variable threshold" plan. Cummins (1981) has hypothesized the existence of two thresholds in first language development. The lower threshold is the minimum amount of first language academic proficiency (knowledge plus literacy) necessary to make a positive impact on second language academic proficiency. The higher threshold is the amount of first language competence necessary to reap the cognitive benefits of bilingualism.

The task of the bilingual educator is to insure attainment of the lower threshold and, whenever possible, help students attain the higher threshold. This plan accomplishes both of these goals.

The plan employs a "variable threshold" approach for the attainment of the lower threshold: As children reach the threshold for a particular subject matter, they then proceed to follow instruction in English in that subject matter, beginning with sheltered instruction. By providing continuing first language development, the plan also provides for the attainment of the higher threshold and its advantages.

The case against bilingual education. Among the most frequent arguments against bilingual education are these:

(1) The research shows it is ineffective;
(2) There is a better option: Immersion;
(3) People succeed without it; and
(4) Even if it works, it will only work when the writing systems are similar in the two languages.

Does the research show bilingual education is ineffective? Basing their conclusions on an analysis of 72 studies that they considered to be methodologically acceptable, Rossell and Baker conclude that the research evidence "does not support transitional bilingual education as a superior form of instruction for limited English proficient children" (1996: 7). They conclude, for example, that in the case of English reading comprehension, transitional bilingual education was superior to submersion in 22% of the studies, worse in 33%, and there was no difference in 45% of the studies (60 studies were examined).

I was not able to re-examine all the studies Rossell and Baker cited because most were unpublished reports. I did, however, read all of the studies that appeared in the professional literature, and found numerous problems with their conclusions. Of the 20 studies in which submersion was claimed to be superior to bilingual education, two were in the professional published literature; I was also able to get information on one other.

MOORE AND PARR 1978. This study examined children in four programs: maintenance, transitional, "minimal" and English-only, and concluded that the latter group scored significantly higher than the others on tests of English reading. We are, however, given no details whatsoever on what went on in the bilingual classes; all we have are labels. In addition, the duration of the study was short: Moore and Parr's oldest subjects had just finished Grade 2. It typically takes longer for bilingual programs to show a positive impact on English language tests. In addition, no raw data is provided, so it is difficult to tell what the real effect of each program was.

CURIEL, STENNING, AND COOPER-STENNING 1980. In this study, seventh graders who had been in bilingual education were compared to students who were not. While Rossell and Baker classify this study as showing submersion to be superior, this is not what Curiel et al. report. For reading comprehension tests given in Grade 6, nonbilingual education students were significantly better. But at Grade 7, there was no significant difference between the groups, although the non-bilingual students were slightly better (mean = 6.35, compared to 5.98). In addition, students in bilingual education had significantly higher grade point averages and fewer of them were retained (30 out of 90 controls had been retained one year in elementary school, compared to 11 out of 86 bilingual education students). Finally, Curiel et al. note that the bilingual program was used as a remedial program "for some students who were previously placed in the monolingual English program ..." (1980: 396)!

Rossell and Baker complain that "no one looks at the future educational success of graduates of bilingual or immersion programs" (1996: 41). Curiel and his associates have attempted to do this. In Curiel, Rosenthal, and Richek

(1986), students who were studied in Curiel et al. up to Grade 7, described just above, were followed to Grade 11. (Rossell and Baker cite this study, but classify it as "methodologically unacceptable.") In the follow-up, Curiel and associates report that students who had been in bilingual programs outperformed comparisons on all measures. While 12 of 90 comparison students had been retained in Grades 7, 8, and 9, only 4 out of 82 bilingual education students had been retained. Fewer bilingual education students dropped out of school (23.5%, compared to 43%). Bilingual students had higher grade point averages, but the difference was not significant. (Note that those who dropped out probably had lower grades.)

EL PASO. Rossell and Baker include the El Paso evaluations of two programs as studies showing submersion to be more effective than bilingual education. This is a bizarre analysis: Neither program was submersion. One, labelled "bilingual immersion" by the El Paso Unified School District, was clearly bilingual education. It contained a "native language cognitive development" component (NLCD), described by the El Paso Independent School District as follows:

> NLCD is taught for 60 to 90 minutes per day. The objective of this component is to develop concepts, literacy, cognition, and critical thinking skills in Spanish. It is during this period that instruction and student-teacher interaction are entirely in Spanish. The more demanding content area concepts are also introduced during NCLD, particularly in the first grade. (1989b: 54)

This program employed the Natural Approach for ESL, a whole language approach to language arts, and sheltered subject matter teaching.

The second program was also considered to be bilingual education, but differed in some important ways. Referred to as SB 477, it used a skills-oriented approach, as described by the El Paso Independent School District:

> It must be understood that BIP (bilingual immersion program) is not an English version of the SB 477 instructional program. SB 477 is built on a philosophy that advocates traditional concepts of teaching language ... SB 477 focuses the child's attention on the details of language such as phonetic sounds and grammar rules. (1987: 9)

While "bilingual immersion" used some whole language and Natural Approach activities, the most commonly used materials in Transitional Bilingual Education (TBE) were basal texts and workbooks (El Paso Independent School District 1987: 18). According to a 1989 report, whole language and comprehensible input-based methodology had been gradually introduced into SB 477 from 1985 to 1987, but "observations indicate that the changes have not been fully implemented by SB 477 teachers" (El Paso Independent School District 1989a: 10).

To summarize, "bilingual immersion" in El Paso combined instruction in the first language with comprehensible input-based methodology, similar to the gradual exit variable threshold plan described earlier in this paper. The "bilingual" program (SB 477) used more instruction in the first language, but focussed more on skill-building.

Gersten, Woodward, and Schneider (1992) published a detailed report on the El Paso programs, limiting their report to students who had been in either program continuously. Gersten et al. confirmed that the "bilingual immersion" students excelled "in all aspects of academic performance" in the fourth grade (1992: 13), "But by the seventh grade, no significant differences were found in any aspect of academic performance" (1992: 13). Far more bilingual immersion students, however, had been placed in the mainstream at Grade 6, and more bilingual immersion teachers were confident about their students' eventual success in the mainstream.

Neither program was particularly successful, however. Sixth-graders did acceptably well on the Language and Math Subtests of the Iowa Test of Basic Skills, but did poorly on the Reading Comprehension test, with bilingual immersion students scoring around the 23rd percentile and transitional bilingual students scoring at the 21st percentile. Vocabulary scores were even lower. The students themselves said that their hardest subjects were Social Studies and Language Arts, those which demand the most competence in academic English (Gersten et al. 1992: 25-26). In addition, although bilingual immersion teachers were more confident of their students' eventual success in the mainstream, only 73% thought they would succeed in the regular program, and only 45% of the transitional bilingual education teachers predicted success for their students. Gersten et al. note that "These levels of performance, sadly, are typical for low-income Hispanic students in the junior high school years" (1992: 29). This may be true, but I think we can do much better. I return to this issue below.

All we can conclude from the El Paso program is that a well-designed bilingual program was better than a less well-designed program up to Grade 4, with no differences by Grade 7. Such studies will help us decide among bilingual education options, but do not address the issue of bilingual education versus submersion.

BERKELEY. Rossell and Baker include a study by Rossell (1990) of Limited English Proficiency (LEP) performance by children in Berkeley as showing that submersion plus ESL was, in one case, superior to bilingual education, and in another, that there was no difference in English reading scores. The programs Rossell compared were labelled bilingual education and pull-out ESL, but no description of Berkeley's bilingual education program was provided, other than the fact that it was labeled "bilingual education" and that instruction was in Spanish 30 to 50 percent of the time.

Rossell also compared Berkeley LEP children's performance on California Assessment for Progress (CAP) tests to performance by LEP children in two districts considered to have "exemplary" bilingual programs, Fremont and San Jose (Krashen and Biber 1988). Rossell reported no significant difference among the children in the three districts in reading, and reported that the Berkeley students excelled in math.

There are problems with this conclusion. First, this analysis does not compare gain scores, nor does it show how rapidly children reached norms. It considers LEP children as a group. The comparison is only valid if, in fact, LEP children in all three districts entered their respective systems at the same level of competence, and if all three districts used similar criteria for exiting children. This may not be the case. According to Rossell's analysis of reclassified children in Berkeley, many children scored very well on the Comprehensive Test of Basic Skills (CTBS) long before they were exited—in CTBS Reading, for example, children in ESL pull-out scored at the 33rd percentile two years before reclassification and at the 54th percentile one year before, while children in bilingual education who were reclassified scored at the 35th percentile two years before reclassification and near the 60th percentile one year before. CTBS Language Scores are similar, and scores in CTBS Math are even higher, with LEP children in Berkeley scoring above the 50th percentile four years before reclassification. Thus, Berkeley scores may look higher because some high-scoring children were retained in these programs longer.

Even if the analysis were a valid one, i.e. if children in all three districts entered at the same level and all three districts had equal reclassification criteria, it is interesting that, according to Rossell's analysis, schools that had bilingual education reported slightly higher CAP scores. The regression coefficients for bilingual education were positive, but did not reach statistical significance ($b = 11.82$; $t=1.02$; $n=108$).

Is immersion better? The term immersion has been used in several different ways. Here, I will focus on just two uses.

Canadian style immersion (CSI): CSI is a program in which middle-class children receive much of their subject-matter instruction through a second language. Efforts are made to insure the language they hear is comprehensible. Children in these programs learn subject matter successfully and acquire a great deal of the second language.

Consideration of the principles of bilingual education presented earlier leads to the conclusion that CSI is similar, if not identical, to bilingual education. Children in CSI receive comprehensible input in the second language and develop literacy and subject matter knowledge in their first language, both outside of school and in school. As noted earlier, children in CSI are typically middle class, and do a considerable amount of reading in English outside of school (suggested by Cummins 1977, and confirmed by Eagon and Cashion 1988). Even in early total immersion programs, a great deal of the curriculum is in English, with English language arts introduced around Grade 2. By Grade 6, half the curriculum of early total immersion is in English. Most important, the goal of CSI is bilingualism, not the replacement of one language with another.

Structured immersion (SI): As described by Gerston and Woodward (1985), SI has these characteristics:

(1) Comprehensible subject matter instruction;
(2) Use of the first language when necessary for explanation, but this is kept to a minimum;
(3) Direct instruction of grammar; and
(4) Pre-teaching of vocabulary.

While the first two characteristics are supported in the research literature, there is little evidence supporting the efficacy of direct grammar instruction (Krashen 1994), and preteaching vocabulary has not been found to be consistently effective (Mezynski, 1983).

Rossell and Baker (1996) claim that "immersion" was more effective than bilingual education for English reading in eight studies. Information concerning six of these studies was available to me.

BARIK, SWAIN AND NWANUNOKI 1977; BARIK AND SWAIN 1978. These are studies of Canadian-style immersion with French as the target language in which early total immersion is compared to partial immersion. In partial immersion, there is less teaching in French; from the beginning, some subjects are taught in English and some in French.

Rossell and Baker claim that the results of such students are relevant to the situation in the United States. I agree that they are, but I interpret their relevance very differently. While Rossell and Baker are not fully explicit about why these studies were included, the idea seems to be that early total immersion is similar to all-English "immersion" for LEP children, and partial immersion is similar to bilingual education. Since Barik et al. and Barik and Swain show that children in early total immersion acquire more French than children in partial immersion programs, "immersion," it is concluded, is better than bilingual education.

But Canadian early total immersion is not the same as an all-English immersion program for LEP children. In fact, both versions of Canadian-style immersion under consideration here, early total and partial immersion, are quite similar to bilingual education. As noted earlier, much of the CSI curriculum is in the first language, English, and children in these programs typically come to school with a great deal of literacy development in the primary language. Since children in both programs come to school so well-prepared, it is reasonable to expect that more exposure to the second language, French, will result in more acquisition of French, because what is heard and read is mostly comprehensible.

Many LEP children in the United States, however, do not come to school with these advantages. All of the all-second language curriculum will be much less comprehensible to them, even if it is carefully "sheltered." While sheltering will clearly help, supplying background knowledge and literacy in the first language is a sure way to ensure that instruction in English will be comprehensible.

Rossell and Baker are clearly aware of this argument. They point out, in defense of their position, that Canadian-style immersion programs have worked for working class students as well as middle class students. A few reports of Canadian-style immersion programs for working class children have been published (e.g., Holobrow, Genesee, Lambert, Gastright and Met 1987). While these children have done well, evaluations so far have been limited to Grade 2 and below. Also, as Genesee notes, none of these children "can be said to come from destitute or 'hard-core' inner-city areas" (1983: 30).

We thus know very little about how well working-class children do in second language immersion programs and nothing about how well under-class children would do. What we do know is that children of lower socioeconomic background experience less print outside of school (e.g., Feitelson and Goldstein 1986), and that the richness of the print environment is related to literacy development (e.g., Krashen 1993).

BRUCK, LAMBERT AND TUCKER 1977. This study compares children in total immersion (CSI) to native speakers of French, and thus has no bearing at all on the question of bilingual education versus immersion.

GENESEE, HOLOBROW, LAMBERT AND CHARTRAND 1989. This project compares fifth-graders in partial immersion, early total immersion, and the performance of English-speaking children in a French school designed for native speakers of French. This third group, however, had methodology that was quite similar to the students in early total immersion, and the population of the school was largely English-speaking. In fact, Genessee et al. refer to it as "super-immersion." Super-immersion students and early total immersion students performed similarly on nearly all measures.

An additional group of a small number of English speaking students in a French school with fewer English-speaking classmates was compared to the super-immersion students; performance was similar, with the "submersion" students doing better only on oral tests. Again, it is not clear why this study is included and how it is supposed to show that structured immersion is better than bilingual education. In my analysis, all groups had the benefits of bilingual education, coming from middle-class homes. We also cannot use the French school-immersion comparison to claim that submersion is equivalent or superior to bilingual education (my interpretation of the Canadian immersion studies) or structured immersion (Rossell and Bakers' interpretation, I assume) because we have no idea how the English speakers were dealt with in French classes in the French school, that is, how much comprehensible input in French they received, in school and outside of school (e.g., tutors).

GERSTEN (1985). Here it is claimed that more students in "structured immersion" scored at or above grade level on standardized tests than children in bilingual education. Gersten's study meets the methodological criteria set out by Rossell and Baker, but is full of other problems:

- Sample size: Gersten only compared 28 structured immersion students to 16 students in bilingual education. Because Gersten does not provide actual scores for the bilingual group, we have no idea how close to grade level students were. (One cohort of SI students scored at the 64th percentile, the other at the 65th percentile.)

- Duration: Gersten examined student performance at the end of second grade. As noted earlier, the impact of bilingual education typically does not show up on standardized tests until much later (Cummins 1981). Gersten included follow-up data on the SI students, and they did very well, with one cohort scoring at the 65th percentile in reading at the end of Grade 4 and the other scoring at the 78th percentile in reading at the end of Grade 3. Each cohort, however, consisted of only nine children!

- Control for socio-economic factors. As noted earlier, SES has a powerful effect on school performance. Gersten informs us that his SI students were "low income" and that the school they attended had "a high proportion of low income, low achieving students, who became eligible for Title I funds" (1985: 188) but provides no supporting evidence of any kind. Nor is SES information provided about the comparison students in the bilingual education program. These children did not attend the same school the SI children attended. (We do not even know the name or location of the school or district studied. All we know is that the school is on the West Coast.)

- Lack of information about the bilingual education program. We are only told that comparison students participated in bilingual education programs in the district. We have no idea what the quality of the program was, what methodology was used, etc. In addition, the comparison students in cohort II included two speakers of Korean, two speakers of Vietnamese, and two speakers of "Samoan or Thai." This implies that this mysterious district provides full bilingual education programs in all of these languages at least up to Grade 2. I know of no districts that are able to do this. Gersten did not include information on the linguistic background of the bilingual education students in the other cohort. Such data, he states, were "unavailable." (!)

- Finally, Gersten notes that the number of LEP students in the school he studied is small; his analysis included "all LEP children who were in the program for at least 8 full months" (1985: 190). These children, thus, were among many English-speaking peers. We do not know what the linguistic environment was like for the children in the bilingual education program.

In short, everything is wrong with this study.

PENA-HUGHES AND SOLIS 1980. This study is unpublished, but it is discussed in several published papers. It is a comparison of two programs in McAllen, Texas. While Rossell and Baker label these programs "immersion" and "bilingual education," Willig (1985, 1987) classified the immersion group as bilingual education, noting that the "immersion" group had instruction in English in the morning and Spanish reading in the afternoon. In addition, the explicit goal of the immersion program was bilingualism—development of both languages.

Also, the group Rossell and Ross label "bilingual education" did not, apparently, have a good program. According to an article in the *Wall Street Journal* (Schorr 1983), classes "were conducted partly in Spanish and partly in English," suggesting concurrent translation, a method shown to be ineffective (Legarreta 1979). What apparently happened in McAllen is that children in a good bilingual program outperformed children in a poor bilingual program.

Success without bilingual education? The most common argument against bilingual education, and against special programs in general, is the observation that many people have succeeded without it. This has certainly happened. In every case, however, the successful person got plenty of comprehensible input, and in many cases they had a de facto bilingual education program.

Probably the most famous case is Richard Rodriguez, the author of *Hunger of Memory* (Rodriquez 1983). Rodriguez succeeded without a special program and acquired a very high level of English literacy. He had two crucial advantages, however, that most LEP children do not have: He grew up in an English-speaking neighborhood in Sacramento, California, and was the only Spanish-speaking child in his class. Rodriguez thus got a great deal of informal comprehensible input from classmates. Many LEP children today only encounter

English at school. In addition, he became a voracious reader, which helped him acquire academic language. Most LEP children have little access to books.

Fernando de la Pena claims that he succeeded without bilingual education (de la Pena 1991). Although he was born in El Paso, he spent his first eight years in Mexico, and came to the U.S. at age nine with no English competence. He reports that he acquired English rapidly, and "by the end of my first school year, I was among the top students." A closer look at his case shows that de la Pena had the advantages of bilingual education: In Mexico, he was in the fifth grade, and was thus literate in Spanish and knew subject matter. In addition, when he started school in the U.S., he was put back two grades and placed in Grade 3. (No wonder he was at the top of his class!) His superior knowledge of subject matter helped make the English input he heard more comprehensible.

Another case is that of Grace Cho. Born in Korea, Grace Cho's family moved to Argentina when she was school age. In school, she was faced with a total submersion situation; schools in Argentina make no provision for limited Spanish-speaking students—there were no Spanish as a second language classes, no sheltered classes, and there was no bilingual education. Nevertheless, she succeeded; she acquired Spanish very well, did well in school, and today, in Los Angeles, works as a bilingual (Spanish-English) teacher.

The conditions underlying successful bilingual education were satisfied outside of school in this case. The first factor is her previous schooling. Unlike so many limited English proficient children who arrive in the U.S., when Cho arrived in Argentina, she was at or above "grade level," and was a success in school in Korea. Thus, she already had considerable subject matter knowledge and literacy development.

Second, her parents hired tutors for her immediately. They worked with her in Korean, primarily assisting her with subject matter, and helping her Korean language competence to continue to develop. In other words, her parents made sure that the second and third characteristics of good bilingual education, subject matter instruction in the primary language and development of literacy in the primary language, were present. Cho reports that because of this help, her school work was much more comprehensible, and this helped her acquire Spanish more easily.

Many people have the perception that Asian students succeed without special programs, while Hispanic students do not. It is true that many Asian children do very well; they often come to the U.S. in the fourth grade with no English, and by the time they are in the sixth grade they are at the top of their class. But not all Asian children do this well. Our Cambodian students, our Hmong students, have a difficult time in our schools: They come with little literacy or schooling in the primary language. It is also true that many Spanish speaking children have a hard time in school. They also come with little literacy or schooling. Occasionally, however, Spanish-speaking children arrive in school here from the urban areas of Spanish-speaking countries, with a good education in the primary language. They come in the fourth grade with no English, but by the time they are in the sixth grade, they are at the top of their class. These children have already had two components of a bilingual education program: both subject matter knowledge and literacy in the primary language. In my view, these children are excellent advertisements for bilingual education.

What about languages other than Spanish? Porter states that "even if there were a demonstrable advantage for Spanish-speakers learning to read first in their home language, it does not follow that the same holds true for speakers of languages that do not use the Roman alphabet" (1990: 65). But it does. The ability to read transfers across languages, even when the writing systems are different. There is evidence that reading transfers from Spanish to English (Mortensen 1984; Buriel and Cardoza 1988), Chinese to English (Hoover 1983), Vietnamese to English (Cummins, Swain, Nakajima, Handscombe, Green, and Tran 1984), Japanese to English (Cummins et al. 1984), and from Turkish to Dutch (Verhoeven 1991); in other words, those who read well in one language, read well in the second language (as long as length of residence in the country is controlled for, to account for the first language loss that is common).

Improving bilingual education. Bilingual education has done well, but it can do much better. The biggest problem, in my view, is the absence of books, both in the first and second language, in the lives of students in these programs. Free voluntary reading can help all components of bilingual education: It is a source of comprehensible input in English, a means of developing knowledge through the first language, a means of promoting first language literacy, and it can help continue first language development.

Students in these programs have little access to books at home (about 22 for the entire family according to Ramirez, Yuen, Ramey, and Pasta 1991) or at school (an average of one book in Spanish per Spanish speaking child in some school libraries in schools with bilingual programs; Pucci 1994). A book flood in both languages is clearly called for. Good bilingual programs have brought students to the 50th percentile by Grade 5 (Burnham-Massey and Pena 1990). But with a good supply of books, both in the first and second languages, we will go beyond the 50th percentile: We will have the Lake Wobegon effect, where all of the children are above average, and we can finally do away with the tests (and put the money saved to much better use.)

REFERENCES

Barik, Henri and Merrill Swain. 1978. "Evaluation of a bilingual education program in Canada: The Elgin study through grade six." Paper presented at the Colloquium of the Swiss Interuniversity Commission for Applied Linguistics. (ED 174 073).

Barik, Henri, Merrill Swain, and E. Nwanunobi. 1977. "English-French bilingual education: The Elgin study though grade five." *Canadian Modern Language Review* 33: 459–475.

Bruck, M., Wallace Lambert, and G. Richard Tucker. 1977. "Cognitive consequences of bilingual schooling: The St. Lambert Project through grade six." *Psycholinguistics* 6: 13–33.

Buriel, Raymond and Desdemona Cardoza. 1988. "Sociocultural correlates of achievement among three generations of Mexican American high school seniors." *American Educational Research Journal* 25: 177–192.

Burnham-Massey, Laurie and Marilyn Piña. 1990. "Effects of bilingual instruction on English academic achievement of LEP students." *Reading Improvement* 27: 129–132.

Cummins, Jim. 1977. "Delaying native language reading instruction in immersion programs; A cautionary note." *Canadian Modern Language Review* 34: 46–49.

Cummins, J. 1981. "The role of primary language development in promoting educational success for language minority students." In *Schooling and language minority students*. Sacramento: California Department of Education. 3–49.

Cummins, Jim, Merrill Swain, Karuko Nakajima, Jean Handscombe, Daina Green, and Chau Tran. 1984. "Linguistic interdependence among Japanese and Vietnamese immigrant students." In C. Rivera (ed.), *Communicative competence approaches to language proficiency assessment: Research and application*. Clevedon, U.K.: Multilingual Matters.

Curiel, Herman, Walter Stenning, and Peggy Cooper-Stenning. 1980. "Achieved reading level, self-esteem, and grades as related to length of exposure to bilingual education." *Hispanic Journal of Behavioral Sciences* 2: 389–400.

Curiel, Herman, James Rosenthal, and Herbert Richek. 1986. "Impacts of bilingual education on secondary school grades, attendance, retentions, and drop-out." *Hispanic Journal of Behavioral Sciences* 8: 357–367.

de la Pena, Fernando. 1991. *Democracy or babel? The case for official English*. Washington, D.C.: U.S. English.

Eagon, Ruth and Marie Cashion. 1988. "Second year report on a longitudinal study of spontaneous reading in English by students in early French immersion programs." *Canadian Modern Language Review* 44: 523–526.

El Paso Independent School District. 1987. *Interim report of the five-year bilingual-education pilot*. 1986–1987 School Year. El Paso, Texas: El Paso Independent School District, Office for Research and Evaluation.

El Paso Independent School District. 1989a. *Bilingual education evaluation: The fourth year in a longitudinal study*. 1987–1988 School Year. El Paso, Texas: El Paso Independent School District, Office for Research and Evaluation.

El Paso Independent School District. 1989b. *Bilingual education evaluation: The fifth year in a longitudinal study*. El Paso, Texas: El Paso Independent School District, Office for Research and Evaluation.

Genesee, Fred. 1983. "Bilingual education of majority-language children: The immersion experiments in review." *Applied Psycholinguistics* 4: 1–46.

Genesee, Fred, G. Richard Tucker, and Wallace Lambert. 1978. "An experiment in bilingual education: Report 3." *The Canadian Modern Language Review* 34: 621–643.

Gersten, Russell. 1985. "Structured immersion for language minority students: Results of a longitudinal evaluation." *Educational Evaluation and Policy Analysis* 7: 187–196.

Gersten, Russell and John Woodward. 1985. "A case for structured immersion." *Educational Leadership* 43: 75–79.

Gersten, Russell, John Woodward, and Susan Schneider. 1992. *Bilingual immersion: A longitudinal evaluation of the El Paso program*. Washington, D.C.: The Read Institute.

Holobrow, Naomi, Fred Genesee, Wallace Lambert, Joseph Gastright, and Myriam Met. 1987. "Effectiveness of partial French immersion for children from different social class and ethnic backgrounds." *Applied Psycholinguistics* 8: 137–152.

Hoover, Wes. 1983. *Language and literacy learning in bilingual instruction*. Austin, Texas: Southwest Educational Development Laboratory.

Krashen, Stephen. 1993. *The power of reading*. Englewood, Colorado: Libraries Unlimited.

Krashen, Stephen. 1994. "The input hypothesis and its rivals." In N. Ellis (ed.), *Implicit and explicit learning of languages*. London: Academic Press. 45–77.

Krashen, Stephen and Douglas Biber. 1988. *On course: Bilingual education's success in California*. Ontario, California: California Association for Bilingual Education.

Legaretta, Dorothy. 1979. "The effects of program models on language acquisition by Spanish speaking children." *TESOL Quarterly* 113 (4): 521–576.

Moore, Fernie and Gerald Parr. 1978. "Models of bilingual education: Comparisons of effectiveness." *The Elementary School Journal* 79: 93–97.

Mortensen, Eileen. 1984. "Reading achievement of native Spanish-speaking elementary students in bilingual vs. monolingual programs." *The Bilingual Review* 11(3): 11–36.

Mezynski, K. 1983. "Issues concerning the acquisition of knowledge: Effects of vocabulary training on reading comprehension." *Review of Educational Research* 53: 253–279.

Porter, Rosalie. 1990. *Forked tongue: The politics of bilingual education*. New York: Basic Books.

Pucci, Sandra. 199s4. "Supporting Spanish language literacy: Latino children and free reading resources in schools." *Bilingual Research Journal* 18: 67–82.

Ramirez, David, S. Yuen, D. Ramey, and D. Pasta. 1991. *Final report: Longitudinal study of structured English Immersion strategy, early-exit and late-exit bilingual education programs for language minority students, Volume I*. San Mateo, California: Aguirre International.

Rodriguez, Richard. 1983. *Hunger of memory*. New York: Bantam.

Rossell, Christine. 1990. "The effectiveness of educational alternatives for limited-English-proficient children." In Gary Imhoff (ed.), *Learning in two languages*. New Brunswick, N.J.: Transaction Publishers. 71–121.

Rossell, Christine and Keith Baker. 1996. "The educational effectiveness of bilingual education." *Research in the Teaching of English* 30: 7–74.

Schorr, B. 1983. "Grade school project helps Hispanic pupils learn English quickly." *The Wall Street Journal*.

Smith, Frank. 1994. *Understanding reading, Fifth edition*. Hillsdale, N.J.: Erbaum.

Verhoeven, Ludo. 1991. "Acquisition of biliteracy." *AILA Review* 8: 61–74.

Willig, Ann. 1985. "A meta-analysis of selected studies on the effectiveness of bilingual education." *Review of Educational Research* 55: 269–317.

Willig, Ann. 1987. "Reply to Baker." *Review of Educational Research* 57: 363–376.

Developing intercultural competence through foreign language instruction: Challenges and choices

Ross Steele
University of Sydney, Australia
National Foreign Language Center, Washington, D.C.

The integration of culture and language has now become a generally accepted explicit objective of foreign language education, but the practical implementation of this objective has proved difficult and elusive. In reality, language and literature still dominate the curriculum of most Foreign Language Departments at the undergraduate level, and usually culture still has a secondary role in supplying contextual tidbits. Culture is rarely integrated into the curriculum in a coherent and systematic fashion.

This is partly due to the difficulty the profession has had in reaching consensus on a definition of culture in foreign language programs and on ways of assessing the learner's cultural competence. It is also due to the fact that culture has been treated as an add-on to language and literature because, it is claimed, the limited time learners spend in class already makes it difficult for them to reach the level of communicative and reading proficiency that they are expected to attain at the end of the course. I would suggest that there are two other, more fundamental, reasons: the popular mind set of what learning a foreign language entails; and the structural division between language and literature in Foreign Language Departments.

Advertisements for commercial language courses in airline magazines can provide insights into the community mind set about language learning. Since these advertisements are a constant in airline magazines, they must presumably achieve their economic purpose. What do they propose? Here are excerpts from one advertisement published in 1996:

The X method and materials have been proven over the last 100 years ... (and only X has) *proven that it's possible to learn a new language so simply and so quickly.* [The students in my classroom don't find learning a foreign language simple and quick. Why?]

The unique X approach has been used by 30 million students and more than half the Fortune 500 companies for their executives going overseas ... [Note the reference to language learning for success in business.]

No endless memorization. No tedious translation. X courses have no vocabulary lists, no grammar drills, no workbooks. [After the elimination of memorization, translation, vocabulary lists, grammar drills and workbooks, what remains in this method?]

The X method is based on immersion and interaction. From the start you'll hear conversations of native speakers. Remarkably, within days you begin to think in their language and speaking it becomes easy and uninhibited. [The definition of "immersion and interaction" as progression from listening, to thinking, to speaking is very succinct and would be considered a caricature by the second language acquisition researchers who study the many variables that can influence the success of immersion programs. Few would agree that limited listening practice (specified later in the advertisement as thirty minutes a day) would within days have the learner thinking in the foreign language. It would indeed be a remarkable osmosis!]

Another 1996 advertisement for a different method has a photo of seven businessmen in dark suits seated around a table under the caption, *You had to pass a lot of hurdles to get this far.* [Note that successful business women are not in the photo!] Under the photo, the text reads: *Now you have just 25 minutes to get your point across—in their language. Discover how quickly barriers fall when you speak a foreign language.* [Once again the proposed goal is to speak a foreign language. Note also the metaphor of barriers falling. Removing the language barrier is a frequent metaphor in such advertisements.] The text continues: *It's no secret. If you want to succeed in the global economy, high school language skills just won't cut it. That's why an estimated 100,000 executives will learn to speak a foreign language this year. And if you're not one of them, watch out. Because they are going to pass you by. And just where will your second language make a difference? You name it. Sell your product. Explain your point of view. Negotiate your terms. Make business or social contacts. Or just make yourself more marketable.* [This advertisement, like the previous one, highlights success in business through a foreign language. The speech events mentioned ("selling," "explaining," "negotiating") are more specific than "making contacts." Performing them successfully doesn't only depend on the use of a linguistic code. Sociolinguistic and discourse appropriateness are important features of language use in these events.]

The third example of a 1996 advertisement has the heading: *Four words for the Best Foreign Language Program Ever!* [If I asked you to list the four words that describe for you the best foreign language program, what would they be?] In this advertisement they are *Free; Fast; Fun; Guaranteed.* [Wouldn't your list have been, rather, words describing content and strategies as well as outcomes?] Again this advertisement features the elements of time and ease under "Fast": *Imagine speaking the language from Day One! It really is that quick and that easy. As you learn at your own pace, you discover how to listen, think, respond and apply the language, literally after the very first lesson. Give it just 30 minutes each day and in 30 days, you'll be functional in that language—speaking and conversing comfortably...guaranteed!* [What would the learner be able to converse about comfortably, we might well ask?]

Just as in everyday conversation you hear adults say that they wish that they could *speak* French (or another foreign language), so these advertisements appealing to adults have as their theme the benefits of *speaking* a foreign language. In everyday conversation you rarely hear adults say that they wish that they could learn about French society and culture when they express the desire to be able to *speak* French. Yet it is the culture that gives the language its meanings. Similarly, culture is not mentioned in these advertisements. Yet, the speaking skill does not exist in isolation from culture which is its content. Culture is the invisible component that becomes visible when foreign language learners begin to converse with a native speaker interlocutor and realize that the linguistic code by itself does not guarantee successful communication. In these advertisements there is an implicit idealized foreign interlocutor who like a machine sends back simple answers to all your questions and requests for information.

In real life the interlocutor is an individual who has both a personal and a cultural identity. This individual belongs to a community of speakers of that language who share a common culture. Some things you say to this individual might be natural in your culture but disturbing or offensive to him or her. Topics raised in private talk and public talk are often different in different cultures. For example, Japanese people do not like talking about their feelings to strangers. The linguistic code by itself can not bridge this cultural gap. The foreign individual also brings to the conversation his or her world knowledge and knowledge of your country and its people. This knowledge, as well as age, gender and socioeconomic factors, will also influence his or her reactions to your behavior and attitudes during the conversation. If the language is an international language spoken in different countries, geographical and ethnic factors will affect the dynamics of the conversation depending on where it takes place. The purpose of the conversation, whether, for example, it is a tourist interaction or a business negotiation, shapes the flow and complexity of the exchange.

Thus, we see that speaking the language is much more than using a linguistic code if the communication is to be successful. Successful communication is culturally contextualized. Intercultural knowledge and skills are essential elements in effective interaction with a foreign language interlocutor. Sociolinguistic competence and communication management are as important as linguistic accuracy. The airline magazine advertisements make promises that are hard to deliver. This is specifically the case in the crucial area of business negotiations where different societies have different cultural conventions, both verbal and non-verbal, to indicate full, partial, or no concluding agreement.

The second reason for the lack of attention to the cultural dimension derives from the traditional structuring of fields of knowledge at the higher education level, where foreign languages are taught in Departments of Language and Literature. Until the 1960's, language was generally taught by a Grammar/translation approach. The purpose of this language learning was primarily to enable students to read the great works of literature, the study of literature being one of the centerpieces of an academic liberal arts education. Grammar/Translation, being an analytic activity, was considered to have a justified place in the academic tradition, as it contributed to the students' expanding knowledge base and analytical capacities. Students learned about the nature and functioning of language, but not necessarily how to use the language in spoken interaction. The impetus for change in language teaching was to come from outside the Language and Literature Departments. When the Soviet Union won the race into space with the successful launch of Sputnik in 1957, the United States responded with the National Defense Education Act, part of which gave substantial funding for the promotion of foreign language education. The emphasis shifted to the ability to speak the foreign language rather than to read and write it, the goals of the Grammar/Translation approach.

During the 1960's, the Audio-lingual Method pioneered by Nelson Brooks, gave the framework for the new emphasis on speaking and listening. Brooks linked the teaching of these skills to a new context. Topics from "small c" culture were seen as the most appropriate context for situations in which the spoken language could be practiced. Brooks elaborated a definition of culture appropriate to language teaching. In his 1968 article, "Teaching Culture in the Foreign Language Classroom," he proposed five meanings of culture: biological growth, personal refinement, literature and the fine arts, patterns for living, and the sum total way of life. He chose to emphasize patterns of living as the most practical approach to teaching culture in the language classroom. "Small c" culture thus became the point of departure in the process of cultural acquisition through language learning.

Whereas up to this time in Language and Literature Departments, language had been taught primarily as the means to gain access to literature, the new emphasis on teaching the listening and speaking skills for social communication gave language teaching a separate objective. The establishment of dual objectives viz. "language for communication" and "language for literature," with the communication objective prioritizing the listening and speaking skills and the literature objective prioritizing the reading and writing skills, created a dichotomy in Language and Literature Departments which became deeply entrenched. This dichotomy had two main consequences for the evolution of the Departments. Firstly, the senior Professors were the literature scholars and the junior faculty taught the communicative language courses. This underscored an uneven power balance in the Departments favoring literature over language. Secondly, culture was a victim of this divide. "Small c" culture was associated with the communicative language courses and "big C" culture was illustrated by literature. "Small c" culture was communicative language. "Big C" culture was the academic prestige language and so invested with superior status. Literature and "Big C" culture were seen as having a rightful place in the scholarly, academic role of the University. Some academics saw communicative language teaching as having a training rather than a scholarly function and thus outside the bailiwick of a University education. By its association with communicative language teaching and learning, "small c" culture was also accorded inferior status by these academics. In practice, the status of "small c" culture was further diminished as a result of the primary aim of communicative language teaching emphasizing the speaking and listening skills. A teaching strategy developed which encouraged learners to use the language by talking about themselves, their family, and friends in interaction with other learners. This focus on personal interaction limited the amount of time available for learning about symbolic features of everyday life in the foreign society, and "small c" culture was often reduced to tourist survival strategies and famous monuments. This did not help claims made by language teaching faculty for the academic acceptance of culture.

Not only did this superficial reductionist presentation of "small c" culture do little to change the usually stereotyped views the learner had of the foreign culture or develop attitudes of sensitivity and openness to that culture, but it also imposed a false separation between "small c" and "big C" culture. The developing social sciences and particularly anthropological studies showed "small c" and "big C" culture are not separate, but form an integrated and dynamic whole which expresses the attitudes, beliefs, and values of a society. In my view, the structural division within Departments of Language and Literature has prevented culture in this holistic form from achieving an accepted place as an object of study on the same level as language and literature in foreign language education at the undergraduate level.

I would suggest that the official recognition of culture as a full part of the curriculum would be a proactive way to reverse the decline in enrollments in French and German Departments, which do not have, in the American context, the sociocultural reasons that are causing rapidly increasing numbers of students to enroll in Spanish. To achieve this, perhaps a name change is necessary from Departments of Language and Literature to Departments of Language, Culture, and Literature in order to make explicit the centrality of culture to language and literature. Students and the community would thus be made aware of the significance of culture as the source of meanings for language and literature. I would personally prefer to use the plural "Department of French Languages, Cultures, and Literatures" in order to underscore the plurality of forms within each rubric and the varieties of language, culture, and literature that constitute Francophone societies. A similar argument can be made for German, Spanish, and indeed most commonly taught languages.

A change of name is of course, not sufficient. It is simply a starting point. The conventional mind set of what culture means in a Foreign Language Department also needs to be transformed. I have already referred to the division between "small c" and "big C" culture and pointed out that the association of "small c" with language courses and "big C" with literature courses has prevented the integration of "small c" and "big C" cultures as a series of interrelationships that explain the coherence of the value systems of the foreign society. For students to start perceiving these interrelationships, culture has to be seen holistically and not as separate, isolated components. At present, in most introductory foreign language textbooks, a "small c" culture topic provides the framework for the dialogue situations in each lesson. Examples of these topics are the family, home, meals, shopping, transport, leisure and vacations, etc. Because the primary purpose of the lesson is to teach language, the treatment of the "small c" culture topic is superficial and often limited to facts about the foreign culture. This presentation of culture as isolated facts which are neither related to the overarching context of the foreign culture nor contrasted with the learner's culture, feeds into the learner's preconception of the foreign culture as strange and bizarre. It does not encourage the learner to compare the two cultures, before making subjective and prejudiced judgements, or to discover the implicit value systems of the native culture that he or she takes as normal. It does not encourage the learner to look beneath the "facts," to explore what they mean within the context of the foreign culture, and to develop skills of interpreting facts and relating them to a sociocultural meaning. It does not encourage the learner to make what is implicit explicit and to discover that what he or she has spontaneously accepted as normal and natural in his or her own society is in fact cultural.

A curriculum to introduce "small c" culture coherently and systematically would develop the relationship between topics which have usually been organized as isolated units in a linear progression. It would also transform the linear progression into a spiral curriculum whereby certain topics are revisited in greater depth. The information and insights that have been gained from relating the topics to each other would allow the learner to interpret elements of the topic from a deeper and more culturally coherent perspective when the topic is revisited. Literary texts also contain illustrations of "small c" culture. These are not generally given much importance in traditional literary analysis. Giving them more importance would be one way of crossing the divide between language and literature courses.

In proposing culture as the organizing principle of Departments of Languages, Cultures and Literatures, I wish to underscore the necessity to perceive culture as composed of numerous sub-cultures. In Departments of Language and Literature, there is a tradition of language and literature having various components. For example, literature has been presented as different genres within prose, poetry, and theater, or as different literary movements across the centuries. Culture, however, has tended to be presented as one standard form that corresponds to the culture of the dominant socioeconomic elite. Factors such as gender, age, urban or regional identity, and ethnicity, which introduce variations in the standard culture, are very often overlooked. Variations of this standard culture that are manifested in sub-cultures throughout the society are constantly neglected. In our daily lives, we all participate in a range of sub-cultures within society. For culture to assume its full place in the Department's course of studies, the plurality of sub-cultures that constitute a culture must be given appropriate attention. Presenting culture not as a monolith but as a network of distinctive sub-cultures helps break down over-generalizations and stereotypes about the foreign society. Moreover, it can increase student motivation and curiosity about the foreign culture. A young learner may not be particularly interested in the standard upper-middle-class culture presented in many introductory textbooks, but could become more interested in the youth culture of different socioeconomic groups in the foreign society. If we genuinely believe in a pedagogy that focuses on the learner and adapts to the learner's interests and objectives, then offering a range of sub-cultures for the learner's interest could stimulate more foreign language learners to continue their studies to a more advanced level.

Students enroll in Foreign Language Departments in higher education for many reasons: to fulfil a language requirement; to learn a language for travel or professional purposes; because they enjoy reading and want to specialize in a foreign literature, etc. However, curricula have usually taken little account of these different reasons. The National Foreign Language Center (NFLC) has defined four basic missions for language teaching/learning in higher education:

- The general education mission seeks to develop, through the study of another language, cultural awareness, intercultural sensitivity, global perspectives, understanding of different modes of apprehending reality, and insights into the workings of language and systems of logic;
- The applied language mission supports the acquisition of task-specific competencies for occupational, recreational, or logistic purposes;
- The specialist mission (i.e. the undergraduate major) ensures the continuity of the profession and the field by preparation for graduate study in language and/or culture and/or literature, and for an academic career; and
- The heritage preservation mission focuses on the maintenance or acquisition of language for the preservation or enrichment of cultural identity.

All four of these missions are extremely important, both from the point of view of the institutions that offer and/or require language study, and from that of the students who enroll in language courses. They are by no means mutually exclusive, and can indeed be mutually reinforcing. However, the NFLC's research in the higher education sector suggests that the relationships among these different missions are often little understood, rarely articulated, and almost never accounted for in programmatic or curricular terms.

In all these missions, however, there is an implicit assumption: the role of the native speaker as a model to be imitated by all learners. Yet, as suggested previously, the interaction between foreign language learner and native speaker involves personal and cultural identities that preclude complete imitation of the native speaker as a goal for the learner. If both language and culture are to play a significant role in the language teaching and learning process, we need to reconsider the goals we set for the learner. Byram and Zarate (1994) have proposed, and I agree with them, that the reference point for the foreign language learner should not be the native speaker but the "intercultural speaker."

Foreign language learners are individuals who bring with them to their learning experience their sociocultural identity as members of their native culture. Even at the most advanced levels of proficiency, this sociocultural heritage plays a part in their interactions. Foreign language learners who speak with what is conventionally called "native speaker fluency"—a linguistic concept—are nonetheless "mediators" between the two cultures. This "mediator" concept is both linguistic and cultural. An analogy could be drawn with a person at the intersecting point of several paths. There are the paths leading from and to the native culture and the paths leading to and from the foreign culture. At this point the learner/mediator has both an insider and outsider perspective. He or she knows his or her own society from within and also knows how his or her society wants to present itself to outsiders. Similarly he or she knows about the foreign culture as an outsider, both from the way that society wants to present itself to outsiders as well as from the developing insights of an outsider getting to understand and experience the behavior, attitudes and values of that society from within. Through the foreign language, the learner is becoming a dual-culture person whose native culture will always be part of his or her identity. This is why the intercultural speaker is a more appropriate goal than the native speaker both from a language and cultural point of view.

Proposing to change the goal from the native speaker to the intercultural speaker should not in any way be seen as lowering the standards of achievement currently expected of the language learner. It is rather a question of setting equally demanding standards of a different kind that reflect the true nature of the foreign language learning experience. Nor is the goal of the intercultural speaker proposed because the limited time available for the classroom foreign language learner makes the goal of the native speaker impossible to achieve. The goal of the intercultural speaker allows learners at different levels to develop skills, knowledge, and attitudes that can be reactivated and expanded throughout their lives whenever required either socially or professionally. The competence of the intercultural speaker is not the same as the native speaker either in linguistic competence or in cultural competence.

In Byram's model (Byram forthcoming), the intercultural speaker possesses four competencies: linguistic competence, sociolinguistic competence, discourse competence, and intercultural competence. Intercultural competence consists of attitudes, knowledge, skills, and critical cultural awareness. He describes these components as:

- Attitudes of curiosity and openness, relativizing self and other, i.e. readiness to suspend belief about one's own culture and other cultures;
- Knowledge of social groups and their products and practices in one's own and in one's interlocutor's country, and of the general processes of societal and individual interaction;
- Skills of interpreting and relating, which are the abilities to interpret a document or action from another culture, to explain it, and relate it to documents or actions from one's own culture;
- Skills of discovery and interaction, which are the abilities to acquire new knowledge of a culture and cultural practices and the ability to operate knowledge, attitudes, and skills under the constraints of real-time communication and interaction; and
- Critical cultural awareness which is the ability to evaluate critically and, on the basis of explicit cultural perspectives, practices, and products, in one's own and other cultures and countries.

The intercultural speaker as defined by Byram has the ability to manage communication and interaction between people of different cultural identities and different languages, and the ability to decenter from one's own perspective; to take up another perspective; to analyze and cope with dysfunctions; and to act as a mediator between different interpretations of reality.

Some foreign language educators have recently made claims that the most effective way for foreign language learners to achieve cultural competence is through reading "text," which is to be understood not only as literature, but text in all its forms. Since the learners are literate native culture learners when they arrive in the classroom, the foreign language program should aim to teach them multiple literacies. By learning to read and interpret the different layers of meaning in the text, the students would discover the cultural attitudes and values that underpin the text. Analyzing and interpreting a range of texts on similar themes would, through intertextual processes, lead students to a deeper and more comprehensive understanding of the network of meaning systems that give coherence to the behaviors, attitudes, and values of the foreign society. While I agree that an important outcome of reading text can be cultural competence, it is my opinion that this is a restricted view of intercultural competence. I believe that intercultural competence is also interaction with people who have an individual and cultural identity and that this interaction involves knowledge, skills, and attitudes. Concentrating on text analysis also emphasizes the distance between the learner and the cultural artifacts of the foreign culture and reinforces the perception of the foreign culture as in another place, disconnected from the learner's culture. In contrast, the learner as intercultural speaker is a mediator between the two cultures, and the interaction is located in the learner and not at some external point in the foreign culture. The concept of the intercultural speaker places the learner at the center of the teaching and learning process. This focus on the learner as intercultural speaker fits with the learner-centered pedagogy that has been widely adopted as the most effective way of teaching a foreign language.

A strategy for developing the skills of intercultural communication which has been experimented successfully by Byram at the University of Durham (Byram, Morgan, et al. 1994) and Robinson-Stuart at the National Language Resource Center (LARC) at San Diego State University, is the ethnographic interview. Learners are given a project to interview foreign native speakers in the community or in the foreign country if they will be visiting or studying there. In the ethnographic interview, the student learns how to establish contact and rapport with a foreign language speaker; ask questions and practice interactive listening; reduce cultural barriers, interpret the non-verbal and get beneath the surface of words; and discover what is important to another person and get an insider's perspective. In learning how to understand another culture, the interviewers learn about themselves and their own cultural environment. This process is very helpful in weakening the students' stereotyped views of the foreign culture.

The levels of proficiency attainable by the foreign language learner are constrained by the instructional setting of the classroom. The use of authentic spoken, written, and visual materials can create a direct link with the foreign culture. Videos of real life situations filmed in the foreign country give opportunities for observing the non-verbal dimension of interactions. Movies reflect a society's evolving values. The ethnographic interview is a way of extending the walls of the classroom and establishing contact with native speakers in the community. The technologically enhanced learning environment resulting from the use of news satellite broadcasts, e-mail, and the Internet allows learners to get information about the foreign country and to ask native speakers about attitudes to events and artifacts in their own society and in the learner's society. The ability of new technology to globalize the classroom can however, run the risk of diverting attention away from the potential of the human resources in the classroom to promote cooperative learning. Group work, collaborative projects, and culture workshops encourage interaction among learners whose different knowledge, experiences, and interests allow them to learn from one another. As learners progress, the instructor increasingly becomes a guide indicating how each learner can develop the knowledge and skills required to take personal responsibility for his or her learning process and move towards the autonomy that will enable life-long learning.

A new paradigm in which culture is the link between language and literature will entail a different approach to teaching literature. Instead of culture being an add-on after the principal activity of literary analysis, the study of literature would grow out of a cultural matrix. This matrix would be created from literary and non-literary works on a chosen theme and might also include a work or works on the same theme in the native language, in order to contrast perspectives from the native and foreign cultures.

A new paradigm of culture-inspired language and literature courses will require new assessment techniques. There are already many sophisticated ways being used to assess the foreign language learner's declarative knowledge, but there has been less research on ways of assessing procedural knowledge. Foreign language instructors have little experience in assessing skills and attitudes. Performance assessment of the learner's speaking skill by the Oral Proficiency Interview is increasingly used, and may be an indicator for the assessment of intercultural competence. The knowledge, skills and attitudes of the intercultural speaker must all be assessed; but assessing each component separately will not give a true measure of the learner's competence, because this is constituted by the interrelationships among the components. Some form of holistic assessment which takes into account these relationships is also necessary. Discrete point accuracy and traditional reliance on other quantification measurements may proportionally decrease as ways of assessing performance outcomes involving more qualitative measurements are devised. A learner's portfolio which records both quantitative and qualitative measurements and documents attitudinal trends may become the most valid way of assessing holistically the intercultural speaker's competence.

As we approach the year 2000, an increasingly borderless world created by new information superhighways and multinational companies becomes the global village of our daily lives. This will perhaps be the next external influence that provokes a major change in the curriculum of Foreign Language Departments at the undergraduate level. Another source of change could be the "Standards for foreign language learning grades K–12" (1996) by a task force established in 1993 under the auspices of four national language organizations (the American Council on the Teaching of Foreign Languages and the American Associations of Teachers of French, German, and Spanish and Portuguese). The purpose of the task force—which consulted widely with educators in a variety of languages at different levels of instruction across numerous geographic regions, and with business leaders, government, and the community on the definition and role of foreign language instruction in American education—was to define content standards, i.e. what students should know and be able to do, in foreign language education. This was the seventh and final subject area to receive federal support to develop national standards. Culture features prominently in these "Standards for foreign language learning," which have the following philosophy:

> Language and communication is at the heart of the human experience. The United States must educate students who are linguistically and culturally equipped to communicate successfully in a pluralistic American society and abroad. This imperative envisions a future in which ALL students will develop and maintain proficiency in English and at least one other language, modern or classical. Children who come to school from non-English backgrounds should also have opportunities to develop further proficiencies in their first language. (1996: 7)

The Standards identify five goals, "the five C's":

(1) Communication—communicate in languages other than English;
(2) Cultures—gain knowledge and understanding of other cultures;
(3) Connections—connect with other disciplines and acquire information;
(4) Comparisons—develop insight into the nature of language and culture; and
(5) Communities—participate in multilingual communities at home and around the world.

The full statement defining the goal of Cultures reads:

> Through the study of other languages, students gain a knowledge and understanding of the cultures that use that language and, in fact, cannot truly master the language until they have also mastered the cultural contexts in which the language occurs. (1996: 27)

There are two specific standards specified for Cultures. They are:

- Students demonstrate an understanding of the relationship between the practices and perspectives of the culture studied:

> This standard focuses on the *practices* that are derived from the traditional ideas and attitudes *(perspectives)* of a culture. Cultural practices refer to patterns of behavior accepted by a society and deal with aspects of culture such as rites of passage, the use of forms of discourse, the social "pecking order," and the use of space. In short, they represent the knowledge of "what to do when and where." (1996: 46)

- Students demonstrate an understanding of the relationship between the products and perspectives of the culture studied:

> This standard focuses on the *products* of the culture studied and on how they reflect the perspectives of the culture. Products may be tangible (e.g., a painting, a piece of literature, a pair of chopsticks) or intangible (e.g., an oral tale, a dance, a sacred ritual, a system of education). Whatever the form of the product, its presence within the culture is required or justified by the underlying beliefs and values *(perspectives)* of that culture, and the cultural practices involving the use of that product. (1996: 47)

Students who have had the types of curricular experiences needed to achieve these standards at Grade 12 and who choose to continue their foreign language studies at the undergraduate level will expect courses that build on these standards.

At the undergraduate level, the "Framework for cultural competence" (American Association of Teachers of French [AATF] 1995) provides an outline for determining standards of competence with respect to foreign cultures. This Framework consists of two main sections: (1) Understanding culture; and (2) Knowledge of French-speaking societies. "Understanding culture" has three components: (a) Empathy toward other cultures; (b) Ability to observe and analyze a culture; and (c) Communication in cultural context (verbal and non-verbal).

The global village, the K–12 Standards and AATF Framework will hopefully provide the additional leverage necessary to have culture accepted as a principal component of studies in Foreign Language Departments. For this to be successful, a new paradigm will be required in which the organizing principle is culture—in its broadest, holistic definition. This paradigm will also have a different reference point, the intercultural speaker, as well as new types of assessment, which we have alluded to in this paper. These changes are required in order to eliminate the structural divide between language/"small c" culture and literature/"big C" culture which presently characterizes many departments of language and literature.

This is the challenge faced by foreign language educators today. Their capacity to institute structural curricular changes in order to redress the current imbalance of academic and administrative power that disadvantages language in favor of literature and compartmentalizes small "c" from big "C" culture will determine the future vitality of their discipline and its ability to attract students and keep them until the senior years. In a society that wants greater accountability from its institutions, enrollments in French and German will continue their current downward trend unless those departments undertake reforms to provide students in their junior as well as in their intermediate and advanced classes with a combination of linguistic and cultural skills that will enhance their professional opportunities and give them the possibility for life-long personal enrichment as intercultural speakers, readers, and viewers. Ways of increasing the learners' repertoires of skills in intercultural communication and interpretation through foreign language instruction is today's challenge for tomorrow.

REFERENCES

American Association of Teachers of French. 1995. "Framework for cultural competence." National Bulletin. January. n.p: AATF.

Brooks, N. 1968. "Teaching culture in the foreign language classroom." *Foreign Language Annals* I: 204–217.

Buttjes, D. and M. Byram (eds.). 1991. *Mediating languages and cultures*. Clevedon, U.K: Multilingual Matters.

Byram, M. In press. *NFLC Occasional Papers Series*. Washington, D.C.: The National Foreign Language Center.

Byram, M. 1989. *Cultural studies in foreign language education*. Clevedon, U.K.: Multilingual Matters.

Byram, M. and V. Esarte-Sarries. 1991. *Investigating cultural studies in foreign language teaching: A book for teachers*. Clevedon, U.K.: Multilingual Matters.

Byram, M., V. Esarte-Sarries, and S. Taylor. 1991. *Cultural studies and language learning: A research report*. Clevedon, U.K.: Multilingual Matters.

Byram, M. and C. Morgan et al. 1994. *Teaching-and-learning language-and-culture*. Clevedon, U.K.: Multilingual Matters.

Byram, M. and G. Zarate. 1994. *Definitions, objectives and assessment of socio-cultural competence*. Strasbourg: Council of Europe.

National Standards in Foreign Language Education Project. 1996. *Standards for foreign language learning: Preparing for the 21st Century*. Lawrence, Kansas: Allen Press, Inc.

Robinson, G. 1988. *Cross cultural understanding*. New York: Prentice Hall.

Robinson-Stuart, G. 1995. Forthcoming. *Ethnographic Interviewing Techniques*. Video training materials. San Diego, California: San Diego State University, National Language Resource Center.

Robinson-Stuart, G. and H. Nicon. Forthcoming. "The role of ethnography in the foreign-language classroom." *The Modern Language Journal*.

Singerman, A. (ed.). 1996. *Acquiring cross-cultural competence*. (AATF National Commission on Cultural Competence). Lincolnwood, Illinois: National Textbook Company.

Steele, R. and A. Suozzo. 1994. *Teaching French culture: Theory and practice*. Lincolnwood, Illinois: National Textbook Company.

Constructions of the learner in second language acquisition research

Michael P. Breen
Edith Cowan University, Western Australia

Introduction. My purpose in this paper is to explore aspects of language learning in the particular context of the classroom. I wish to address variation in the language learning process and its outcomes which may be at least partially explained with reference to the nature of classroom discourse. My central argument is that the classroom makes a difference in language learning and that second language acquisition (SLA) research has, to date, adopted a limited perception of the context of learning which renders only partial its explanation of certain prevailing characteristics of the process with which it is concerned.[1]

I cannot claim that the particular features of the classroom context which I describe will meet all the challenges of an adequate explanatory account of language learning. The influences of the context of learning are only one set of variables in the broader picture. However, I intend to assert that an account of such influences that is more precise than current views of the classroom in mainstream SLA research can inform and enrich both the research enterprise and its future contributions to language pedagogy.

The classroom provides particular opportunities for and specific constraints upon language learning. These opportunities and constraints can be identified through a view of the discourse of language lessons which I will explore in this paper. A prevailing feature of language learning is the differential achievement of learners. I believe that a crucial variable that can account for the relative success or failure of learners is the nature of the discourse in which they participate in classrooms.

If we see discourse broadly as the ways in which we structure knowledge and social practices (Foucault 1972 and 1984; Fairclough 1992), we can view the classroom—its subject matter, procedures, and participants—as a very particular arena which is far from being neutral and is inevitably selective in its impact upon the learning process. The same can be said of SLA research. The

---

[1]Although SLA theory and research generally assert a difference between "acquisition" and "learning"—one which on the basis of different theoretical frameworks is much debated and articulated in various terminology—throughout this paper I use the term "learning" in its generic sense to cover both learning and acquisition.

relative youth of the discipline inevitably means that the ways we plan and do the research and the ways we theorise about what we discover are piecemeal, lack the caution of mature hindsight, and, as a result, often express strongly competing positions. The emergent discourse of SLA research, despite its struggles to be dispassionately objective, is itself socially constructed and grows out of the belief systems of the academic culture or cultures in which the research is undertaken. The preoccupations, enthusiasms and tenets of SLA research a generation from now will be different and the discourse of the discipline through which it operates will evolve in ways we cannot clearly anticipate at the present time.

Starting from this assumption, and being aware that I too am constrained in what I have to propose by the currently prevailing discourse of SLA research, I will briefly summarise its achievements to date by considering how such research constructs the learner. I will use this heuristic in order to uncover the relationship of these constructs to how learners are actually positioned and constructed *as learners* in the reality of the classroom. A consideration of the discursive process through which the classroom frames or shapes language learning will form the main part of the paper, and I will conclude with a number of deductions for future SLA research and classroom pedagogy. First, however, I start in a hopefully less controversial space by identifying what most SLA researchers would agree upon as the purposes of their endeavour.

Explaining second language acquisition. It appears that we have reached a watershed in SLA research where, emboldened by over twenty years of investigation, a lively debate is currently underway concerning the kind of theory which might best explain the accumulated "facts" derived from research, and this debate has been interpreted by some as an indication of the emerging maturity of the discipline (Spolsky 1989, 1990; Hatch et al. 1990; Crookes 1992; Long 1990, 1993; Beretta 1993; and Gregg 1993). Most participants in this debate would agree that any adequate theory of SLA has to account for three key factors and, crucially, their interrelationship: (1) what the learner brings or contributes to the process, from innate predispositions through the activation of certain psychological processes such as attention or memory, to strategic behaviour which may render the process more manageable or, at least, pleasant; (2) the actual process through which language is learned; and (3) the outcomes from the process in terms of linguistic or, more broadly, communicative competence in the target language.

In exploring this relationship, SLA research to date has primarily focused upon the interaction between what learners contribute, particularly their innate templates for language or their cognitive processes, and the language data made available to them. Taking the very comprehensive review of SLA research offered by Ellis (1994) as a possible indicator, more than two thirds of the chapters in his account refer to work which assumes this interaction to be paramount. Elsewhere Ellis also overviews the less prevalent work on individual differences and the strategic behaviour of learners. And he fairly reflects the more recent and possibly less developed perspective which locates the interaction between the learner and the target language in the context of interpersonal or social situations. His account reveals that context has been defined or framed in particular ways by SLA research. It is addressed as a diversity of "social factors"—from identification by the learner with the target language group to different types of language programs—or as the specific features of classroom interaction, or as the impact of formal instruction. Ellis himself concludes that "the relationship between social factors and L2 achievement is an indirect rather than a direct one" (1994: 239). In referring to classroom interaction studies, he concludes that they have "contributed little to our understanding of how interaction affects acquisition" (1994: 607). And he deduces that formal instruction can, at most, be credited with "facilitating natural language development" in terms of increased accuracy and accelerated progress (1994: 659).

So, although we may agree or disagree with Ellis's general interpretations of the research, it appears that much of it attributes to the variable of context a relatively minor role, a mere backdrop perhaps, for the main business of the learner's relationship with target language data. My intention in this paper is to suggest that a closer examination of, in particular, the classroom as context will allow the possibility that (1) what the learner contributes, (2) how the interaction between learner and data unfolds, and (3) what the outcomes from this process may each be significantly shaped and circumscribed by social context. In other words, if we discovered and could implement all those ideal conditions which we may deduce from current SLA research as optimal for language learning, learners will still differentially achieve. They will continue to learn mostly different things, at different rates, and to different levels of proficiency. Clearly a part of this variation in outcomes will be due to diversity in the contributions of the learners to the process. But variation will also have to be explained with reference to the context in which the learning occurred so that input, process, and outcomes are seen as extensions of how the learners variously defined that context and acted in it. I will try to justify these claims in what follows, but first I return to what SLA research seems to confirm regarding the pivotal relationship between the learner and target language data. This leads me to consider how SLA research constructs the learner.

Constructing the learner. Taking the interaction between learner and language data as pivotal in the whole process, one way of summarising the main themes of SLA research to date is to consider how we may perceive the learner's active roles within this interaction. Recognising that SLA research articulates a momentarily dominant paradigm, such a consideration may enable critical reflection on the extent and limits of our current explanations of how language is learned. It can serve as a heuristic for identifying fuller or alternative explanations for what we claim to be true and, perhaps, lead us to consider what we may have overlooked.

I propose that SLA research has, to date, provided us with three constructs of the learner: the interpretative learner, the accommodating learner, and the strategic learner. I will briefly describe each of these in turn. It needs to be said at the outset, however, that researchers and theoreticians appear to attribute different weight to each of these constructs and may assert the primacy of one over the other two. Also, in constructing learners in these ways and thereby attributing to the learner a clearly active role when relating to language data, the research appears to indicate that learners interpret, accommodate, and adopt strategies more or less efficiently and only rarely does it seem necessary for them to be conscious of doing such things.

The interpretative learner. Despite vigorous debate relating to falsifiability of the claim (Gregg 1984; Krashen 1985), the place of comprehension in SLA is generally accepted as the crucible from which the acquisition process flows. Even those researchers who assert that input must be seen in the context of negotiated interaction in order to guarantee its necessity and sufficiency base their research on the assumption that comprehensible input is what learners negotiate for (Long 1981, 1985; Lightbown 1985; Pica et al. 1986; Pica et al. 1987). And the recent work which argues for the explicit focus on form for those learners whose interlanguage sustains resilient nontarget-like structures appears to conclude either that form can only be processed when meaning is already clear or that drawing a learner's attention to form can be most effective when learners already know what they are trying to say (Doughty 1988; Van Patten 1989; Lightbown 1992).

The interpretative learner clothes the language which is addressed to her with meaning, even if a good proportion of the noises she hears is incomprehensible. The effort to make sense is the catalyst of language learning. As Slobin (1973) observed over twenty years ago, developmental changes in the grammatical system are most likely to occur when learners want to understand something which seems important or want to say something which is important to them but are aware that they need further resources in order to achieve this. That they appear to be aided in this task by learner-friendly formal features in the messages communicated to them by more proficient users of the language is one of the basic tenets of SLA research. The interpretative learner devotes her conscious energy to creating meaning, and even interlocutors who have no knowledge of the theory most often adhere to the criterion of comprehensibility in what they say as if intuitively participating in a joint communicative conspiracy.

A glance at some of the dominant concerns of SLA research over a decade later reveals the interpretative learner still at centre stage. The search for the kinds of learning tasks which best generate negotiation for meaning (Long 1985; Pica et al. 1993) and recognition of the demands and potential of learners' own comprehensible output, not least as an opportunity to "notice the gap" between their own interlanguage and target forms (Swain 1985; Schmidt and Frota 1986), both rest on the assumption that it is the learner's interpretative work which coaxes the interlanguage system into more flexible and advantageous shapes. However, the efforts of SLA research to further *explain* how this striving for meaning serves as a synapse between the learner's innate linguistic capacity or, more broadly, the learner's mental processing and the target language data, have resulted in the construction of the learner as not merely interpretative but also accommodating.

The accommodating learner. I here use the term "accommodating" as deriving from Piaget's (1926) claim that adaptation of the learner's conceptual architecture to what is to be learned and, crucially, the restructuring or reinventing of the new knowledge by the learner are the dual prerequisites for the occurrence of real learning. Whilst few SLA researchers would claim Piaget as a mentor, this adaptive interaction between the learner's mental capacities and the creation of interlanguages has been a central theme of the discipline. From its infancy in the early 1970's, SLA has been fascinated by the accommodating learner. Applying Chomsky's (1965) radical theory on the relationship between language and the mind, the seminal studies of Brown (1973) on the child's construction of grammar and Slobin (1973) on psycholinguistic operating principles were strongly echoed in the interpretations of child second language learning by Dulay and Burt (1974, 1975). Their ground-breaking work on creative construction encouraged SLA research to take its first tentative steps.

The early work which perceived errors as traces of emerging competence and revealing the learner's creative reduction of the target language to manageable proportions (Dulay and Burt op.cit.) coincided with Corder's (1967) and Selinker's (1972) articulation of the notion that learners appear to reinvent the language they are learning as a series of systematic and relatively stable interlanguages. Research which built upon these ideas grappled with the reasons why some learners revealed the irritating tendency to stop accommodating and allow their language to fossilise. And explanations ranged from the loss of plasticity in the brain (Scovel 1988), through lack of input (Bickerton 1975), to lack of desire to embrace membership of the target language community (Schumann 1978).

A debate still rages in SLA research as to whether the accommodating learner is someone who places high priority on what is manageable at a particular time and is therefore unable to learn new forms of language until ready to do so or, alternatively, can be encouraged to be more open to explicit instruction of forms not yet acquired (Anderson 1979, 1990; Felix 1981; Pienemann 1989; Johnston and Pienemann 1986; White et al. 1991). A significant body of SLA theory has tried to explain the stages and variations in learners' accommodation of new forms in terms of the distinction between what learners have to consciously or explicitly work upon and those unconscious or innate mental capacities which appear not to require adaptation but merely activation of an internal mechanism for language acquisition to occur (Krashen 1981,1982; Bialystok 1979,1983; Ellis 1985; Klien 1986).

Whilst there may be disagreement as to the actual nature and extent of the accommodating learner's mental predisposition to language data, there is little doubt that recent SLA research puts a great deal into the head of such a learner. Not satisfied with the determinism and opaqueness of mentalist models, some researchers have mobilised the insights of cognitive psychology to account for the tendency of real learners to vary in the pace and attainment of their efforts. Two areas of recent research activity illustrate a view of learners as cognitively engaged in imposing order upon the chaos of the new. McLaughlin (1990; McLaughlin et al. 1983), for example, has argued that learners actively restructure new data in order to accommodate precisely because they have limited capacity to deal with all the information that may be available in that data.

Relating to the notion that learners approach their task with established "frames" or "scripts" (Minsky 1988) and reflecting the current interest in how learners integrate knowledge from exposure to the bits and pieces of performative data so that they construct minitheories of the target language and its use, Schmidt (1988) and MacWhinnery and Bates (1989) have recognised the possible contributions of models of parallel distributed processing. Rumelhart and McClelland's seminal work (Rumelhart et al. 1986) in this area suggests that language learners are likely to be in the process of constructing fairly complex networks of links between established and new knowledge and that incoming language data is tagged, like a spider forming a web, to these links. What is interesting about this model is that any pre-existing—perhaps even innate—or data-driven concepts which are formed as "nodes" in the network appear not to become so fixed or resistant to adaptation as earlier models of the mind suggested. Computer simulations of the workings of the mind undertaken by Rumelhart and colleagues reveal that these concepts exist as a loose and flexible tracery which is constantly evolving. It therefore seems that the accommodating learner is even more accommodating than we have previously assumed. The fuller implications of these ideas for our views of the Language Acquisition Device or the distinctions between acquired or learned and unanalysed or analysed language knowledge have yet to be fully explored.

There is a school of research in SLA that, while appearing to acknowledge the interpretative and accommodating nature of learners, seeks to explain the differences between learners and the differences in the pace and outcomes of learning with reference to variables seen as more tangible than mentalist or cognitive metaphors of the mind. Adherents of this school, possibly reflecting a contemporary impatience with what they perceived as a construction of the learner as a computer waiting to be switched on by incoming data, place control of the learning process primarily in the hands of the learner.

The strategic learner. Here learners are seen as actively channelling their energies in order to make the learning process manageable. The research suggests that this effort towards control of the process is expressed in two broad ways. A learner will adopt *learning strategies* that mobilise cognitive processes such as attention or memory, metacognitive planning and decision-making, and overt socio-affective behavior in ways which the learner believes will reduce the complexity of the learning task (Wenden and Rubin 1987; O'Malley and Chamot 1990; Oxford 1990). Learners' inclination to be strategic is also revealed in *communication strategies* which they employ on becoming aware that their own linguistic resources do not match the communicative demands of a particular situation or interaction. Confronted by complexities of sharing meaning, learners appear to reduce the size of the problem either by avoiding or side-stepping it or, more creatively perhaps, mobilising whatever linguistic resources they already have to produce a kind of interlanguage communicative dialect (Tarone 1977; Faerch and Kasper 1980; Poulisse 1990; Kellerman et al. 1990).

The strategic learner is a relative infant on the SLA research scene, lacking the theoretical ancestry of the interpretative and accommodating learner. There has been some debate concerning the validity of evidence derived from learners' own articulations of the strategies they use (Seliger 1983; Grotjahn 1991). Relatively few strategies are available to observation and, while inferring communication strategies from conversational data appears more acceptable to mainstream SLA—after all the interpretative and accommodating learners have largely been constructed on the basis of inferences from the linguistic production of learners—some scepticism surrounds models of strategic behavior which appear heavily reliant on learner self-reports. That successful learners appear to use more strategies and with greater flexibility could be a function of the fact that they are better able to talk about what they do reminds us of the chicken-and-egg problem concerning whether higher participation in the classroom leads to, or derives from greater proficiency. The recent efforts to train learners to clothe themselves with strategies borrowed from successful learners might also be regarded as premature given that the strategic learner appears still to be a rather speculative and unpredictable being (Cohen and Aphek 1981; Ellis and Sinclair 1989; O'Malley 1987; Wenden 1991).

This is, of course, a useful discovery in itself. And the research is beginning to suggest that learners differ in their strategy use according to age, motivation, personality type, the language being learned, the type of task being undertaken, and—significant for my present purposes—according to the social context in which they are learning (Oxford and Nyikos 1989; Ehrman 1990; Chamot et al. 1987; O'Malley et al. 1985). Furthermore, the strategic learner has been given more substance recently, either by recognising that communicative strategies are revealing expressions of how the accommodating learner works within conversation (Bialystok 1990) or that learning strategies are a function of how learners conceptually and affectively locate the learning process which they are experiencing within their beliefs or theories about language and language learning (Bialystok 1981; Wenden 1987; Horwitz 1987; Grotjahn 1991).

Noticing the gap. At the start of this inevitably brief historical interpretation of SLA research, I indicated my purpose was to enable critical reflection on the extent and limits of our explanations of how language is learned. Seeing constructs of learners as a heuristic for identifying fuller or alternative explanations for what we claim to be true might lead us to consider what we may have overlooked. The short history of SLA research with its competing theories and emergent investigative methods understandably provides us with a fragmented image of the learner. On the other hand, we might regard the three constructions of the learner as the beginnings of a possible synthesis; the foundations for a more holistic view of the language learning process. Clearly interpretative, accommodating, and strategic learners are related one to each other. Trusting the research, we could argue that the learner is all of these things and simultaneously so.

Moreover, the three constructions of the learner which I have reviewed also allow me to propose a further construction of the learner which may reveal ways in which the other three are related during the learning process. The construction of the learner which I will describe also offers one explanation for the prevailing phenomenon of variation in the processes and outcomes of language learning *despite* the interpretative, accommodating, and strategic efforts of learners. Indeed, I suggest that the learner's active engagement is significantly shaped by the fact that much of learning and, therefore, the evidence on which we base our explanations, is fashioned by the context in which it occurs.

Taking variation in the processes and outcomes of learning as something demanding an adequate explanation, we might hypothesise that differentiation between learners is least likely to be revealed between interpretative learners, more likely to be perceived between accommodating learners, and most transparent between strategic learners. In other words, locating constructs of the language learner on a continuum, we might propose that explanations of why some learners succeed while other learners fail are more likely to derive from studies of their strategic behavior than from research on accommodation. And studies of the interpretative nature of learning have less potential to account for this kind of variation. I suggest that, as we focus more on the interaction between learner and data as *actually occurring in context*, explanations for differential achievement in language learning become more possible. In order to justify such a claim, I need to begin by offering my interpretation of the context of learning.

Putting SLA research in place. I believe it is fair to say that mainstream SLA research which focuses upon the relationship between the learner and language data is conducted and reported on in ways that take for granted the social contexts in which the research is done. Dyadic encounters between caretakers and young learners or between native-speaker researchers and non-native-speaking informants, interactions in experimental situations using elicitation techniques, or closely observed interactions in classrooms are never socially neutral. The actual nature of the evidence we obtain will be a function of the social space within which we obtained it.

If we unpack the notion of the context of learning, we can see it as a unity of affective, physical, and interpersonal or collective characteristics. And there is a long tradition of research which has explored the impact of context in these terms. We might take it for granted that learners will learn better if they are working under conditions that are non-threatening and make them feel happy and relaxed. Seminal studies of remembering confirm that when we are happy, or slightly inebriated, or are deep sea divers out of the water we are better at remembering things at some later time when we are also happy, slightly inebriated, or out of the water. However, such studies also tell us that when we are sad, sober, or deep sea divers under the water we remember just as well so long as we are required to recall what we originally learned in *the same conditions* of sadness, sobriety, and in deep water (Godden and Baddeley 1975; Smith et al. 1978; Lowe 1980; Bower 1981). We might deduce from all this that relaxed classroom conditions are the least appropriate location for preparing students for examinations!

More pertinently perhaps, recent studies of first language acquisition, building on the influences of sociolinguistics, discourse analysis and the work of Vygotsky (1962), explore complexities of the interpersonal context of learning as essential ingredients of the whole process (Donaldson 1978; Bruner 1981; Lock 1980; Schiefelbusch and Pickar 1984; Wells 1981, 1985; Foster 1990). Hatch brought this kind of perspective into SLA research in revealing how learners extend their grammatical repertoires on the basis of the "scaffolding" provided for them by proficient speakers during conversations (Hatch 1978, 1992; Hatch et al. 1986). Her work has had some influence upon those in SLA research who claim a social interactionist perspective in studying speech modifications when there is communication breakdown between learners or learners and their teachers (Long 1981, 1985; Lightbown 1985; Pica et al. 1986;

Pica et al. 1987). However, as I have argued elsewhere (Breen 1985), analysis of the discourse or, more accurately, the text of social interaction alone is a rather superficial way of tracing the deeper and more complex influences of the social within the learning process.

European traditions in the study of learning seem not to have made an impact on SLA research and this fact confirms that the research is itself rooted in a particular cultural and academic milieu. A European perspective is fairly represented by Leont'ev who, like Vygotsky, saw learning as, in essence, a sociocultural activity; an interpsychological undertaking between those who have mastered knowledge or capability and those who are learning. Leont'ev identifies learning in a classroom, for example, as an activity equivalent to other social activities in the wider world such as work, family life, or participation in other everyday institutions. For Leont'ev, even an individual interpreting a text or painting a picture is participating in a social process:

> ... if we removed human activity from the system of social relationships and social life, it would not exist and would have no structure. With all its varied forms, the human individual's activity is a system in the system of social relations. It does not exist without these relations. The specific form in which it exists is determined by the forms and means of material and mental social interaction ... (Leont'ev 1981: 47)

If we focus on the learning and use of *language*, wherein social structure and system may be seen to permeate their whole texture (Halliday 1978), the relative neglect of the context of learning in SLA research seems even more surprising.

This kind of perspective suggests not only that the object of our learning is a social and cultural construct, but our participation in the activity of learning is social action. If we learn in the company of others in a language classroom, then the nature of this social action is not merely a superficial frame for our work on language data, but it permeates what is made available for learning, how learning is done, and what we achieve. The data made available to learners are socially filtered through the discourse of the classroom and, thereby, rendered distinctive from what we might describe as naturally occurring language data in a different context. Furthermore, because the data made available to learners in a classroom are a collective product with which learners interact actively as both creators and interpreters, because what learners actually learn from the classroom is socially rather than individually constructed, any explanation of how language is learned must locate learners as active participants in the discourse of language lessons. Therefore, a fourth and complementary construction of the learner *as discursive practitioner* seems to me an essential element in future SLA theory and research.

The concept of the learner as discursive practitioner requires further elaboration and I will offer this by looking more closely at some of the prevailing features of classroom discourse. I will then try to support my claim concerning the relevance of such a construction of the learner with reference to a number of findings from SLA research.

The discourse of language lessons. Discourse is a difficult concept because, like SLA research, discourse analysis is a relatively young discipline and there are several conflicting and overlapping definitions deriving from a range of theoretical and analytical positions (van Dijk 1985; Macdonell 1986). Early work was motivated by the need to uncover pattern and system at a higher level of organisation than the sentence and to analyse the properties of dialogue such as speech acts, turn-taking, topicalisation, and so on. Descriptive work was also undertaken in relation to what were seen as distinctive discourses such as media discourse, medical discourse, or legal discourse. More recently, the ideas of social theorists such as Foucault (1971, 1972) and Bordieu (1991) have led to an extension of such work to refer to how knowledge and everyday social practices are themselves constructed and sustained by discourse.

In endeavouring to synthesise earlier discourse analysis with social theory, Fairclough (1989, 1992) provides a three-dimensional perspective on discourse. For him, any instance of discourse can be seen as being simultaneously a piece of text, an instance of discursive practice, and an instance of social practice. If we applied such a framework to the language classroom, the *text* of lessons is all the available language or communicative data, be they spoken, written, or in other visual media from diagrams to facial expressions. The *discursive practices* are how texts are produced and interpreted and how different types of texts are combined. Clearly, teachers and learners in the classroom produce, interpret, and combine texts. But the teaching materials in whatever medium are also produced, interpreted, and combined by people not present in the classroom. Finally, *social practice* refers to the institutional and organisational circumstances of classroom discourse, not only those broader cultural and situational factors which locate classrooms as having a particular function and identity, but also those seemingly trivial manifestations of social practice which determine how the furniture is organised in the room or how long a lesson should last. Social practice also refers to the routines and procedures which teachers and learners jointly establish and which I have described elsewhere as expressing the underlying culture of the language class (Breen op. cit.). In other words, the social practices or the particular culture of the classroom shapes the discursive practices of teacher and learners, and these discursive practices generate and relate to the text of classroom interaction.

If we accept this three-dimensional view of discourse, and if we turn to the contributions of SLA research to our understanding of classroom language learning, we find that researchers have focused almost solely upon the *text* of classroom interaction. From this focus, however, we know that the text of language lessons, like lessons in other subjects, appears to have a consistent pattern in which teachers initiate, learners respond, and teachers follow up their responses by repetition, reformulation or evaluation (Sinclair and Coulthard 1975). McTear (1975) has pointed out that, in the language class, learners often repeat verbatim a teacher's reformulation, interpreting it as a model to be imitated. Van Lier (1988) also points out that, as many of the teachers' utterances in a lesson are not directed at particular individuals, learners can self-select and offer their own responses, some of which may include questions for clarification.

Chaudron's (1988) review of research on teacher talk in the language class reveals that a good proportion of the input made available to learners in classrooms has very specific characteristics. Teachers appear to have two-thirds more practice in the target language than all the learners put together. They also modify their speech in ways similar to the characteristics of caretaker speech to young children or native-speaker speech to non-native speakers. And such modification appears more emphatic when addressing individual learners whom they regard as having lower proficiency (Dahl 1981; Griffiths 1991; Hamayan and Tucker 1980; Henzel 1979; Kliefgen 1985; Ellis 1985; Wong-Filmore 1982).

Generally, teachers appear to be inconsistent in their reactions to learner errors with the result that learners often either disregard the opportunity to incorporate into their own interlanguages the corrections that teachers do offer or fail to recognise the force of teacher's illocutions that they should do this (Allwright and Bailey 1991; Edmondson 1985; Nystrom 1983; Van Lier 1988). Underlining Van Lier's observations about the teacher's discursive control of classroom interaction, research reveals that a remarkably high proportion of teacher utterances are interrogatives (Johnston 1990; Long and Sato 1983). And a high proportion of these are closed display questions in which learners are required to provide information which the teacher already knows rather than open referential questions which genuinely seek information from the learners (Long and Sato op. cit.). We might conclude from these general patterns in the contributions of teachers to the interactive text of language lessons that learners are not actually required to do much discursive work. What do we know about the learner's contribution to the text of lessons?

Navigating the discourse. There are few studies of learner input in the classroom apart from the body of work on conversational modifications during group or dyad work on tasks. Perhaps this is not surprising when, if we examine the research on learner participation and, by implication, their construction of the text of lessons as discursive practitioners, we find that learners are most often positioned by the discourse in a responsive role (Politzer et al. 1981). Strong (1983, 1984) discovered that a high response rate among certain learners correlated with their achievement in tests based upon the grammar, pronunciation and vocabulary of classroom speech. Seliger (1977) suggested that those learners identified as "high input generators" in the classroom performed better on an aural comprehension task than did less participating learners. In their classic study of the good language learner, Naiman et al. (1978) found that learners who raised their hands more and responded more often did better on tests. However, Day's replication of Seliger's study (1984) and Ely's (1986) investigation of learner-initiated utterances found no relationship between overt learner participation and later test attainment.

Generally, it seems that, through their control of the discursive practices of lessons, through their use of questions, explanations, commands and, crucially, their evaluation of much of the language produced by learners immediately after it is uttered, teachers significantly shape classroom discourse. We might fairly deduce that learners are positioned in certain ways by teachers' discursive practices; that they are constituted *as* learners in a primarily responsive role.

But the picture becomes more complicated if we look within the text of lessons. Much of the work on classroom interaction in SLA has identified what we might call the intertextual nature of language data in classroom talk. Allwright (1980) analyses classroom talk into three types: "samples" or instances of the target language, "guidance" where communication occurs about the target language, and "management" wherein procedural talk facilitates the optimal occurrence of samples and guidance. And Van Lier (1988) elaborates upon this intertextuality by identifying four types of interaction: small talk or student asides, teacher instructions, teacher's highly structured elicitations of student responses, and procedurally structured learner activity such as small group or dyadic tasks. Van Lier suggests that these different types of talk reflect different degrees of teacher control over topics or activities. What is clear from this work is that the data made available to the learner in the classroom is an ongoing amalgam of communication through the target language, metacommunication about the target language, and communication about the teaching-learning process, its procedures and classroom routines. And, as discursive practitioners, learners have to work within this intertextuality, identifying the textual cues which signal transitions from one kind of talk to another, sometimes with mixed success and sometimes with little help from the teacher's rapid shifting.

However, this is still not the full story. If we look beneath the surface text of classroom language learning, we may see that learners selectively work through the discourse of the classroom not only as discursive practitioners within the immediate lesson but also on the basis of (i) their definition of the teaching-learning situation; (ii) their history of experience with other realms of discourse beyond that of the particular classroom; and (iii) the social practices of the classroom at a given time or, in other words, their understanding of and contributions to the emerging culture of the classroom group. I have suggested that this culture is not only asymmetrical in terms of who controls the discourse or normative in terms of the teacher's judgements of correctness or appropriacy, but that learners *jointly conspire* with teachers in maintaining the routines and procedures of the surface text of lessons (Breen op. cit.). They navigate through classroom discourse in ways that will enable them to avoid trouble or looking foolish in public. Learners navigate the discourse to minimise its costs and sometimes to maximise its benefits on the basis of their experience that the social practices within classrooms construct knowledge, teachers, and learners in very specific ways.

Learners therefore anticipate that classrooms will frame *what counts* as valid interpretation, what counts as knowledge worth accommodating, and what counts as appropriate overt strategic behavior. Relative success or failure in learning from language lessons may therefore be related to the skill or determination with which individual learners undertake such navigation. We therefore need to consider how learners as discursive practitioners seem obliged to work through classroom discourse in selective ways. And this may provide further clues as to the different outcomes they achieve.

Discursive practices and variation in learning. So far, on the basis of language classroom research, I have suggested that the discourse of lessons is significantly shaped by the teacher, that learners are positioned in particular ways by this, that the discourse manifests a complex intertextuality, and that learners appear obliged to undertake pragmatic navigation both within this intertextuality and within certain social practices which are special to the classroom. In this section, I will identify several features in the discourse of the language classroom which also may be seen as contributory factors in the differential achievement of learners. I will refer briefly to variables in classroom input, variations in the discursive practices of learners, and variation in the circumstances of instruction.

Studies by Larsen-Freeman (1976a, 1976b), Hamayan and Tucker (1980), Lightbown (1983), and Long (1980) suggest that the frequency of occurrence of certain linguistic forms in classroom input is likely to correlate with the accurate production of these forms by learners. And further studies by Lightbown (1980, 1991), Snow and Hoefnagel-Höhle (1982), and Trahey, Spada and Ranta (1991) not only confirm this but show higher retention rates of question forms while speech directed specifically at individual learners correlates with higher individual gain scores. It appears that, while it may not be surprising that frequent occurrences of certain features in the text of lessons render them more accessible, types of teacher utterances which place what we may describe as *discursive pressure* upon learners, such as questioning or nominated turns, also shape what is learned from lessons by particular learners.

Recent research on the kinds of classroom tasks which most facilitate interaction among learners confirms the significance of discursive pressure.

Tasks that entail an information gap between interlocutors, tasks that engage learners in social exchanges about particular experiences rather than those that are explicitly pedagogic in focus, and tasks that demand a single, closed solution for successful completion are found to encourage learners to have longer turns, produce more complex language, and devote more time to negotiating for meaning than any other kinds of tasks (Berwick 1990; Long 1989). Furthermore, Tanaka (1991) and Yamazaki (1991) have suggested that learners' work on modifying particular input data through their own interaction provides for greater gains in learning than either unmodified or premodified input. In addition, Lightbown's studies of corrective feedback (Lightbown 1991) and Swain's work on the functions of learner output (Swain 1995) confirm that feedback is most likely to have an impact on the learner's interlanguage if it occurs at times when the learner is working hard to convey a particular message.

However, I have suggested earlier that learners will differently navigate through the discourse of lessons depending upon individual variations in their definitions of the situation, previous experiences of classrooms, and understanding of the dynamic social practices or culture of the classroom group. Overt discursive pressure upon particular learners does not alone account for differences in what learners learn from a lesson. For example, in tracing learner's immediate "uptake" from lessons of previously unknown vocabulary, Slimani (1989) made the interesting discovery that low participating and even non-participating learners often recalled as much if not more new information from lessons than did high-participating learners. And, significantly, learners recalled more items from lessons if they were topicalised or introduced into the text of the lesson by *learners* rather than those topicalised by the teacher. Slimani deduced that low-participating learners were directly benefiting from their high-participating colleagues. A recent replication of Slimani's study by Dobinson (1996) confirmed these findings and suggested that differences between learners in what they recalled from lessons was due to a whole range of factors and that some of the vocabulary which they not only recalled but also retained over a longer period never actually cropped up in the overt interactive text of the lesson. Some learners found that items occurring in the spoken or written texts of the lesson triggered, by association, their own deduction of new words, some of which were target forms and some not so. In other words, learners appear to be capable of navigating the discourse in ways that reflect their own different purposes and agendas (Allwright 1984). It therefore appears that some learners will deliberately avoid discursive pressure so that they can devote their attention to other things. And it appears likely that learners will differentially gain from such practices.

The interesting studies of Beebe and Zuengler (Beebe 1977; Beebe and Zuengler 1983) and of Young (1988, 1991) reveal that the learners will actually vary the style of their production depending upon whom they are addressing and, in particular, their perception of the relative status and linguistic competence of their interlocutors. Of direct relevance to the classroom, Takahashi's research suggests that learners will be more hesitant and briefer in their utterances when addressing someone whom they perceive as highly competent in the target language (Takahashi 1989) and Rampton (1987) reveals that learners, while capable of more complex language, may actually revert to earlier features of their interlanguage precisely in order to signal that they *are* learners. In other words, learners may undertake a kind of impression management in their discursive practices which expresses their own construction of themselves as learners and their construction of whom they interact with. Therefore, variations in how learners participate in the text of lessons may also be a reflection of their self-assessment and their assessment of both the teacher's language and the teacher's likely reactions to their own production.

Finally, if we turn to the different pedagogic circumstances within which learning takes place, we know that different types of classroom activities and tasks will permit different outcomes for different learners (Larsen-Freeman 1976; Tarone 1988; Schmidt 1980; Bahns and Wode 1980; Hyltenstam 1984; Lightbown 1991). We also know that different types of classrooms in terms of their overt routines and procedures or, more broadly, their social practices will generate different learning outcomes as well (Wong-Filmore 1982; Enright 1984; Spada 1987; Allen et al. 1990). And, if we widen our lens to examine the effects of different types of language programs, it appears that segregated or submersion programs, or language being taught as a separate school subject, are far less beneficial to learners than mother-tongue maintenance or immersion bilingual programs (Ellis 1994: 222–229). Clearly there is a complex of reasons for this. Communicating about subject matter which is of immediate educational or social relevance to learners entails discursive pressure. But more significant perhaps will be the impact of different programs on the learners' definition of the learning situation, particularly in terms of how their identities are recognised or constituted both as learners and members of language communities.

The learner as discursive practitioner. The foregoing review of classroom language learning research has illustrated some of the ways in which the interaction between the learner and target language data is situated within social action. We have seen that, when participating in the discourse of lessons, the learner has to act as a discursive practitioner in, at least, the following ways:

(1) Adopt a responsive role in relation to the teacher's management of the discourse;
(2) Constantly adapt to the varying inter-textuality of lessons;

(3) Define the situation on the basis of past experience, present an understanding of the culture of the classroom group, and act in ways that are seen as appropriate to the culture;
(4) Participate with the teacher and other learners in the ongoing construction of lessons and the maintenance of classroom routines and procedures;
(5) Navigate the discourse of the classroom—its specific texts, discursive practices, and particular social practices—with reference to personal costs and benefits;
(6) Act in relation to discursive pressure within teacher-learner interaction and within tasks and activities during lessons;
(7) Exploit classroom discourse as opportunities to serve own purposes and learning agenda;
(8) Manage self-identity and the presentation of self through the discourse according to own definition of the situation; and
(9) Adapt to the demands and opportunities inherent in different tasks, different types of classroom organisation, and different language programs.

Deductions for research and language pedagogy. My focus in this paper has been upon learners in classrooms. My argument has been that the social context in which learning occurs will shape the discursive practices of different learners. Because of varying factors in the discourse of the classroom—the particular text of lessons, the demands upon learners and their discursive reactions to these demands, and their definitions of the social practices or culture of the classroom—it is not at all surprising that learners will differentially achieve. In fact, these variables in social context are an important explanation for such differentiation. I am not claiming that they constitute the only explanation, but that any adequate account of the reasons why learners succeed or fail in language learning needs to locate the learner as an active discursive practitioner within context.

My intention has been to offer this construction of the learner as a complementary facet to the interpretative, accommodating, and strategic learner. It also reveals certain relationships between these activities because much of the interpretative work and communication strategies of learners are themselves discursive practices. However, I further suggest that learners in classrooms will differentially interpret, accommodate, and adopt strategies largely on the basis of what classroom discourse provides as text, what practices it requires of teacher and learners, and how it constructs both the knowledge to be learned and the unfolding teaching-learning process. I therefore believe that future SLA research would significantly benefit from an exploration of the kinds of deeper though pervasive aspects of the context of learning which I have tried to identify.

There are, of course, a number of pedagogical implications to be drawn from the perspective I have offered. We need to consider how learners are actually constructed by the discourse of lessons and the impact upon learning of the different discursive practices they may adopt. However, I will conclude by highlighting just one pedagogic implication which I see as crucial. There is a growing body of evidence which suggests that the discourse of the language classroom is distinctive. And it is distinctive in many ways from the discourse in which we participate in other contexts (Riley 1977; Gremmo et al. 1978; Edmondson 1985; Kramsch 1985; Glahn and Holman 1985; Kasper 1986; Ellis 1992). If, for most learners perhaps, language learning is embedded in the discourse of the classroom, if they learn how to *become* members of a new language community through the discursive practices which they adopt or are obliged to adopt in the classroom, how are they to transcend the specific constraints of this discourse in order to participate as speakers of the new language in other realms of discourse?

A key issue for language pedagogy is how it may facilitate the *disembedding* of language learning from the prevailing discourse of lessons. In raising this issue I am not intending to imply that all the features of the classroom discourse inhibit the learner's capacity to participate in other kinds of discourse. However, I believe it does imply that we need to consider closely how we might mobilise the beneficial discursive work of learners and also push back the mutable constraints of the current discursive and social practices of many language classrooms. This means focusing upon the *opportunities* provided by classroom discourse and seeing them as the foundations for a full range of interpretative, accommodating, strategic, and discursive ways of working. These ways of working may, in turn, enable learners to exercise responsibility for their own learning and to be active, collaborative partners in the learning process of the classroom community.

REFERENCES

Allen, P., M. Swain, B. Harley, and J. Cummins. 1990. "Aspects of classroom treatment: Toward a more comprehensive view of second language education." In B. Harley et al., *The development of second language proficiency*. Cambridge, U.K.: Cambridge University Press.

Allwright, R. 1980. "Turns, topics and tasks: Patterns of participation in language teaching and learning." In D. Larsen-Freeman (ed.), *Discourse analysis in second language research*. Rowley, Massachusetts: Newbury House.

Allwright, R. 1984. "Why don't leaners learn what teachers teach? The interaction hypothesis." In D. Singleton and D. Little (eds.), *Language learning in formal and informal contexts*. Dublin: IRAL.

Allwright, R. and K. Bailey. 1991. *Focus on the language classroom: An introduction to classroom research for language teachers*. Cambridge, U.K.: Cambridge University Press.

Anderson, R. 1979. "Expanding Schumann's Pidginisation Hypothesis." *Language Learning* 29: 105–119.

Anderson, R. 1990. "Models, processes, principles and strategies: Second language acquisition inside and outside of the classroom." In B. VanPatten and J. Lee (eds.), *Second language acquisition–foreign language learning*. Clevedon, U.K.: Multilingual Matters.

Bahns, J. and H. Wode. 1980. "Form and function in L2 acquisition." In S. Felix (ed.), *Second language development: Trends and issues*. Tübingen: Gunter Narr.

Beebe, L. 1977. "The influence of the listener on code-switching." *Language Learning* 27: 331–339.

Beebe, L. and J. Zuengler. 1983. "Accommodation theory: An explanation for style shifting in second language dialects." In N. Wolfson and E. Judd (eds.), *Sociolinguistics and second language acquisition*. Rowley, Massachusetts: Newbury House.

Beretta, A. 1993. "'As God said, and I think, rightly...' Perspectives on theory construction in SLA: An introduction." *Applied linguistics* 14: 221–224.

Bialystok, E. 1979. "Explicit and implicit judgements of L2 grammaticality." *Language learning* 29: 81–104.

Bialystok, E. 1981. "The role of conscious strategies in second language proficiency." *Modern Language Journal* 65: 24–35.

Bialystok, E. 1983. "Inferencing: Testing the 'hypothesis-testing' hypothesis." In H. Seliger and M. Long (eds.), *Classroom-oriented research in second language acquisition*. Rowley, Massachusetts: Newbury House.

Bialystok, E. 1990. *Communication strategies: A psychological analysis of second-language use*. Oxford: Basil Blackwell.

Bickerton, D. 1975. *Dynamics of a Croele system*. Cambridge, U.K.: Cambridge University Press.

Bordieu, P. 1991. *Language and symbolic power*. Cambridge, U.K.: Polity Press.

Bower, G.H. 1981. "Mood and memory." *American Psychologist* 36: 128–149.

Breen, M.P. 1985. "The social context for language learning: A neglected situation?" *Studies in second language acquisition* 7: 135–158.

Brown, R. 1973. *A first language: The early stages*. Cambridge, Massachusetts: Harvard University Press.

Bruner, J. 1981. "The pragmatics of acquistion." In W. Deutsch (ed.), *The child's construction of language*. New York: Academic Press.

Chamot, A. 1987. "The learning strategies of ESL students." In A. Wenden and J. Rubin (eds.), *Learner strategies in language learning*. Englewood Cliffs, N.J.:Prentice Hall. 71–84.

Chamot, A., J. O'Malley, L. Kupper, and M. Impink-Hernandez. 1987. *A study of learning strategies in foreign language instruction: First year report*. Rosslyn, Virginia: Interstate Research Associates.

Chaudron, C. 1988. *Second language classrooms: Research on teaching and learning*. Cambridge, U.K.: Cambridge University Press.

Chomsky, N. 1968. *Language and mind*. New York: Harcourt, Brace and World.

Cohen, A. and E. Aphek 1981. "Easifying second language learning." *Studies in second language acquistion* 3: 221–236.

Corder, S.P. 1967. "The significance of learners' errors." *International Review of Applied Linguistics* 5: 161–169.

Crookes, G. 1992. "Theory format and SLA theory." *Studies in Second Language Acquisition* 14: 425–429.

Dahl, D. 1981. "The role of experience in speech modifications for second language learners." *Minnesota Papers in Linguistics and Philosophy of Language* 7: 78–93.

Day, R. 1984. "Student participation in the ESL classroom, or some imperfections in practice." *Language Learning* 34: 69–102.

Dobinson, T. 1996. *The learning of vocabulary in the language classroom.* Unpublished M.A. dissertation, Edith Cowan University, Western Australia.

Donaldson, M. 1978. *Children's minds.* London: Fontana.

Doughty, C. 1991. "Second language instruction does make a difference: Evidence from an empirical study of SL relativization." *Studies in Second Language Acquisition* 13: 431–469.

Dulay, H. and M. Burt. 1974. "Errors and strategies in child second language acquisition." *TESOL Quarterly* 8(1): 129–136.

Dulay, H. and M. Burt. 1975. "Creative construction in second language learning and teaching." In M. Burt and H. Dulay (eds.), *On TESOL '75: New directions in second language learning, teaching and bilingual education.* Washington, D.C.:TESOL. 21–32.

Edmondson, W. 1985. "Discourse worlds in the classroom and in foreign language learning." *Studies in Second Language Acquistion* 7: 159–168.

Ehrman, M. 1990. "The role of personality type in adult language learning: An ongoing investigation." In T. Parry and C. Stansfield (eds.), *Language aptitude reconsidered.* Englewood Cliffs, N.J.: Prentice Hall.

Ellis, G. and B. Sinclair. 1989. *Learning to learn English: A course in learner training.* Cambridge, U.K.: Cambridge University Press.

Ellis, R. 1985. "Teacher-pupil interaction in second language development." In S. Gass and C. Madden (eds.), *Input in second language acquisition.* Rowley, Massachusetts: Newbury House.

Ellis, R. 1992. "Learning to communicate in the classroom." *Studies in Second Language Acquisition* 14: 1–23.

Ellis, R. 1994. *The study of second language acquisition.* Oxford, U.K.: Oxford University Press.

Enwright, D. 1984. "The organisation of interaction in elementary classrooms." In J. Handscombe et al. (eds.), *On TESOL '83: The question of control.* Washington, D.C.: TESOL. 23–38.

Faerch, C. and G. Kasper. 1980. "Processes and strategies in foreign language learning and communication." *Interlanguage Studies Bulletin* 5: 47–118.

Fairclough, N. 1989. *Language and power.* London: Longman.

Fairclough, N. 1992. *Discourse and social change.* Cambridge: Polity Press.

Felix, S. 1981. "The effect of formal instruction on second language acquisition." *Language Learning* 31: 87–112.

Forster, S. 1990. *The communicative competence of young children.* London: Longman.

Foucault, M. 1971. *L'Ordre du discours.* Paris: Gallimard.

Foucault, M. 1972. *The archeology of knowledge.* London: Tavistock Publications.

Foucault, M. 1984. "The order of discourse." In M. Shapiro (ed.), *Language and politics.* Oxford: Basil Blackwell.

Glahn, E. and A. Holman. (eds.) 1985. *Learner discourse.* Anglica et Americana 22. Copenhagen: University of Copenhagen.

Godden, D.R. and A.D. Baddeley. 1975. "Context-dependent memory in two natural environments: On land and under water." *British Journal of Psychology* 66. 325–331.

Gregg, K. 1984. "Krashen's monitor and Occam's razor." *Applied Linguistics* 5: 79–100.

Gregg, K. 1993. "Taking explanation seriously; or, let a couple of flowers bloom." *Applied Linguistics* 14: 276–294.

Gremmo, M., H.Holec, and P. Riley. 1978. "Taking the initiative: Some pedagogical applications of discourse analysis." Melanges Pedagogiques, University of Nancy, France: CRAPEL.

Griffiths, R. 1991. "Pausological research in an L2 constext: A rationale and review of selected studies." *Applied Linguistics* 12: 276–294.

Grotjahn, R. 1991. "The research programme subjective theories: A new approach in second language research." *Studies in Second Language Acquisition* 13: 187–214.

Halliday, M.A.K. 1978. *Language as social semiotic.* London: Edward Arnold.

Hamayan, E. and R. Tucker. 1980. "Language input in the bilingual classroom and its relations to second language achievement." *TESOL Quarterly* 14(4): 453–468.

Hatch, E. 1978. "Discourse analysis and second language acquisition." In E. Hatch (ed.), *Second language acquisition*. Rowley, Massachusetts: Newbury House.

Hatch, E. 1992. *Discourse and language education*. Cambridge, U.K.: Cambridge University Press.

Hatch, E., Y. Shirai, and C. Fantuzzi. 1990. "The need for an integrated theory: connecting modules." *TESOL Quarterly* 24: 697–716.

Henzl, V. 1979. "Foreigner talk in the classroom." *International Review of Applied Linguistics* 17: 159–165.

Horwitz, E. 1987. "Surveying student beliefs about language learning." In A. Wenden and J. Rubin (eds.), *Learner strategies in language learning*. Englewood Cliffs, N.J.: Prentice Hall. 119–129.

Hyltenstam, K. 1984. "The use of typological markedness conditions as predictors in second language acquisition: the case of pronominal copies in relative clauses." In R. Anderson (ed.), *Second language: A crosslinguistic perspective*. Rowley, Massachusetts: Newbury House.

Hyltenstam, K. and M. Pienemann (eds.) 1985. *Modelling and assessing second language acquisition*. Clevedon, U.K.: Multilingual Matters.

Johnston, S. 1990. "Teacher questions in the academic language-content classroom." Unpublished paper, Temple University, Tokyo, Japan.

Johnston, M. and M. Pienemann. 1986. *Second language acquisition: A classroom perspective.* Wales: New South Wales Migrant Education Service.

Kasper, G. (ed.) 1986. *Learning, teaching and communication in the foreign language classroom.* Aarhus: Aarhus University Press.

Kellerman, E., A. Amerlaan, T. Bongaerts, and N. Poulisse. 1990. "System and hierarchy in L2 compensatory strategies." In R. Scarcella, E. Anderson, and S. Krashen (eds.), *Developing communicative competence*. New York: Newbury House.

Kliefgen, J. 1985. "Skilled variation in a kindergarten teacher's use of foreigner talk." In S. Gass and C. Madden (eds.), *Input in second language acquisition*. Rowley, Massachusetts: Newbury House.

Klien, W. 1986. *Second language acquisition* Cambridge, U.K.: Cambridge University Press.

Kramsch, C. 1985. "Classroom interaction and discourse options." *Studies in Second Language Acquisition* 7: 169–183.

Krashen, S. 1981. *Second language acquisition and second language learning*. Oxford: Pergamon.

Krashen, S. 1982. *Principles and practice in second language acquisition*. Oxford: Pergamon.

Krashen, S. 1985. *The Input Hypothesis: Issues and implications*. London: Longman.

Leont'ev, A. N. 1981. "The problem of activity in psychology." Quoted in J. Wertsch. 1985. *Vygotsky and the social formation of mind*. Harvard: Harvard University Press.

Lightbown, P. 1980. "The acquisition and use of questions by French L2 learners of English." In S. Felix (ed.), *Second language development: Trends and issues*. Tübingen, Germany: Gunter Narr.

Lightbown, P. 1983. "Exploring relationships between developmental and instructional sequences in L2 acquisition." In H. Seliger and M. Long (eds.), *Classroom oriented research in second language acquisition*. Rowley, Massachusetts: Newbury House.

Lightbown, P. 1985. "Can language acquisition be altered by instruction?" In K. Hyltenstam and M. Pienemann (eds.), *Modelling and researching second language acquisition*. Clevedon. U.K.: Multilingual Matters.

Lightbown, P. 1991. "What have we here? Some observations on the effect of instruction on L2 learning." In R. Phillipson et al. (eds.), *Foreign/second language pedagogy research*. Clevedon, U.K.: Multilingual Matters.

Lightbown, P. 1992. "Getting quality input in the second/foreign language classroom." In C. Kramsch and S. McConnel-Ginet (eds.), *Text and context: Cross-disciplinary perspectives on language study*. Lexington, Massachusetts: D.C. Heath and Co.

Lock, A. 1980. *The guided reinvention of language*. New York: Academic Press.

Long, M. 1980. *Input, interaction and second language acquisition*. Unpublished Ph.D. dissertation, University of California at Los Angeles.

Long, M. 1981. "Input, interaction and second language acquisition." In H. Winitz (ed.), *Native language and foreign language acquisition*. Annals of the New York Academy of Sciences, 379.

Long, M. 1985. "A role for instruction in second language acquisition: Task-based language teaching." In K. Hyltenstam and M. Pienemann (eds.), *Modelling and assessing second language acquisition*. Clevedon, U.K.: Multilingual Matters.

Long, M. 1989. "Task, group, and task-group interactions." *University of Hawai'i Working Papers in ESL* 8: 251–286.

Long, M. 1990. "The least a second language acquisition theory needs to explain." *TESOL Quarterly* 24(4): 649–666.

Long, M. 1993. "Assessment strategies for SLA theories." *Applied Linguistics* 14: 225–249.

Long. M. and C. Sato. 1983. "Classroom foreigner talk discourse: forms and functions of teachers' questions." In H. Seliger and M. Long (eds.), *Classroom oriented research in second language acquisition*. Rowley, Massachusetts: Newbury House.

Lowe, G. 1980. "State-dependent recall decrements with moderate doses of alcohol." *Current Psychological Research* 1: 3–8.

Macdonnel, D. 1986. *Theories of discourse*. Oxford: Basil Blackwell.

MacWhinnery B. and E. Bates. 1989. *A cross-linguistic study of sentence processing*. Cambridge, U.K.: Cambridge University Press.

McLaughlin, B. 1990. "Restructuring." *Applied Linguistics* 11: 113–128.

McLaughlin, B., T. Rossman, and B. McLeod. 1983. "Second language learning: An information processing perspective." *Language Learning* 33: 135–158.

McTear, M. 1975. "Structure and categories of foreign language teaching sequences." In R. Allwright (ed.), *Working Papers: Language Teaching Classroom Research*. University of Essex, Department of Language and Linguistics.

Minsky, M. 1988. *The society of mind*. London: Pan Books.

Naiman, N., M. Frohlich, H. Stern, and A. Todesco. 1978. *The good language learner. Research in Education Series 7*. Toronto: The Ontario Institute for Studies in Education.

Nystrom, N. 1983. "Teacher-student interaction in bilingual classrooms: Four approaches to error feedback." In H. Seliger and M. Long (eds.), *Classroom oriented research in second language acquisition*. Rowley, Massachussets: Newbury House.

O'Malley, J. 1987. "The effects of training in the use of learning strategies on acquiring English as a second language." In A. Wenden and J. Rubin (eds.), *Learner strategies in language learning*. Englewood Cliffs, N.J.: Prentice Hall. 133–144.

O'Malley, J., A. Chamot, G. Stewner-Manzanares, R. Russo and L. Kupper. 1985. "Learning strategy applications with students of English as a second language." *TESOL Quarterly* 19(2): 285–296.

O'Malley, J., and A. Chamot. 1990. *Learning strategies in second language acquisition*. Cambridge: Cambridge University Press.

Oxford, R. 1990. *Language learning strategies: What every teacher should know*. Rowley, Massachusetts: Newbury House.

Oxford, R., and M. Nyikos. 1989. "Variables affecting the choice of language learning strategies by university students." *Modern Language Journal* 73: 291–300.

Piaget, J. 1926. *The language and thought of the child*. London: Routledge and Kegan Paul, 1955.

Pica, T. 1983. "Adult acquisition of English as a second language under diferent conditions of exposure." *Language Learning* 33: 465–497.

Pica, T., C. Doughty, and D. Young. 1986. "Making input comprehensible: Do interactional modifications help?" *International Review of Applied Linguistics* 72: 1–25.

Pica, T., R. Young, and C. Doughty. 1987. "The impact of interaction on comprehension." *TESOL Quarterly* 21(4): 737–758.

Pienemann, M. 1989. "Is language teachable? Psycholinguistic experiments and hypotheses." *Applied Linguistics* 10: 52–79.

Politzer, R., A. Ramirez, and S. Lewis. 1981. "Teaching standard English in the third grade: classroom functions of language." *Language Learning* 31: 171–193.

Poulisse, N. 1990. *The use of compensatory strategies by Dutch learners of English*. Enschede: Sneldruk.

Rampton, B. 1987. "Stylistic variability and not speaking 'normal' English: Some post-Labovian approaches and their implications for the study of interlanguage." In R. Ellis (ed), *Second language acquisition in context*. London: Prentice Hall International. 47–58.

Riley, P. 1977. "Discourse networks in classroom interaction: Some problems in communicative language teaching." Melanges Pedagogiques, University of Nancy, France: CRAPEL.

Rumelhart, D., J. McClelland, and the PDP Research Group (eds.) 1986. *Parallel distributed processing: Explorations in the microstructures of cognition, Volume 2. Psychological and biological models*. Cambridge, Massachusetts: MIT Press.

Schiefelbusch, R., and J. Pickar (eds.). 1984. *The acquisition of communicative competence*. Baltimore, Maryland: University Park Press.

Schmidt, M. 1980. "Coordinate structures and language universals in interlanguage." *Language Learning* 30: 397–416.

Schmidt, R. 1988. "The potential of parallel distributed processing for SLA theory and research." *University of Hawai'i Working Papers in ESL* 7: 55–56.

Schmidt, R., and S. Frota. 1986. "Developing basic conversational ability in a second language: a case-study of an adult learner." In R. Day (ed.), *Talking to learn: Conversation in second language acquisition*. Rowley, Massachusetts: Newbury House.

Schumann, J. 1978. "The acculturation model for second language acquisition." In R. Gingras (ed.), *Second language acquisition and foreign language teaching*. Arlington, Virginia: Center for Applied Linguistics. 27–50.

Scovel, T. 1988. *A time to speak: A psycholinguistic enquiry into the critical peroid for human speech*. Rowley, Massachusetts: Newbury House.

Seliger, H. 1977. "Does practice make perfect? A study of interaction patterns and L2 competence." *Language Learning* 27: 263–278.

Seliger, H. 1987. "The language learner as linguist: Of metaphors and realities." *Applied linguistics* 4: 129–158.

Selinker, L. 1972. "Interlanguage." *International Review of Applied Linguistics* 10: 209–231.

Sinclair, J., and M. Coulthard. 1975. *Towards an analysis of discourse*. Oxford: Oxford University Press.

Slimani, A. 1989 "The role of topicalisation in classroom language learning." *System* 17: 223–234.

Slobin, D. 1973. "Cognitive prerequisites for the development of grammar" In C. Ferguson and D. Slobin (eds.), *Studies of child language development*. New York: Appleton-Century-Crofts.

Smith, S. M., A. Glenberg, and R. Bjork. 1978. "Environmental context and human memory." *Memory and Cognition* 6: 342–353.

Snow, C. and M. Hoefnagel-Höhle. 1982. "School age second language learners' access to simplified linguistic input." *Language Learning* 32: 411–430.

Spada, N. 1987. "Relationships between instructional differences and learning outcomes: A process-product study of communicative language teaching." *Applied Linguistics* 8: 181–199.

Strong, M. 1983. "Social styles and second language acquisition of spanish-speaking kindergarteners." *TESOL Quarterly* 17(2): 241-258.

Strong, M. 1984. "Integrative motivation: cause or result of successful language acquisition?" *Language Learning* 34: 1-14.

Swain, M. 1985. "Communicative competence: some roles of comprehensible input and comprehensible output in its development." In S. Gass and C. Madden (eds.), *Input in second language acquisition.* Rowley, Massachusetts: Newbury House.

Swain, M. 1995. "Three functions of output in second language learning." In G. Cook and B. Seidlhofer (eds.), *For H.G. Widdowson: Principles and practice in the study of language.* Oxford: Oxford University Press.

Takahashi, T. 1989. "The influence of listener on L2 speech." In S. Gass, C. Madden, D. Preston, and L. Selinker (eds.), *Variation in second language acquisition, Volume II: Psycholinguistic issues.* Clevedon, U.K.: Multilingual Matters.

Tanaka, N. 1988. "Politeness: some problems for Japanese learners of English." *JALT Journal* 9: 81-102.

Tarone, E. 1977. "Conscious communication strategies in interlanguage: A progress report." In H. Brown, C. Yorio, and R. Crymes (eds.), *On TESOL '77.* Washington, D.C.: TESOL.

Tarone, E. 1988. *Variation in interlanguage.* London: Edwards Arnold.

van Dijk, T. 1985. *Handbook of discourse analysis, Volumes 1-4.* London: Academic Press.

Van Lier, L. 1988. *The classroom and the language learner.* London: Longman.

VanPatten, B. 1989. "Can learners attend to form and content while processing input?" *Hispania* 72: 409-417.

Vygotsky, L. 1962. *Thought and language.* Cambridge, Massachusetts: MIT Press.

Wells, G. 1981. *Learning through interaction: The study of language development. Language at home and school, Volume 1.* Cambridge, U.K.: Cambridge University Press.

Wells, G. 1985. *Language development in the preschool years. Language at home and school, Volume 2.* Cambridge, U.K.: Cambridge University Press.

Wenden, A. 1987. "How to be a successful language learner: Insights and prescriptions form L2 learners." In A. Wenden and J. Rubin (eds.), *Learner strategies in language learning.* Englewood Cliffs, N.J.: Prentice Hall. 103-118.

Wenden, A. 1991. *Learner strategies for learner autonomy.* New York: Prentice Hall.

Wenden, A. and J. Rubin (eds.) 1987. *Learner strategies in language learning.* Englewood Cliffs, N.J.: Prentice Hall.

White, L., N. Spada, P. Lightbown, and L. Ranta. 1991. "Input enhancement and question formation." *Applied Linguistics* 12: 416-32.

Wong-Filmore, L. 1982. "Instructional language as linguistic input: Second language learning in classrooms." In L. Wilkinson (ed.), *Communicating in the classroom.* New York: Academic Press.

Yamazaki, A. 1991. "The effect of interaction on second language comprehension and acquisition." Unpublished paper. Temple University, Tokyo, Japan.

Young, R. 1988. "Variation and the interlanguage hypothesis." *Studies in Second Language Acquisition* 10: 281-302.

Young, R. 1991. *Variation in interlanguage morphology.* New York: Peter Lang.

The Cognitive Academic Language Learning Approach: Theoretical framework and instructional applications

Anna Uhl Chamot
The George Washington University

The Cognitive Academic Language Learning Approach (CALLA) is an instructional model designed to increase the school achievement of students who are learning through the medium of a second language. The original model has continued to be developed and refined as it has been tried out in classrooms during recent years (Chamot and O'Malley 1986, 1987, 1989, 1994, 1996). CALLA is now being implemented in twenty-six school programs in the United States.

The CALLA model fosters language and cognitive development through its integration of language and content and its explicit instruction in learning strategies. The model is based on cognitive learning theory in which learners are viewed as mentally active participants in the teaching-learning interaction. The mental activity of learners is characterized by the application of prior knowledge to new problems, the search for meaning in incoming information, higher level thinking, and the developing ability to regulate one's own learning. The CALLA model suggests ways in which teachers can tap these mental processes through activities in which students reflect on their own learning, and learn how to learn more effectively.

This paper describes the theoretical background of the CALLA model, which incorporates major findings of current research and effective practice for all students in both first and second language learning contexts. I present the components of the CALLA model and discuss instructional practices congruent with its research base.

Theoretical framework. The development and refinement of the CALLA model has been based on research conducted with both language minority and language majority students. Much of this research has sought to understand learning processes in order to improve instruction, especially for students who are not encountering success in school.

In his study of immigrant students in Canada, Cummins (1981, 1984) found that whereas conversational skills in English were generally learned in about two years, students' ability to handle academic language demands lagged far behind, and students typically needed five to seven years of exposure to English in school before they could be successful academically. Cummins postulated that both the task difficulty and the context of language use have an impact on language comprehension and use. Language that is supported by contextual clues is easier to understand than language without such support, and language that is used for social interaction about familiar topics is easier than language that contains new or difficult information. The language of the academic classroom tends to be both reduced in context and cognitively demanding, so it is not surprising that students learning a second language need a longer period of time to acquire academic language than to acquire social language. Collier (1987, 1989) conducted similar research with immigrant students in the United States and not only confirmed Cummins' findings, but also found that the age of arrival in the U.S. was related to the number of years students needed to reach reasonable achievement levels in academic subjects, with students arriving at the age of twelve or older faring the worst. While these students are engaged in the slow process of learning the type of English needed for subject matter classes, their native English-speaking peers are moving ahead with increasingly complex academic courses. For the secondary English as a second language (ESL) learner, it becomes almost impossible to catch up.

Both Cummins and Collier have argued for the need to provide continuing instruction through students' native language while they are acquiring English so that they do not fall behind in subject matter concepts. Concepts and skills developed in the native language can readily be transferred to English once students have learned the language with which to express them.

Another line of research influencing the development of the CALLA model was work on modifications to the ESL curriculum that was standard in the 1970's and 1980's in most schools. This standard curriculum focused on linguistic aspects of English and stressed the vocabulary and grammatical structures needed for conversational encounters—very much as foreign language courses tend to be designed. Mohan (1979, 1986) suggested that the language and vocabulary of content subjects such as social studies and science would be a useful addition to ESL courses. DeAvila and Duncan (1984) and Cohen, DeAvila, and Intili (1981) conducted research with bilingual science/mathematics materials and found that children using the materials not only outperformed control group children in developing science and math concepts, but also significantly improved their skills in English. In addition, research on Canadian French immersion programs found that children were acquiring high levels of academic proficiency in French in classes that focused on content rather than language (Genesee 1987).

A third area of research, conducted with both native English-speaking students of various ages and second language learners, began by investigating the mental processes and learning strategies of effective learners (Naiman, Frohlich, Stern, and Todesco 1978; O'Malley et al. 1985a; Rubin 1975, 1981). This line of research has led to studies comparing more effective with less effective language learners, finding that, in general, more effective language learners are more adept at selecting and deploying appropriate strategies for a language learning task than are less effective students (Abraham and Vann 1987; Chamot, Küpper, and Impink-Hernandez 1988a, 1988b; Nagano 1991; O'Malley, Chamot and Küpper 1989; Vandergrift 1992; Vann and Abraham 1990). An early experimental study on learning strategy instruction with ESL students found that students receiving strategies instruction significantly improved the coherence and organization of oral reports and also showed improved comprehension on some of the listening tasks presented (O'Malley, Chamot, Stewner-Manzanares, Russo, and Küpper 1985a). Subsequent learning strategies studies with both second and foreign language students have reported moderate success in improving language proficiency (e.g., Chamot, Robbins, and El-Dinary 1993; Chamot, Barnhardt, El-Dinary, and Carbonaro 1993; Rubin, Quinn, and Enos 1988; Thompson and Rubin 1993). However, studies reporting success with learning strategies interventions have been reported with native English-speaking students for a variety of learning activities, including reading comprehension, problem-solving, and written composition (e.g., Brown and Palincsar 1982; Garner 1987; Harris and Graham 1992; Palincsar and Brown 1984; Pressley and Associates 1990; Silver and Marshall 1990).

The development of CALLA has been based on these complementary strands of research. In addition, the cognitive learning theoretical model developed by Anderson (1983, 1985) and applied to school learning by Gagné (1985), has provided considerable explanatory power for an information-processing perspective on second language learning. (See O'Malley and Chamot 1990 and O'Malley, Chamot, and Walker 1987.)

Instructional applications. Instructional practices recommended in CALLA include extensive use of students' prior conceptual and linguistic knowledge, cooperative learning, teacher modeling and scaffolding, and an emphasis on interactive dialogue on thinking and learning strategies.

In integrating content subject matter, academic language, and learning strategy instruction, the CALLA model advocates beginning with high priority content topics, adding academic language development activities to them, and then teaching learning strategies that can help students understand and remember both the content and language. Therefore, content includes topics from academic subjects such as science, mathematics, social studies, and literature. The rationale for the emphasis on content subjects is that language, as the medium of communication, permeates all aspects of the curriculum. In other words, language is essential for activities such as scientific experiments, solving mathematics problems, finding out about historical events and geographical information, and writing about a novel. By focusing on important content subject topics, language teachers can help students acquire the vocabulary and linguistic structures they will need to perform successfully in other subjects.

It is important for students learning English to experience how academic language is used in a variety of disciplines, not just in the discipline of English language arts. As students move up through different grade levels from elementary to secondary school, the language demands of different subjects increase substantially. For example, in lower grades science can be taught with activities, discussion, and demonstration, while the secondary level adds reading science texts for information and writing more formal lab reports. In social studies, the demand for literacy skills appropriate to the subject increases as students enter upper elementary and secondary grades. Even mathematics, which used to be seen as a language-free subject, has changed in the last years and now requires students to communicate mathematically, read and solve story problems, and explain solutions verbally or in writing. (See, for example, National Council of Teachers of Mathematics 1989.). Language, therefore, is necessary for all content areas in school. Teachers of all subjects can help their students—both second language learners and native English speakers—by engaging them in language activities related to the subjects they teach.

By the same token, language teachers—whether ESL or grade-level English and language arts teachers—can help all students become more successful academically by showing them how to listen to explanations in different subject areas, how to read expository and discipline-specific texts as well as literary ones, how to answer questions about content subjects and explain reasoning and problem solutions, and how to write reports and informational summaries as well as creative and personal experience compositions. Thus language teachers bring into their classrooms a taste of how language is used functionally in other disciplines.

Trying to deal with both content and academic language at the same time is daunting to second language learners, yet simultaneous processing of both information and language is required in grade-level classrooms. Techniques for more effective learning can help students cope with this double demand. The third component of CALLA specifies instructional techniques for explicitly teaching learning strategies that second language learners can apply to both language and content tasks. Learning strategies tend to be mental processes over which students have conscious control and which they can choose to deploy for challenging tasks. Learning strategies have been classified into three general types which interact with and support each other (O'Malley and Chamot 1990). The first type of learning strategy has to do with metacognitive processes in which students reflect on and identify their own abilities and approaches to learning. The metacognitive strategies include as *planning*, *monitoring*, and *evaluating* strategies. That is, learners set a goal for and decide how to organize a task before embarking on it, regulate their performance as they engage in the task, and check their performance after completing it. These metacognitive strategies are useful for any learning task and can assist students in reflecting about the task and about their own learning approaches. Allied to these metacognitive strategies are *cognitive strategies*, in which students use specific strategies to accomplish both language and content tasks. Some of the most useful cognitive strategies include *elaboration of prior knowledge*, in which students actively recall what they already know about the lesson's topic; *making inferences*, in which students use context clues to make logical guesses at new words or phrases; *imagery*, in which they use actual or imagined pictures as an aid to comprehension or production; and *linguistic transfer*, in which students recognize and use similarities between their native language and English. Finally, *social* and *affective* strategies can be used by students to help them complete a learning or communication task. For example, a student may ask *questions for clarification*, *cooperate* with classmates, or use *positive self-talk* to allay anxiety.

Metacognitive and social/affective learning strategies are closely tied to student motivation. By using metacognitive strategies, students come to understand that they have power over their own learning and can choose to be successful by effort and appropriate strategy use. They learn how to regulate a learning task themselves, rather than being dependent on the teacher. By using social and affective strategies, students come to value team work in socially-mediated learning, and develop feelings of self-efficacy as learners. Self-efficacy is at the root of self-esteem, motivation, and self-regulation (Bandura 1992; Zimmerman 1990). Thus, strategies instruction can not only help students achieve cognitive learning goals but can also increase their motivation and self-confidence.

Learning strategies are best taught as part of an ongoing lesson, rather than separately. When students are shown how to use one or more strategies for a specific classroom task, they easily see the immediate application of the strategy. The task itself needs to be complex enough to make the use of learning strategies result in better learning. A very easy task may be accomplished without conscious learning strategies, but a challenging one can profit from appropriate strategies use. For example, developing a report based on extensive reading about a topic is a complex task that can more easily be achieved with strategies such as *planning*, *selective reading*, *making inferences*, *cooperation*, and *evaluation*. Strategies are learned more easily when the teacher models how to use them, often by thinking aloud through a task similar to the one students will be working on. When the teacher models processes such as reading comprehension and writing, students can observe how an expert reader or writer thinks and interacts with the task (Chamot and O'Malley 1994). At this point, the teacher should give names to the strategies being taught so that students can discuss and analyze their own strategies use. Many opportunities for practice with new strategies are needed before students become completely comfortable with them. Once students have developed a repertoire of strategies, they should be encouraged to select the strategies that work best for them and are most appropriate for a given task. The goal of strategies instruction is for students to become independent, self-regulated learners. When students become self-efficacious learners, they become, in Cummins' (1986) words, *empowered*.

Conclusion. The CALLA instructional model can be used by both ESL and content teachers to develop academic language, subject matter knowledge, and how-to-learn procedures for all students. Although all students can benefit from an approach which seeks to develop and enhance the type of language and learning approaches that will lead to greater academic success in school, students who do not speak English as their native language are in critical need of such instruction.

A CALLA classroom can become a learning community in which the prior knowledge that students bring from diverse linguistic and cultural backgrounds is valued for its role in constructing new knowledge for all students. Teachers can help all their students by sharing the secrets of effective learning through modeling and practice with learning strategies in English and all other subjects. By helping students become better learners, teachers will be developing the sense of self-efficacy and empowerment that students need for educational achievement.

REFERENCES

Abraham, R.G. and R.J. Vann. 1987. "Strategies of two language learners: A case study." In A. Wenden and J. Rubin (eds.), *Learner strategies in language learning*. Englewood Cliffs, N.J.: Prentice-Hall. 85–102.

Anderson, J.R. 1983. *The architecture of cognition*. Cambridge, Massachusetts: Harvard University Press.

Anderson, J.R. 1985. *Cognitive psychology and its implications. Second edition*. New York: Freeman.

Bandura, A. 1986. *Social foundations of thought and action: A social cognitive theory*. Englewood Cliffs, N.J.: Prentice-Hall.

Brown, A.L., and A.S. Palincsar. 1982. "Inducing strategies learning from texts by means of informed, self-control training." *Topics in Learning and Learning Disabilities* 2(1). 1–17.

Chamot, A.U. and J.M. O'Malley. 1986. *A cognitive academic language learning approach: An ESL content-based curriculum*. Washington, D.C.: National Clearinghouse for Bilingual Education.

Chamot, A.U. and J.M. O'Malley. 1987. "The Cognitive Academic Language Learning Approach: A bridge to the mainstream." *TESOL Quarterly* 21(2): 227–249.

Chamot, A.U. and J.M. O'Malley. 1989. "The Cognitive Academic Language Learning Approach." In P. Rigg and V.G. Allen (eds.), *When they don't all speak English*. Urbana, Illinois: National Council of Teachers of English. 108–125.

Chamot, A.U. and J.M. O'Malley. 1994. *The CALLA handbook: How to implement the Cognitive Academic Language Learning Approach*. Reading, Massachusetts: Addison-Wesley.

Chamot, A.U. and J.M. O'Malley. 1996. "The Cognitive Academic Language Learning Approach (CALLA): A model for linguistically diverse classrooms." *The Elementary School Journal* 96 (3): 259–273.

Chamot, A.U., S. Barnhardt, P.B. El-Dinary, and G. Carbonaro. 1993. *Methods for teaching learning strategies in the foreign language classroom and assessment of language skills for instruction: Final report.* Available from ERIC Clearinghouse on Languages and Linguistics.

Chamot, A.U., L. Küpper, and M.V. Impink-Hernandez. 1988b. *A study of learning strategies in foreign language instruction: The third year and final report.* McLean, Virginia: Interstate Research Associates. Available from ERIC Clearinghouse on Languages and Linguistics.

Chamot, A.U., M. Dale, J. M. O'Malley, and G.A. Spanos. 1993. "Learning and problem solving strategies of ESL students." *Bilingual Research Journal* 16 (3/4): 1–38.

Chamot, A.U., J. Robbins, and P.B. El-Dinary. 1993. *Learning strategies in Japanese foreign language instruction. Final Report.* Available from ERIC Clearinghouse on Languages and Linguistics.

Cohen, E.G., B. DeAvila, and J.A. Intil. 1981."Executive summary: Multicultural improvement of cognitive ability." Report to State of California Department of Education.

Collier, V.P. 1987. "Age and rate of acquisition of second language for academic purposes." *TESOL Quarterly* 21: 617–641.

Collier, V.P. 1989. "How long? A synthesis of research on academic achievement in a second language." *TESOL Quarterly* 23: 509–531.

Cummins, J. 1981. "Age on arrival and immigrant second language learning in Canada: A reassessment." *Applied Linguistics* 2: 132–149.

Cummins, J. 1984. *Bilingualism and special education: Issues in assessment and pedagogy.* San Diego, California: College-Hill Press.

Cummins, J. 1986. "Empowering minority students: A framework for intervention." *Harvard Educational Review* 56(1): 18–36.

Cummins, J. 1992. "Language proficiency, bilingualism, and academic achievement." In P.A. Richard-Amato and M. A. Snow (eds.), *The multicultural classroom: Readings for content-area teachers.* White Plains, New York: Longman. 16–26.

DeAvila, E.A., and S.E. Duncan. 1984. *Finding Out/Descubrimiento. Training Manual.* San Rafael, California: Linguametrics Group.

Ellis, N.C. 1994. *Implicit and explicit learning of languages.* London: Academic Press.

Garner, R. 1987. *Metacognition and reading comprehension.* Norwood, N.J.: Heinemann.

Genesee, F. (ed.) 1994. *Educating second language children: The whole child, the whole curriculum, the whole community.* New York: Cambridge University Press.

Harris, K.R. and S. Graham. 1992. *Helping young writers master the craft: Strategy instruction and self-regulation in the writing process.* Cambridge, Massachusetts: Brookline Books.

Mohan, B.A. 1979. "Relating language teaching and content teaching." *TESOL Quarterly* 13: 171–182.

Mohan, B.A. 1986. *Language and content.* Reading, Massachusetts: Addison-Wesley.

Nagano, K. 1993. *Investigating FL listening comprehension strategies through thinking aloud and retrospection.* Unpublished paper.

National Council of Teachers of Mathematics. 1989. *Curriculum and evaluation standards for school mathematics.* Reston, Virginia: National Council of Teachers of Mathematics.

Naiman, N., M. Fröhlich, H.H. Stern, and A. Todesco. 1978. *The good language learner.* Toronto: Ontario Institute for Studies in Education.

O'Malley, J.M. and A.U. Chamot. 1990. *Learning strategies in second language acquisition.* Cambridge: Cambridge University Press.

O'Malley, J.M. and A.U. Chamot. 1994. "Learner characteristics in second language acquisition." In A.O. Hadley (ed.), *Research in language learning: Principles, processes, and prospects.* Lincolnwood, Illinois: National Textbook Company. 96–123.

O'Malley, J.M., A.U. Chamot, G. Stewner-Manzanares, L. Küpper, and R.P. Russo. 1985a. "Learning strategies used by beginning and intermediate ESL students." *Language Learning* 35: 21–46.

O'Malley, J.M., A.U. Chamot, G. Stewner-Manzanares, R.P. Russo, and L. Küpper. 1985b. "Learning strategy applications with students of English as a second language." *TESOL Quarterly* 19: 285–296.

O'Malley, J.M., A.U. Chamot, and L. Küpper. 1988. "Listening comprehension strategies in second language acquisition." *Applied Linguistics* 10(4): 418–437.

O'Malley, J.M., A.U. Chamot, and C. Walker. 1987. "Some applications of cognitive theory to second language acquisition." *Studies in Second Language Acquisition* 9: 287–306.

Oxford, R. 1990. *Language learning strategies: What every teacher should know*. New York: Newbury House.

Palincsar, A.S., and A.L. Brown. 1984. "Reciprocal teaching of comprehension-fostering and comprehension-monitoring activities." *Cognition and Instruction* 1: 117–175.

Pressley, M. and Associates. 1990. *Cognitive strategy instruction that really improves children's academic performance*. Cambridge, Massachusetts: Brookline Books.

Rubin, J. 1975. "What the 'good language learner' can teach us." *TESOL Quarterly* 9: 41–51.

Rubin, J. 1981. "Study of cognitive processes in second language learning." *Applied Linguistics* 11: 117–131.

Rubin, J., J. Quinn, and J. Enos. 1988. *Improving foreign language listening comprehension*. Report to International Research and Studies Program, U.S. Department of Education, Washington, D.C.

Silver, E.A. and S.P. Marshall. 1990. "Mathematical and scientific problem solving: Findings, issues, and instructional implications." In F. F. Jones and L. Idol, (eds.), *Dimensions of thinking and cognitive instruction*. Hillsdale, N.J.: Lawrence Erlbaum. 265–290.

Thompson, I. and J. Rubin. 1993. *Improving listening comprehension in Russian*. Report to International Research and Studies Program, U.S. Department of Education, Washington, D.C.

Vandergrift, L. 1992. "The comprehension strategies of second language (French) listeners." Unpublished doctoral dissertation, University of Alberta, Edmonton, Alberta, Canada.

Vann, R.J. and R.G. Abraham. 1990. "Strategies of unsuccessful language learners." *TESOL Quarterly* 24(2): 177–198.

Zimmerman, B.J. 1990. "Self-regulated learning and academic achievement: An overview." *Educational Psychologist* 25: 3–17.

The effect of participation structure on second-language acquisition and retention of content

Mary Ann Christison
Snow College

Introduction. Once there were two linguists who were selected to participate in a special space project. They were going to the moon. One of the linguists said to the other, "You know, I don't really want to go to the moon. I want to do something different, something unique. Everybody goes to the moon." "No," said the other linguist, "we need to follow our instructions. If we don't, we'll get in trouble. Besides, if we don't go to the moon, where would we go." "Well," said the first linguist, "I've been thinking about it, and I have an idea." "Okay," said the second linguist, " what's your idea?" "No one has done what I am thinking about doing. It is something unique and different. I think we should go to the sun." "The sun? Are you kidding?" "No," said the first linguist. "I have it all figured out. We can go at night!" (adapted from Heyer 1992).

This story makes us laugh because the linguist's suggestion of going to the sun creates problems that seem so immediately obvious based on the information that we possess. Yet, the problems did not seem so obvious to the linguist who made the suggestion. One linguist was focused on one way of looking at the information, and the other linguist focused on another. Second- and foreign-language teachers often feel like the linguist who suggested going to the sun. They have many creative and exciting ideas for the language classroom, but they may not have all the information they need to make the best choices in selecting materials, content, tasks, and activities for the language classroom. How can language teachers get the information they need about language classrooms? One important way to get more information about the language class is by looking at classroom-based research. Classroom-based research attempts to provide confirming or disconfirming evidence for claims about the influence of language instruction and its effect on classroom interaction, retention of content, and second-language acquisition (Chaudron 1988).

The chief factor motivating this study is the desire for information about language classrooms. If language classrooms can have a positive influence on second-language acquisition, and if second-language learners can learn and make gains in the target language as a result of classroom activity, then there are several questions that need to be answered: What kind of classes do learners need if they are to make optimal gain in the target language? What patterns of interaction are best? What kind of input do language learners need to acquire the target language? What environments make the input conducive to language acquisition? Understanding classroom interaction and patterns of communication in the language classroom is central to the process of teaching and learning (Johnson 1995).

Review of the literature. This study will look at the effect of participation structure on second-language acquisition and retention of content. The shift in second- and foreign-language classrooms from teacher-fronted, teacher-centered classrooms to interactive, student-centered ones has been receiving a growing amount of attention (Chaudron 1988; Ramirez 1995; Ellis 1994). It has also received theoretical and empirical support (Long 1981, 1983; Long and Porter 1985; Pica and Doughty 1985, 1986; Christison 1986). Researchers such as Long and Porter (1982) have suggested that through these conversational adjustments speakers and second-language learners make the most dramatic advances. Long (1981) has stated that the interaction adjustments that native speakers make with each other are now considered the most crucial to second-language acquisition. Conversational adjustments can be defined as natural psychological units in comprehension and memory (Long 1981). These units include paraphrase, confirmations, comprehension checks, clarification, agreement, arbitration, self-repair, repairing others, and elaboration. They require negotiation of the input between and among speakers.

Content-based instruction is the integration of content learning with language teaching aims (Briton, Snow, and Wesche 1989). Many language teaching professionals now claim that a second language is learned most effectively when used as the medium to convey informational content that is of interest and relevance to the learner (Cantoni-Harvey 1987; Crandall 1987; Mohan 1979, 1986; Shih 1986). This trend, with its broad-based pedagogical implications, has gained wide acceptance in language teaching in recent years (Briton, Snow, and Wesche 1989). Although it is possible to discover the impetus of this claim by examining the last decade when language educators and researchers argued for looking at language teaching in the boarder context of language across the curriculum, few studies have actually demonstrated the effect of participation structure and content-based teaching on retention of the content (Christison 1986).

The study I present here attempts to do the following.

(1) Provide a more thorough definition of the differences in participation structures normally used in classrooms;
(2) Evaluate the possible effect of participation structure on the interactional process; and

(3) Utilize research methodology that may help us make predictions about the effect of input on second-language acquisition and retention of content.

Methods.

Subjects. The subjects in this study were fifty international students who ranged in age from eighteen to twenty-eight. The mean age was 20.76. They came from eleven different language backgrounds. There were eleven females and thirty-nine males. The two teachers selected to participate in the study had both previously taught ESL, but neither could be considered an experienced teacher. They were similar in their years of formal education and teaching experience. The subjects were randomly assigned to one of the eight groups.

Design. The design was a 2 (Teacher 1 vs. Teacher 2) X 2 (teacher-fronted vs. interactive) X 2 (Group 1 vs. Group 2) factorial design. There were six dependent measures: native language background, length of time spent studying in the United States, Michigan Proficiency Scores, Pretest 1, and two delayed learning measures, Posttests 1 and 2.

Materials. Two typical language activities were used to collect the data. (See Appendix.) Each teacher taught four groups and two activity types. These activities were defined as either teacher-fronted or interactive. Inherent in the different activity types were changes in participation structure and task type, although the content of both activity types remained the same. The teacher-fronted groups sat in straight rows, while the interactive groups formed small circles. Both groups were asked to solve a problem. Subjects in the teacher-fronted groups were all given the same information and then asked to solve a problem. Subjects in the interactive groups were given part of the information. They were asked to synthesize the information and share the most important parts with the group. They were then asked to make a decision collectively.

Procedure. Preliminary data were collected first. All subjects completed a short questionnaire that included name, native language background, and time spent studying in the United States. Subjects were also given a Michigan Proficiency test. A pretest on the content was administered. The subjects were randomly assigned to eight groups. Each teacher taught two teacher-fronted groups and two interactive groups. The eight groups were videotaped, with each session lasting fifty minutes. Posttest 1 was given immediately after the videotaping; Posttest 2 was given two weeks later; both posttests were timed.

Scoring. The two areas of consideration in the scoring were patterns of interaction and types of propositions. Patterns of interaction are the direction of conversation within the group—who initiates the conversation, who receives the conversation. Each student was assigned a number for tracking purposes. The eight groups were analyzed in the following way:

(1) Who was involved in the turn?
(2) How much time did each turn take? and
(3) How many turns did the subjects take?

Written transcripts were also made of each videotaped group in order to understand the different propositional types being used.

Results. Analyses showed that students placed within a ten-point raw score range on the Michigan Tests. Analyses on the Pretest showed no significant differences among the fifty students in their knowledge of the content being covered. The first analyses were all concerned with time—teacher interaction time, student interaction time, and interaction time that did not involve the teacher.

Teacher interaction time. The eight groups were first analyzed for teacher interaction time. The results of this analysis appear in Table 1 (right). In the teacher-fronted group, teachers participated in 90.5% to 100% of the total interaction time. In the interactive group, teachers participated in less of the total interaction time, 36.7% to 56.8%.

Table 1. Teacher interaction time

Teacher-fronted	Interactive
90.5%–100% of the total time	36.7%–56.8% of the total time

Percentages include both teacher-initiated and teacher-received time

Student interaction time. The eight groups were also analyzed for student interaction time. The results of this analysis appear in Table 2 (right). In the teacher-fronted group, students participated in 14.8% to 19.5% of the total time. The percentages increase with the interactive group with percentages ranging from 19.7% to 28.8% of the total time.

Table 2. Student interaction time

Teacher-fronted	Interactive
14.8%–19.5% of the total time	19.7%–28.8% of the total time

Percentages include student-initiated and student-received time.

Interaction time without the teacher. The interaction time in groups without the teacher was also calculated. In the teacher-fronted group the teachers were not involved in 0% to 2.17% of the interactions. In the interactive groups, teachers were not involved in 11.21% to 21.82% of the total interaction time. These results appear in Table 3 (right).

Table 3. Interaction time without the teacher

Teacher-fronted	Interactive
0%–2.17% of the total time	11.21%–21.82% of the total time

Turn-taking totals. Each group was analyzed for turn-taking in three different ways: total turns, total teacher turns, and total student/student turns. In the teacher-fronted group there were 261 turns compared to 339 turns in the interactive group. Total teacher turns in the teacher-fronted group were 251, dropping to 144 in the interactive group. The most noticeable difference between participant structures was the number of student/student turns. All the teacher-fronted groups had only 10 student/student turns while the interactive groups had 195. These results appear in Table 4 (below).

Table 4. Turn-taking totals

Teacher-fronted		Interactive	
Total turns	261	Total turns	339
Teacher turns	251	Teacher turns	144
Student/Student turns	10	Student/Student turns	195

Student/Student = interaction without teachers

Number of Propositions. The number of propositions across groups was also analyzed. There were 525 more propositions in the teacher-fronted group than in the interactive group. The number of propositions for the teacher in the teacher-fronted group was quite dramatic. There were 2,342 in the teacher-fronted group and 787 in the interactive group. The case was reversed for the students. There were only 387 proposition for students in the teacher-fronted group. For the interactive group, this figure rose to 1,417. The data used in these analyses of numbers of propositions appear in Table 5 (below).

Table 5. Number of propositions

Teacher-fronted		Interactive	
Teacher	2,342	Teacher	787
Students	387	Students	1,417
Total	2,729	Total	2,204

Subject performance on posttests. The results of subject performance on Posttests 1 and 2 appear in Tables 6 and 7 (below). The raw score means on Posttest 1 were 18.12 for the teacher-fronted and 21.72 for the interactive. There was a standard deviation of 8.10 and 7.60 respectively. A one-way analysis of variance indicated that the difference between the means was not significant at the $P > .05$ level. The raw score means on Posttest 2 increased for both groups to 20.80 and 25.28. A one-way analysis of variance indicated that the difference between the means of 8.20 and 6.60 was significant at the $P < .05$ level.

Table 6. Subject performance on Posttest 1

	T-F	I
M	18.12	21.72
SD	8.10	7.60

Note: $\underline{F}$ (1,48)=4.48, $P > .05$

Table 7. Subject performance on Posttest 2

	T-F	I
M	20.80	25.28
SD	8.20	6.60

Note: $\underline{F}$ (1,48)=4.48, $P < .05$

Conversational adjustments. The final area of analysis concerned the conversational adjustments. Table 8 (right) shows the final analysis. In the teacher-fronted groups, there were 242 conversational adjustments—201 from teachers and forty-one from subjects. The interactive groups had only 117 conversational adjustments for teachers, but conversational adjustments from students went up to 171.

Table 8. Conversational adjustments

Teacher-fronted		Interactive	
Teacher . .	201	Teacher . . .	117
Students . . .	41	Students . .	171
Total	242	Total	288

Discussion. The analyses showed many differences between teacher-fronted and interactive groups. Interactive groups could be defined as more student-centered. Students in interactive groups spent more time engaged in interaction in terms of turn-taking time and time involved in the turn. In addition, students in the interactive groups were involved in more conversational adjustments. According to Long (1981), they had greater opportunity to make gains in the target language. If the difference between interactive and teacher-fronted classrooms is defined in this way, it seems that one possible effect of participation structure would be greater opportunity for language acquisition.

There was no significant difference among students on the Pretest on content. Because a different kind of classroom experience should result in a different outcome, and there were significant differences between the teacher-fronted and interactive groups in the ways suggested above, one would expect there to be a significant difference between the groups on Posttest 1. The reverse turned out to be true. There were no significant differences between interactive and teacher-fronted groups on Posttest 1. The interactive group did better than the teacher-fronted group, but not significantly better. The increase in subject time, subject turns, number of propositions, and number of conversational adjustments are all important factors to consider according to the hypothesis for second-language acquisition; yet, all these differences did not result in a significant difference on Posttest 1.

Although many facets of this study added to my understanding of second-language classrooms, the most interesting was the Posttest 2. One goal of this research was to utilize research methodology that would help predict the effect of input on retention of content. When the learners were tested at the end of two weeks, the scores between teacher-fronted and interactive groups were significantly different. Interactive groups did significantly better than the teacher-fronted groups. What could account for this difference? It seems that in the long run the subjects in the interactive groups were able to improve and make greater gains in their understanding of the content involved in these activities.

The combination of factors seems to give the subjects in the interactive groups the strategies necessary for making significant gains in the mastery of content once they leave the classroom and must rely on input and interaction in the outside world. While we have no way of knowing exactly what happened between the administration of Posttest 1 and Posttest 2, it seems highly unlikely that all the interactive subjects could have participated in something the teacher-fronted subjects had not. The results suggest that interactive groups gained some important skills or strategies that assisted them in finding support for certain hypotheses that they generated about the material. If we look at the preceding results carefully, we find that the most outstanding features of the differences between these groups pertain to the type of interaction the subjects were involved in. Rather than content questions and answers, which were the principal propositions from the teacher-fronted groups, subjects in the interactive groups had more opportunities for conversational adjustments. They spent more time finding ways to negotiate meaning—do comprehension checks, elaborate, clarify, etc. These skills will certainly be more useful in real-life situations where students must find methods for extracting meaning from conversation and confirming their own hypotheses and guesses about the language with which they are presented. We have no way of knowing, of course, but if this trend continues for the interactive groups, we might begin to see an even greater advantage for retention of content in interactive groups.

Obviously, more research needs to be done over a longer span of time in order to fully understand the effect of participation structure on the retention of content. It is also important to continue to investigate language acquisition and retention of content through classroom-based research in order to make well-informed decisions about language education and language pedagogy.

REFERENCES

Brinton, D.M., M.A. Snow, M.B Wesche. 1989. *Content-based second language instruction*. Boston, Massachusetts: Heinle and Heinle.

Cantoni-Harvey, G. 1987. *Content area language instruction: Approaches and strategies*. Reading, Massachusetts: Addison-Wesley.

Chaudron, C. 1988. *Second language classrooms*. New York: Cambridge University Press.

Christison, M.A. 1986. *The effect of participation structure in second and foreign language classrooms*. Unpublished Ph.D. dissertation, University of Utah.

Crandall, J. (ed.) 1987. *ESL through content-area instruction: Mathematics, science, social studies*. Englewood Cliffs, N.J.: Prentice-Hall Regents.

Ellis, R. 1994. *Instructed second language acquisition*. Cambridge, Massachusetts: Blackwell Publishing.

Heyer, S. 1992. *Picture stories in beginning composition*. Englewood Cliffs, N.J.: Prentice-Hall.

Johnson, K.E. 1995. *Understanding communication in second language classrooms*. New York: Cambridge University Press.

Long, M.H. 1981. "Input, interaction, and second language acquisition." In H. Winitz (ed.), *Native language and foreign language acquisition*. Annals of the New York Academy of Sciences 379.

Long, M.H. 1983. "Does second language instruction make a difference? A review of research." *TESOL Quarterly* 17(3): 359–382.

Long, M.H. 1985. "Input and second language acquisition theory." In S. Gass and C. Madden (eds.), *Input in second language acquisition*. Rowley, Massachusetts: Newbury House. 377–393.

Long, M.H. and P. Porter. 1985. "Groupwork, interlanguage talk, and second language acquisition." *TESOL Quarterly* 19(2): 207–228.

Mohan, B.A. 1979. "Relating language teaching and content teaching." *TESOL Quarterly* 13(2): 171–182.

Mohan, B.A. 1986. *Language and content*. Reading, Massachusetts: Addison-Wesley.

Pica, T. and C. Doughty. 1985a. "Input and interaction in the communicative classroom: A comparison of teacher-fronted and group activities." In S. Gass and C. Madden (eds.), *Input in second language acquisition*. Rowley, Massachusetts: Newbury House. 115–132.

Pica, T. and C. Doughty. 1985b. "The role of group work in classroom second language acquisition." *Studies in Second Language Acquisition* 7(2): 233–248.

Ramirez, A.G. 1995. *Creating Contexts for second language acquisition*. White Plains, N.Y.: Longman Publishers.

Shih, M. 1986. "Content-based approaches to teaching academic writing." *TESOL Quarterly* 20(4): 617–648.

APPENDIX

Who should adopt? Sample Instructional Activity: Interactive Group.

Who should adopt?

Instructions: You are a member of the social services adoption committee for the state. The following six applicants have applied to adopt this child. Only one child is available for adoption. Your task is to decide which of the following six applicants would make the best parents(s). The remaining five applicants would be ineligible for adoption in the future, so make your decision very carefully. The child's future depends on the parent(s) you choose. Your group must decide on only one applicant. Each member of your group will have a piece of the information. You must listen to each group member give his/her part of the information in order to gain all of the facts. Your information appears below.

Applicant #1: Bill and Mary Smith have been married for 10 years. Bill is 40 and Mary is 38. Both are college graduates. Their combined income is $45,000 with Mary making $30,000 as a public school teacher and Bill making $15,000 as an author of children's books. They own their own home and one car, a 1976 Volkswagen. The Smiths have never been able to have children, so this adoption is very important to them because they have waited may years. Bill would take care of the baby at home. They would not use day care. Although the Smiths are not wealthy, they manage their money well and would be able to give a child most of the material things it wanted. In their spare time, they like to read and go bowling.

Who should adopt? Sample Instructional Activity (partial): Teacher-fronted Groups

Who should adopt?

Instructions: You are a member of the social services adoption committee for the state. The following six applicants have applied to adopt this child. Only one child is available for adoption. Your task is to decide which of the following six applicants would make the best parents(s). The remaining five applicants would be ineligible for adoption in the future, so make your decision very carefully. The child's future depends on the parent(s) you choose. Your group must decide on only one applicant. Each member of your group has all of the information. Listen and share the information you feel is essential with your group.

Applicant #1: Bill and Mary Smith have been married for 10 years. Bill is 40 and Mary is 38. Both are college graduates. Their combined income is $45,000 with Mary making $30,000 as a public school teacher and Bill making $15,000 as an author of children's books. They own their own home and one car, a 1976 Volkswagen. The Smiths have never been able to have children, so this adoption is very important to them because they have waited may years. Bill would take care of the baby at home. They would not use day care. Although the Smiths are not wealthy, they manage their money well and would be able to give a child most of the material things it wanted. In their spare time, they like to read and go bowling.

Grammaticality judgment tasks and second-language development

Ronald P. Leow
Georgetown University

Introduction. The grammaticality judgment (or metalinguistic) task in second-language acquisition (SLA) has its roots in the procedures used by early descriptive and theoretical linguists (especially generative grammarians), who primarily used this type of task to explore first-language (L1) or second-language (L2) intuitions about the grammaticality of specific sentences or structures. The theoretical assumption underlying the use of the grammaticality judgment task in both first- and second-language acquisition has been that it provides a relatively direct window into learners' implicit knowledge or grammatical competence of the L1/L2 language (Kellerman 1986), thereby allowing researchers to investigate the mental structures and processes that make learning possible (Bley-Vroman, Felix, and Ioup 1988). This intuitive perspective is reflected in studies that have employed the task mainly to address hypothesis testing under the framework of Universal Grammar (e.g., Bley-Vroman, Felix, and Ioup 1988; Lakshmanan and Teranishi 1994; White 1985) and markedness theory (e.g., Mazurkewich 1985; Tanaka 1987). However, the validity of this task in addressing learners' linguistic competence, especially in the second or foreign language, has come under scrutiny (e.g., Birdsong 1989, 1990; Chomsky 1986; Cowan and Hatasa 1994; Ellis 1991). The presence of variation in learners' responses appears to suggest that the grammaticality judgment task may be more of a performance task rather than one that reflects competence (Ellis 1991).

Even if we were to accept that grammaticality judgments do not provide direct evidence of learners' competence, there is still some controversy as to (1) whether grammaticality judgments are reliable measures of performance (e.g., Ellis 1991; Christie and Lantolf 1991, cited in Gass 1994; Gass 1994); (2) whether there exists any relationship between learners' performance on grammaticality judgment tasks and that on other types of production tasks (e.g., Arthur 1980; Chaudron 1983; Ellis and Rathbone 1987; Liceras 1983); and, as a corollary of (2), (3) whether modality of task plays a differential role in this relationship. This study seeks to address these three issues in SLA.

Grammaticality judgments and reliability. Ellis (1991) is one of the first to address the reliability of grammaticality judgments in SLA by employing a test-retest research design in his study. In the first part of the experiment, twenty-one adult advanced ESL Chinese students were asked to discriminate and correct a total of forty sentences involving dative alternation in English. In the second part (one week later), a subset (eight) of the subject population was selected to perform a subset (ten) of the items used on the first part. In addition, the eight subjects were also requested to perform a think aloud task. Based on the considerable inconsistency found in his subjects' grammaticality judgments, Ellis tentatively suggests that "learners' judgments can be inconsistent, and, therefore, unreliable, when they are unsure" (1991: 181). However, as Gass (1994) correctly points out, this study is not without statistical and methodological problems; only descriptive statistics were provided and the numbers of subjects and linguistic items were not held constant for both parts. Consequently, Ellis's study does not provide a definitive answer to the issue of the reliability of grammaticality judgments in SLA.

Christie and Lantolf (1991) attempted to investigate English-speaking L2 learners' grammaticality judgments of properties of the *Pro*-drop Parameter in Italian. Their study included an oral narrative task (describing the events of a film) along with the grammaticality judgment task and, like Ellis' study, was administered in two parts, the second part taking place fifteen months later on a subset of the original total. In addition, during the second part two subjects performed an oral task (not specified in the write-up of the study). Based on the findings that one of the two subjects demonstrated no change in performance on the grammaticality judgment task and a substantial change on the oral task, Christie and Lantolf concluded that "judgment data may not necessarily inform us of a learner's changing interlanguage grammar" (1991: 18). However, this study, like Ellis's, shares both statistical and methodological problems.

Gass (1994) attempted to address the issue of the reliability of grammaticality judgments by considering reliability as a function of syntactic constraints. Her subjects were twenty-three Asian students who were attending mandatory English classes before pursuing studies in other disciplines. The linguistic structures were relative clauses in English, carefully chosen for their positions on the accessibility hierarchy assumed to be capable of making predictions on the frequency and occurrence of these clauses in languages (based on Keenan and Comrie 1977 and Comrie and Keenan 1979). Subjects were requested to make grammaticality judgments on thirty sentences and given a scale of +3 to –3 to record their degree of confidence while making the judgments. Like the other two studies, there were two parts, with one week separating the two administrations. In the second part, four subjects were also interviewed to elicit their reasons for making changes on that part. Gass found statistical correlations for both dichotomous judgments (discrimination) and data on the seven-point scale. She also found a graphic relationship between the comparison of reliability data and an experimentally non-motivated oral production task in which subjects combined two sentences to form a relative clause (taken from an earlier study, Gass 1979). Gass concludes that, based on her results, the issue of reliability of grammaticality judgments cannot be separated from issues of indeterminacy, that is, learners' partial knowledge or absence of knowledge of certain aspects of the L2 grammar, and that grammaticality judgments "are indeed reflective of patterns of second-language use" (1994: 320).

Gass's study is methodologically and statistically superior to the first two studies due to the substantially greater number of subjects, control of the same number of subjects in both parts, and use of statistical analyses to interpret her data. However, her statement that grammaticality judgments reflect patterns of second-language use is limited to only a period of one week of learners' interlanguage. Research also needs to investigate patterns of second-language use from different stages beyond one week to truly address potential changes in learners' L2 interlanguage. In addition, her effort to compare, though not statistically, learners' performance on the grammaticality judgment task with that on an oral production task also needs to be addressed statistically at both stages to reflect more precisely learners' patterns of second language use at different stages of their interlanguage. This relationship between learners' performance on a grammaticality judgment task and other L2 production tasks will be discussed in the next section.

Grammaticality judgments and L2 production. Studies that have attempted to investigate the relationship between learners' performance on grammaticality judgment tasks and production data are quite inconclusive in their findings. On the one hand, some studies have claimed that learners' metalinguistic judgments generally reflect their oral production (e.g., Arthur 1980) and that these judgments by both native speakers and non-native speakers tend to be validated by their performances on other measurement tasks. (See Chaudron's 1983 comprehensive review of research on grammaticality judgment studies.) On the other hand, studies have also revealed mismatches between learners' performances on grammaticality judgment tasks and their production (e.g., Liceras 1983; Ellis and Rathbone 1987). For example, Liceras investigated both beginning and advanced Spanish students' performances on a grammaticality judgment task, a translation task, and a fill-in-the-blank task. Results indicated that there were mismatches in percentage scores between the beginning students' performance on the grammaticality judgment task and those demonstrated on the other two written production tasks, mismatches not found for students of superior language experience. Similar results appear in Ellis and Rathbone (1987), who found no correlation between the performances of 39 beginning learners of German on a grammaticality judgment task (measuring three word order rules in German) and a task designed to measure their ability to correctly use these rules in spontaneous production.

The apparent lack of relationship between grammaticality judgment tasks and learners' production seems more evident when learners are required to verbalize the underlying grammatical rules. Some studies have claimed that performance on grammaticality judgment tasks do not predict learners' performance on production tasks (e.g., Hulstijn and Hulstijn 1984; Green and Hecht 1992; Sorace 1985). For example, Green and Hecht provided 300 German learners of English at different levels of proficiency with twelve sentences containing errors commonly committed by German pupils. They were asked to state the rules for the errors and to correct the errors. They found that while learners were able to produce correct corrections in almost all cases for which they had a rule available, a lack of rule knowledge did not impact on their ability to produce such corrections. In other words, the results appear to indicate that there is no simple relationship between corrections and explicit rules. However, like many of the studies cited above, these studies either had validity problems (e.g., Hulstijn and Hulstijn 1984), or low number of subjects (e.g., Sorace 1985), or did not employ inferential statistical analyses to interpret the data (Green and Hecht 1992), leaving unknown whether the differences found in learners' performances on the different tasks were significant or not.

Modality and tasks. The issue of modality has not attracted much attention in SLA studies. The few studies that have addressed modality in SLA research have viewed it from two perspectives. It can refer to the type of (1) L2 input (written or aural) learners are exposed to (e.g., Danks 1980; Danks and End 1987; Leow 1995; Lund 1991); and (2) output (written or oral) learners produce in the L2 (e.g., Terrell, Baycroft, and Perrone 1987; Sanz 1994; VanPatten and Sanz 1995). Although these studies strongly suggest further research on the role of modality in SLA for both theoretical and pedagogical purposes, to my knowledge, there is no published study that has empirically explored the role of modality with respect to the relationship between learners' grammaticality judgments and their performances on two tasks that address different modes. This potential role certainly warrants empirical consideration.

As can be seen, even within the paucity of studies that have attempted to address the reliability of grammaticality judgments and their relationship to performances on L2 production tasks, there is no conclusive direction regarding the usefulness or predictive power of this task due to both methodological and statistical problems. An additional factor contributing to this situation appears to be the inconsistency or variation found in learners' performances on grammaticality judgment tasks as found in both Ellis's (1991) and Christie and Lantolf's (1991) studies over two different time periods (one week separating the first and fifteen months separating the second, respectively). However, variation in learners' performance is not an uncommon feature in SLA (although Gass

1994 revealed quite a remarkable lack of inconsistency) and may actually reflect learners' changing interlanguages (e.g., Gass 1983). For example, Gass referred to research that indicates that variation or inconsistency in performance on grammaticality judgment tasks and oral production tasks are found with both experienced and inexperienced language learners. Indeed, if grammaticality judgments tasks are viewed as performance tasks, the variation demonstrated between and within L2 learners' performances on such tasks should be quite acceptable and expected.

In light of the potential presence or role of variation in learners' performance, this study takes a slightly different approach to the issues discussed above. In this study, I address reliability in terms of the relationships between learners' performances on a grammaticality judgment task administered at two substantially different stages of their L2 development and their performances on two production tasks, using statistical analyses to arrive at an interpretation of the data. If it can be shown that there is a significant relationship between learners' grammaticality judgments and their performances on production tasks at each distinct stage of their L2 development, it can be argued that the grammaticality judgment task is a reliable tool that can be useful in SLA research. In addition, the present study will also explore the role of modality in the relationship between grammaticality judgments and different production tasks, one written and the other oral.

The Present Study.

Subjects. Subjects were thirty college-level undergraduate students enrolled in the first semester of Spanish language study who participated in both stages of this study and completed all six tasks. These subjects entered a four-semester program and met three times a week for fifty minutes each session. Their formal exposure to Spanish at stage one was approximately six hours (approximately three weeks of formal exposure) while they had received approximately thirty-five hours (approximately fourteen weeks of formal exposure) by Stage 2.

Linguistic item. The linguistic item selected for this study was agreement in Spanish between nouns/noun phrases and adjectives or past particles (that function like adjectives in Spanish). This phenomenon has frequently been referred to as a late acquired feature of Spanish due to its absence in English and low communicative value. Because this study is methodological in nature and does not attempt to address the ongoing debate concerning this feature, no review of the relevant literature is provided.

The grammaticality judgment task was designed to address both the Spanish copulas *ser* and *estar* "to be" and noun phrase-adjective/past participle agreement, although subjects' attention primarily focused on the copulas. (Only the findings of the agreement data are presented in this study.) Learners were required to (1) discriminate between grammatically correct and incorrect sentences, (2) correct the errors, and (3) to provide a grammatical rule. More specifically, subjects were asked to do the following:

> *Read the following sentences. Select one of the multiple-choices,* ***A*** *(grammatically correct),* ***B*** *(grammatically incorrect), or* ***C*** *(not sure).*
> *If you select A (grammatically correct), please give a REASON(S) why you think it is correct.*
> *If you select* ***B*** *(grammatically incorrect), please make the appropriate correction(s), and then give a REASON(S) why you made this correction.*
> *If you select* ***C*** *(not sure), you don't need to give a REASON(S).*

The type of response being elicited in this study was analytic, that is, both verbalizable knowledge and production (cf. Ellis 1991 for an elaboration of the nature of response required by different types of task requirements). There were thirty-three items, of which twenty contained a noun phrase followed by an adjective or past participle. All these sentences were ungrammatical for agreement (cf. Appendix 1 for a sample of the grammaticality judgment task).

Tasks. There were two production tasks, one written and the other oral (semi-spontaneous). Both production tasks were designed to elicit learners' responses to questions based on a series of drawings. (See *Materials* Section below.) The questions, presented in English to avoid possible provision of the correct forms of the targeted items to the subjects, were designed to encourage the use of these targeted items in the responses, either orally or written. There were forty-one items on each task, with twenty-one distractors (cf. Appendices 2 and 3 for samples of the written and semi-spontaneous oral production tasks, respectively).

Materials. Two series of drawings depicting similar everyday episodes that lent themselves naturally to the use of the targeted linguistic form in learners' production were chosen for the experiment. These two series were used for both the oral and written production tasks, that is, the series used in Stage 1 for the oral task was then used for the written production task in Stage 2. For the oral tasks, both series were then divided into individual frames and transposed onto clear transparencies. Vocabulary words and their glosses were also provided before the experiment, on the overheads and written tasks, to minimize the impact of processing for vocabulary on the tasks. (Adjectives were presented in their singular masculine form.)

Method. The study was divided into two stages. Stage 1 took place during the third week of classes (out of a fourteen-week semester). Subjects agreed to participate in the study and then proceeded to perform the grammaticality judgment task in their classroom. They were told to take as long as they wanted to complete the task. The next class session they reported to the language laboratory to perform the oral and written production tasks, in that order. Before beginning each task, subjects were asked to answer each question in Spanish with complete sentences (i.e., including the subjects, verbs, and adjectives). For the oral production task, subjects were shown on an overhead a series of drawings (each frame presented separately) followed by questions in English provided by an assistant. Subjects answered the questions which were recorded on their individual recorders. For the written production task, subjects were provided with a different series of drawings with questions on a separate sheet. To approximate the duration of time between the two tasks in order to ensure a truer comparison between them, subjects were also requested to do the questions in the order they were presented and not to return to any number already answered. The average amounts of time spent to complete the two tasks were seven minutes for the oral production task and eight and a half minutes for the written production task.

Stage 2 took place in the fourteenth week of the semester. A similar procedure was followed with three exceptions. The items on the grammaticality judgment task were randomly reordered while the order of the tasks and the series of drawings was interchanged, that is, subjects first performed the written production task, followed by the oral production task. The average times spent to complete the production tasks were eight minutes and seven minutes for the written production task and oral production task, respectively.

Scoring procedure. The grammaticality judgment task was scored one point for each item that was judged ungrammatical and followed by a correct grammatical reason or metalinguistic explanation for a total of twenty. The production tasks were scored one point for each correct agreement produced by the subjects for a total of twenty. Interrater reliability for the oral production task was approximately 89%.

Results and discussion. In order to address the relationship between learners' performance on a grammaticality judgment task and their performances on production tasks at two different stages of their L2 development, the raw scores obtained on the grammaticality judgment tasks and the written and oral production tasks for both stages were submitted to separate Pearson Product-Moment Correlations. These results are found in Table 1 and graphically displayed in Figure 1.

Table 1. The relationship between the grammaticality judgment task (GJT) and the written and oral production tasks at Stage 1 and Stage 2.

STAGE 1 GJT and Written Production		STAGE 2 GJT and Written Production	
r	*p*	*r*	*p*
.737 % of variance: 54%	<.0001	.733 % of variance: 54%	<.0001

STAGE 1 GJT and Oral Production		STAGE 2 GJT and Oral Production	
r	*p*	*r*	*p*
.515 % of variance: 27%	<.0036	.602 % of variance: 36%	<.0004

Figure 1. Reliability coefficients of production tasks at Stage 1 and Stage 2.

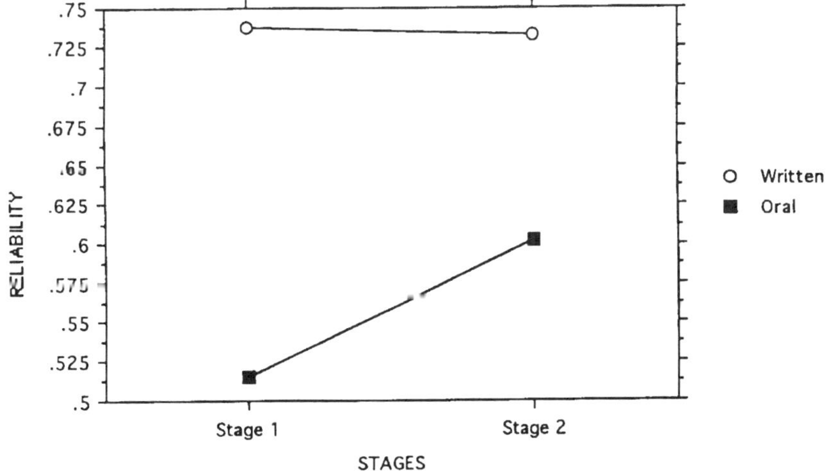

Correlations for all four relationships were significant at the level of $p<.01$. The results also revealed an almost identical significant relationship between learners' performance on the grammaticality judgment task and their performances on the written production task performed at two substantially different stages of their L2 development ($p=.0001$ for both stages). Significant though not similar relationships for each stage were also found for the oral production task ($p=.0036$ and $p=.0004$ for Stages 1 and 2, respectively). Overall, these significant relationships lend support to the reliability of grammaticality judgment tasks in reflecting stages of learners' L2 development.

Consequently, the findings of this study do not lend support to studies that have found low nonsignificant correlations or mismatches between learners' performances on grammaticality judgment tasks (verbalized or nonverbalized) and oral production (e.g., Ellis and Rathbone 1987; Green and Hecht 1992; Sorace 1985) or written production tasks (e.g., Liceras 1983). Plausible explanations for these differences may lie in the method used in the studies to elicit grammaticality judgments, the scoring of these judgments, the linguistic items being tested, the tasks themselves, and the use or lack of use of statistical analyses to interpret the data. Future research can elucidate the precise influence of these factors.

The results also revealed that the role of modality needs to be considered in any relationship between grammaticality judgment tasks and beginning learners' performances on production tasks. The relationship between learners' grammaticality judgments and their performance on a written production task appears to be substantially stronger at both stages of their L2 development when compared with this relationship and performance on a semi-spontaneous oral production task. As can be seen in Table 1, the relationship between the grammaticality judgment task and the written production task at both stages accounted for 54% of the variance, while the amounts of variance for the relationship between the grammaticality judgment task and the oral production task are substantially less, that is, 27% and 36% for Stages 1 and 2, respectively. In other words, it appears that the grammaticality judgment task is more predictive of performance on written production tasks when compared with oral production tasks. It is also interesting to note that the reliability coefficient for the relationship between the grammaticality judgment task and the oral production task reveals a relatively substantial increase in Stage 2. This increase may be due to the language experience factor and appears to support Sorace (1985), who found a growing and proportional association between metalinguistic ability and improvement of L2 proficiency.[1]

---

[1]Mean scores also revealed this proportional increase on all three tasks. For Stage 1 and Stage 2, the GJT was 4.68 and 9.13, the written production task 8.68 and 11.17, and the oral production 9.50 and 12.60, respectively.

Conclusion. This study has attempted to address the reliability of grammaticality judgment tasks in SLA in light of the statistical relationships between beginning L2 learners' performance on a grammaticality judgment task and their performances on two production tasks at two substantially different stages of their L2 development. Given that these relationships were found for both stages of learners' L2 development and for both production tasks, these results lend support to Gass (1994) who stated that grammaticality judgments appear to reflect behavioral patterns of L2 development and, consequently, may be used as a reliable instrument for SLA research. The results also appear to indicate that modality may play a role in the relationship between grammaticality judgments and production tasks. More specifically, the grammaticality judgment task may be relatively more reliable for performances on written production tasks when compared to oral production tasks. Using two tasks that elicited both written and oral responses furthers our understanding of the differential role of modality on learners' performances and behavioral patterns on different tasks, and the findings lend support to the use of multiple assessment tasks in SLA research (e.g., Sanz 1994; Shook 1994).

REFERENCES

Arthur, Bradford. 1980. "Gauging the boundaries of second language competence: A study of learner judgments." *Language Learning* 30: 177–194.

Birdsong, David. 1989. *Metalinguistic performance and interlinguistic competence*. New York: Springer.

Birdsong, David. 1990. "Universal grammar and second language acquisition theory: A review of a research framework and two exemplary books." *Studies in Second Language Acquisition* 12: 331–340.

Bley-Vroman, Robert, Sascha Felix, and Georgette L. Ioup. 1988. "The accessibility of Universal Grammar in adult language learning." *Second Language Research* 4: 1–32.

Chaudron, Craig. 1983. "Research on metalinguistic judgments: A review of theory, methods and results." *Language Learning* 33: 343–377.

Chomsky, Noam. 1986. *Knowledge of language: Its nature, origin and use*. New York: Praeger.

Christie, K. and James Lantolf. 1991. "The ontological status of learner grammaticality judgments in UG approaches to L2 acquisition." Paper presented at Second Language Research Forum, Los Angeles.

Comrie, Bernard and Edward L. Keenan. 1979. "Noun phrase accessibility revisited." *Language* 55: 649–664.

Cowan, Ron and Yukiko Abe Hatasa. 1994. "Investigating the validity and reliability of native speaker and second-language learner judgments about sentences." In Elaine E. Tarone, Susan M. Gass and Andrew Cohen (eds.), *Research methodology in second-language acquisition*. Hillsdale, N.J.: Lawrence Erlbaum: 287–302.

Danks, Joseph H. 1980. "Comprehension in listening and reading: Same or different?" In Joseph H. Danks and K. Pezdek (eds.), *Reading and understanding*. Newark, Delaware: International Reading Association. 1–39.

Danks, Joseph H. and Laurel End. 1987. "Processing strategies for reading and listening." In Rosalind Horowitz and S. Jay Samuels (eds.), *Comprehending oral and written input*. San Diego, California. 271–294.

Ellis, Rod. 1991. "Grammaticality judgments and second language acquisition." *Studies in Second Language Acquisition* 13: 161–186.

Ellis, Rod and M. Rathbone. 1987. *The acquisition of German in a classroom context*. Mimeograph, London: Ealing College of Higher Education, London.

Gass, Susan M. 1979. "Language transfer and universal grammatical relations." *Language Learning* 29: 327–344.

Gass, Susan M. 1983. "The development of L2 intuitions." *TESOL Quarterly* 17(2): 273–291.

Gass, Susan M. 1994. "The reliability of second language grammaticality judgments." In Elaine E. Tarone, Susan M. Gass and Andrew D. Cohen (eds.), *Research methodology in second-language Acquisition*. Hillsdale, New Jersey: Lawrence Erlbaum. 303–322.

Green, Peter S. and Karlheinz Hecht. 1992. "Implicit and explicit grammar: An empirical study." *Applied Linguistics* 13: 168–183.

Hulstijn, Jan H. and Wouter Hulstijn. 1984. "Grammatical errors as a function of processing constraints and explicit knowledge." *Language Learning* 34: 23–43.

Keenan, Edward and Bernard Comrie. 1977. "Noun phrase accessibility and Universal Grammar." *Linguistic Inquiry* 8: 63–99.

Kellerman, Eric. 1986. "An eye for an eye: Crosslinguistic constraints on the development of the L2 lexicon." In Eric Kellerman and Michael Sharwood Smith (eds.), *Crosslinguistic influence in second language acquisition*. Oxford: Pergamon. 35–48.

Lakshmanan, Usha and Keiko Teranishi. 1994. "Preferences versus grammaticality judgments: Some methodological issues concerning the governing category parameter in second-language acquisition." In Elaine E. Tarone, Susan M. Gass and Andrew Cohen (eds.), *Research methodology in second-language acquisition*. Hillsdale, N.J.: Lawrence Erlbaum: 185–206.

Leow, Ronald P. 1995. "Modality and intake in second language acquisition." *Studies in Second Language Acquisition* 17: 79–89.

Liceras, Juana M. 1983. *Markedness, contrastive analysis and the acquisition of Spanish syntax by English speakers*. Unpublished doctoral dissertation, University of Toronto.

Lund, Randall. 1991. "A comparison of listening and reading comprehension." *Modern Language Journal* 75: 196–204.

Mazurkewich, Irene. 1985. "Syntactic markedness and language acquisition." *Studies in Second Language Acquisition* 7: 15–36.

Sanz, Cristina. 1994. "Multiple assessment of an input-based approach to explicit instruction in grammar." Unpublished Doctoral dissertation, University of Illinois at Urbana-Champaign, Illinois.

Seliger, Herbert W. 1979. "On the nature and function of language rules in language teaching." *TESOL Quarterly* 13(3): 359–369.

Shook, David. 1994. "FL/L2 reading, grammatical information, and the input-to-intake phenomenon." *Applied Language Learning* 5: 57–93.

Sorace, Antonella. 1985. "Metalinguistic knowledge and language use in acquisition-poor environment." *Applied Linguistics* 6: 239–254.

Tanaka, Shigenori. 1987. "The selective use of specific exemplars in second language performance: The case of dative alternation." *Language Learning* 37: 63–88.

Terrell, Tracy D., Bernard Baycroft, and Charles Perrone. 1987. "The subjunctive in Spanish interlanguage: Accuracy and comprehensibility." In Bill VanPatten, Trisha Dvorak, and James F. Lee (eds.), *Foreign language learning: A research perspective*. Rowley, Massachusetts: Newbury House. 19–32.

VanPatten, Bill and Cristina Sanz. 1995. "From input to output: Processing instruction and communicative tasks." In Fred Eckman, D. Highland, P. Lee, J. Mileham, and R. Rutkowski

(eds.), *Second language acquisition: Theory and pedagogy*. Mahwah, N.J.: Lawrence Erlbaum. 169–185.
White, Lydia. 1985. "The 'pro-drop' parameter in adult second language acquisition." *Language Learning* 35: 47–62.

APPENDIX 1: Sample of the grammaticality judgment task

1. Mi computadora está muy rápido.
A grammatically correct B. grammatically incorrect C. not sure
REASON(S): ____________________

2. María está ambicioso.
A grammatically correct B. grammatically incorrect C. not sure
REASON(S): ____________________

3. Al oír las malas noticias, mis padres son triste.
A grammatically correct B. grammatically incorrect C. not sure
REASON(S): ____________________

4. La oficina está cerrado durante el fin de semana.
A grammatically correct B. grammatically incorrect C. not sure
REASON(S): ____________________

5. La clase de español es mi favorito.
A grammatically correct B. grammatically incorrect C. not sure
REASON(S): ____________________

6. Después de la bomba, muchas personas son ansioso.
A grammatically correct B. grammatically incorrect C. not sure
REASON(S): ____________________

7. Isabel es dormido.
A grammatically correct B. grammatically incorrect C. not sure
REASON(S): ____________________

8. ¿Sabes que recibió una A Rebecca? Es muy contento.
A grammatically correct B. grammatically incorrect C. not sure
REASON(S): ____________________

9. Mi profesora está besado por sus estudiantes.
A grammatically correct B. grammatically incorrect C. not sure
REASON(S): ____________________

10. Mis estudiantes están inteligente.
A grammatically correct B. grammatically incorrect C. not sure
REASON(S): ____________________

APPENDIX 2: Sample of the written production task

In this task, you have a series of drawings that will be accompanied by some questions in English. After each question, please answer the questions in SPANISH with COMPLETE SENTENCES (that is, including the subjects, verbs and adjectives)—this is very important. Also, when you have finished each item/number, please do not return to it. In other words, do 1 to 41 without stopping to return to an item you have already completed. Are you ready? ¡Vamos!

Dibujo A

1. Where is this scene taking place (*la habitación*)? ______________________________

2. Are they both awake (*despierto*)? ______________________________

3. Who is awake (*despierto*)? ______________________________

Dibujo B

4. Look at her face. Is it tired (*cansado*)? ______________________________

5. Look at his face (*la cara*). It is tired (*cansado*) also, don't you think? ______________________________

Dibujo C

6. In this drawing, do you think the woman is seated (*sentado*) or not? ______________________________

7. Their clothes (*la ropa*) are full of colors (*lleno de colores*), don't you think so? ______________________________

8. Would you say that his shirt (*la camisa*) is striped (*rayado*)? ______________________________

Dibujo D

9. Is the woman kissed (*besado por*) by the man? ______________________________

10. The suitcase (*maleta*) the woman is carrying is a little small (*pequeño*), don't you think? ______________________________

APPENDIX 3: Sample of the oral production task

In this activity, you are going to see a series of drawings that will be accompanied by some questions in English. Please answer the questions with COMPLETE SENTENCES (that is, including the subjects, verbs, and adjectives—this is very important). Are you ready? ¡Vamos!

1. Where is this scene taking place?

2. What is the man waken up by?

3. Is his wife waken up by the clock also?

4. Are they both awake?

5. Who is not awake?

6. Look at her face. She is contented, don't you think?

7. What about her nose? It is small, isn't it?

8. Is the woman served by the man?

9. Look at his wife. Is she tall or short?

10. Describe his suitcase. It is a little small, isn't it?

Second language speech/pronunciation: Acquisition, instruction, standards, variation, and accent

Joan Morley
University of Michigan

Background. Over the past few years one important development in the field of second language education has been a renewed interest in the importance of oral communication skills. Perhaps most apparent in programs for adult and adolescent second language learners, this new interest has been operationalized by the introduction of more and (more importantly) *different* instructional measures focused on strengthening the learning and teaching of the speech/pronunciation component of oral communication. It has been encouraging to see increasingly serious attention concentrated on this area of second language acquisition and education. Such attention has long been out of fashion, long swept under the proverbial rug—in other words, it has been virtually "out of sight and out of mind" in the field since the decline of a once omnipresent audiolingualism. Indeed, until relatively recently, neither teachers nor researchers in the second language field appeared to have much interest in the learning and teaching of second language speech/pronunciation, much less enthusiasm about it.

The fact that the phrase "speech/pronunciation," (hereafter, SP/PR), is used throughout this paper reflects the need to find a way to demarcate clearly—for second language educators who may not be keenly aware of the changes taking place—that today there is a "new age" view of this component of language learning and teaching. This change in terminology reflects a profoundly revisionist view—indeed an activist view—that has been developing among a number of applied linguists/language teachers who specialize in second language SP/PR theory and practice.

The fundamental tenet of this view is this: *Speech/pronunciation in the second language curriculum is an integral part of communicative language learning*. Today's SP/PR instruction is *not set aside from the mainstream of communicative language learning, namely, from meaning, discourse, context, and situation*, nor is today's SP/PR instruction *drill-based sets of minimal-pairs exercises—a misleading myth, a hold-over perspective, falsely perpetuated by those who are unaware of the fact that we are, today, far beyond the wholesale use of such audiolingual-only techniques.*

Traditional pronunciation teaching practices focused primarily—often exclusively—on the competence area that Canale and Swain (1980) define as *linguistic competence* (here, phonetic-phonological competence). Current SP/PR instructional protocol, on the other hand, is concerned first and foremost with the **macrolevel**—with procedures whose goal is *discourse competence* and those global elements of communicability central to communicative competence, ones that must be integrated with goals of *sociolinguistic competence* and *strategic competence*. *Within* this larger instructional framework, there remains, of course, a continuing focus on the **microlevel** (i.e., *linguistic competence*) with attention to the discrete segmental and suprasegmental elements of pronunciation (Morley 1995).

As Pennington and Richards note:

> pronunciation in a second language involves far more than the correct articulation of individual sounds. Pronunciation is not simply a surface performance phenomenon but is rather a dynamic component of conversational fluency ... The acquisition of the phonology of the second or foreign language involves learning how to produce a wide range of complex and subtle distinctions which relate sound to meaning at several different levels. (1986: 212)

In *Discourse Intonation and Language Teaching*, Brazil and his associates (1980: 2) clearly set out their view on the central importance of a discourse focus in this statement: "... it is doubtful that above some rehabilitative motivation, there is little merit in massive drilling through stress and/or intonation exercises which are at sentence level and decontextualized." And in the preface to this same volume, Candlin notes that "In essence the argument hinges on the inseparability of the meaning of intonation from discoursal context" (1980: xi). He comments further that the emphasis needs to be placed

> on the use of intonational signals to indicate such discoursally significant information as awareness by speaker of common ground, speaker's choice of presenting information as known or unknown to the hearer, speaker's assessment of the relative information load carried by particular elements in the utterance, role-relationships between speaker and hearer, degrees of solidarity and apartness and so on. (1980: xi)

Ross, in a review of Brown (1991), observed that:

> The problematic status of pronunciation teaching is probably due to two related factors. To begin with, many instructors may associate pronunciation pedagogy with phonetics and phonology, which, of all the linguistic fields,

come closest to being "hard" sciences and, hence, inaccessible to the average liberal-arts-inclined teacher. Secondly, many instructors cling to an outdated model of pronunciation teaching theory that demands too much from the teacher and produces too little fruit from the student. (1992: 441)

These and other contemporary views will be examined in this paper with the specific purpose of reviewing recent developments in SP/PR instruction and presenting some "revisionist" views in three areas of second language theory and pedagogy: (1) current research in second language phonology and applied phonetics (according to Pennington 1995); (2) current directions in SP/PR instruction; and (3) issues involving standards, goals, instructional models, variation, and accent.

Trippingly on the tongue.[1] Suppose I set out to learn a second language (L2), and my cherished dream is one day to *master* its spoken form (i.e., its SP/PR) for competent, effective oral communication.

The first thing I need is "informants"—models—and, more specifically, individuals who speak the particular dialect of the language that I wish to learn. In a formal setting, in all probability, my informants will be professional teachers or tutors. In an informal setting, they will likely be friendly native speakers with patience and goodwill toward a nonnative "wannabe" speaker of their language—and goodwill is a particularly key condition (Lippi-Green 1994: 166).

What I need, in Corder's (1967) words, is a source of language "input" in order for me to "intake," as I can and as I wish. And then, probably after much travail, "Voila!" I am an L2 speaker of that language! But alas, I'm told that I have such a "bad accent" that my SP/PR is well-nigh unintelligible, much less attractive, and clearly will interfere with my getting and keeping a job in which I must use the second language. Moreover, with a "heavy accent" it very well may be that I will encounter neither much patience nor much goodwill from the world of native speakers with whom I wish to communicate. My cherished dream of being a competent, effective second language speaker is dashed.

An "accent" is an interesting thing. Each of us has an accent, yet in our conventional wisdom, we often think it is others who have accents, who "talk funny," while *our* speech is the *right* speech—so of course we are not the ones with accents.

As described by Matsuda:

[1]From William Shakespeare, "Hamlet's speech to the players." *Hamlet*, Act III, Scene II.

> Your accent carries the story of who you are—who first held you and talked to you when you were a child, where you have lived, your age, the schools you attended, the languages you know, your ethnicity, whom you admire, your loyalties, your profession, your class position. Traces of your life and identity are woven into your pronunciation, your phrasing, your choice of words. Your self is inseparable from your accent. Someone who tells you they don't like the way you speak is quite likely telling you that they don't like you ... Every person has an accent. Yet, in ordinary usage, we say a person "has an accent" to mark difference from some unstated norm of non-accent, as though only some foreign few have accents. (1991: 1329–1330)

"Treatment of accent" is often a focus of both foreign language and second language programs, and its goals may be variously stated as "accent improvement," "accent correction," or "accent reduction." Increasingly, advertisements from commercial programs guarantee "accent-free" pronunciation, "perfect pronunciation," "native-like pronunciation" or, the goal of all goals, "irradication of accent."

Certainly there are knotty problems for the second language teacher who specializes in non-native speakers' accents and presumes to "teach" pronunciation. Indeed, the word "teach" is presumptuous: whether one is persuaded by von Humboldt's philosophy that we cannot really teach language, but can only create conditions in which it will develop spontaneously in the mind in its own way; whether one heeds the words of Lebanese poet Gibran on teaching, "If he ... is indeed wise he [the teacher] does not bid you enter the house of his wisdom, but rather leads you to the threshold of your own mind" (1923: 56); whether one incorporates into one's teaching scheme an explicit focus on learning strategies in support of the belief that one of teachers' major responsibilities is to help learners gain their *own* insights and develop their *own* skills for helping themselves, in short to learn to monitor their own language to teach themselves (Oxford 1990; Wenden 1991); or whether one follows Corder (1976) in believing in the centrality of the learner in the language learning process, i.e., that the learner is the prime mover in his or her own learning, it clearly is more accurate to look upon the SP/PR teacher's role as that of a learning facilitator and manager, a speech "coach" who, like sports and drama coaches, guides learners toward the actualization of specific skills.

The SP/PR teacher who is willing to accept the role of facilitator-manager-coach, not drill-leader, must have a host of prerequisite information in order to meet the demands of revisionist SP/PR teaching. Chief among these are:

- Knowledge of phonetics and phonology, and applied phonetics;
- Knowledge of discourse phonology and the structure of oral discourse;
- L2 teacher preparation in current directions in SP/PR; and

- Current information on issues involving standards, goals, instructional models, and accents.

As this inventory of requirements for the professionally trained SP/PR instructor clearly indicates, the "treatment of accent" can no longer be trivialized, no longer relegated to a peripheral corner of the second language field. SP/PR is a fundamental component of a communicative approach to second language learning, and the instruction is a complex enterprise—one of the most challenging in foreign and second language teaching.

Second language phonology: Pennington research review. The neuromotor-cognitive act of "pronunciation" is a truly complex human behavior. Its very complexity may be one of the reasons so little research attention has been given to second language phonology until relatively recently. In the last ten years, however, interest in this area has emerged among applied linguists and second language acquisition scholars, and a small but respected body of literature is developing, one that includes attention to a variety of dimensions of second language phonology.

In my view the feature that sets pronunciation aside from all other aspects of language is that it is a motor habit. As one studies the anatomy, physiology, and neurology of speech production, one cannot but come away in awe of the complexity and delicacy of this motor act—with its strong dependence on "muscle memory." As Scovel describes it:

> It is obvious that pronunciation is the only part of language which is directly "physical" and which demands neuromuscular programming. Only pronunciation requires an incredible talent for sensory feedback of where the articulators are and what they are doing. And only pronunciation forces us to time and sequence motor movement. All other aspects of language are entirely "cognitive" or "perceptual" in that they have no physical reality. (Scovel 1988: 62)

In a comprehensive review of recent research in second language phonology Pennington (1995: 94) discusses six "...partially autonomous and partially overlapping themes ..." which have emerged in recent years, "... as important foci of attention." Each of these six themes from Pennington's work is summarized below:

Phonology in context. Pennington observes that, in current theory, patterns of oral discourse are conceptualized as a linguistic level of spoken language that lies between the content and the sound segment; that is, this level acts as a bridge connecting the meaning encoded in the spoken discourse to the phonetic level. From this view it follows that informed instructional planning for phonological instruction in an L2 must focus first on the discoursal context in which speech is embedded and second on appropriate prosodic patternings at various levels (e.g., phrasal, clausal, sentential, and larger segments of discourse).

Phonological parameters. This term refers to the set of features that comprise an L1 speaker's underlying linguistic model, whose values govern the surface structure (that is, the phonetic level) of speech actualization. These parameters appear to be language specific and are believed to exert a powerful underlying influence on a speaker's production of L2 sound segments. In Pennington's (1995: 95) words, these features " ... may be defined in terms of parameters carried over from the L1 to the L2 and in need of readjustment for phonological fluency and accuracy in an L2." This process, which has come to be called a parameter-resetting model, may be a useful way to introduce learners to L1 and L2 values and help learners understand L1/L2 differences.

Transfer and development. Here Pennington presents a synopsis of Major's (1987) views on interlanguage phonology and the related work of other researchers. Central to Major's model is the thesis that there is a series of predictable stages in the acquisition of L2 phonology. In the first stages of the learning process, the most prominent feature is interference from the L1. In subsequent stages, this influence appears to diminish, giving way to what Major calls developmental processes, noting that these processes decrease further in later stages of L2 phonological acquisition. These two processes (transfer and developmental levels) affect L2 acquisition in ways that are manifest in the different types of error patterns learners exhibit as they move through stages in their individual acquisition of L2 phonology. Pennington stresses the importance of recognizing these influences so that appropriate teaching materials and activities can be developed to provide different instructional frameworks at different times.

Speech perception and production. The key focus here is the critical interrelationship between speech perception and production. Pennington reviews research on learners' needs to adjust and readjust their categories of both perception (sensory features) and production (motor features).

Maturational constraints. Pennington examines issues relating to the controversial topic of age and language acquisition and suggests that teachers may want to design different kinds of practice experiences that accommodate to learners' capabilities at different ages.

Psychological and social influences on L2 pronunciation patterns. In this important final section of her paper, Pennington discusses several new studies that have investigated psychological and social influences on L2 learners' speech. The research reported focuses on the examination of factors of self-image and language identity that appear to have a very strong influence on the nature of L2 pronunciation patterns.

Throughout this informed and insightful discussion, Pennington includes comments on implications for SP/PR teaching.

Current directions in SP/PR instruction. A fundamental characteristic of a "revisionist" SP/PR program is an expanded conceptualization that views SP/PR as a critical component of the entire act of speech communication, namely, an integral part of *meaning, discourse, context,* and *situation*. SP/PR can no longer be divorced from reality and relegated to a few moments of meaningless exercises performed in classrooms or laboratories.

Debunking myths. Above all, it is time L2 teachers and instructional programs that consider themselves responsive to current theory and pedagogy no longer evoke the following four myths of *misguided conventional wisdom* as reasons for denying students access to the SP/PR instruction they need.

MYTH: PRONUNCIATION ISN'T IMPORTANT. This belief is patently false from any perspective. The speaker's verbal message rides the wave of the SP/PR stream of speech and, together with the non-verbal aspects of communication, forms a vehicle for transmitting the speaker's meaning. If the listener does not understand the message, no communication takes place, and while there are indeed other speaker/listener factors involved, one of the chief aspects is the level of intelligibility of the speaker's pronunciation. In short, intelligible pronunciation is an essential component of communicative competence.

MYTH: STUDENTS WILL PICK IT UP ON THEIR OWN. Some will learn to pronounce the second language intelligibly; many will not. In any case, withholding SP/PR instruction not only deprives learners of systematic attention to improving their oral communication skills, but also denies them access to systematic approaches to developing personal oral language learning strategies.

MYTH: PRONUNCIATION IS TOO HARD TO TEACH. Too hard to teach? In this regard, Marks (1986: 9) makes the case for SP/PR: "Few teachers, probably, would claim that they do not teach grammar or vocabulary, on the grounds that they are either too difficult or else not sufficiently important. Yet these are the kinds of comments which many teachers make with regard to the teaching of phonology [pronunciation]."

MYTH: I DON'T HAVE THE TRAINING TO TEACH IT, SO I JUST WON'T BOTHER (AND, I'LL JUST SAY PRONUNCIATION ISN'T IMPORTANT). This is the one myth that can be eliminated, once and for all, with two measures: first, a profession-wide recognition of the critical importance of SP/PR as a primary feature of communicative competence; and second, a profession-wide focus on redesigning second language teacher preparation programs to include appropriate modern-day theory and practice in SP/PR instruction (supplemented by in-service presentations locally or at national and international conferences and institutes). Two new publications in this area will be of significant assistance to programs: Pennington (1996) and Celce-Murcia, Brinton, and Goodwin (1996). In addition, many excellent teacher reference books and student texts have appeared over the last ten years. (For a review of key SP/PR publications, see Morley 1991.)

Two key factors involved in the movement toward changing SP/PR instruction. Two factors have figured prominently in the movement toward changing traditional pronunciation classrooms into "new look" SP/PR programs. First, more and louder voices are being raised about *learner problems and unmet learner needs*. This concern is not going to go away, because the speakers who need specialized SP/PR instruction are not going to go away—and their needs demand responsible action by the profession. Second, *important revisions in curriculum design* and significant changes in SP/PR instruction are developing rapidly today, and these revisions are increasingly informed by current learning/teaching research.

FACTOR 1: LEARNER PROBLEMS AND UNMET LEARNER NEEDS. Many adult and near-adult learners have unintelligible speech patterns that may place them at serious risk educationally, occupationally, professionally, and socially. As noted elsewhere (Morley 1995, 1991, 1988; Wong 1985), significant numbers of potentially disadvantaged speakers of English can be found in a variety of settings. For the field to dismiss the needs of these learners is, in my estimation, an abrogation of professional responsibility. As witness to the fact that the English language teaching field has neglected pronunciation, one need look no further than the enormous proliferation of commercial accent reduction packages now on the market.

While some accent reduction programs are offered by solidly trained language professionals, many are operated by less well-informed entrepreneurs. For all L2 learners in special need of attention to pronunciation, a broadly-constructed communicative approach to teaching SP/PR is mandatory. Such a program must take into account not only linguistic competence, but just as importantly discourse competence, sociolinguistic competence, and strategic competence (Canale and Swain 1980).

In addition, the critical importance of the non-linguistic competencies cannot be ignored, as expressed in the following comment by sociolinguist Lippi-Green (1994):

> ... accent is most likely to pose a barrier to effective communication when two elements are lacking ... These elements are (1) a basic level of communicative competence on the part of the speaker, independent of phonology and intonation; and (2) the listener's goodwill. (1994: 166)

Lippi-Green considers the latter more important as well as more difficult to assess. She expresses the view that:

> Without that goodwill, the speaker's command of the language, i.e., his or her degree of communicative competence, is irrelevant. Prejudiced listeners cannot hear what a person has to say, because accent, as a mirror of social identity and a litmus test for exclusion, is more important. (1994: 166)

All things considered, an informed revisionist SP/PR program that actively attends to all competencies has a much better chance of being effective than a narrowly constructed articulatory phonetics approach whose main focus is on "correcting" the speaker's segmentals (i.e., consonant and vowel "errors"). In broadly based competence-oriented programs, certainly segmentals are not neglected, but a host of other elements are integrated into the instructional plan. These will be discussed in the last part of this section.

It is possible to identify a number of kinds of learner problems and unmet learner needs in SP/PR, including the following (Morley 1995):

- *Complete breakdown in communication.* Speech is incomprehensible, resulting in a complete breakdown in communication. Verbal patternings are such that they prohibit functional oral communication. Often these nonnative speakers exhibit extensive breakdown at the *microlevel* (i.e., that aspect of SP/PR which involves speech production and attention to discrete points of pronunciation such as sounds, stress, intonation, etc.), which, in fact, precludes assessment at the *macrolevel* (i.e., that aspect of SP/PR involving speech performance and global patterns of speech communicability). (See Morley 1992.)
- *Ineffectual speech performance.* Speech patterns result in basically ineffectual performance, whatever the intended interlocutor role, whether the discourse function is an interactional or transactional one (in Brown and Yule's 1983 terms). Speakers are judged to lack

credibility and not to inspire confidence in either their knowledge of "content" or their persona. Breakdowns usually combine micro- and macrolevel features and may lead to negative judgments about personal qualities. Speech patterns result in negative judgments about personality traits and "foreignerism" stereotyping. Beebe (1978: 2) reports that native speakers described pronunciation errors as sounding " ... comical', 'cute', 'incompetent', 'not serious', 'effeminate', or 'childish.'"

- *Anticipatory-apprehensive listener reactions*. When engaging in a conversation with a nonnative speaker who has poor SP/PR intelligibility, native speakers report having very uncomfortable, apprehensive feelings as the interaction proceeds. They report that even though they *seem* to understand what the nonnative speaker is saying *at the moment*, they feel a continual undercurrent of anxiety, apprehensive that they will not understand as the interaction moves along. Moreover, they report that often they keep to superficial, "social" topics (i.e., interactional discourse, in Brown and Yule's 1983 terms), shift topics frequently, speak more loudly and slowly, and often move to terminate the interaction as soon as possible.
- *Pejorative stereotyping*. Listener-perceived aberrant speech patterns result in an even more serious negative-judgment problem, i.e., nonnative speakers often are assigned to a variety of undesirable socioeconomic categories based on pronunciation. The research of Lambert in Montreal (1967) and Labov in New York (1972) demonstrated that listeners will judge speakers they have never seen nor met before as to their personality, intelligence, ethnic group, race, social status—even their height—simply from listening to the way they pronounce a few words.
- *Accent discrimination*. The 1964 U.S. Civil Rights Act clearly forbids an employer from discriminating against a job applicant on the basis of linguistic traits linked to national origin. However, employers have considerable latitude in matters of language and employer violations are widespread in the United States, perhaps at a level as high as 10% of businesses, although only a very small percentage of these violations result in litigation. Cases are often settled out of court, and the general tendency is that plaintiffs have a low success rate in winning their cases. (See the section on accent later in this paper.)

FACTOR 2. MAJOR CHANGES IN SP/PR INSTRUCTION. The second factor in the spread of interest, indeed excitement, in SP/PR has been the emergence of new instructional designs in teaching. The hallmark of the model followed in many revisionist SP/PR programs is two-fold: (1) a considerably broadened conceptualization of what constitutes the domain of "pronunciation"; and (2) practices which are anchored firmly in current language learning and teaching theory.

These programs do not slavishly follow rigid methodologies; they develop their own. The basic plan includes the following four elements:

- Careful needs analysis: diagnostic assessment of learner needs at both the *microlevel* (i.e., that aspect of SP/PR which involves speech production and attention to discrete points of pronunciation such as sounds, stress, intonation, etc.) and the *macrolevel* (i.e., that aspect of SP/PR which involves speech performance and global patterns of speech communicability) (Morley 1992);
- Careful planning of short-term and long-range goals in consultation with the learner;
- Careful preparation of group and individualized instructional syllabi; and
- Implementation of the plan through a variety of instructional activities and appropriate SP/PR communicative tasks.

Implementation, of course, is the most challenging of these four elements. One functional approach to implementation is a three-cycle system combining imitative, rehearsed, and extemporaneous practice. These three modes allow learners to move through speech practice activities suited to their needs along a continuum of dependent, partially dependent, and independent experiences (Morley 1992):

- *Imitative speaking practice* provides for controlled production of selected SP/PR features;
- *Rehearsed speaking practice* provides for stabilization of modified pronunciation through the use of relatively "fixed" texts, both oral reading scripts and pre-planned talks; self-study rehearsals, in-class presentations, and individual "work-out" sessions with the teacher (i.e., the "speech coach") enable students to have a variety of learning/practice opportunities; and
- *Extemporaneous speaking practice* provides for the integration of modified speech patterns into naturally occurring creative speech in both partially planned and unplanned talks (monologues), panel discussions, and audience participation in an interactive collaborative question-and-answer format (dialogues).

Eight major changes in pronunciation instruction. The following eight features are the most important shifts in SP/PR instruction that have taken place over the past ten years (Morley 1995):

- *A communicative focus:* one that views the proper place of pronunciation in the L2 curriculum as an integral part of communication, not as a separate drill-based component set aside from the mainstream of spoken discourse;
- *Increased attention to suprasegmentals:* a redirection of priorities within the sound system to focus more on the critical importance of suprasegmentals; in particular, a discourse perspective on intonation, rhythm, and stress, and how they are used to communicate meaning in spoken discourse, as well as the importance of segments (vowels and consonants), their combinations both within and across word boundaries, and their reduced, elided, and assimilated forms;
- *An expanded domain for pronunciation:* a focus on an expanded concept of pronunciation incorporating attention to (1) segmentals; (2) suprasegmentals; (3) voice quality features, articulatory settings, and other paralinguistic areas; and (4) elements of body language used in oral communication (i.e., extralinguistic features);
- *Changing perspectives on the roles of learner and teacher:* a focus on revised expectations for both learner and teacher involvement, with an emphasis on the development of learner self-help strategies, including speech awareness, self-awareness, and self-monitoring under the guidance of a SP/PR teacher-facilitator;
- *Practice activities contextualized for specific purposes:* a focus on practice activities and speaking-task experiences matched to the communicative needs of learners in personalized, real-life contexts;
- *Increased attention to the reciprocal listening-speaking connection:* a stronger focus on the link between listening comprehension and SP/PR.
- *Attention to sound-spelling relationships:* a focus on a range of important sound-spelling relationships and specific guidance for students in using English orthography as a key tool in predicting pronunciation patterns; and
- *Individualization and the uniqueness of each learner:* a focus on individualization in the SP/PR, specifically on the uniqueness of each ESL learner. Since each learner has a personal pattern of spoken English which is unlike that of anyone else in the world and the product of a variety of influences, instruction needs to guide him or her toward effective communication while simultaneously modifying distracting SP/PR elements that may interfere with intelligibility.

Overall, learners need to be consciously involved in the SP/PR modification process as they work to become intelligible, confident speakers of English. It is essential that they develop learner awarenesses and attitudes, including the following:

- Speech awareness;
- Self-awareness of features of speech production and performance;
- Self-observation skills and a positive attitude toward self-monitoring processes;
- Speech-modification skills (i.e., self-"correction") and the elimination of the negative feeling that correction is a punitive thing;
- Awareness of the learner role as one of a "speech performer" who modifies, adjusts, or alters a feature of SP/PR; awareness of the teacher role as one of assisting students as a "speech coach" who gives suggestions and cues for speech modification, as well as support, encouragement, and constructive feedback;
- A sense of personal responsibility for one's own learning, not only for immediate educational and occupational needs, but for future career, social, and personal goals;
- A feeling of pride in one's own accomplishments; and
- Building a personal repertoire of speech monitoring and modification skills in order to continue to improve speaking effectiveness in English when the formal instructional program is finished.

Standards, goals, variation, and accent.

Traditional expectations, unrealistic goals, and false standards. Many traditional pronunciation texts exhort students to strive for perfect pronunciation, near-native pronunciation, or mastery of pronunciation—and if these expectations are not stated explicitly, they are almost certainly implied. Although these goals may sound attractive to many students and teachers, they are unrealistic standards.

At best, perfectionist performance goals are unrealistic because they are virtually unattainable for the vast majority of learners. At worst, they have been instrumental in imposing and perpetuating false standards, and aspiring to false standards can be devastating. It can defeat students who feel they cannot measure up and frustrate teachers who feel they have failed in their job.

In fact, there is a widely held consensus that few persons, especially those who learn to speak an L2 in their adolescence or later, can ever achieve nativelike pronunciation in that language. It is fortunate that perfect or nativelike pronunciation is not a necessary condition for fully functional communication in an L2. This is particularly significant in today's world, where English has become an increasingly useful international lingua franca.

Communicative learner goals. Careful goal-setting, with a program developed by teachers and students is essential in SP/PR curricula. The following three-part statement of goals has been a useful guideline in developing the curriculum of the advanced SP/PR courses in the English for Academic Purposes (EAP) program at the University of Michigan.

LEARNER SP/PR GOALS.

- Functional intelligibility: The intent is to help learners develop spoken English that is (at least) reasonably easy to understand and not distracting to listeners.
- Functional communicability: The intent is to help learners develop spoken English that serves their individual communicative needs effectively for a feeling of communicative competence.
- Increased self-confidence: The intent is to help learners become more comfortable and confident in using spoken English, and to develop a positive self-image as a nonnative speaker of English and a growing feeling of empowerment in oral communication.
- Speech-monitoring abilities and speech modification strategies for use beyond the classroom: The intent is to help learners develop speech awareness, personal speech-monitoring skills, and speech adjustment strategies that will enable them to continue to develop intelligibility, communicability, and confidence outside as well as inside class.

COMMUNICATIVE COMPETENCE GOALS. The four goals listed above are intended to move learners toward developing communicative competence, including linguistic competence, discourse competence, sociolinguistic competence, and strategic competence (Canale and Swain 1980).

LANGUAGE-LEARNING STRATEGIES. These four SP/PR goals also encompass a focus on helping learners develop a variety of language-learning strategies including metacognitive, cognitive, communication, global practice , affective, and social strategies. (See Oxford 1990; Wenden 1991.)

Accent and accent discrimination. Lawyer Mari Matusda in "Voices of America: Accent, Antidiscrimination Law, and a Jurisprudence for the Last Reconstruction" observes that, "Someone who tells you they don't like your accent is quite likely telling you that they don't like you" (1991: 1329). Lippi-Green begins her comprehensive and thought-provoking article, "Accent, Standard Language Ideology, and Discriminatory Pretext in the Courts," with the following statement:

> Title VII of the U.S. Civil Rights Act clearly forbids an employer to discriminate against persons of color for reasons of personal or customer preference. Similarly, a qualified job applicant may not be rejected on the basis of linguistic traits linked to national origin. In contrast to racial discrimination, however, an employer has considerable latitude in matters of language, provided in part by a judicial system which recognizes in theory the link between language and social identity, but in practice is often confounded by blind adherence to a standard language ideology. (1994: 163).

Lippi-Green (1994: 166) uses the term language-trait focused (LTF) discrimination in referring to accent discrimination. She explains that LTF discrimination is based upon "the acceptance of a standard language ideology (a term coined by Milroy and Milroy 1985)." Standard language ideology is defined as "a bias toward an abstracted, idealized, homogeneous spoken language which is imposed from above and which takes as its model the written language." She also observes that "the most salient feature is the goal of suppression of variation of all kinds."

In discussing the question of the magnitude of LTF discrimination, Lippi-Green reports that:

> The General Accounting Office of the United States Government conducted a carefully designed statistical study of a stratified random sampling of employers nationwide, and reported that 10% of their sample, or 461,000 companies employing millions of persons, openly if naively admit that they "discriminated on the basis of a person's foreign appearance or accent." (1994: 174)

According to Price (1996: 13A), the Equal Employment Opportunity Commission (EEOC) reported the following: " ... in 1994, the EEOC ... had 120 active charges pending against 67 employers based on English-language rules." In a preliminary report for fiscal year 1995, 8,738 cases were reported as awaiting action for national origin discrimination and most English-only cases fall under this jurisdiction.

Matsuda (1991: 1367) proposes a Title VII analysis for accent cases, one that "considers both the legitimate concerns of employers and the societal goal of eliminating discriminatory employment practices." She suggests that courts consider four separate questions in accent cases:

- What level of communication is required for the job?
- Was the candidate's (or employee's) speech fairly evaluated?
- Is the candidate intelligible to the pool of relevant, nonprejudiced listeners, such that job performance is not unreasonably impeded? and

- What accommodations are reasonable given the job and any limitations in intelligibility?

Assessing intelligibility and communicability. Responsible SP/PR programs today use a variety of evaluations beginning with a needs analysis of SP/PR as an entrance test, and ending with an exit test devised to measure progress and final SP/PR proficiency level. No evaluation, however, is more important than the assessment of intelligibility. Yet "intelligibility" is a very slippery concept.

Judgments about intelligibility are related directly to listeners' preconceived ideas about nonnative speakers in general (including their accents) and the personalities and accents of individual nonnative speakers in particular. Thus, in the final analysis, judgments about intelligibility are as much in the minds of listeners as the mouths of speakers.

Chastain (1980), looking at the general concept of comprehension judgments of nonnative speakers by native speakers, makes some revealing discoveries. He finds that, depending upon native speaker factors such as linguistic tolerance, insight, interest, and patience, student language error will be viewed as (1) comprehensible and acceptable, (2) comprehensible but not acceptable, or (3) incomprehensible (in the case of failure to comprehend). Chastain notes that while these reactions will vary from person to person and situation to situation, this does not diminish the importance of contributions made by listeners in the communicative process.

A University of Michigan study (Ayala and Bell 1995) using the University of Michigan Intelligibility/Communicability Index (see Appendix) obtained the following results. Two groups of undergraduate subjects rated the same nine nonnative speakers quite differently based on the conditions established by the researchers. Group One listeners were told to assess the speakers on the video tape as if they were International Teaching Assistants (ITAs) delivering a lecture in a math class. Group Two listeners were told to assess the speakers as if they were people whom the listeners had just met and engaged in passing, friendly, conversation. Predictably the subjects in Group One scored the speakers much lower than those in Group Two. Clearly, the findings from this study showed that students have very high expectations for the speaking abilities of ITAs whom they might encounter in a classroom setting.

With increasing numbers of accent discrimination cases in the courts, it is essential that second language SP/PR experts and applied linguists perfect their skills in assessing the qualities of intelligibility and, indeed, attend to quantifying decision-making in this critical area. Two kinds of potential need (perhaps demand) for our services are: (1) being summoned as expert witnesses in intelligibility assessment to give testimony in accent discrimination cases; and (2) being called upon to provide services when SP/PR classes are ordered by courts as a contingency for plaintiffs being reinstated in their place of employment. An example of the latter situation can be found in the cases of

ITAs who are conditionally rejected for teaching, with the provision that they receive instruction in SP/PR teaching and classroom management.

Learner outcomes. Overall, learner outcomes in an updated SP/PR program must take the form of three patterns:

- **Learner Process**. Learners must work toward becoming positively self-involved, becoming active forceful partners in their own learning, and developing personal skills and strategies for monitoring and altering their own speech patterns.
- **Learner Product**. Learners must demonstrate satisfactory levels of intelligibilityand nondistracting patterns of speech (microlevel features) and/or increasingly satisfactory levels of communicability in spoken discourse (macrolevel features). They must have command of speech-monitoring abilities and speech modification strategies that they can use beyond the classroom, both during the instructional period and beyond.
- **Adaptation Attitude**. Learners also need guidance in developing an attitude of SP/PR adaptation. Adaptation is complex; certainly it is one part each of linguistic, discourse, sociolinguistic, and strategic competence—but it must also have one part *goodwill* and an open philosophy toward adapting one's own English dialect when in contact with other dialect speakers of the many Englishes across the globe.

Variation and adaptation: Crosscultural communication in speaking English internationally. Finally, for both *second language* speakers of English and *first language* speakers of the myriad dialects of English—for everyone who will use English "internationally"—it is essential to broaden the base of our philosophy toward speech-monitoring and speech modification (as listed above). Learners need to be guided to considering the importance of developing these skills to adapt their mode of speaking English internationally in the reciprocal communicative context where their interlocutors can be expected to use different dialects of SP/PR. Developing an attitude of openness and adaptation, in both linguistic and nonlinguistic patterns of behavior, will help them become more comfortable crossdialect, crosscultural speakers.

As noted by Baxter:

> Adaptation is not an easy process, requiring in the speaker a variety of communicative skills and an awareness of what is entailed in cross-cultural communication. It also requires a willingness to modify, temporarily or even permanently, one's cultural identity. (1980: 66)

A not-unusual situation is that of transplanted native speakers of a World English dialect different from the one of the speech community in which they find themselves. A clear example of this is ITAs in North American universities who may need guidance from their SP/PR teacher in addressing the need to adjust their attitude as well as to adapt their SP/PR monitoring and modification skills. Other examples are professionals who are employed in North American companies, businesses, industries, educational institutions, etc., whether they find themselves in subordinate or leadership roles in research, production, and/or business management. They, too, need specific training in all three areas of the three A's: language adaptation, cultural adaptation, and attitude adjustment.

These three areas are important considerations for both nonnative and native speakers of any given dialect of world English when they travel and/or work in countries where English is used as a lingua franca. They will find themselves needing to attend to adaptation and accommodation in order to communicate comfortably and successfully. No speakers are exempt from considering seriously the roles they play in the two-way street of international, intercultural communication. How they play these roles, both linguistically and culturally, will effect the outcomes of their communicative encounters.

REFERENCES

Ayala, Claudia A., and Katherine L. Bell. 1995. "Non-native English speaker assessment of intelligibility." Unpublished research paper.

Baxter, James. 1980. "How should I speak English? American-ly, Japanese-ly, or internationally?" In Adam Brown (ed.), *Teaching English pronunciation*. London: Routledge. 53–71.

Beebe, Leslie. 1978. "Teaching pronunciation (why we should be)." *IDIOM* 9(1): 2–3.

Bolinger, Dwight. 1986. *Intonation and its parts*. Palo Alto, California: Stanford University Press.

Brazil, David, Malcolm Coulthard, and Catherine Johns. 1980. *Discourse, intonation and language teaching*. London: Longman.

Brown, Adam (ed.) 1991. *Teaching English pronunciation: A book of readings*. London: Routledge.

Brown, Gillian, and George Yule. 1983. *Discourse analysis*. New York: Cambridge University Press.

Canale, Michael, and Merrill Swain. 1980. "Theoretical bases of communicative approaches to second language teaching and testing." *Applied Linguistics* 1(1): 1–47.

Celce-Murcia, Marianne, Donna Brinton, and Janet Goodwin. 1996. *Teaching pronunciation: A reference for teachers of English as a second language*. New York: Cambridge University Press.

Chastain, Kenneth. 1980. "Native speaker reactions to instructor-identified student second-language errors." *The Modern Language Journal* 34: 210–215.

Corder, S. Pit. 1967. "The significance of learners' errors." *International Review of Applied Linguistics* 5(4): 161–170.

Corder, S. Pit. 1976. "The study of interlanguage." In Gerhard Nickel (ed.), *Proceedings of the Fourth International Congress of Applied Linguistics*. Stuttgart, Germany: Hochschul-Verlag. 9–34.

Gibran, Khalil. 1923. *The prophet*. New York: Alfred Knopf.

Labov, William. 1972. *Sociolinguistic patterns*. Philadelphia: University of Pennsylvania Press.

Lambert, William. 1967. "A social psychology of bilingualism." *Journal of Social Issues* 23(1): 91–109.

Lippi-Green, Rosina. 1994. "Accent, standard language ideology, and discriminatory pretext in the courts." *Language in Society* 23(1): 163–198.

Major, R. 1987. "A model of interlanguage phonology." In G. Ioup and S. Weinberger (eds.), *Interlanguage phonology: The acquisition of a second language sound system*. New York: Newbury House/Harper and Row. 101–124.

Marks, J. 1986. "All language teaching is phonology teaching." *IATEFL Phonology: Special Interest Group Newsletter* 1: 8–9.

Matsuda, Mari J. 1991. "Voices of America: Accent, antidiscrimination law, and a jurisprudence for the last reconstruction." *The Yale Law Journal* 100(1): 1329–1407.

Milroy, James, and Lesley Milroy. 1992 [1985]. *Authority in language: Investigating language prescription and standardisation, Second revised edition*. London: Routledge.

Morley, Joan. 1988. "How many languages do you speak? Perspectives on pronunciation-speech-communication in EFL/ESL." *Nagoya [Japan] Gakuin University Roundtable on Linguistics and Literature Journal* 19(1): 1–35.

Morley, Joan. 1991. "The pronunciation component in teaching English to speakers of other languages." *TESOL Quarterly* 25(3): 481–520.

Morley, Joan. 1992. *Extempore speaking practice*. Ann Arbor, Michigan: The University of Michigan Press.

Morley, Joan. 1995. "A multidimensional curriculum design for speech/pronunciation instruction." In Joan Morley (ed.), *Pronunciation theory and pedagogy: New views, new directions*. Alexandria, Virginia: TESOL Publications. 64–91.

Oxford, Rebecca. 1990. *Language learning strategies: What every teacher should know*. New York: Newbury House.

Pennington, Martha C. 1996. *Phonology in English language teaching: An international approach*. New York: Addison Wesley Longman

Pennington, Martha C. 1995. "Recent research in L2 phonology: Implications for practice." In Joan Morley (ed.), *Pronunciation theory and pedagogy: New views, new directions*. Alexandria, Virginia: TESOL Publications. 92–108.

Pennington, Martha C., and Jack Richards. 1986. "Pronunciation revisited." *TESOL Quarterly* 20(2): 207–225.

Price, David Andrew. 1996. "English-only rules: EECO has gone too far." In *USA Today*, March 28, 1996: 13A.

Ross, David A. 1992. "Review of 'Teaching English Pronunciation: A book of Readings by Adam Brown.'" *Language Learning* 42(3): 441–444.

Scovel, Thomas. 1988. *A time to speak: A psycholinguistic inquiry into the critical period for human speech*. Cambridge, Massachusetts: Newbury House.

Wenden, Anita. 1991. *Learner strategies for learner autonomy*. London: Prentice-Hall International.

Wong, Rita. 1985. "Does pronunciation teaching have a place in the communicative classroom?" In Deborah Tannen and James E. Alatis (eds.), *Georgetown University Round Table on Languages and Linguistics 1985*. Washington, D.C.: Georgetown University Press. 17–28.

APPENDIX

University of Michigan Speech Intelligibility/Communicability Index: Describing Speech and Evaluating its Impact on Communication

Level	Description	Impact on Communication
1	Speech is basically unintelligible; only an occasional word/phrase can be recognized.	Accent precludes functional oral communication.
2	Speech is largely unintelligible; great listener effort is required; constant repetitions and verifications are required.	Accent causes severe interference with oral communication.
	--------------- COMMUNICATIVE THRESHOLD A ---------------	
3	Speech is reasonably intelligible, but significant listener effort is required due to speaker's pronunciation/grammatical errors which impede communication and cause listener distraction; on-going need for repetitions and verifications.	Accent causes frequent interference with communication through the combined effect of the individual features of mispronunciaiton and the global impact of the variant speech pattern.
4	Speech is largely intelligible; while sound and prosodic variances from NS norm are obvious, listeners can understand if they concentrate on the message.	Accent causes interference primarily at the distraction level; listener's attention is often diverted away from the content to focus instead on the novelty of the speech pattern.
	--------------- COMMUNICATIVE THRESHOLD B ---------------	
5	Speech is fully intelligible; occasional sound and prosodic variances from NS norm are present but not seriously distracting to the listener.	Accent causes little interference; speech is fully functional for effective communication.
6	Speech is "near-native"; only minimal features of divergence from NS can be detected; near-native sound and prosodic patterning.	Accent is virtually nonexistent.

NOTES ON SPEECH EVALUATION:

1. Elicit a speech sample of several minutes. The sample should be sustained impromptu speech, not just answers to simple questions or "rehearsed" biographical comments. The sample should be spontaneous speech, perhaps on a topic such as: (a) what the student wants to be doing in 5 years; (b) what makes the student's life interesting; (c) what makes a happy family.
2. Try to listen to the speech sample as if you were an untrained language listener. Err on the conservative side with consideration of the "lay" listeners whom the student will meet.
3. In a few descriptor phrases summarize the student's strengths and weaknesses in three areas: (a) use of vowel and consonant sound segments, their combinations, and reductions, contractions, elisions, assimilations, etc.; (b) use of features of stress, rhythm, and intonation, and vocal quality features, rate, volume, etc.; (c) features of general "communicability." (Comment on how each of these factors impacts communicative intelligibility, and assign a level number as Speech Intelligibility Level (SIL), using [+] and [-] notations as necessary. Monitor student progress through periodic SIL re-evaluation.

Morley (1992:xv). Intensive Consonant Practice (Chart 3). Ann Arbor, Michigan: University of Michigan Press.

From communicative competence through bilingualism to metalinguistic development: Some theoretical pointers and research perspectives

Renzo Titone
University of Rome and University of Toronto, Ontario

The purpose of my discussion is to clarify some important contemporary issues in psycholinguistics applied to language teaching, where confusion or neglect are dominant and endanger sound educational practice. In particular, I want to share some reflections about the notion of "communicative competence" which is the pivot of language learning and teaching but all too often misunderstood or subjected to reductive thinking. At the same time, I consider the relation of communicative competence to bilingual education in its deepest and richest meaning. Both notions are, in turn, related to a very important educational goal on the horizon of language pedagogy today, namely, what modern educational psycholinguists call "metacognitive/metalinguistic development."

My thesis is that real "bilingual competence" implies mastering two languages not only on the tactical level of sensory-motor skills in decoding and encoding verbal communication but, above all, on the strategic and ego-dynamic levels of adequate cognitive comprehension and analytic awareness of language structures and functions. Most of all, bilingual competence implies the linguistic and personal consciousness of the human values of language and culture. In short, we can state that linguistic-communicative competence in two languages/cultures becomes an invaluable asset of the human communicator if, and only if, the total human personality, in its performative, cognitive, and deeply conscious dimensions, is involved in the command of the two communication systems.

My discussion is divided into two parts: (1) What is the meaning and significance of a "personological" view of language and "communicative competence"? and (2) Does research ascertain that true "bilingual competence" generates a high degree of "metacognitive/metalinguistic development"?

How does the notion of "communicative competence" fit in with a personological view of language?

Some implications for "humanistic language pedagogy." Since the late 1960's, there has been a great deal of talking about "communicative competence" as opposed to "linguistic competence." This discussion has become more heated as language teaching specialists have adopted the notion of "communicativeness" as the pivotal concept of language pedagogy, especially vis-à-vis second language acquisition. The so-called communicative approach in its various forms—such as the Council of Europe's proposal for the widely applied "notional-functional" syllabus—has become the dominant trend in many countries. Heated discussions usually beget chaos and conceptual confusion, which has been the case in the the field of applied psycholinguistics.

What is the problem? If, on one hand, the notion of "communicative competence" is strong on the side of the adjective "communicative," it may be reductive on the side of the noun, "competence." My contention here is that the notion of "competence" completely overcomes the limitations of the behavioral view of language learning, i.e. learning as a mechanistic, stimulus-response bonding process, in that it embodies essentially cognitive contents beyond even the cognitive concept entailed in the "linguistic competence" of the Chomskyan tradition. In other words, "competence" deals with cognitive command of both linguistic rules and pragmatic constraints. On the other hand, an ill-defined notion of "competence" risks falling into two parameters, namely that cognition is reduced to (1) "declarative knowledge" of an abstract and static nature, or, conversely, to mere "operational knowledge" of an essentially concrete nature, for example, practical skills; or (2) from a strictly rational perspective, "pure cognition," thereby ignoring the role of affective, deeply personal factors, clustered around the deep core of the Ego/Self. The former definition views the communicator merely as a "thinking intellect" or, vice versa, as a mechanically-operating system; the latter considers the communicator to be a pure intellect devoid of emotions, motivations and attitudes, in short, as a cold, frozen, insensitive individual, a fully living Person.

Is there a way out of such an impasse? Yes, if we redefine "competence" and "communication" in deeper and richer terms, namely, by taking account of the essential structural and dynamic components of the "communicating personality." I discuss this proposal by (1) redefining the notion of "competence"; (2) considering "communicative" competence to include structural and dynamical "linguistic" competence; (3) placing "communicative competence" in its appropriate role, viz. as an asset of the "Speaking Person"; and, finally, (4) proposing a "holodynamic" view of "communicative competence" in light of the Holodynamic Model of language behavior and language learning.

REDEFINING THE NOTION OF "COMPETENCE." "Competence" essentially means the mastery of both knowledge and skill. It implies that speakers know the rules and paradigms of action, but at the same time are capable of using instrumental strategies and tactics aimed at definite objectives. In sum, "competence" is tantamount to a dynamically structured system of awareness and skillfulness, both essential prerequisites to any successful operation.

Not only must both declarative and operational knowledge be present in the acting organism, but it must also be able to carry on and out well-conceived operations according to the demands of accuracy and fluency. In the case of language competence, speaker-hearers must master on all its levels (phonology-phonetics, morphology-syntax, semantics-lexicon) the rules specific to a particular language system and, at the same time, command the automatic performance of language units and sequences. Moreover, the planning, previewing, and connecting of language sequences must be carried out under the conscious control of the speaker's Ego or Self, at least at the starting moment of these operations. In addition, the fact that the Ego/Self is not an isolated monad breathing out pure self-expressions, but uses language to send out messages, i.e. to "communicate," with an interlocutor in a vital dialectic exchange between Ego and the World, urges the consideration of the interactional character of communication. This demands consideration of and agreement with the social rules governing communicative interaction. All of this amounts to saying that both the knowledge and skills constituting "competence" work on all the systemic levels of the language system but also, no less, in the sphere of pragmatic relations. Hence, I view the enlarged notion of "communicative competence" as encompassing the more restricted notion of "linguistic competence."

"COMMUNICATIVE COMPETENCE" > "LINGUISTIC COMPETENCE." It would be wrong to oppose "communicative competence" to "linguistic competence" as if they were non-inclusive and heterogeneous notions. In reality, no communication is possible without the use of linguistic (and non-linguistic) tools. Language as performance (*parole*) prerequires the existence and availability of language as a system (*langue*).

Therefore, linguistic competence must be mastered before one is able to communicate verbally. Communication is a wider pale containing language. But if they are devoid of the knowledge of social rules ensuring and governing effective communication, language and linguistic command are not alone sufficient to ensure interpersonal contact, or real communication. The "pragmatic" component of competence adds an essential element to the procedural knowledge, or the "how," of the communication process.

It is precisely this attention to the pragmatic rules and conditions of communicating that call imperiously for the active participation of all levels of the communicator's entire personality: conscious, subconscious, and unconscious. If one can imagine a speaking machine programmed to produce linguistic "objects" (like automatically produced "sentences"), it is absurd to imagine an unconscious or mechanical emission of messages, which by their very nature imply the intention to communicate with another person. In short, no communication can take place without the conscious, intentioned participation of at least two people; there is no such thing as non-personalized communication, although most improperly, one could speak of "impersonal messages" in quite a different sense.

"COMMUNICATIVE COMPETENCE" AS AN ASSET OF THE SPEAKING PERSON. The pivotal terms involved in authentic communication are therefore: *person*, *intention*, *context*, and *message*. Interesting speculations developed by Malinowsky (1935), Morris (1946), Gumperz and Hymes (1964), Halliday (1973), and others have helped define the elements of "communicative competence," from the role of social context, to the meaning of message, to the role of intentions and functions in the pragmatic use of language. But very few have perceived the basic relevance of the role of the Person in the act of human communication.

This view is substantialized into an integrated model of the acting Personality, which I discuss next.

A "HOLODYNAMIC" VIEW OF COMMUNICATIVE COMPETENCE. I introduced the term "holodynamic" together with the term "Model" (1973 and ff.) while trying to define the dynamics of human activity in all areas, especially in the linguistic-communicative area, viewed from the perspective of the structure of Human Personality. The adjective means that all (*holos*) the essential components of personal activity (*dynamis*) are present in human behavior and human learning. This is especially relevant in the case of language and communication as human activities.

Beyond a merely cybernetic view, implying both strategic and tactical operations, the Human Being needs initiative power and deep-seated control of the Self or Ego (not in the Freudian sense) to perform whatever action in the fullness of humanity. This means that all worthy human behavior and learning, more so when language is involved, needs the simultaneous participation of the three operational levels, viz. the Tactic Level (of sensory-motor performances, like encoding and decoding), the Strategic Level (of mental programming, selecting, ordering, controlling, reviewing, and/or correcting, through all sorts of feedback operations), and the Ego-dynamic Level (of deep conscious and unconscious motivations, desires, attitudes, intentions, decisions, which fall under the control of self-consciousness and language awareness, and over social rules of interpersonal contact).

Where does "communicative competence" lie? Where is the source and performance of communicative acts located? Why is Man responsible for all his words? Why, in sum, is speech so tremendously important with respect to human existence and destiny? Certainly, neither linguistics nor psychology can give answers to these questions: They belong on a higher level, the level of philosophical wisdom.

Concretely speaking, the source theory of my proposal is explained by the merging of two Models: the psychological Holodynamic Model and the neurological Bimodal Model (see Figure 1 in Appendix). The teaching/learning process entailed in the achievement of competence is specified on the three basic levels of the Active Personality (see Figure 2 in Appendix), while a Person-centered Communicative Competence Model implies cross-breeding between personality levels on one side and structure and function components of competence, both on the linguistic level and the communicative levels, on the other.

Linguistic competence represents structure in its basic microsystems (semantic, morphosyntactic, phonetic-phonological), while communicative competence works through the control of basic functions (instrumental, regulatory, interactional, personal, hueristic, imaginative, mathematic, and metalinguistic/metacommunicative; Halliday 1973). Basically, the Communicator's Personality governs and fertilizes communicative competence, which will be all the richer and more effective the greater it is permeated by the Person's deep existential and experiential contents. *Loquor, ergo sum*—"I speak, therefore I exist"—I like to repeat by paraphrasing Decartes' axiom, *Cogito, ergo sum*—"I think, therefore I am." Existing as a full experience, enriched, enlivened, and supported by language/communication, communicative competence becomes identified with the Word, in its fullest meaning, or, as Wilhelm von Humboldt said, as *energeia*, or "vital power."

Bilingual education and the development of metalinguistic abilities: A research project. To begin with, we must acknowledge that bilingual competence represents the summit of communicative ability. Furthermore, the vital connection between bilingualism as a psychological state and metacognition/metalinguistic consciousness has recently been emphasized and repeatedly confirmed by research (cf. Titone and Pinto 1989). Theoreticians and researchers from different countries and more or less complex linguistic and cultural settings have adduced evidence for a positive correlation between the two individual states, provided certain social, psychological, and educational conditions have been ensured. The purpose of my contribution is to bring to the attention of educational psycholinguistics the results of some investigations and experiments carried out in linguistic and cultural settings where Italian is the first spoken language of bilingual and diglossic individuals (beginning in pre-school and primary level).

After summarizing the main features of the research on metalinguistic abilities that my colleagues and I have been conducting, I outline our basic hypotheses, clarify a few terminological assumptions, and present the results of several specific investigations carried out in Italian settings.

An ongoing research project on metalinguistic development.

ITALIAN SETTINGS: MONOLINGUALISM, DIGLOSSIA, BILINGUALISM. Italy is a multilingual country, with over one hundred dialects of a very different origin and four languages added to the national language, Italian, viz. French, German, Slovenian, and Albanian. These four second languages are currently used and taught, beginning in kindergarten, in special-statute Regions: Valley of Aoste, Alto Adige, Friuli, and Puglia-Calabria/Sicily. (I should add that a fifth language, Ladino, is semi-officially used and taught in a restricted area of the Province of Trento.) Accordingly, we have truly bilingual areas protected by special laws and enjoying bilingual schooling from kindergarten, or at least primary-school, levels.

Besides these cases of societal bilingualism, Italy has a high percentage of diglossic speakers who, outside of school, use both the local dialect and the standard national language according to varying social situations. In some cases dialects have been recaptured and also literarily reintegrated, with a spreading tendency toward teaching them in certain elementary schools. In these cases, besides maintaining oral competence, the goal of some supporters is to develop writing skills and, where the dialect has been studied with modern linguistic methods, even to teach some formal grammar.

A third situation is that of monolingual speakers who since early childhood have only spoken the national language, Italian, although with unavoidable regional inflections and a slightly peculiar regional lexicon (Italo-Sicilian, Italo-Neapolitan, Italo-Piedmontese, Italo-Lombard, Italo-Venetian, etc.). But in their formal education, all monolingual speakers, at least up to Junior High School (Scuola Media: ages eleven to fourteen), are required to study at least one foreign language and, after Junior High School, even two or three foreign languages. (One should note that the current Italian Elementary School Syllabus, approved in 1985, enforces the acquisition of one foreign language from Grade I, or at least Grade III.) This means that, even if we cannot speak of real acquired bilingualism, we are at least entitled to a sort of "enriched monolingualism."

From this developing perspective, we have launched a research project aimed at checking the educational and psycho-social outcomes of such a multilingual and pluricultural situation by testing the degree of metacognitive and metalinguistic development of students exposed to bilingual education, or at least diglossic behavior. Our subjects represent very different age levels and educational curricula: kindergarten (ages three to five), elementary schools (ages six to eleven), middle schools (ages eleven to fourteen), and secondary schools (ages fifteen to nineteen). In order to evaluate the degree of metalinguistic development we have devised a special test, the Metalinguistic Abilities Test (TAM), that has been developed and standardized in three forms (Form A: kindergarten; Form B: elementary and middle school; Form C: secondary school). TAM has been correlated with several other measures and variables, namely, linguistic aptitude, age, sex, social class, educational level, and, in particular bilingual and/or diglossic competence.

The investigations I report on here deal with monolingual, diglossic, and bilingual/trilingual subjects.

EXTENSION TO OTHER COUNTRIES. In order to check on the validity of our hypotheses and evaluation tools, we are now trying to extend our research to other national settings: in Spain, to speakers of Castilian and Catalan (Barcelona), and speakers of Castilian and Andalusian (Huelva); and in Canada, to speakers of Italian and English or French (Toronto, Ottawa, Montreal). We are in the process of translating and adapting our test of metalinguistic abilities, which was drawn from an earlier draft formulated by Hakes (1980), and further articulated into special metalinguistic abilities and subtests (Titone and Pinto 1989). Our conviction that bilingualism is from a very early age a powerful factor in the special development of metalinguistic abilities and consciousness has already been confirmed and supported not only by other investigations (e.g., Bowey and Tunmer 1984; Cummins 1978; Hake 1980) in Canada, Australia, and the U.S., but also by the results of our investigations in Italy since 1985.

Some basic hypotheses. We can distinguish three main cases where the relationship between linguistic competence and metalinguistic consciousness exists: (1) diglossic competence versus monolingual education; (2) early L2 acquisition versus monolingual education; and (3) bilingual education versus monolingual education. Our hypotheses are defined as follows:

(1) Monolingual education has the lowest chance of producing a high degree of metacognition, having as its only resource the factors tied with literacy, specifically, learning to read and intensive/extensive reading as a reflective activity.

(2) Diglossic competence, provided it is systematically submitted to special teaching strategies, can become a source for analytic reflection of language texts. But to become effective from the point of view of reflective ability, teaching must be oriented towards a deep comparative/contrastive analysis of the two codes, both the low and high varieties (to use Ferguson's 1959 terminology).

(3) Bilingual education has the highest chance of providing food for thought, in that it can stimulate, spontaneously or systematically, analytic reflection about the structures and functions of the two languages and their cultures. This is the case because it is both actively present and working within the minds of the bilingual speakers and,

above all, it is equally present in the media and content of a rich educational process. The level of effectiveness of bilingual education *stricto sensu* can be approached by a very productive teaching/learning of a foreign language. (Experiences in this regard consider intensity and extensiveness of time of instruction and appropriateness of teaching methodology to be essential factors for attaining significant results).

Next to bilingual education we have found that conscious and systematic exploitation of diglossic competence, by focussing the student's attention upon the structure of the dialectal code, can have a particular effect upon metalinguistic consciousness. But what do we mean by the terms "language awareness," "metalinguistic consciousness," and "metalinguistic abilities" (and, incidentally, "epilinguistic awareness")?

Terminological assumptions. Writers frequently fall into ambiguity or haziness in using these terms, with great damage to the definition of research objectives and the interpretation of results.

I usually (Titone 1985) distinguish language awareness from metalinguistic consciousness. The former I characterize as implicit, caused by cognitive maturation and appearing prior to formal schooling; the latter I characterize as the formal, rational, intentional, and declarative knowledge of the sign and symbol systems common to languages. Metalinguistic consciousness appears at about the age of twelve, after exposure to formal schooling.

As reported in Titone (1985), Tunmer and Harriman (1984) suggest that major views of metalinguistic awareness include those who (1) see it as part and parcel of the language acquisition process; (2) see it as distinct, and of unique importance; (3) employ the information processing metaphor to describe and explain this concept; and (4) see it as a consequence of reading and grammar skills. Indeed, the notion of metalinguistic consciousness is a higher-order ability that follows the attainment of a certain level of proficiency in reading and grammar.

The interesting point here is that bilingualism, as a psychological state involving intelligence factors and motivational attitudes, seems to be a particularly powerful factor in influencing development of metalinguistic consciousness, even in very young children growing up in a state of simultaneous bilingualism. And this happens independently of the type of first and second languages acquire and used. (For further discussion of terminological definitions see MacClaren 1989: 5–18.) We should add here one more concept proposed more recently, i.e. "Epilinguistic Awareness". As Gombert states: "We shall employ the term 'Epilinguisitic' to designate the 'unconscious metalinguistic activities,' supposing by definition that a reflective, intentional character is inherent in metalinguistic activity in the strict sense of the term"

(1990/1992: 10). Thus we could say that "epilinguistic awareness" is an implicit reference to the working of languages, a sort of intuitive knowledge following or governing the elements of speech acts. But, if this notion has relevance in the analysis of language acquisition processes in children, I think that it is almost null in the case of advanced bilingual behavior, especially where the case involves school-directed acquisition. Here "metalinguistic consciousness" may be more important and pertinent.

Some investigations in Italian settings. For the sake of illustration, I consider here only eight cases studied by my co-researchers.

CASE I. "Early bilingual education and cognitive flexibility" (Veccia 1989).

(1) Objectives: The following are the preliminary questions asked by the researcher: Does L2 competence improve competence in the L1? What is the degree of metalinguistic development acquired by young bilingual children? Is bilingualism a factor enhancing the disappearance of egocentrism? and Is cognitive flexibility (and intellectual creativity) enhanced by bilingual acquisition?

(2) Sample: An experimental group of nineteen children and a control group of eighteen children, ages 3:4–4:4. Their social extraction was mixed class. The second language taught was French in a Southern area of Italy (Avellino kindergartens).

(3) Tools: An intelligence test (Terman-Merrill) with IQ as a result; tests of oral comprehension and production in the L1; a test on nominal realism and cognitive flexibility; a test of oral comprehension in L2 (French).

(4) Results: Both the awareness of the conventional nature of names and the ability to invent new semantic contents and new words were very high (87.5% in the experimental group vs. 50% in the control group). Therefore, it appears that these two traits mark some important aspects of metalinguistic consciousness. In this case, they were stimulated by the acquisition of a second language (French), very different from the first language (Italian/Neapolitan).

CASE II. "Metalinguistic development in elementary school children speaking Italian and Albanian" (D'Errico 1988).

(1) Objectives: To determine the influence of the comparative analysis of Italian and Albanian on metalinguistic development.

(2) Sample: Twenty bilingual children from two Grade V classes from the Province of Cosenza.

(3) Tools: A teaching method based on the analytic comparison of the two languages starting from Grade II. The evaluation was made on the basis of a questionnaire on the social perception of the two codes, translation of texts from Italian into Albanian, and TAM.

(4) Results: With regard to the control group, the children tested showed superiority, especially in certain metalinguistic abilities, viz. comprehension, semantic disambiguation, and semantic acceptability. Therefore, the choice of pedagogical method seems to be highly relevant, namely guiding the children to a comparative analysis of the structures of the two language systems.

CASE III. "Trilingual education in the elementary schools and cognitive development" (Pilotti 1990).

(1) Objectives: To measure the correlation between diglossic and bilingual competence and metacognitive abilities.

(2) Sample: Two hundred forty-four subjects comprising four Grade I classes plus five Grade III classes in a mountain village in the province of Turin (North Italy) studying Italian, English, and the local dialect; distributed into experimental and control groups.

(3) Tools: A questionnaire on the social class of the subjects, an intelligence test, and linguistic tests in the four skills of all three languages. An evaluation of sociolinguistic attitudes toward the three codes provided an additional measure the children's trilingual competence.

(4) Results: Cognitive development appeared to be higher after one year of instruction in all experimental groups, both in Grade I and Grade III. Language development was also significantly higher in all experimental groups: The subjects demonstrated better oral production (especially with regard to lexical competence), better written production (also with regard to lexicon), and fewer morphosyntactic errors.

CASE IV. "Cognitive development and trilingual competence" (Punxeddu 1989).

(1) Objectives: To measure the degree of cognitive development in trilingual children speaking Sardinian (Cagliari), Italian, and studying English in elementary schools.

(2) Sample: Thirty students from two Grade V classes, from a low social class (agricultural).

(3) Tools: Reading tests and oral translation from and into the three languages; also written production in Italian.

(4) Results: First, the use of the Sardinian language did not represent any obstacle to competence in Italian or the acquisition of English. Social factors also did not appear to handicap to the acquisition of L1 and L2. The "transfer effect" (Cummins 1978) was altogether evident.

CASE V. "Metalinguistic development in junior adolescents (middle schools)" (Ottavi 1988).

(1) Objectives: To measure the interrelation of different language and cognitive abilities as a function of the level of schooling (Grades VI, VII, and VIII).

(2) Sample: Sixty students, all monolingual, from Grades VI, VII, and VIII in the Italian middle-school system.

(3) Tool: TAM.

(4) Results: No significant differences among the three grades were noted. (Grade VII seems to be the culminating point of cognitive development.) Metalinguistic consciousness depends on global intellectual development. The absence of influence from foreign language study seems to be one of the reasons for lack of significant metacognitive growth.

CASE VI. "Metalinguistic development in students of junior high school (middle school)" (Elia 1991).

(1) Objectives: To ascertain the dependence of metalinguistic development on social class level. (The use of the local dialect is implied but not considered a teaching goal.)

(2) Sample: Thirty-six students in Grade VI (age 11:5), from varying social classes, with some diglossic component.

(3) Tool: TAM.

(4) Results: The level of social class seems to determine metalinguistic consciousness to some degree through the national language, Italian, as a dominant medium both in the home environment and school. The higher the social class of the home, the more sophisticated the level of cognitive/ metacognitive development, although this appears limited to certain conditions (like use of the language, reading habits, contact with a second language).

CASE VII. "Metalinguistic abilities and L2 learning in the elementary school" (Di Bernardino 1996).

(1) Objectives: To ascertain the degree of metalinguistic development in elementary school children studying a foreign language and determine the impact of properly planned teaching strategies on this development.

(2) Subjects: One hundred and twenty-one children, half studying foreign languages and half following a monolingual curriculum, during a three-year period (Grades III, IV, and V).

(3) Measurements: Entrance examinations consisting of an IQ Test (WISC) and a linguistic aptitude test for children (TALB) by Titone; final assessment based on proficiency tests in FL comprehension and production, mainly oral, and especially a metalinguistic abilities test (TAM, second level; ages nine to thirteen), devised and standardized by Titone and Pinto.

(4) Instructional approach: Special teaching strategies aimed at developing levels of language awareness; these strategies combined aspects of the communicative approach (specifically, the "notional-functional syllabus") with

procedures designed to guide the pupils to reflect upon (analytically and comparatively) patterns assimilated in the L2 (English, French, or German in comparison with L1, Italian).

(5) Results: In all subtests of the TAM, the students in the experimental group were significantly superior to the students in the control groups, even in the case where language abilities were equal in both groups.

CASE VIII. "Metalinguistic development and L2 learning in the middle school (Junior High School)" (Gambellini 1996).

(1) Objectives: To ascertain the cognitive advantages of L2 learning at the middle school level (especially Grades VI and VIII) after different periods of time studying the L2 at the elementary-school level.

(2) Subjects: Students at the high-school level with prior L2 learning in elementary school (experimental group) and L2 beginners at the junior high school level (control group). The sample of subjects involved one hundred and forty two of which sixty were in Grade VI and eighty-two in Grade VIII; 50% had studied a L2 previously, and 50% had not. The languages studied were English, French, or Spanish.

(3) Measurement tools: At the outset, a questionnaire, the Standard Progressives Matrices 38 by Raven; at the end the TAM 2.

(4) Results: One global result concerned the level of metalinguistic ability: an average score of 50.8 in the experimental group, and 42.2 in the control group. The conclusion was that the longer period of time devoted to L2 learning (starting in elementary school) was a decisive factor in metalinguistic progress whereas, independently of previous L2 contact, natural progress in age and schooling was not significantly influential.

Conclusions. As noted above, we are, at present, developing further applications of our objectives and experimental tools to other samples of learners and settings. Having the opportunity to conduct longitudinal investigations in all grades of Italian elementary schools—from the kindergartens in different regions and provinces of Italy all the way through secondary schools in which at least one foreign language is taught, or where bilingual education programs are being developed—we will be able to compare results in metalinguistic development. At the same time, ascertainment of the same variables in different countries (Spain, Canada) will make cross-linguistic and cross-cultural comparisons possible. We believe in the effectiveness and meaningfulness of this perspective because it highlights the primary importance of language acquisition, not merely as a communicative tool, but above all as a formative factor in the development of the learner's whole personality. This, in turn, appears to be the highest objective of basic education in the modern world.

REFERENCES

Ben Zeev, S. 1975. "Mechanism by which childhood bilingualism affects understanding of language and cognitive structure." In P.A. Hornby (ed.), *Bilingualism: Psychological, social, and educational implications*. New York: Academic Press.

Ben Zeev, S. 1977. "The influence of bilingualism on cognitive strategy and cognitive development." *Child Development* 48: 1009–1018.

Berthoud-Papandropoulou, I. 1978. "An experimental study of children's ideas about language." In J. Sinclair, H. Jarvella, and H. Levelt, *The child's conception of language*. Berlin: Springer. 55–82.

Bialystok, E. 1991. *Language processing in bilingual children*. Cambridge: Cambridge University Press.

Bonnet, C.E. and J. Tamine-Gardes. 1984. *Quand l'enfant parle du langage. Connaissance et conscience du langage chez l'enfant*. Brussels: Mardaga.

Bowey, J.A. and W.E. Tunmer. 1984. *Word awareness in children*. Berlin: Springer Verlag. 73–91.

Cummins, J. and M. Gulutsan. 1974. "Some effects of bilingualism cognitive functioning." In S. Carey (ed.), *Bilingualism, biculturalism, and education*. Edmonton: University of Alberta Press.

Cummins, J. 1978. "Bilingualism and the development of metalinguistic awareness." *Journal of Cross-cultural Psychology* 9: 131–149.

Cummins, J. and M. Danesi. 1990. *Heritage Languages: The development and denial of Canada's linguistic resources*. Toronto: Our Schools/Ourselves Education Foundation and Garamond Press.

Danesi, M. 1993. "Metalinguistic awareness and the role of grammar in second language teaching." *Scientia Paedagogica Experimentalis XXXI*.

Danesi, M. 1988. *Studies in Heritage Language learning and teaching*. Toronto: Centro Canadese Scuola e Cultura Italiana.

D'Errico, S. 1988. "Abilità metalinguistiche e educazione bilingue." Report. Faculty of Psychology, University of Rome.

Di Berardino, A.R. 1996. "Abilità metalinguistiche e seconda lingua. Un'indagine in soggetti di scuola elementare." M.A. Dissertation, University of Rome.

Donaldson, M. 1978. *Children's minds*. Glasgow: Collins.

Elia, L. 1991. "Lo sviluppo delle abilità metalinguistiche: Una ricerca nella scuola media." Report. Faculty of Psychology, University of Rome.

Ervin, S. and C.E. Osgood. 1954. "Second language learning and bilingualism." *Journal of Abnormal and Social Pyschology* 49: 139–146.

Ferguson, C.A. 1959. "Diglossia." *Word* 15: 325–340.

Gambellini, R. 1996. "Sviluppo metalinguistic e apprendimento scolastico delle lingue." M.A. Dissertation, University of Rome.

Gandolfi, M. and B. Benelli. 1979. "Il bilinguismo e il problema della convenzionalità del linguaggio: Uno studio sperimentale del realismo nominale in soggetti bilingui e non bilingui." *Quaderni per la promozione del bilinguismo* 25/26: 2–23.

Giannelli Campana, M.V. 1978. "The pragmatic theory of linguistic 'functions' in M. A. K. Halliday and its possible applications to FLT." *Annali, Anglistica, Instituto Orientale di Napoli* 1–2: 4–8.

Gombert, J.E. 1990/1992. *Metalinguistic development*, Translated from French. New York and London: Harvester Wheatsheaf.

Gombert, J.E. 1990. *Le développement métalinguistique*. Paris: Universitaires de France.

Gumperz, J. and D. Hymes. 1964. "The ethnography of communication." *American Anthropologist LXVI*: 86–102.

Hakes, D.T. 1980. *The development of metalinguistic abilities in children*. Berlin: Springer Verlag.

Hakuta, K. 1984. *The causal relationship between the development of bilingualism, cognitive flexibility, and social-cognitive skills in hispanic elementary school children*. Final Report. Part C. Washington, D.C.: National Clearing House for Bilingual Education.

Hamers, J. and M.H.A. Blanc. 1989. *Bilinguality and bilingualism*. Cambridge: Cambridge University Press.

Jakobson, R. 1966. *Saggi di linguistica generale*. Milano: Feltrinelli.

Karmiloff-Smith, A. 1995. *Oltra la mente modulare*. Bologna, Il Mulino.

Karmiloff-Smith, A. 1979. *A functional approach to child language*. Cambridge: Cambridge University Press.

Halliday, M.A.K. 1973. *Explorations in the functions of language*. London: Arnold.

Leopold W.F. 1939. "Pattern in children's language learning." In S. Saporta (ed.), *Psycholinguistics*. New York: Holt, Rinehart and Winston. 41–59.

Morris, C. 1946. *Signs! Language and behavior*. New York: Prentice Hall.

Malinowsky, B. 1935. *Coral gardens and their magic*. London: Allen and Unwinn.

MacLaren, R.I. 1989. "The distinction betwen linguistic awareness and metalinguistic consciousness: An applied awareness." *Rassegna Italiana di Linguistica Applicata*, Anno XXI(1–2): 5–18.

Mininni, G. 1989. "Note sui tratti psiosemiotici della consapevolezza metalinguistica." *Rassegna Italiana di Linguistica Applicata*, Anno XXI, (1–2): 41–58.

Nesdale, A.R., M.L. Herriman, and W.E. Tunmer. 1984. *Phonological awareness in children*. Berlin: Springer Verlag.

Ottavi, I. 1988. "Lo sviluppo delle abilità metalinguistiche negli studenti di scuola media." Report. Faculty of Psychology, University of Rome.

Papandropoulou, J. and H. Sinclair. 1974. "What's a word? Experimental study of children's ideas on grammar." *Human Development*. 241–258.

Peal, E. and W.E. Lambert. 1962. "The relationship of bilingualism to intelligence." *Pscychological Monographs: General and Applied*. 76: 1–23.

Piaget, J. 1975. *La presa di coscienza*. Milano: ETAS Libri.

Piaget, J. 1977. *Recherches sur l'abstraction reflechissante, Volume 2*. Paris: PUF.

Pilotti, U. 1990. Educazione trilingue: Italiano/Dialetto/Inglese nelle Scuole Elementari. Report. Faculty of Psychology, University of Rome.

Pinto, M.A. and R. Titone. 1989. "Uno strumento di misurazione delle abilità metalinguistiche: il T.A.M." *Rassegna Italiana di Linguistica Applicata* 1–2: 59–128.

Pinto, M.A. 1993. "Le développement metalinguistique chez les enfants bilingues. Problématiques théoriques et résultats de recherche." *Scientia Paedagogica Experimentalis* XXX, 1: 119–148.

Pinto, M.A. 1995. "Abilità metalinguistiche. Teoria sviluppo e strmenti di misurazione." *Rassegna Italiana di Linguistica Applicata* 3. 90–120.

Pinto, M.A., T. Taeschner, and R. Titone. 1995. "Second language learning in primary educationin Italy." In H. Johnstone and J. Edelembos (eds.), *Teaching foreign langauges in Europe*. Cambridge: Cambridge University Press.

Pratt, C. and A.R. Nesdale. 1984. *Pragmatic awareness in children*. Berlin: Springer Verlag.

Pratt, C. and R. Grieve. 1984. *The development of metalinguistic awareness: An introduction*. Berlin: Springer Verlag.

Puxeddu, M.R. 1989. "Competenza trilingue nel Cagliaritano." Report. Faculty of Psychology, University of Rome.

Raven, J.C. 1982. *Progressive matrices 1938. Manuale di istruzione*. Firenze: Organizzazioni Speciali.

Reynolds, A.G. 1991. "The cognitive consequence of bilingualism." In A.G. Reynolds (ed.), *Bilingualism, multiculturalism, and second language learning: The McGill conference in honour of Wallace E. Lambert*. Hillsdale, N.J.: Erlbaum.

Ricoeur, P. 1990. *Soi-même comme un autre*. Paris: Ed. du Seuil.

Titone, R. 1973. "The Glossodynamic model of language behavior and language learning." *Rassegna Italiana di Linguistica Applicata* V(1): 1–23.

Titone, R. 1972. *Bilinguismo precoce ed educazione bilingue*. Rome: Armando.

Titone, R. 1981. *La ricerca in psicolinguistica applicata e in glottodidattica*. Rome: Bulzoni.

Titone, R. 1985. "A crucial prerequisite to reading: Children's metalinguistic awareness." *Rassegna Italiana di Linguistica Applicata* XVII: 1–20.

Titone, R. and M. Danesi. 1985. *Introduzione alla psicpedagogia del linguaggio*. Rome: Armando.

Titone, R. 1989. "The Holodynamic Model of language learning." *The Canadian Modern Language Review* 1: 10–21.

Titone, R. and M.A. Pinto. 1989. "Uno strumento di misurazione delle abilità metalinguistiche; il TAM." *Rassegna Italiana di Linguistica Applicata* 1(2): 29–128.

Titone, R. 1990. *La lingua staniera nella scuola elemantare, Guida didattica*. Roma: Armando.

Titone, R. 1993a. "A crucial psycholinguistic prerequisite to reading: Children's metalinguistic awareness," *Scientia Paedagogica Experimentalis* XXX (17): 81–96.

Titone, R. 1993b. *La psicolinguistica ieri e oggi. Seconda edizione*. Roma: LAS.

Tunmer, W.E., C. Pratt, and M.L. Herriman. 1984. *Metalinguistic awareness in children: Theory, research, and implications*. Berlin: Springer Verlag.

Tunmer, W.E. and M.S. Herriman. 1984. *The development of metalinguistic awareness: A conceptual overview*. Berlin: Springer Verlag.

Tunmer, W.E. and R. Grieve. 1984. *Syntactic awareness in children*. Berlin: Springer Verlag.

Yelland, G.W., J. Pollard, A. Mercuri. 1993. "The metalinguistic benefits of limited contact with a second language." *Applied Psycholinguistics* 14: 423–444.

Veccia, R. 1989. "Educazione bilingue precoce e flessibilità cognitiva." Report. Faculty of Psychology, University of Rome.

Vygotsky, L.S. 1962. *Thought and language*. Cambridge, Massachusetts: MIT Press.

APPENDIX

Figure 1.

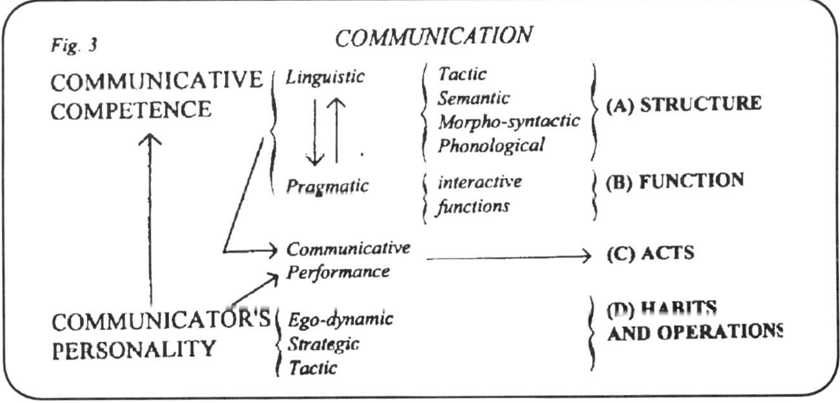

Figure 2. An integrated descriptive/operational model of language behavior and language learning (a neuropsycholinguistics framework).

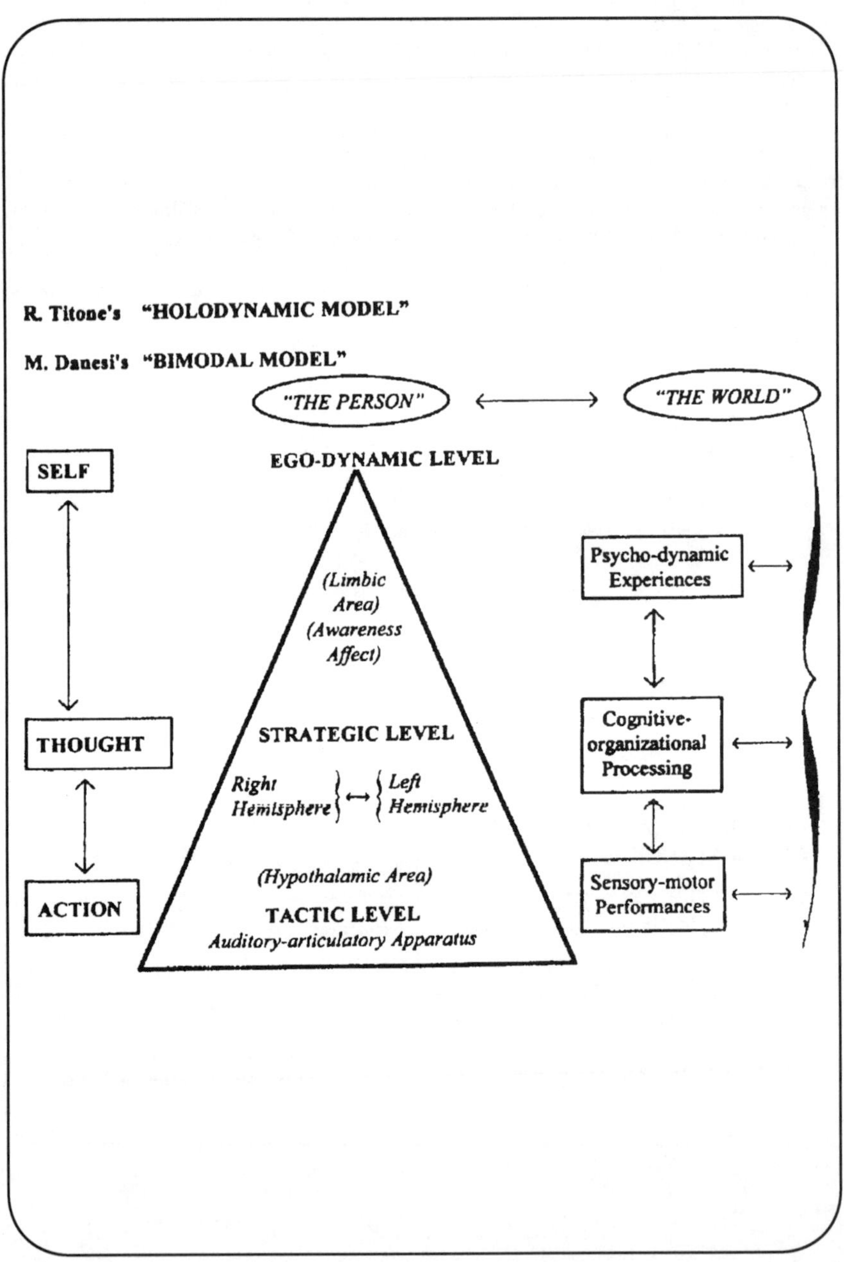

Figure 3. Renzo Titone's "Teaching/ Learning Holodynamic Model" (Toronto 1990).

I. EGO-DYNAMIC LEVEL

"TEACHER"	*"STUDENT"*
* Self-awareness	* Self-perception
* Affectuve sets as initiators	* Affective sets as followers
* Mature experiences	* Developing experience
* Will to teach (from competence)	* Will to learn (toward competence)

II. STRATEGIC LEVEL

* Intention to transmit	* Intention to receive
* Selection of cognitive contents	* Acception of information contents
* Programming communicative operations	* Following leads/perceiving cues
* Choosing verbal/nonverbal signs	* Understanding meanings
* Evaluating student responses	* Learning feedback
* Programming follow-up	* Accepting feedforward

III. TACTIC LEVEL

* Focusing on encoding media	* Focusing on decoding media
* Producing instructional messages	* Perceiving auditory/visual messages
* Controlling output	* Accepting input
* Ensuring continuing interaction	* Reacting to instructional stimuli (recoding)

Culture, variation, and languages of wider communication: The paradigm gap

Yamuna Kachru
University of Illinois at Urbana-Champaign

The aim of this paper is to look at language variation, particularly variation in languages of wider communication (LWC, hereafter), from the perspective of critical linguistics (e.g., Fairclough 1992; Hodge and Kress 1993 [1979]). By LWC, I mean languages such as Arabic, Bengali, Chinese, English, French, Hindi-Urdu, Ki-Swahili, Portuguese, and Spanish that are utilized to serve communicative purposes of diverse speech communities, some separated by linguistic and cultural boundaries, others by political boundaries as well. Sociolinguistic research has shown that the structural variations observed in LWCs around the world have resulted from a number of well-defined processes. (See, e.g., B. Kachru 1983, 1992b; Y. Kachru 1982, 1988; Lowenberg 1984; Pakir 1992; Pandharipande 1986, 1992; Platt and Webber 1980; Tay 1993; Teh 1986.) The same is true of discourse structures and strategies across languages and cultures (e.g., Y. Kachru 1991, 1993, 1995a, 1995b; Smith 1987). There is, however, a great deal of resistance to according equal status to all varieties of LWCs, and the questions of "standards" and "norms" are still being debated widely and passionately. (See, e.g., the debate with regard to English in B. Kachru 1988, 1991; Quirk 1988; Tickoo 1991; and Hindi in Rai 1991.) The debate with regard to varieties of English is nothing new; it started in the last quarter of the eighteenth century with the disapproval of American English and is still as prevalent as ever. The quotes in the first chapter of Mencken (1936), such as the one given below, bear a striking similarity to what is being said now by both American and British ELT specialists about the Outer Circle[1] varieties:

---

[1]B. Kachru (1985) divides the English-using world into three concentric circles. The Inner Circle consists of the native English-speaking countries, e.g., Australia, Canada, New Zealand, the U.K. and the U.S.A. The Outer Circle comprises the former colonies or spheres of influence of the U.K. and the U.S.A., e.g., India, Kenya, Nigeria, the Philippines, and Singapore, among others. In these countries, nativized varieties of English have achieved the status of either official languages, or of languages widely used in education, administration, legal system, etc. The Expanding Circle consists of countries where English is fast becoming a dominant second language in the domains of education, science, and technology, e.g., China, Japan, Taiwan, Thailand, and the countries of Europe.

(1) It is extremely desirable, to say the least, that every necessary effort should be made to preserve some standard of pure idiomatic English. But from what quarter is the preservation of such a standard in any way threatened? The answer is "solely from America." Yet we are asked to collaborate with the Americans on the problem ... that their huge hybrid population of which only a small minority are even racially Anglo-Saxons should use English as their chief medium of intercommunication is our misfortune, not our fault. They certainly threaten our language, but the only way in which we can effectively meet that threat is by assuming—in the words of the authors of "The King's English" [by H.W. and F.G. Fowler, Oxford, 1908] that "Americanisms are foreign words and should be so treated." (*New Statesman*, June 25, 1927, quoted in Mencken 1936: 33)

Recent remarks by Prince Charles about American English being a "corrupting" influence (reported in *Chicago Tribune,* March 24, 1995, Section 1:4) show that even an established Inner Circle variety is not free from the criticism of "purists" worried about the changing "norms" of the language. A critical linguistic perspective helps us in examining the societal and attitudinal factors that result in such resistance and downgrading of varieties of LWCs.

I focus here on two aspects of the topic: (a) characterization of the competence required in LWCs for successful cross-cultural interaction, and (b) planning to achieve the educational goal of acquiring such competence. I discuss the situation with special reference to English as a LWC, since it is impossible to deal with all the LWCs in this short paper. Approaching the issues involved in English across the world from a critical linguistic perspective will be helpful in planning effective language education for cross-cultural communication rather than combating resistance to what is increasingly being viewed as "linguistic imperialism" (Phillipson 1992).

The points I wish to emphasize in this paper are the following:

- LWCs, used as they are by various populations, necessarily develop varieties in the course of their spread. This was true of ancient languages such as Sanskrit, and is true of modern languages such as English, Hindi, and Ki-Swahili;
- There are attitudes toward these varieties which have very little basis in linguistic facts. Standardization and norm creation are societal acts;
- All varieties, native or institutionalized, have both dialectal (i.e., geographic) and diatypic (i.e., social) variations;
- Acquiring communicative competence in a LWC does not necessarily entail native-like linguistic competence. In fact, some LWCs have no native speakers in the sense in which French and Spanish have native speakers, e.g., Hindi and Ki-Swahili. A majority of users of Hindi and Ki-Swahili are

bi- or multilinguals, and the small number of "native speakers" play only a minor role in setting the standards in these languages;

- Awareness and familiarity with several, if not all, varieties of English are more useful in intercultural communication than adhering to any particular standard model, as studies have shown (e.g., Smith 1992);
- Such awareness includes appreciation of variation at all linguistic levels, including the level of discourse;
- Variation in the LWCs, including English, is attributable to sociocultural factors, and issues of identity are crucially involved in preferences for varieties; and
- The ELT profession has to become sensitive to issues raised by variation. ELT may have been promoted as "cultural propaganda" (Pennycook 1994: 147) and there may still be emphasis on keeping "the local variants of second-language English within limits of comprehensibility" (Pennycook 1994: 150, quote from British Council Report 1959-60: 9). ELT, however, is no longer the exclusive domain of the Inner Circle; both the Outer and Expanding Circle institutions are making their presence felt in English education.

Variation in English. I start this discussion with a look at the status of varieties of English around the world. Sociolinguistic research on varieties of English and the range and depth they have acquired in different speech communities shows clearly that it is no longer justified to look at them as reflecting acquisitional deficiency.[2] Concepts of "interlanguage" and "fossilization" are irrelevant in characterizing the institutionalized varieties of the Outer Circle, and are fast becoming so in accounting for the acrolectal forms of performance varieties of the Expanding Circle. The observations of Quirk (1985) about the "monochrome" standard go against the sociolinguistic realities in the Outer as well as Expanding Circle contexts:

(2) I believe that the fashion of undermining belief in standard English has wrought educational damage in the ENL [Inner circle] countries, though I am ready to concede that there may well have been compensating educational gains in the wider tolerance for an enjoyment of the extraordinary variety of English around us in any of these countries. But then just such an airy contempt for standards started to be exported to EFL and ESL countries, and for this I can find no such mitigating compensation. *The relatively narrow range of purposes for which the nonnative needs to*

---

[2]Range refers to the functional allocation of the language in terms of its users, and depth refers to the penetration of the language in various strata of society across cultures and languages (B. Kachru 1986).

use English (even in ESL countries) is arguably well-catered for by a single monochrome standard form that looks as good on paper as it sounds in speech. There are only the most dubious advantages in exposing the learner to a great variety of usage, no part of which he will have time to master properly, little of which he will be called upon to exercise, all of which is embedded in a controversial sociolinguistic matrix he cannot be expected to understand. (Quirk 1985: 6, emphasis added)

In view of the push by Australian English in Asia,[3] the question of standards and models for ELT is going to get more rather than less controversial; in addition to the American and the British models, the Australian model is likely to compete at providing the norm and the ELT "experts" in the Asian context.

Be that as it may, the observable differences among and between the Inner Circle and the Outer and Expanding Circle Englishes result from the needs of the speech communities that use them. There is enough research to show that variation in lexicogrammar, discourse strategies, and literary styles results from the relevant speech communities attempting to express their own meanings in English.[4] This is as true of the Outer and Expanding Circle varieties as it is of the Inner Circle Englishes.

Competence and performance in world Englishes. For successful communication in world Englishes across languages and cultures, we need to pay attention to some major factors.

The first relevant factor is that not all users of world Englishes in the three circles need to communicate across regional and national boundaries. Those who are required to participate in intercultural communication, for whatever purposes, need to be sensitized to variation that exists in the language so that issues of intelligibilitydo not assume proportions such that successful interaction becomes impossible. Intelligibility includes not only the ability to decode incoming messages in terms of sounds, words and grammatical structures, but also in terms of comprehending utterances and interpreting the intentions of encoders of messages. The distinction that Smith (1992) makes in terms of intelligibility, comprehensibility, and interpretability is crucial here. Intelligibility refers to utterance recognition, comprehensibility to recognition of utterance meaning, and interpretability to recognition of the illocutionary forces

[3]The Macquarie Dictionary Project has just announced a series of conferences on "English is an Asian Language" in several locations in Southeast Asia.

[4]For variation in lexicogrammar, see Bamgboṣe (1992), Bokamba (1992), B. Kachru (1983), Lowenberg (1992a), Tay (1993); for discourse strategies, see Y. Kachru (1987), Teh (1986); and for literary styles, see Dissanayake (1985, 1990), B. Kachru (1986), Thumboo (1985, 1986, 1992).

of utterances. Obviously, for the users of different varieties to be intelligible in this sense requires a great deal of awareness of linguistic as well as cultural context. The linguistic factors that are involved are phonological, lexicogrammatical, and discoursal. I would like to discuss variation in each of these areas in world Englishes in some detail to see what is involved in acquiring competence in more than one variety.

Phonology. It has been claimed that more than segmental sounds, the rhythmic patterns in speech are responsible for ensuring interpretability. This means that unfamiliar stress and intonational patterns can lead to breakdowns in communication. (See Gumperz 1982a, 1982b for examples.) It is also a well-known fact that stress assignment in words differs across varieties. For instance, word stress in the American English (AE) and British English (BE) varieties differs significantly. In the Outer and Expanding Circle varieties, stress placement is different from the Inner Circle varieties in one crucial respect. Most Outer and Expanding Circle varieties have a syllable-timed rather than a stress-timed rhythm (Bamgboṣe 1992; B. Kachru 1983). As such, stress assignment follows the values attached to the "mores" (weight of syllables in terms of duration) in these varieties. This seems to be the case in Nigerian English (NE) and Indian English (IE). Variation in stress placement across select varieties is as follows:

(3) Stress placement, e.g., AE: *pri'marily* vs. BE: *'primarily*; *te'legraph* vs. *'telegraph*; IE: *'success* for AE: *su'ccess*, IE: *recog'nize* for AE: *'recognize*

Stress placement in IE and NE follows from the principle of syllable weight. In *success*, both syllables are short; therefore, the default rule of placing the stress on the first syllable applies. In *recognize*, however, since the vowels in *re-* and *-cog-* are short and not as weighty as the diphthong in *-nize*, the primary stress goes with the heavier syllable. Rhythm in these varieties is based on the mores of the syllables; long syllables are twice as long as short ones, but the quality of the vowel in long as well as short syllables remains the same. In the case of a word with several long syllables, all the syllables are pronounced long irrespective of their stressed or unstressed character. In the Inner Circle Englishes, the stressed syllable has a longer duration than the unstressed syllable; in fact, the rhythmic pattern of these Englishes is such that in a multisyllabic word, the duration of the several unstressed syllables is roughly equivalent to the one stressed syllable. Consequently, vowel quality has a strong correlation with stress. To the Inner Circle speakers of English, the other varieties sound as though they have a staccato rhythm. In situations of reasonably long-term contact, however, users of different varieties seem to adjust well to each other's rhythm and manage to communicate successfully. This is obvious when one looks at the educational, financial, media-related, and political and diplomatic institutions around the world.

Lexicogrammar.

LEXICON. Most varieties have their own characteristic lexicon, developed in response to local contexts. Well-known examples of this phenomenon are innovations that take place in a variety as a response to local needs, items that are borrowed from the substratum languages, and hybrid items that are formed by juxtaposing such a borrowed item and an English item. Some examples from both Inner and Outer Circle varieties are as follows:

(4) Lexicon. American innovations: *affiliate*, *endorse*, *collide*, *jeopardize*, *predicate*, *itemize*, *boomer*, *boom-town*, *bouncer*, *roller-coaster*, *fill the bill*, *fizzle out*, *make tracks*, *peter out*, *keep tab*, etc.
African English (Bokamba 1992) innovations: *be on seat* (be in one's place of work), *been-to* (one who has been to England), *be coupled* (find a partner at dance), *me-and-my-darling* (love seat), *bush meat* (game), *tight friend* (close friend), *small room* (toilet)

GRAMMAR. Grammatical features that vary noticeably in performance are the following: the article system, uses of infinitives and gerunds, and systems of tenses and question answering. I will discuss the article system in some detail here.

The conventions for using articles with nouns can be stated as follows:

(5) *a(n)*: indefinite non-specific, or indefinite specific, or generic (with count nouns in the singular);
the: definite specific (with count and mass nouns), or non-specific generic (with count nouns only);
some: indefinite non-specific, or indefinite specific (with count nouns in the plural, with mass nouns); and
Ø: generic (with count nouns in the plural, with mass nouns).

The above description makes it clear that there is considerable overlap among the forms of articles and the meanings they signal. Of course, the generic reference is not signaled by the articles exclusively; the tense-aspect of the utterance is relevant, too (cf. *A tiger roars* vs. *A tiger is roaring* or *A tiger roared*).

There are three factors that complicate learning the above system of articles in areas where English is not acquired as the first language. First, there is no one-to-one correlation between the forms (i.e. *a*, *the, some*) and the meanings they signal. Second, there are inconsistencies in the use of articles even with the count nouns, as has been pointed out by Ilson (1995) and McArthur (1994). For instance, there is variation in the use of articles in American and British English which manifests itself in the dropping of *a(n)* or replacing *an* with *a*:

(6a) Dropping a(n):
The Sunday Times, 13 June 1993: "He was decent, caring man who was disgusted by the vandalism." (McArthur 1994: 2)
International Herald Tribune, 15 April 1993, quoting an American: "It is virulent strand of racism." (McArthur 1994: 2)
The Observer: "The point is that it is platform for good journalism with differing views." (Ilson 1995: 43)

In addition, the norms of article use in American English seem to be undergoing a change (Stewart and Fawcett 1994):

(6b) *an* > *a* in American English (Stewart and Fawcett 1994: 20–22)

President Carter	*a election process* (1976)
President Bush	*a internal* (1990)
Dick Cavett	*a emergency* (1986)
Phil Donahue	*a upper class* (1986)
Robert Ballard (scientist)	*a unqualified success* (1985)
Jana Williams (educator)	*a interesting game* (1982)

Third, in many languages of the world, only the indefinite noun is marked with a determiner or an affix; the definite is unmarked, and the generic is a function of the definite. This is true of all the major languages of South Asia, Persian, and several other languages of the world. In view of these facts, it is not surprising that the Outer and Expanding Circle Englishes do not use articles in the way that the existing English grammars prescribe.

The picture is further complicated by the fact that, depending upon speaker intentions, article choice may vary in what appears to learners to be identical linguistic and communicative contexts. For instance, both the utterances by B in (6c)—one with *some* and the other with the zero article—are appropriate in response to A's remark:

(6c) A: I am thirsty.
B: There is (some) orange juice in the fridge.

Except for the implication of quantity in the use of *some* as opposed to the zero article, no difference in referential meaning is signaled by this choice.

A related complication is that according to grammars, nouns are said to be inherently either count or mass and the use of articles is determined by these properties of the nouns. In fact, grammatical descriptions differ from each other considerably. According to Allan (1980), in terms of countability, there are eight different classes of nouns in English in view of (a) their potential for combining with the following types of determiners: the zero determiner; unit determiners such as *a(n)*, *one*; fuzzy quantifiers such as *several*, *about fifty*; the determiner *all* in the sense of "completely"; and (b) their potential for being marked as plural, either inflectionally or in terms of agreement features. According to Huddleston (1984: 245), there are six classes of nouns exemplified by *equipment* (fully mass), *knowledge* (almost mass, but occur with *a*, e.g., *a good knowledge of Latin*), *clothes* (occur with fuzzy quantifiers such as *many*, *few*, hence are more count-like), *cattle* (occur with fuzzy quantifiers and large round numbers), *people* (collective noun, have plural forms, e.g., *peoples*, but are not fully countable in that these nouns do not occur in a singular form), and *dog* (fully count). Inner Circle varieties seem to treat nouns differently in terms of countability:

(7a) Countability of nouns: *lettuce*, *attendance*, *entertainment*, non-count in AE, count in BE; *knowledge*, *evidence*, used as countable by reputed linguists in AE, but non-count in BE. (Lowenberg 1992b)

It is clear that the English system of countability is complex. Moreover, the conventions of marking countability differs across languages. In English, mass nouns (*equipment, sugar*) are inherently singular, but in Sinhalese and Ki-Swahili, they are treated as plural. In many languages, there is no distinction between a *shirt* and (*a pair of) trousers*. Thus, there does not seem to be any conceptual basis for treating several categories of nouns in any particular way, grammatically speaking.

In African, Caribbean, East, South and South-East Asian varieties of English, the complex system of marking count/mass distinction in English is simplified. Perceptually countable items such as *furniture*, *equipment*, *luggage* are regularly used with a plural marker to denote more than one piece. (See the papers in B. Kachru 1992b.) Since neither the determiner nor the countability system is clearly described in any language learning/teaching text, there is a great deal of variation in the Outer and Expanding Circle varieties in the usage of determiners and the categorization of nouns. In some varieties, such as Singaporean and Thai, inflectional marking of the plural is not always consistent, partly as a result of phonological processes such as final consonant cluster simplification. According to the several generations of American MATESL candidates with whom I have had the privilege to interact, these inconsistencies do not cause problems of intelligibility,even though they identify spcakcrs as nonnative users of English.

The assertion that grammatical differences are responsible for lack of intelligibility in native-nonnative interaction is only partially true. I would like to contrast some differences between Inner Circle Englishes with those between Inner and Outer Circle Englishes. Consider the examples given in (7b–c):

(7b) Reversal of meaning in restrictive vs. non-restrictive relative clauses (Newbrook 1992):
AusE: The students who had finished left the hall. [all the relevant students]
The students, who had finished, left the hall. [only a subset]

BE: The students who had finished left the hall. [a subset of students]
The students, who had finished, left the hall. [all the relevant students]

(7c) Question-Answering system (in IE, AfrE (Bokamba 1992), PhE [Philippino English] (Gumperz 1982)):

Isn't your car running?
Yes (implication: It isn't running)
No (implication: It is)

One wonders why (7c) is likely to cause more problems in intelligibility than (7b). The differences in both sets are equally salient from the point of view of meaning.

Lexical differences are readily observable and there have been numerous compilations of glossaries for familiarizing American and British English speakers with each other's word stock. Some lexical borrowings in Inner and Outer Circle varieties are listed below:

(7d) Lexical items and idioms
Borrowings in American English: *canyon*, *corral*, *plaza*, *tornado*, *patio* [from Spanish]
Borrowings in Malaysian English: *gotong-royong* (communal operation), *adat* (traditional law)
Borrowings in Indian English: *karmacari* (office workers), *shariyat* (traditional Muslim law), *gobar gas plant* (cow dung gas plant)

These borrowings are a natural result of language contact. The communicative needs of the populations who use a specific variety dictate what sources will be tapped for such borrowings.

Discourse.

SPEECH ACTS. Communicative competence across varieties of English depends a great deal on familiarity with cultural conventions of language use. English is used in a particular variety to express the sociocultural meanings that the users of that variety have and that are unfamiliar to those who are outside the context. One example may make this clear. There is a Hindi speech genre *saugandh khānā* or *qasam khānā* which is roughly translatable as "to swear." It is, however, different from the English item "swear" in that it only shares the following meanings with it: "to assert, promise, agree to, or confirm on oath." The other, more negative meanings of the English item are not shared by the Hindi item. Another difference is that one can "swear" by anything dear or valuable to one, e.g., one's own self, one's kin, and, of course, the sacred text, *Bhagvadgītā,* or God. It has the illocutionary force of strong assertion, persuasion, challenge, promise, or entreaty, depending upon the context. Two examples of how *saugandh khānā* is used in Indian English with the illocutionary forces of strong assertion and persuasion, respectively, are given in (8a) and (8b) below:

(8a) "Hé, brother, what is it all about?"
"Nothing. I think it's about the quarrel between Ramaji and Subbaji. You know about the Cornerstone?"
"But, *on my mother's soul*, I thought they were going to the court?"
(Raja Rao. 1978. *The Policeman and The Rose*. Delhi: Oxford University Press: 17)

The context is that one villager is trying to find out from another what the bailiff's drum meant. The first villager "swears" in order to convince the second that he had a certain piece of information which he really believed to be true.

In the second example (8b), an older sister is scolding a younger brother for arguing with her:

(8b) "... And Ramu," she cried desperately, "I have enough of quarreling all the time. *In the name of our holy mother* can't you leave me alone!"
(Raja Rao. 1978. *The Policeman and The Rose*. Delhi: Oxford University Press: 88)

The expression *holy mother* in the above example does not refer to any deity; it refers to the female (biological) parent of the siblings. The sister is trying to persuade her brother to drop the topic they have been arguing about.

These examples make it clear that the cultural meaning of *saugandh khānā* is very different from "to swear" in the native English-speaking context. The two instances of swearing are interpretable only in the context of a society or culture that shares the specific meanings with South Asian society and culture. Notice that it is not the meaning of assertion or persuasion that is unfamiliar to other variety users; it is the linguistic device of using "swear" to accomplish assertion or persuasion that is unfamiliar. Some further patterns of familiar speech genres are given below.

(8c) Pattern of greetings and response (If B is older in age or relationship)
A: Greeting
B: Blessing

(8d) Pattern of compliment-response
A: Compliment
B: Not deserving the compliment OR lowering of head in humility OR silence

(8e) Pattern of invitation-response
A. Invitation
*B. Initial unwillingness to cause trouble
*A. Insistence
B. Acceptance
[There may be more exchanges of * in an interaction]

(8f) Patterns of expressing gratitude (Y. Kachru 1995c)
Informal situations: Blessing (if expressing gratitude to a younger person), appreciation of inherent qualities or effort or help rendered (if equal), expression of one's helplessness and grateful acceptance of favor (if superior in status)
Formal situations: Thanks.

To ensure success in intercultural communication, it is necessary to be aware of these conventions.

Writing Conventions. Nonnative writing has been a source of great concern to educators in the Inner Circle institutions. The problem is that most Outer Circle and Expanding Circle writers would agree with Chinua Achebe—substituting their own region for "African"—when he says:

(9a) Most African writers write out of an African experience and of commitment to an African destiny. For them that destiny does not include a future European identity for which the present is but an apprenticeship. (Achebe in Jussawalla and Dasenbrock 1992: 34)

Writing from one's own experience means that conventions of writing differ across varieties. Some of the conventions of writing personal and business letters are listed in (9b):

(9b) Formulas for opening and closing letters: Compare the following from Indian English with the Inner circle norms (B. Kachru 1992a: 313): "If the writer is senior in age, the use of blessings seems excessive to a person who is not part of the culture ... " Consider, for example, the following:
"I always send my love and prayers to you all everyday: unseen unheard. May Lord Shiva always protect you all and look after you." Bamgbọse (1992: 159) claims that in the context of Nigerian English, "one has little choice but to mix formulas for opening and closing letters (i.e., open with *Dear Sir* [instead of Dear surname or first name] and close with *Yours sincerely*), since it will be considered impolite to address an older person by his surname, and positively disrespectful, if not impudent, to use his first name."

One good example of a culturally different business letter is in (9c) (Jenkins and Hinds 1987: 349):

(9c) Dear sir,

In Japan, fall has deepened, and the trees have begun turning colors. As exchange students, we believe you are busy studying every day.

Well, getting right into it. We are carrying out the 1984 business evaluation with the material described below. We hope that you will please fill out the enclosed evaluation card and send it to us.

We believe that this will cause you some inconvenience, but since winter is coming near, we will hope that you will take care of yourself.

Sincerely,

The Japanese letter reflects the dominant cultural value of emphasis on what Jenkins and Hinds (1987) term "space"; i.e., the relationship between the reader and the writer. The opening situates the letter in a shared season, and its implication for the addressee. The transition is provided by the first sentence of the second paragraph, which is followed by the request. The third paragraph acknowledges the "imposition" made by the request and attempts to establish the desired harmonious relationship by expressing concern about the addressee's well-being.

One of the conventions of Outer Circle English that has been discussed much in Inner Circle academic institutions is that of ornateness and deferential or "high" style in prose. That such a style is important for cultural identity is supported by the following fact: An Inner Circle speaker of English, Chuck, who became Acyutananda Svami, expresses his gratitude to his "guru" or "spiritual teacher" in the following words:

(10) I offer my prostrate obeisance first unto all the devotees that have surrendered unto his divine lotus feet and next unto the devotees who will in the future take shelter of his lotus feet, and I then offer my humble obeisances unto his lotus feet again and again. May he bless this first translation attempt so that it may be accepted by the *Lord Sri Kṛṣṇa,* and may he engage me in the service of the six *Gosvāmīs of Vṛndāvana, Lord Caitanya*, and *Rādhārāṇī*. (*Acyutānanda Svāmī: Songs of the Vaiṣṇava Ācāryas*. Los Angeles, 1974: xviii)

That there are adverse reactions to such styles in the Inner Circle is well-documented. In fact, there are strong reactions against regional varieties of Inner Circle Englishes, too, as illustrated by the events that followed the award of the Booker Prize to the Scottish writer James Kelman.

The author, reacting to the response to his novel *How Late it Was, How Late*, which was called a "disgrace" by one of the judges, Rabbi Julia Neuberger, and "literary vandalism" by Simon Jenkins, had this to say in *The Times of London* :

(11) "A fine line can exist between eliticism and racism," he said. "On matters concerning language and culture, the distinction can sometimes cease to exist altogether."
Recalling times when Glaswegian accents were banned from the radio or when his two daughters were "reprimanded" in school for using the Scotts "aye" instead of the English "yes," he said it was wrong to call the language of his work "vernacular" or "dialect."
"To me, those words are just another way of inferiorizing the language by indicating that there's a standard," he said. "The dictionary would use the term 'debased.' But it's the language! The living language and it comes out of many different sources, including Scotland before the English arrived." (Reported in *The New York Times*, November 29, 1994: B1–2)

In academic writing there are also several myths. One is that indirection is bad, all good writing must be direct and linear and, in the absence of the capability to write in this preferred manner, no scientific or technological progress is possible. In view of the fact that almost all styles of writing—German, Russian, African, Asian—have been shown to be indirect or circular or digressive, one wonders how any scientific progress was possible in the centuries preceding the latter half of the twentieth century. After all, the so-called direct, linear style of writing is, historically speaking, a recent phenomenon in the literate English-speaking world (see Y. Kachru 1995a and 1995b for a detailed discussion of this point).

Challenges for English education. I will address this question from the perspective of a teacher-educator involved in the higher education of ESL and EFL teachers. As important as courses in teaching methodologies, psychology of learning and second language acquisition are for prospective teachers of English, no less important are courses that provide a comprehensive view of world Englishes and their uses and users. This is especially important since there is little awareness of LWCs in the SLA literature. The perspective on language variation and its implications for language learning and teaching presented in this paper is almost totally absent in SLA literature. There is resistance to acknowledging the social reality of varieties and their relevance for human interaction across languages and cultures. This attitude is reflected in the quote from Quirk (1985) in (2) above. It is also reflected in the lack of courses in the area of language variation in general and world Englishes in particular in the MATESL programs of the Inner Circle institutions of higher education (Vavrus 1991). There seems to be little understanding of the fact that awareness of variation does not preclude teachers helping learners acquire whichever variety the educational system of a particular region or nation prefers. On the contrary, it leads both teachers and students to assess realistically what motivates such preferences, and prepares them to respond professionally to performance requirements in a responsible manner.

The critical linguistic perspective advocates student empowerment by making it possible for them to become aware of language variation, attitudes toward variation, and societal consequences of these attitudes (Rampton 1992). A wealth of material is now available on varieties of English and some attempts have been made to suggest ways of making ESL professionals aware of these resources (e.g., B. Kachru 1995, Tawake 1993). There is no excuse for not using these resources to raise the consciousness of all ESL professionals. Educational practices are cultural practices. Language education does not and should not mean perpetuation of outdated prejudices and attitudes that result from them.

As a result of the explosion of technology and developments in international business and commerce, the dream of the world being a "global village" is closer to reality. There is no denying the fact that all over the world, educators feel the need for English education, and international students flock to American, Australian, British, and Canadian universities in ever larger numbers.

However, we must not forget that they represent the majority of English users and come with their own identities and worldviews. As an experienced writing teacher says (Fox 1994: 74), these "world majority students," who find "the [Inner Circle] academic form dull or dry ('like a skeleton, there's no juicy, meaty part in it,' said a Japanese student) or who are disheartened by its implicit competitiveness could join legions of U.S. graduate students who, for a time at least, resist the veiled attacks on other authors, the name-dropping, the abandonment of common-sense vocabulary, the surrender of voice." Fox goes on to suggest:

(12) ... there are ways to see and experience the world that most of us have never dreamed of, ways of creating and communicating knowledge that are vastly different from what we have long been convinced is "good writing," "good thinking," and "proper understanding." As teachers, we have an obligation to help world majority students [international students] find a voice at the university by explaining in respectful, knowledgeable ways how we expect them to think, investigate, and express themselves in the U.S. context. And if we listen closely to what they have to tell us, we will not only teach more completely but deepen the meaning of our own intellectual lives as well. (Fox 1994: 126)

And as Geertz (1983: 234) says in the context of anthropological research, "the world is a various place" and it is "various" in many ways: " ... various between lawyers and anthropologists, various between Muslims and Hindus, various between little traditions and great, various between colonial thens and nationalist nows ..." Nevertheless, "much is to be gained, scientifically and otherwise, by confronting that grand actuality rather than wishing it away in a haze of forceless generalities and false comforts."

The English language, as an LWC, has become pluricentric, and carries the weight of various sociocultural identities. Consequently, the language teaching profession faces a situation which provides both a challenge and an opportunity. The challenge is to see and appreciate the pluricentricity of LWCs, and the opportunity is to educate future generations of language professionals in dealing with the complexities of these languages.

REFERENCES

Allan, Keith. 1980. "Nouns and countability." *Language* 56(3): 541–567.

Bamgboṣe, Ayo. 1992. "Standard Nigerian English: Issues of identification." In Braj B. Kachru (ed.), *The other tongue: English across cultures, Second edition*. Urbana, Illinois: University of Illinois Press. 148–161.

Bokamba, Eyamba G. 1992. "The africanization of English." In Braj B. Kachru (ed.), *The other tongue: English across cultures, Second edition*. Urbana, Illinois: University of Illinois Press. 125–147.

Dissanayake, Wimal. 1985. "Towards a decolonized English: South Asian creativity in fiction." *World Englishes* 4: 233–242.

Dissanayake, Wimal. 1990. "Self and modernism in Sri Lankan poetry in English." *World Englishes* 9(2): 225–236.

Fairclough, Norman. 1992. "Critical linguistics." In William Bright (ed.), *Oxford international encyclopedia of linguistics, Volume 1*. New York: Oxford University Press. 314–316.

Fox, Helen. 1994. *Listening to the world: Cultural issues in academic writing*. Urbana, Illinois: National Council of Teachers of English.

Geertz, Clifford. 1983. *Local knowledge*. New York: Basic Books.

Gumperz, John J. (ed.). 1982a. *Language and social identity*. Cambridge, U.K.: Cambridge University Press.

Gumperz, John J. 1982b. *Discourse strategies*. Cambridge, U.K.: Cambridge University Press.

Hodge, Robert and Gunther Kress. 1993 [1979]. *Language as ideology*. New York: Routledge.

Huddleston, Rodney. 1984. *Introduction to the grammar of English*. Cambridge, U.K.: Cambridge University press.

Ilson, Robert. 1995. "A(n)-dropping." *English Today* 11(1): 42–44.

Jenkins, Susan and John Hinds. 1987. "Business letter writing: English, French and Japanese." *TESOL Quarterly* 21(2): 327–349.

Jussawalla, Feroza and Reed W. Dasenbrock. 1992. *Interviews with writers of the post-colonial world*. Jackson and London: University Press of Mississippi.

Kachru, Braj B. 1983. *The Indianization of English: The English language in India*. Delhi: Oxford University Press.

Kachru, Braj B. 1985. "Standards, codification and sociolinguistic realism: The English language in the outer circle." In Randolph Quirk and Henry Widdowson (eds.), *English in the world*. Cambridge, U.K.: Cambridge University Press. 11–30.

Kachru, Braj B. 1986. *The alchemy of English: The spread, functions and models of non-native Englishes*. Oxford: Pergamon Press.

Kachru, Braj B. 1988. "The spread of English and sacred linguistic cows." In Peter Lowenberg (ed.), *Georgetown University Round Table on Languages and Linguistics 1987*. Washington, D.C.: Georgetown University Press. 207–228.

Kachru, Braj B. 1991. "Liberation linguistics and the Quirk concern." *English Today* 7(1): 3–13.

Kachru, Braj B. 1992a. "Meaning in deviation: Toward understanding non-native English texts." In Braj B. Kachru (ed.), *The other tongue: English across cultures, Second edition*. Urbana, Illinois: University of Illinois Press. 301–326.

Kachru, Braj B. (ed.). 1992b. *The other tongue: English across cultures. Second edition*. Urbana, Illinois: University of Illinois Press.

Kachru, Braj B. 1995. "World Englishes: Approaches, issues and resources." In H.D. Brown and S. Gonzo (eds.), *Readings on second language acquisition*. Englewood Cliffs, N.J.: Prentice-Hall Regents. 220–261.

Kachru, Yamuna. 1982. "Syntactic variation and language change: Eastern and Western Hindi." *Studies in the Linguistic Sciences* 12(2): 87–96.

Kachru, Yamuna. 1987. "Cross-cultural texts, discourse strategies and discourse interpretation." In Larry Smith (ed.), *Discourse across cultures: Strategies in world Englishes*. London: Prentice-Hall International. 87–100.

Kachru, Yamuna. 1988. "Implications of teaching a standard variety as mother tongue: Evidence from the Hindi area." Keynote speech at the International Conference on Language and National Development: The Case of India, Osmania University, Hyderabad, India, January 5, 1988.

Kachru, Yamuna. 1991. Guest Editor, *World Englishes* 10(3). Symposium on Speech Acts in World Englishes. Oxford: Pergamon Press. 295–340.

Kachru, Yamuna. 1993. "Social meaning and creativity in Indian English." In James E. Alatis. (ed.), *Georgetown University Round Table on Languages and Linguistics 1992*. Washington, D.C.: Georgetown University Press. 378–387.

Kachru, Yamuna. 1995a. "Contrastive rhetoric in world Englishes." *English Today* 11(1): 21–31.

Kachru, Yamuna. 1995b. "Cultural meaning and rhetorical styles: Toward a framework for contrastive rhetoric." In Barbara Seidlhofer and Guy Cook (eds.), *Principles and practice in applied linguistics: Studies in honor of Henry G. Widdowson*. London: Oxford University Press. 171–184.

Kachru, Yamuna. 1995c. "Lexical exponents of cultural contact: Speech act verbs in Hindi-English dictionaries." In Braj B. Kachru and Henry Kahane (eds.), *Cultures, ideologies, and the dictionary: Studies in honor of Ladislav Zgusta*. Tübingen, Germany: Max Niemeyer Verlag. 261–274.

Lowenberg, Peter. 1984. "English in the Malay archipelago: Nativization and its functions in a sociolinguistic area." Unpublished Ph.D. Dissertation. University of Illinois, Urbana.

Lowenberg, Peter. 1992a. "The marking of ethnicity in Malaysian English literature: Nativization and its functions." *World Englishes* 11(2–3): 251–258.

Lowenberg, Peter. 1992b. "Teaching English as a world language: Issues in assessing non-native proficiency" In Braj B. Kachru (ed.), *The other tongue: English across cultures, Second edition*. Urbana, Illinois: University of Illinois Press. 108–121.

McArthur, Tom. 1994. "Is it a new way of speaking? Comment." *English Today*, 10(4): 2.

Mencken, H.L. 1936. *The American language, Fourth edition*. New York: Alfred Knopf.

Newbrook, Mark. 1992. "Unrecognized grammatical and semantic features typical of Australian English: A checklist with commentary." *English World-Wide* 13(1): 1–32.

Pakir, Ann (ed.). 1992. *Words in a cultural context*. National University of Singapore, Singapore: UniPress.

Pandharipande, Rajeshwari. 1986. "Language contact and language variation: Nagpuri Marathi." In Bh. Krishnamurti, et al. (eds.), *South Asian languages: Structure, convergence and diglossia*. Delhi: Motilal Banarsidass. 218–231.

Pandharipande, Rajeshwari. 1992. "Defining politeness in Indian English." In Larry E. Smith and S.N. Sridhar (eds.), *The extended family: English in global bilingualism (Studies in honor of Braj B. Kachru)*. Special Issue of *World Englishes* 11(2–3): 241–250.

Pennycook, Alastair. 1994. *The cultural politics of English as an international language*. London: Longman.

Phillipson, Robert. 1992. *Linguistic imperialism*. London: Oxford University Press.

Platt, John and Heidi Webber. 1980. *English in Singapore and Malaysia: Status, features, functions*. Kuala Lumpur: Oxford University Press.

Quirk, Randolph. 1985. "The English language in a global context." In Randolph Quirk and Henry G. Widdowson (eds.), *English in the world: Teaching and learning the language and literatures*. Cambridge, U.K.: Cambridge University Press. 1–6.

Quirk, Randolph. 1988. "The question of standards in the international use of English." In Peter Lowenberg (ed.), *Georgetown University Round Table on Languages and Linguistics 1987*. Washington, D.C.: Georgetown University Press.

Rai, Amrit. 1991. *A house divided: The origin and development of Hindi-Urdu*. Delhi: Oxford University Press.

Rampton, M.B.H. 1992. "Scope for empowerment in sociolinguistics?" In Deborah Cameron, E. Frazer, P. Harvey, M.B.H. Rampton and K. Richardson (eds.), *Researching language: Issues of power and method*. London: Routledge. 29–64.

Smith, Larry E. (ed.). 1987. *Discourse across cultures: Strategies in world Englishes*. London: Prentice-Hall International.

Smith, Larry E. 1992. "Spread of English and issues of intelligibility." In Braj B. Kachru (ed.), *The other tongue: English across cultures, Second edition*. Urbana, Illinois: University of Illinois Press. 75–90.

Stewart, Penny and Richard C. Fawcett. 1994. "'An' to 'A' in American speech: Language change in progress." *English Today* 10(1): 18–24.

Tawake, Sandra. 1993. "Reading *The Bone People*—cross-culturally." *World Englishes* 12(3): 325–333.

Tay, Mary Wan Joo. 1993. *The English language in Singapore: Issues and development*. Singapore: National University of Singapore, UniPress, Center for the Arts.

Teh, G.S. 1986. "An applied discourse analysis of sales promotion letters." Unpublished M.A. Thesis. National University of Singapore, Singapore.

Thumboo, Edwin. 1985. "Twin perspectives and multi-ecosystems: Tradition for a commonwealth writer." *World Englishes* 4(2): 213–221.

Thumboo, Edwin. 1986. "Language as power: Gabriel Okara's *The Voice* as a paradigm." *World Englishes* 5(2–3): 249–264.

Thumboo, Edwin. 1992. "The literary dimension of the spread of English." In Braj B. Kachru (ed.), *The other tongue: English across cultures, Second edition*. Urbana, Illinois: University of Illinois Press. 255–282.

Tickoo, Makhan Lal. (ed.). 1991. *Languages and standards: Issues, attitudes, case studies*. Singapore: SEAMEO Regional Language Centre.

Vavrus, Frances K. 1991. "When paradigms clash: The role of internationalized varieties in language teacher education." *World Englishes* 10(2): 181–195.

Variation and the Mesolect in Jamaican Creole

Peter L. Patrick
Georgetown University

Whether one is primarily concerned with language teaching, language acquisition, or structural analysis of language data, a basic question in the study of language is: What do we know when we know a language? I ask this in the context of a creole speech community, the Caribbean nation of Jamaica, where an English-related creole has been spoken for three hundred years. This language, which linguists call Jamaican Creole (JC) but practically all Jamaicans call *di Patwa*, is spoken to varying degrees by people at all levels of society, alongside a local standard variety, Standard Jamaican English (SJE). Full competence in the standard is limited to a small fraction of society; however, because it is nominally the language of all education, because there is no popularly-accepted orthography for JC, and because both local and foreign standard-language mass media are ubiquitous, most Jamaicans have at least a minimal competence in SJE as well.

This is the usual description of Jamaica on a bilingual model, but it is not a typical bilingual community. It resembles diglossia—in fact some creolists (especially native creole-speaking ones) have labeled Caribbean English Creole communities like Jamaica diglossic situations (Winford 1985)—but it is not. Jamaica is instead generally described as having a *creole continuum*. This label was invented by DeCamp (1971) just for Jamaica but has since been widely applied, with some controversy over the precise nature of the continuum (Rickford 1987) and its application to particular cases. The term suggests a graded, intermediate dimension between two distinct poles. I will focus on the intermediate portion: what creolists have called the *mesolect*, taking from the Greek *meso-* for "situated in the middle, intermediate," and *-lect*, for "a variety or way of speaking." The exact nature of the mesolect, of the grammar or grammars that govern it (if any), and the proper description of the speech that mesolectal speakers produce, is my topic. Other questions radiate from this, typical of pole-and-continuum phenomena: Is the middle a version of (one of) the poles, or a distinct element in a class of its own? Does it exist merely as a predictable product of interaction of the two poles, or are its properties unpredictable and unique?

I will consider these questions from a variationist perspective on language. This position need not be described afresh, but I wish to highlight a few of its characteristics that are useful to oppose to other linguistic approaches that have been labelled *categorical*. To notice the existence of language variability is not enough to make one a variationist, since all linguists are aware of it; what you do with the variation once you have noticed it makes all the difference. Categorical linguistics (including most American structuralists and generative grammarians) may be defined by its inability to reconcile variable data with a systematic concept of grammar, following Chambers (1995: 12) "The axiom of categoricity [is] the simplifying assumption that data for linguistic analysis must be regularized to eliminate real-world variability."

Variationist linguistics, on the other hand, assumes the linguist's task is not to enforce orderliness by excluding data, but rather to discover the existing order within the complex and apparently chaotic language data of situated utterances. In doing so, it is often quite necessary to violate two other, incidental tenets of categorical linguistics: first, by exploring the connection between linguistic behavior (narrowly defined) and the social world, and second by making use of quantification where it illuminates the nature of language data, especially continuous data. While the search for order is also part of the mandate of categorical linguistics, the latter excludes data of certain extremely common types: "If we find continuous-scale contrasts in the vicinity of what we are sure is language, we exclude them from language" (Hockett 1955: 17). Again: "All continuities, all possibilities of infinitesimal gradation, are shoved outside of linguistics in one direction or the other" (Joos 1950: 702; the more remarkable for appearing in a phonetics journal!). Finally, Chomsky's (1965: 3) famous dictum concerning the object of linguistic theory isolates the language of "an ideal speaker-listener in a completely homogeneous speech community," unaffected by the many factors that help produce real-world variability, which Chomsky dubs "grammatically irrelevant."

Categorical linguistics, which rejects continuity and external factors, has proven incapable of describing mesolectal speech in a creole continuum, yet most linguists studying creoles embrace assumptions of categorical linguistics. Thus, beyond identification and labelling of the phenomena, little progress has been made in discovering the grammatical basis of the mesolect and the creole continuum. It falls to variationist linguistics to solve this difficult problem. Here, I outline the need for a solution, identify obstacles faced by categorical approaches, and show why several such models are necessarily inadequate. I also present data that are difficult for categorical models to assimilate, which invite resolution in a variationist model instead.

The description of language variation in mesolectal creole languages was one of the earliest problems in the field of variation studies, and has been a persistent one. DeCamp began research on JC in the 1950s, before variationist principles were explicitly enunciated; he was followed by Labov (1971), Winford (1972), Bickerton (1973, 1975), and Rickford (1979, 1987), among others. However, difficulties in the very identification and basic description of these language situations, not to mention their explanation, remain. Mesolectal creoles are often ignored as language varieties deserving attention in their own right. The mesolect is typically defined as a range of non-discrete language variation between two poles. These poles, nearly always idealized, are isolated and referred to as the *acrolect* or (local) standard, and the *basilect*, often simply called "the creole." Each of these notions is also fraught with problems, which cannot be addressed here. It is clear that *acrolect* refers to a variety heavily influenced by formal, foreign standards and distinct in grammar from the basilect. The *basilect's* two defining features are that it is recognized where African-derived features occur, and where speech does not coincide with features of European standards. Yet it is difficult in practice to find so-called true basilect or true creole speakers, since stretches of speech that can be wholly defined in this way are rare to nonexistent.

Creole research in general has paid lip service to the importance of the mesolect and yet, perhaps because of conceptual difficulties, concentrated on the basilect, inadvertently confirming it as the legitimate object of investigation. It is tremendously important to study basilectal speech, but this valorization process has had some unfortunate byproducts. If only the basilect is a true creole, then the mesolect is relegated to limbo—not a creole, certainly not a standard. In the case of Jamaica, the prototype of the creole continuum, it cannot be treated as a non-standard vernacular dialect of the related standard because of the well-known observation that no clear dialectal boundaries seem to exist between acrolect and mesolect, or between mesolect and basilect (DeCamp 1971).

A more extreme version of the same tendency to idealize language description, and to privilege only varieties that are maximally distant from European standard languages as true creoles, was common in the early years of modern creole studies. Such influential scholars as Stewart (1962), Taylor (1963), and Bailey (1966) considered restricting the term *creole* to just those language situations where no linguistic continuum existed to muddy the waters—i.e., where creole and standard could be cleanly distinguished. Vestiges of that position still linger, e.g. in the recent debate over whether Barbadian speech (which is considerably closer to Standard Englishes than Guyanese or Jamaican) constitutes a true creole—a debate resolved only by the fieldwork of scholars who obtained "more basilectal" data from present-day Barbadians (Cassidy 1980, Hancock 1980, Roy 1986, Rickford 1992).

Outside of Suriname and the Guianas, few Caribbean creole-speakers have been located (or at any rate tape-recorded) who could qualify as monolectal speakers of a basilect. The vast majority of people do in fact speak a variety most creolists agree to call mesolectal. There is wide agreement in the literature on the bipolar definition mentioned above. Bickerton (1975: 24) defines the mesolect as "all intermediate varieties" between the acrolect and basilect, following Stewart (1965). In textbooks from the 1980s, Mühlhäusler (1986) applies the label to "varieties intermediate between the two," while Romaine (1988: 158) says it is "transitional, mediating between the polar opposites of basilect and acrolect," and has emerged through decreolization as part of a continuum (on which she quotes Bickerton). More recently, de Rooij (1995: 53) speaks of "transitional varieties," and Muysken and Smith (1995: 5) single out "intermediate forms" existing in the middle range of a creole continuum—"forms such as *did*" (de Rooij 1995: 54), the pre-verbal past marker in Jamaica.

With this intermediate definition I concur happily. Frequently, however, such descriptions cast aspersions on the creole-ness of the middle range, as when Muysken and Smith (1995: 5; emphasis in the original) discuss "a continuum of speech-forms varying from the creole at one end of the spectrum (the *basilect*) through intermediate forms (*mesolectal* varieties), to the lexifier language (the *acrolect*)." Alleyne (1980: 192) earlier described "the continuum as it exists in Jamaica ... in terms of three codes (creole, intermediate and standard)"; he leaves *mesolect* aside as a term he associates with Bickerton, but it is quite clear where it would fit in this scheme.

In proposing his model of a linguistic continuum, DeCamp (1971: 350ff) does not use the term *mesolect* (apparently it was not yet in wide use at the 1968 conference from which this paper comes), but refers to intermediate varieties, arguing powerfully that more attention ought to be paid them as "the speech actually used by almost all Jamaicans" (1971: 351). In keeping with the variationist insistence on the primacy of the vernacular as data for structural analysis, and the evident ubiquity of the mesolect in spontaneous everyday speech, I argue that if a creole is to be found in Jamaica, the mesolect must surely belong to it.

Several other models have been employed to further flesh out the notion of the mesolect, but most recent authors of textbooks on pidgins and creoles (Arends et al. 1995, Holm 1989, Mühlhäusler 1986) do not appear to state their positions with any great conviction, and some (e.g. Romaine 1988) are quite careful to quote others rather than assert their own beliefs. If not valor, this may reflect a collective wisdom on the part of creolists—the kind of wisdom that recognizes our ignorance and, where we cannot be silent, inclines us to express it only softly. According to some of these various views, the mesolect:

- Is characterized by *separate forms*, distinct from those used in the basilect and acrolect for the same linguistic functions;
- Is the synchronic product of *code-switching* between two distinct grammars;
- Is the synchronic product of *code-mixing* between two distinct grammars, one of which is the dominant frame;
- Is the diachronic product of *decreolization*, a linguistic convergence process; or

- Consists of an infinite series of graded dialects differing only minimally from each other and ordered on some social dimension (the *creole continuum*).

A folk position can easily be elicited from many speakers in Jamaica who assert the existence of "Patwa" (JC) and "English," two polar opposites, but do not recognize intermediate varieties. If pressed, they will answer that sometimes people "mix them," but this label conveys no firm sense of alternative identity for the mesolect (and so resembles the code-switching and -mixing linguistic analyses). There is some truth to each of these positions, and I will touch on each below (except decreolization, which deserves a longer discussion). But none is adequate to characterize the daily practice of millions of mesolectal creole speakers in all its range and variety.

In this investigation, I accept the defintion of the Jamaican mesolect as the variety, or range of varieties, intermediate between the acrolect and the basilect, with a narrow definition of these polar varieties leaving room for a broad view of the mesolect. Thus whenever a standard variety of English is being spoken, whether it is the emerging local Standard Jamaican English (SJE), or a foreign variety learned through formal education and/or time abroad, the mesolect is not.[1] This is often, in practice, a clear and easy distinction, since the occasions permitting the standard and the ability to speak it consistently are both rather rare in everyday Jamaican life, while public recognition of its salient features is high.

Similarly, whenever the basilect is being spoken, the mesolect is not. Again, in practice this is rarely problematic. As noted, linguists have not done very well in capturing extended passages of speech which conform to creolists' descriptions of basilectal JC in all respects, i.e. passages in which elements attributable to English, or elements which are classically described as mesolectal, are altogether absent. Consequently, in any approach to Jamaican language that allows for intermediate varieties at all, it seems fair to say that a large proportion of the speech commonly heard in Jamaica and available for linguistic analysis must be assigned to the mesolect. Since much of the data examined below was collected in an urban environment by a well-educated white foreigner known to speak a standard variety of English (in addition to my JC, which is quite fluent since I have spoken it nearly all my life), I do not hesitate to describe the data as broadly mesolectal. This liberal identification, however, raises several important questions:

---

[1]Speaky-Spoky, a local style, is not considered a standard variety (Patrick, forthcoming), while Formal Educated Jamaican English and the accent known as the Upper St. Andrew Drawl are (Irvine 1988, Miller 1987, Shields 1989).

- Is the mesolect properly characterized as a creole (like the basilect), rather than a local dialect of a standard language (like the acrolect)?
- Does the mesolect possess any unique characteristics, or is it in some way predictable or derivable from the properties of the acrolect and basilect? and
- Is there a unity to the mesolect such that it can be characterized as a single variety, or more precisely as possessing a single grammar?

I propose answers to the first two questions below, and suggest one to the third. (The third question requires additional comparative study of data from two or more sources, each of which can plausibly be identified as mesolectal independently of the other.) All are, in my view, empirical problems best resolved by the study of naturally-occurring speech data in a framework capable of recognizing variability and addressing its social and linguistic context. Much of the data considered below comes from a study of a single, mixed-class urban neighborhood of Kingston, which I have described in detail elsewhere (Patrick 1992). I will now consider attempts to model mesolectal variation along three main lines: code-switching, code-mixing, and variable grammar. Each implies a different position on the relations of the basilectal and acrolectal grammars to the mesolectal speech which I am interested in describing and explaining.

Mesolect as code-switching. One common approach to the mesolect is to see it as a synchronic product of code-switching between two well-defined, invariant, and essentially incompatible grammars, Standard English and basilectal Jamaican Creole, both occurring in a contact situation. Many speakers are fully competent in one (usually the basilect) and competent to a great degree in the other. Mesolectal utterances are seen as the product of switching between two lexicons and their associated grammars, in much the same way that speakers of Spanish and English, or French and German, might code-switch.

Curiously, there is very little literature explicitly testing or arguing for this view, yet it occurs often as an assumption in arguments, or as an offhand characterization of mesolectal data. The view's strength is that it accords well with the reported perceptions of many creole speakers (particularly the elite, including creole-speaking linguists, who are more likely to be fluent speakers of the standard than the majority of native creole speakers) that English and Creole are separated by a great gulf, and typically used in different domains. There is ample support for this point, both sociolinguistic and structural, yet I do not believe it is sufficient to support a code-switching analysis.

Most description of Jamaican Creole has been aimed at the basilect, and has been done in a structural or generative framework assuming categoricity and denying variability. This sort of linguistics assigns any token of language variation to one or another idealized, invariant model of a language, denies significance to the choice of a particular variant in its context, and considers quantitative facts about the proportions of choices, or of contexts, to be grammatical irrelevancies, mere matters of performance. This tradition of linguistic investigation has been seriously challenged for speech communities and regions where many studies have uncovered and examined linguistic variation, demonstrating patterns which have yet to be accounted for by categorical approaches; but such is not yet the case of Jamaica, or of most creole-speaking areas, where it remains dominant. The most descriptive influential works on JC have characterized an invariant basilect that is maximally different from an invariant English, and have interpreted any stray features from the other pole as errant "interference," i.e. as flaws of performance.

Sociolinguistically, there is sharp functional stratification between the basilect and standard in Jamaica, such that the use of one in a situation where the other is widely recognized as appropriate may produce an incongruous or laughable situation. As social norms for the polar varieties are quite distinct, they typically occur in complementary distribution. As one descends the scale of social prestige, however, while sensitivity to contrasting social values does not diminish, the practical knowledge speakers have of the educated standard shrinks rapidly. Consequently, there is a great blurring of the lines between varieties so that one person's "English," when described in structural terms, resembles another person's "Patwa." Yet while speakers' perceptions of the contrast between English and Jamaican Creole are very real and important data with great sociolinguistic significance, they do not constitute a structural linguistic analysis of the two varieties. Social reality does not mirror linguistic reality. The folk tendency is to confuse the two, focusing on social conditions rather than structure. Linguists' analyses, on the other hand, have all too often been conducted in frameworks that discount social data, and that offer no model but a contrastive or oppositional one. The tendency of creole-speaking linguists has also been to polarize their descriptions—not because of any lack of linguistic training but in part because of the nature of that training. Categorical linguistics is insensitive to, and incapable of incorporating, the commonsense, everyday social and functional pressures on language use which are part of every speaker's experience. Linguistic ideology, then—the beliefs of linguists about the nature of language—interferes with our analyses, as Crystal (this volume) notes.

I offer these speculations about why a code-switching analysis of the mesolect has proven so attractive on perceptual, attitudinal, and ideological grounds only because it seems to me so unlikely linguistically. I do not deny that code-switching takes place between standard English and Jamaican Creole—certainly it does. But the vast majority of utterances I have collected and analyzed, or those that may be heard any day in Kingston by an observer, cannot simply be accepted as "code-switches" for several reasons. First is the absence of an adequate model, theory, or procedure for identifying switch points and assigning them to the grammar of JC or SJE. Invoking and demonstrating a mechanism for code-selection, and reconciling natural speech with the grammars of the two codes, are the twin responsibilities of any linguist who wishes to claim that the mesolect is the output of this process. As Labov noted a quarter of a century ago, "The statement that opposing variants belong to different systems is not enough: it is necessary to show how the speaker moves from one system to another, and under what conditions" (1971: 461).

Second is the requirement that distinguishes code-switching from code-mixing, namely sustained co-occurrence. A code-switching analysis must show that when elements from English occur, they generally do so in a continuous string. That is, when the grammar of Jamaican Creole gives way to that of standard English, all or most elements for some stretch of time must be drawn from English and not from Jamaican, and vice versa. If this analysis is only supported in rare occasions, we must reject the hypothesis of code-switching; for code-switching, so defined, is not true language *mixture* at all, but rather *alternation* between languages which do not change to accommodate each other.

In an article attempting to quantify the distance between JC and English, Bailey (1971) attacked the problem of the mesolect by estimating the number of translation rules that would need to be applied to make a spoken text conform with either SJE or basilectal JC. This effort was motivated by her "uncanny feeling" that a much-cited collection of Jamaican narratives, DeCamp (1960), "used language which was at some point midway in the continuum, and that *some means had to be found for justifiably assigning [it] to the creole rather than the standard* end of the continuum" (1971: 342, my emphasis). Bailey was, incidentally, the author of the earliest complete generative grammar of a Caribbean Creole, *Jamaican Creole Syntax* (1966)—the Bible of the basilect, and still the standard reference description of it. Bailey's words indicate both the dilemma and the solution: Variable mesolectal speech is seen as an anomaly, and the categorical linguist's task is to analyze it in a way that brings it into conformity with the basilect, "the idealized construct which I described in [Bailey 1966], the construct which I here assume lies at the core of all borrowing and interference as manifest in the continuum" (ibid.). In other words, it must be shown that the grammar underlying intermediate (i.e. mesolectal) speech is really a basilectal one.

One of the two samples Bailey analyzed contained the sentences given below in (1), with translations in (2), from a narrative "told by a 60-year-old grandmother in an isolated hill village" (1971: 343, lines 12–14 given below; this text was collected by Bailey, and is not from DeCamp 1960). The sentences are in the usual orthography for JC (Cassidy and LePage 1980). I have marked them in two typefaces, indicating English in *italics* and Jamaican in **bold**, and placed an E or J under each clearly identifiable element. I followed Bailey's own rules wherever they were noted, but had to extend them as well: She only gave a few examples of rules and substitutions distinguishing the two polar varieties on lexical, phonological, and syntactic levels. Some elements belong both to

English and JC; these I did not label switches, but left in the same typeface as the elements which precede them.

(1)

Bot luo,	***aafta***	*shi*	*got*	***mari,***	***insted***	*it*	*woz*	*a*	*man,*
J		E	E	*J*	*J*		E	E	

it	*woz*	*a*	***bul-kou.***	*And*	*evribadi*	***[0]***	*telin*	*har*	*Dat*
	E	E	*J*	E	E	*J*	E	E	E

dat	*woznt*	*a*	*gud*	*man,*	*bot*	*shi*	***huol***	***aan***	***opan***	***di***	***man***
J	E	E				E	*J*	*J*	*J*	*J*	

(2) "But lo, after she got married, instead of its being a man, it was a bull. And everybody was telling her that that wasn't a good man, but she held on to the man..."

Switch points were identified on the basis of such JC features as the downglide in /luo/, lack of participial inflection in /mari/, absence of preposition after /insted/, the lexical item /bul-kou/, absence of copula in the progressive construction, etc.; regular verbs show no evidence of past-tense inflection, and /woz/ *was* occurs only with noun complements, not in auxiliary constructions. English features serving to indicate switch points include the pronoun /shi/, copular /woz/, consonant clusters in /and/ and negative suffix /-nt/, and so on. These two sentences, when conservatively judged for features specific to JC or English, require ten switches from one variety to the other under a code-switching analysis. However, this is not one of Bailey's problematic texts with intermediate language! This is one she describes as "well within the SJE end of the continuum, and far removed from the JC end" (1971: 347). It is all the more surprising to find so many "switches" in a text that she labels "obviously English, and not creole" (1971: 344). While one can find short strings of co-occurring English and JC features, every clause contains some elements that Bailey's rules would assign to JC and some that would be assigned to SJE. This example is not untypical of upper mesolectal speech, and it is clear that "sustained co-occurrence" does not describe it well.

In her 1971 article, Bailey does not in fact give a code-switching account of the above data, but rather implies what I shall next characterize as code-mixing, claiming that JC elements are used within a matrix of English rules.[2]

---

[2]Elsewhere, Bailey (1966:1) has stated the code-switching position clearly, describing the typical Jamaican speaker as one who "is likely to shift back and forth from Creole to English or something closely approximating English within a single utterance, without ever being conscious of

My point, however, is that code-switching does not seem a plausible way to account for every (non-)occurrence of a lexical item, verb inflection, particle or preposition, auxiliary, or phonological variant associated with the "other" variety. Labov (1971) and Bickerton (1975: 12ff) have given further criticisms of the code-switching model—criticisms which might also hold of Bailey's procedure as I have applied it here—in classic arguments against describing creole systems as composed of multiple invariant grammars.

My third objection to this type of analysis, then, is that it leaves large sections of actual Jamaican speech in a grammatical limbo, frequently without a predictable or definable system which speakers use to project (or hearers use to interpret) the stream of speech. Everyday speech, typical of many Jamaican speakers most of the time, is treated as a random oscillation between two invariant grammars with little in common and no systematic relation to each other, despite centuries of co-existence. It seems odd that such behavior should occur in the same speech community that assigns profound social meaning to the choice of the two codes in question, which is surely evidence for the evolution of specific norms. We should not accept such an analysis without more compelling arguments and stronger evidence, both of sustained co-occurrence on the grammatical level, and of its social interpretation.

It is a common solution of categorical linguistics to ignore data which cannot be neatly housed in existing invariant systems, or to multiply the number of invariant systems to house these homeless data (e.g. the spurious "dialects" discovered whenever two generative syntacticians disagree on grammaticality judgments). The variationist response is to assume that structure and order underlie such data, and seek to explain them in a grammar that explicitly allows for variation. In search of such an explanation, then, we press on.

Mesolect as code-mixing. The second model I consider for the mesolect is *code-mixing*. This term is sometimes used interchangeably with *code-switching*, but here I make a crucial distinction about the nature of the underlying grammar in operation. If code-switching consists of alternation between two distinct underlying grammars and their respective surface elements, then code-mixing refers to the case when there is only one underlying grammar, but surface elements from two distinct varieties occur. Fasold (1984), following Hill and Hill (1980), notes that although this distinction may be quite difficult to make in practice, theoretically it is important. In the Jamaican case, mesolectal utterances contain features associated with both SJE and the basilect, but a speaker would be following the rules and constraints of only one grammar: either basically speaking Creole with some English mixed in or (as Bailey

---

this shift."

suggested for the example above) basically speaking English with Creole mixed in.

Again, I know of no detailed test of the applicability of this model to a body of Caribbean English Creole data. However, it has been assumed to hold by many creolists, and has even been incorporated into theories of creole development and change as the basic mechanism of decreolization. The diachronic changes that occur are said to move the creole in the direction of the standard, affecting either its basic grammar, the repertoires of its speakers, or both (Rickford 1983); eventually it "transform[s] the creole... into a dialect of the standard" (Whinnom 1971:111). Many creolists believe this type of contact-induced change has gone on continually since the earliest days of creoles, and is directly responsible for the very existence of intermediate varieties, i.e. of the mesolect. Bickerton (1975: 69–70) defines this "characteristic strategy of the decreolisation process" in Guyanese English Creole as one of replacement: "[N]ew, 'English-looking' morphemes are simply slotted into place in creole structures—semantic as well as syntactic." This is the same process as code-mixing: elements of one variety, here English, appear in the midst of a string of elements of the other, Creole, and are governed by the Creole grammatical rules. (Replacement, where "new" forms are assigned to the same underlying structure as "old" ones, is the converse of reanalysis, where the same "old" forms are assigned "new" structures.)

This description of mesolectal variation resembles the previous one in that it maintains a binary opposition between English and Creole, reflecting the language attitudes of the native speaker, which are based on social function and value. These attitudes are social products, and not to be given the evidentiary status that intuitions receive in generative grammar. Far from being Platonic insights into the true nature of language, such attitudes are in part products of what Crystal (this volume) calls "the largest and most successful exercise in popular brainwashing that I know of," namely the imposition of Standard English norms throughout the English dialect-speaking world. This binary opposition is maintained, once again, at the expense of any independent identity for the mesolect.

While the code-mixing approach has not been established empirically either, it does not share two other defects of the code-switching model. It explicitly does not require sustained co-occurrence (indeed, that would tend to weigh against it), and it asserts the operation of a single systematic grammar governing the behavior of most speakers most of the time. In the first respect, it seems to be closer to the facts; in the second, it provides an explanation which is simpler and a degree more orderly. There is a key difficulty, however: The grammar asserted by the code-mixing hypothesis is not one that on its face accounts for many of the forms of the language observed. A key tenet of this view is that *despite appearances*, and contrary to the alleged tendency of linguists to interpret English-like forms as being governed by English-like grammatical constraints and semantic categories, SJE-like forms in mesolectal Jamaican speech are constrained by basilectal grammar.

Considerable literature tests and contests such assertions in the area of verbal tense-aspect marking for Atlantic creoles (e.g. Edwards and Winford 1991, Patrick 1992, Rickford 1987, Singler 1990), while less is known about noun-phrase phenomena such as plural-marking (Mufwene 1986, Patrick, Carranza and Kendall 1993, Poplack and Tagliamonte 1994). Results, sometimes controversial, suggest that a variety of complex constraints are at work on several linguistic levels. Some may be characterized as functional, and thus perhaps likely to apply in unrelated systems; others suggest historical links between creoles and standard varieties of English; yet others offer the kind of simple contrast between the two polar grammars that code-mixing asserts as the general case. Much room exists for further examination of the claim by accountable empirical investigation of natural speech data.

Yet there is a further degree of order that the code-mixing hypothesis cannot provide, due to its framing as a categorical approach. We do not yet know whether or why the elements of English which crop up in an essentially creole text might do so with any particular frequency, nor whether the context exercises any constraining influence on their occurrence. Not only does code-mixing not provide any reason to ask *quantitative* questions such as this—as a variationist would like to do—it gives us no reason yet to ask *any* questions, for this model still assumes no system-level relation between the grammar of the code-mixed English items and that of the Creole matrix. The English items are lost at sea, grammar-less, then claimed by a basilectal grammar which somehow recognizes their equivalence and deploys them appropriately.

Mesolect as variable grammar. Let us hypothesize, instead, that choices of a certain sort (say, between English past *-ed* and JC past pre-verbal *did*) occur because they are favored by linguistic processes or tendencies embodied in contextual factors of a certain sort (e.g., narrativity, stativity). We then need to discover and specify higher-level relations between the grammatical modules in which the forms are embedded; we also need to consider whether functional requirements (e.g., disambiguation of past-reference) are held in common between the two polar systems, while other local and historical grammatical differences favor the choice of one or the other item in a given context. Such an approach, while admittedly presenting difficulties in description, is more consonant with the perhaps imperfect, yet considerable, knowledge Jamaicans have of the polar varieties than the oil-and-water image suggested by the simple model of code-mixing, which like code-switching allows only one monolithic set of rules to be in operation at any time.

It does not seem plausible that more than three hundred years after JC crystallized as a variety, during which time it has remained in contact with local standard Englishes, there are no regular accommodations between the two grammars, no normative patterns of constraints governing the integration of salient and contrasting features from one system into the other. Indeed, the concept of decreolization is fueled by the idea that just such accommodations have taken place and may be generalized about—and the concept, however poorly defined, is widely accepted by creolists. Why, then, maintain a model in which the only varieties granted grammatical structures are the polar ones? If such constraints exist, they ought to be described and then linked to general linguistic and sociolinguistic explanatory theories. The existence and nature of such constraints may then serve as the basis for substantive characterization of an independent variety, or related set of varieties, to be labelled the mesolect.

I now turn to an examination of mesolectal Jamaican data, to see how a variationist description fares in comparison to the approaches found unsatisfactory so far. A variationist approach is quantitative, asking "How often ...?" as a basic descriptive question. One productive way to ask this concerns the distinct forms that are often said (e.g. Alleyne 1980) to characterize the mesolect, differing on the surface from both basilectal and acrolectal forms but accomplishing many of the same functions. How often do these distinct forms occur in speech identified as mesolectal? I consider three elements of the grammar that have been studied by several creole scholars: progressive aspect, TD-Deletion, and the past-marking of verb phrases.

Jamaicans mark progressive aspect by three main constructions. The basilectal form uses an invariant pre-verbal marker, /a/, which precedes the bare verb in sentences like:

(3) *Dem a waak an luk roon* A + Verb + 0
They are walking and looking around

The acrolectal variant, identical to English, uses an inflected form of the verb "Be" and the suffix "ING":

(4) *They are walkin' an' lookin' around.* Infl. BE + Verb + ING

The variant usually assigned to the mesolect is literally intermediate. It makes use of the ING suffix only:

(5) *Dem waakin an lukin roon* 0 + Verb + ING

This (Zero + ING) option is typical of mesolectal compromises, in that the form adopted is acrolectal. The verb is not inflected, however, and the marker itself is invariant, features which resemble the basilect. In an analysis of 17 diverse Jamaican speakers recorded in 1958 by DeCamp, I found the following distribution of 125 tokens of progressive marking over a total 90 minutes of speech (Patrick 1988):

(6)	A + Bare Verb	56	45%
	Zero + Verb + ING	34	27%
	Inflected "Be" + Verb + ING	29	23%
	Other forms + Verb + ING	6	5%

For these speakers, the dominant form is (A + Verb), the basilectal construction. The other two options are almost equally chosen; together the constructions with ING, which we can safely label non-basilectal, slightly outnumber the basilectal variant. Let us temporarily exclude from consideration speakers with very small amounts of data (fewer than five tokens) in their brief extracts of speech, which were typically three to seven minutes long. Strikingly, seven of the nine remaining speakers use *both* the basilectal A and the non-basilectal ING forms (although never together).

Two observations come to mind. Speakers alternate forms in all but the briefest interviews, making it unlikely that code-switching or style-shifting underlie their behavior. In fact, the two briefest interviews in which sufficient tokens occur are two minutes forty seconds and two minutes fifty-three seconds long; these are the only ones in which categorical behavior occurs, with speakers employing the ING form exclusively (nine and seven tokens of it). In every interview of three minutes or longer, the forms used vary. One might counter that such an interview is an unnatural speech event. Another view, however, is that even the pressure of an interview by a white foreigner is insufficient to discourage frequent use of the basilectal variant, or to induce regular use of the acrolectal variant. I take these data, incomplete as they are, to indicate that most JC speakers commonly alternate between at least two of the three options in brief stretches of speech on a single topic with the same interlocutor.

The data allow another interesting suggestion, which I will investigate by looking at other linguistic features: Where the standard forms are inflected and enter into relations of agreement, zero-marking may be a common mesolectal option. This does not contradict the claim that the mesolect is marked by distinct forms—in fact, it complements it by proposing another characteristic pattern—but zero-marking has its own peculiar properties. The lack of overt inflection where the standard requires one (in this case, on the verb "Be") is not in itself evidence for the absence of underlying grammatical relations of agreement since inflections are occasionally absent for many features of spoken English, and yet linguists maintain that the usual rules are underlyingly in force. Similarly, the lack of an overt invariant pre-verbal marker (in this case, pre-verbal A) where the creole has one does not prove that we are not dealing with a creole rule-system.

In settling such a question, hard categorical evidence of ungrammaticality such as (6) above would be most helpful. In its absence, however, and in the presence of variability, let us call on the methods of variation analysis. Where choice of a given linguistic element is possible, e.g. the realization of one or another phonetic variant or the variable application of a linguistic process, a specific variant or choice is often favored by properties of the linguistic context. Some properties favor a particular outcome more than others. When measured on a suitable body of data, the ordering of properties may form a statistically reliable pattern; and, if there is a linguistic explanation for the ordering, one can plausibly claim that the contextual factors constrain the choice of linguistic elements.

Take, for example, the variable process of final consonant cluster simplification sometimes called TD-Deletion, which operates to make the words *bust, told, played* homophonous with the words *bus, toll, play*. Linguists have considered the effect of the surrounding phonological context on the deletion process. The effect is not categorical, i.e. simplification occurs variably in all contexts; but it happens more often before a following consonant than a following vowel, as numerous studies of English dialects have found (Labov et al. 1968; Guy 1980, 1991; Santa Ana 1991). Strong and regular patterns have been identified for several constraints across many varieties of English. In descending order of strength:

(7) Major constraints favoring TD-Deletion :

Following Segment: consonant > liquid > glide > vowel
Grammatical Status: mono-morpheme final > semi-weak verb suffix > regular past-tense suffix
Preceding Segment: sibilant > stop > nasal > fricative > liquid

(Adapted from Labov 1989)

The question is to what extent these patterns hold in the Jamaican continuum. One might expect that they would hold in acrolectal speech, which is a dialect of English, but not in the basilect, which is not. In fact, some creolists have claimed it is not even appropriate to speak of "deletion" in the basilect, which does not possess final clusters in underlying representations. (Consequently, I will refer to TD-Absence in order not to prejudge the question.) What pattern does the mesolect show? Is it creole-like, with no final clusters? If so, one would not expect to find the same constraints that operate on deletion processes in North American Englishes.

TD-Absence was examined for the urban Jamaican mesolectal speech community described earlier. Fifteen hours of data were analyzed for ten speakers who span a wide range of the creole continuum and the social spectrum, and over two thousand tokens of the feature were tabulated. (Exact numbers vary for each constraint analyzed; see Patrick 1991.) Consider the influence of the following phonetic environment:

(8) Rate of TD-Absence in Mesolectal JC by following segment:

Following:	Consonant	/r/	Glide	Vowel	Total
percent:	88%	78%	74%	63%	76%
probability:	0.66	0.43	0.45	0.34	
no. tokens:	960	55	237	793	2,045

The order of phonological constraints closely matches the phonetic conditioning patterns found in North American Englishes and indicated above, except that it applies at a much higher level of absence in JC. (The figures labeled "probabilities" represent the output of the Varbrul-2S multivariate analysis program; see Guy 1980, Sankoff 1988.)

But following segment is the strongest constraint, and it has been suggested that it is in fact a separate process, a post-lexical operation having to do with resyllabification, possibly a phonetic universal—in which case it would be no surprise if it operated in JC. Let us consider the preceding phonetic environment, for which these caveats do not hold since it addresses the internal structure of the word and resyllabification is irrelevant:

(9) Rate of TD-Absence in Mesolectal JC by preceding environment:

Preceding:	Sibilant	Stop	Nasal	Fricative	/l/	Total
percent:	85%	80%	67%	75%	58%	72%
probability:	0.67	0.60	0.42	0.56	0.35	
no. tokens:	462	162	907	73	168	1,772

The results again generally confirm those found in North American Englishes. There is one deviation, with fricatives favoring simplification more than nasals. Against this, it must be said that preceding segment has consistently been found to be a weaker constraint than following segment, perhaps because consonants are less different from each other than from vowels. In any case, this too is a favoring result, one which confirms that a deletion process is at work in JC. Taken together, these results indicate that the JC mesolect shows significant resemblances to English, from similar underlying representations at the lexical level to more abstract phonological principles and processes.

The grammatical constraint, however, reveals a different picture. In English dialects, final /t/ or /d/ in words like *belt*, as in *belt buckle*; the past verb *told*, as in *I told her*; and the past verb *billed*, as in *My doctor billed me*, all have different morphological statuses. In *belt*, final /t/ is part of the monomorphemic root; in *told*, final /d/ is a redundant indication of past tense; and in *billed*, final /d/ is the sole indicator of past-marking. Study after study has found that TD-Absence applies to these three classes at different rates, with mono-morphemic clusters being most likely to undergo simplification, and regular past-tense verbs being least likely. Various accounts of this phenomenon have been given (cf. Guy 1980, 1991), but the ordering is very robust.

The Jamaican data show the following pattern:

(10) Rate of TD-Absence in Mesolectal JC by grammatical status:

Status:	Mono-morphemes (e.g. *belt*)	Semi-weak verbs (e.g. *told*)	Regular verbs (e.g. *billed*)	Total
percent:	71%	59%	79%	75%
no. tokens:	1,358	44	370	1,772

This reverses the expected order: Regular past-tense verbs show a markedly higher rate of absence than even mono-morphemes. No natively-spoken English dialect has shown this pattern. The explanation, however, is simple. The high rate of absence in regular past-tense verbs is not due entirely to a deletion process—something else is at work. Not all verbs which occur with past reference in mesolectal JC are underlyingly marked with past morphology. This can be seen by inspecting other regular verbs where consonant cluster simplification does not apply, both syllabic verbs such as *want/wanted* and vowel-final verbs such as *cry/cried*; these classes are past-marked only about 50% of the time in past-reference contexts. (Data are from the same speakers; see Patrick 1991.) Irregular verbs like *give/gave* which mark past by ablaut in English received past-marking even less often, about 30% of the time. Some large proportion of consonant-final regular past verbs, then, are never suffixed to begin with, and the rest are subject to the operation of TD-Deletion. This combination of variable linguistic processes explains the high rate of absence in regular verbs shown in (10).

What does this say about the mesolect? Phonological findings seem to group the mesolect with dialects of English. Yet the pattern of the grammatical constraint, caused by variable past-marking, is not shared with any native dialect known to me. On the other hand, no published analysis of the Jamaican basilect describes it as applying an English-like, inflectional model of past-tense marking even part of the time—creolists all agree that it is organized along quite different and incompatible principles.

Any attempted retreat to the code-switching and -mixing models—where at least one can maintain that English grammar rules sometimes and Creole grammar at other times—proves insufficient, however. Variable past-marking applies at the morphological level, while rules of pan-English phonology must apply to condition TD-Deletion both word-internally (for preceding segments) and post-lexically. If words are underlyingly English (which they need be in order to possess clusters), how can variable past-marking, the Creole process, apply? And if this Creole rule applies, how can dialectal English rules apply to words at a later level of derivation? What sort of code-switching could this be, where switches must take place between abstract levels of rule application? Code-mixing faces a similar problem. Suppose English words, with underlying consonant clusters, are inserted into speech which is ruled by JC grammar. This works fine for the non-inflection of past tense, but one is forced again to go beyond the bounds of basilectal JC grammar for the English rules of TD-Deletion which potentially apply to such clusters.

The simplest solution involves a single variable grammar with both JC and English rules. I argue that the mesolect is a system itself, variable in nature, incorporating some processes from both basilect and acrolect within a grammar that constrains possible outputs and has evolved its own norms. Distinct mesolectal forms find a place in this conception, but we may expect to find them alternating with zero forms (as with the progressive). Forms and constraint patterns that might have diffused from English (as with TD-Deletion), or indeed developed historically along parallel lines, should be expected to accommodate basilectal influences as well. Two final examples from past-marking illustrate these points.

The form *did* is often cited as a distinctly mesolectal form in JC (e.g., Alleyne 1980: 182; de Rooij 1995: 54), which also has basilectal *ben* and its many variant forms. Like *ben* and other creole indicators of tense, mood or aspect, *did* occurs as an invariant pre-verbal marker before a bare verb.[3] In a study of mesolectal JC past-marking (Patrick 1992), *did* was the most often-used of these markers for past reference, and it tended to co-occur with stative verbs as creolists have predicted, following the pattern of *ben* as first identified by Bickerton (1975). *Did* was offered by many urban speakers as a form characteristic of city speech, as opposed to rural use of *ben*. While *did* use was known to everyone in the study, it was only used frequently by speakers over

[3]In the same environments in which English has emphatic affirmative *did*, although the JC particle is never stressed and is not emphatic.

forty-five years old and, even for them, it occurred in less than 10% of past-reference clauses.

(11) Relative frequency of common methods of Past-marking in Mesolectal JC:

		did +Verb		0 +Verb		Verb + Inflection	
		N	*percent*	*N*	*percent*	*N*	*percent*
Older	(>45)	98	6%	993	64%	455	29%
Younger	(<25)	3	0.4%	358	53%	315	47%

Not only does the distinct intermediate form alternate with the standard form of verb inflection, but both are dominated by the zero-marking option. If anything can be said to characterize the urban mesolect portrayed here, it is the use of zero-marking.

The English past negative adverb *never* also occurs in JC with the same meaning. In both varieties it may appear before the verb, but in English the verb must be inflected for past, while in basilectal JC it is not. In JC, however, *neva* has a wider distribution: It can be also used as a simple past negator where English would require *didn't* + Verb.

(12) *A neva sii soch a big gon in aal mi laif.*
I never saw such a big gun in all my life.

(13) *Ai neva av no tiivii fi riili watch it.*
I never had/didn't have a TV to watch it on, actually.

(14) *A wa im go ina palitiks, im neva waan no moni.*
Why did he go into politics, he didn't lack money.

Except for the lack of inflection on the verb, *neva* is used the same way in (12) as it would be in English; the concluding phrase confirms the exclusive nature of the negation. (13) is ambiguous, however: The hearer cannot be sure whether the speaker had ever owned a TV set, only that she did not at the moment in question. In (14), the speaker refers to a relative who started life out poor, made a lot of money, and subsequently went into politics. The exclusive reading of English *never* is simply false. (All three utterances are by the same speaker.)

Not only is the exclusive reading of *neva* optional for JC speakers, but it appears to have different co-occurrence patterns within the mesolect. The ten speakers in this sample are divided into three groups (4-2-4) representing different levels of the creole continuum. That is, the groups are ordered by the frequency of their English or basilectal forms along a scale which generally corresponds to aspects of their social position. These groups show different patterns in their use of *neva*. The High group (those speakers with the most English-like speech and the highest social status) frequently inflects the following verb for past, about half the time—a rate which is close to their normal rate of past-marking:

(15) Past-marking with *Neva* for three groups of Mesolectal JC speakers

Speakers	Bare Verb	Inflected Verb	Percent Inflected	Overall Inflection (Regular Verbs)	
High	8	9	53%	57%	N=228
Middle	11	0	0%	32%	N=225
Low	44	2	4%	11%	N=270

In other words, their tendency to past-mark the verb does not seem to be affected by the occurrence of the negator. The other two groups show an identical strong tendency to avoid inflection on the verb following *neva* (combined, they differ significantly from the High group at $p<.001$). This is not a function of their general tendency towards lower past-marking, however, for they differ markedly in their overall rates, and both groups inflect the general class of regular verbs significantly more often than verbs following *neva*. In other words, they appear to have a constraint against inflecting a verb preceded by *neva*: They treat it just like a basilectal preverbal tense-aspect marker.

Overall, in their variable rates of past-marking, the speakers show a stratification which recalls DeCamp's continuum, a pattern of continuous gradation; but alongside it, this sharp distinction in their handling of the past negator *neva* stands out. The dividing line does not separate basilect from mesolect, however, but distinguishes the upper reaches of the mesolect from the lower. The form of the negator undoubtedly diffused from English, but has accommodated the requirements of two very different grammars.

Conclusion. I have argued that a truly mixed model is needed to account for the forms and grammatical relations observed in mesolectal data, a model which must allow for variable processes and variable realizations of elements. Accordingly, I rejected the code-switching and code-mixing models as unsuccessful efforts to derive variable data from invariant grammars. The progressive and *did* past-marking data gave evidence of the general mixture of forms within the mesolect; the *neva* past-marking data testified to the availability of both basilectal and acrolectal rules; the TD data gave evidence of variable processes at work, and the constraining effects of linguistic context, much as in English varieties with unified grammars; and the extract from Bailey (1971) demonstrated the difficulty variable data present for the code-switching model.

The mesolect ought to be recognized as creole in nature, partly on social grounds, since it is what most people speak most of the time in an allegedly creole-speaking society; and partly on historical grounds. Most creolists agree that a creole language is one which mixes elements of its source languages into a unique product that develops according to natural linguistic processes, and is strongly influenced by social factors. This certainly describes the mesolect as presented here, and consequently it, too, should be considered a creole alongside the basilect. While the mesolect is clearly different in kind from the acrolect, it remains to be seen in future work how different it is from the basilect, when the latter is analyzed in a variable framework.

I have also argued that the mesolect is best explained as a variable system, ruled by a single grammar which incorporates components from both English and basilectal JC. On this count code-switching is ruled out, again, and code-mixing, although it postulates a single grammar and combines JC and English surface forms, fails to allow the required combination of English and JC properties at the level of abstract rules. The TD data were evidence that variable processes may truly be incorporated deeply into a single grammar, and the *neva* data demonstrated that grammatical components of both systems appear to be underlying the use of an ambiguous form alongside the variable past-marking that occurs throughout the mesolect. In addition, both invariant solutions seem implausible when compared to the integration and development of norms for JC and English at the sociolinguistic level that has resulted from their long history of interaction in Jamaica.

Finally, I have presented evidence that the mesolect is essentially variable in a way that the standard and basilect are not. The standard has its agreement and obligatory inflections; the basilect has its preference for overt forms that are shunned as one moves up the creole continuum; but the mesolect has, in particular, high levels of zero forms which are constrained by contextual linguistic factors. These zero forms occur in alternation with overt forms which may be unique to the mesolect, or may be shared either with the acrolect or basilect. The distinguishing features are not the uniqueness of forms, but the level and patterns of variability.

Earlier I echoed Crystal's evocation of the intersection between linguistic ideology and linguistic analysis. But there is another way in which I believe ideology affects linguistic analysis: our social and political beliefs. In a recently independent, post-colonial nation such as Jamaica, powerful ideological pressures oppose the African to the European, the rural to the urban, the local to the foreign. In support of independence—and independence is not a single political event in such a country, but an ongoing national voyage of discovery—it may be important to create a nationalist discourse emphasizing difference and autonomy from major cultural influences (first Britain, now the U.S.A.) in nearly every area of life, including language. This position supports a segregation and opposition of grammars: The more invariant and idealized the basilect, the more clearly JC can be seen to stand on its own from the foreign standard, linguistically. This is not a trivial point or passing fad of politicization, incidentally; Alleyne (1994: 13) notes that "the perception of differences ... is the basis of language loyalty, which is one of the attitudes standardization ... is designed to cultivate." Language loyalty to creoles, even among a small elite, is significant progress for languages which until recently were routinely denigrated even by linguists.

American and European creolists, generally trained in a categorical, non-social linguistics like their Caribbean counterparts, are unlikely to challenge the ideology of opposition for other reasons, not least of which is that it coincides nicely with the orthodox position of universal linguistic adequacy. This position asserts the communicative and intellectual adequacy of all natural languages, and has been responsible for linguists' passionate defense of countless endangered languages, despised social dialects, accents, and ethnic varieties which are discriminated against—in short, much of what good linguists have tried to do in the wider society has been inspired by this doctrine. Creoles have only been covered by it for a few decades, and creolists may not wish to lose the ground that has been gained for creoles and their speakers. Consequently, all parties seem to have an investment in structural analyses that minimize the mixed or intermediate nature of creole varieties, and maximize the gap between basilect and acrolect.

But is the cost misrepresenting or ignoring the actual language use of the majority in a speech community? Must the defense of an academic doctrine, even one which is universally subscribed to by modern linguists, be opposed to the accurate depiction of speakers' own language use, their real voices? Surely this uncomfortable position is unnecessary. Our basic responsibility as researchers in the discipline is to describe the facts correctly, or at least adequately, and I have argued that a variationist approach is required to do that for the mesolect in the Jamaican creole continuum. Our responsibility to society includes, among other things, supporting linguistic tolerance with the findings of our research. Creolists should not have to argue for laudable goals with poor analyses.

As a final example, the choice of standard orthography is a major language planning problem confronting creole continuum societies, where standardization efforts are practically nonexistent. Alleyne (1994: 12) has questioned "whether standardization should serve the function of emphasizing the autonomy of the creole or whether it should reflect socioeconomic realities that place urbanized forms of the creole language in a dominant position." In practical terms, this amounts to asking whether to codify the basilect or the mesolect. In order to even have a choice, it is important to continue research on structural properties of the mesolect. To answer the question of which is more likely to succeed with the population of speakers, the variation studies argued for here, though perhaps crucial, will not be enough. A research program that not only directly addresses linguistic structure and language use, but situates them in the broader context of communicative behavior, social institutions, and language ideology, is required if we hope to comprehend variation and the mesolect.

REFERENCES

Alleyne, Mervyn C. 1971. "Acculturation and the cultural matrix of creolization." In Dell Hymes (ed.), *Pidginization and creolization of languages*. Proceedings of a conference held at the University of the West Indies in Mona, Jamaica, April 1968. Cambridge, U.K.: Cambridge University Press. 169-186.

Alleyne, Mervyn C. 1980. *Comparative Afro-American*. Ann Arbor, Michigan: Karoma Publishers.

Alleyne, Mervyn C. 1994. "Problems of standardization of creole languages." In Marcyliena Morgan (ed.), *Language and the social construction of identity in creole situations*. Los Angeles: Center for Afro-American Studies Publications. 7–18.

Arends, Jacques, Pieter Muysken, and Norval Smith (eds.). 1995. *Pidgins and creoles: An introduction*. Amsterdam/Philadelphia: John Benjamins.

Bailey, Beryl L. 1966. *Jamaican Creole syntax*. Cambridge, U.K.: Cambridge University Press.

Bailey, Beryl L. 1971. "Jamaican Creole: Can dialect boundaries be defined?" In D. Hymes (ed.) *Pidginization and creolization of languages*. Proceedings of a conference held at the University of the West Indies in Mona, Jamaica, April 1968. Cambridge, U.K.: Cambridge University Press. 341–348.

Bickerton, Derek. 1973. "The nature of a creole continuum." *Language* 49: 640–669.

Bickerton, Derek. 1975. *Dynamics of a creole system*. Cambridge, U.K.: Cambridge University Press.

Cassidy, Frederic G. 1980. "The place of Gullah." *American Speech* 55(1): 3–15.

Cassidy, Frederic G. and Robert B. LePage (eds.). 1980. *Dictionary of Jamaican English*. Cambridge, U.K.: Cambridge University Press.

Chambers, J.K. 1995. *Sociolinguistic theory: Linguistic variation and its social significance*. Language in Society 22. Cambridge, Massachusetts: Blackwell Publishers.

Chomsky, Noam. 1965. *Aspects of the theory of syntax*. Cambridge, Massachusetts: MIT Press.

Crystal, David. This volume. "Playing with linguistic problems: From Orwell to Plato and back again."

de Rooij, Vincent. 1995. "Variation." In J. Arends, P. Muysken and N. Smith (eds.), *Pidgins and creoles: An introduction*. Amsterdam/Philadelphia: John Benjamins. 53–64.

DeCamp, David. 1960. "Four Jamaican Creole texts." In R.B. LePage (ed.), *Jamaican Creole: An historical introduction. Creole Language Studies 1*. London: Macmillan.127–179.

DeCamp, David. 1971. "Towards a generative analysis of a post-creole speech continuum." In D. Hymes (ed.), *Pidginization and creolization of languages*. Proceedings of a conference held at the University of the West Indies in Mona, Jamaica, April 1968. Cambridge, U.K.: Cambridge University Press. 349–370.

Edwards, Walter F. and Donald Winford (eds.). 1991. *Verb phrase patterns in Black English and Creole*. Detroit, Michigan: Wayne State University Press.

Fasold, Ralph. 1984. *The sociolinguistics of society*. Oxford, U.K.: Basil Blackwell Ltd.

Guy, Gregory R. 1980. "Variation in the group and the individual: the case of final stop deletion." In William Labov (ed.), *Locating language in time and space*. New York: Academic Press. 1-36.

Guy, Gregory R. 1991. "Explanation in variable phonology: An exponential model of morphological constraints." *Language Variation and Change* 3(1): 1-22.

Hancock, Ian F. 1980. "Gullah and Barbadian: Origins and relationships." *American Speech* 55(1): 17-35.

Hill, Jane and Kenneth Hill. 1980. "Metaphorical switching in modern Nahuatl: Change and contradiction." *Papers from the 16th Regional Meeting of the Chicago Linguistic Society*. Chicago: Chicago Linguistic Society. 121-133.

Hockett, Charles F. 1955. *A manual of phonology*. Baltimore, Maryland: Waverly Press.

Holm, John. 1989. *Pidgins and Creoles, Volume II: Reference survey*. Cambridge Language Surveys. Cambridge, U.K.: Cambridge University Press.

Hymes, Dell (ed.). 1971. *Pidginization and creolization of languages*. Proceedings of a conference held at the University of the West Indies in Mona, Jamaica, April 1968. Cambridge, U.K.: Cambridge University Press.

Irvine, Grace Alison. 1988. "A study of the linguistic markers of social differentiation in two Jamaican communities." Unpublished M. Phil. thesis, University of York.

Joos, Martin. 1950. "Description of language design." *Journal of the Acoustical Society of America* 22: 701-708.

Labov, William. 1971. "The notion of 'system' in creole languages." In D. Hymes (ed.) *Pidginization and creolization of languages*. Proceedings of a conference held at the University of the West Indies in Mona, Jamaica, April 1968. Cambridge, U.K.: Cambridge University Press. 447-472.

Labov, William. 1989. "The child as linguistic historian." *Language Variation and Change* 1(1): 85-97.

Labov, William, Paul Cohen, Clarence Robins, and John Lewis. 1968. *A study of the non-standard English of Negro and Puerto Rican speakers in New York City*. (Cooperative Research Project no. 3288). Philadelphia: U.S. Regional Survey.

LePage, Robert B. (ed.). 1960. *Jamaican Creole: An historical introduction*. Creole Language Studies 1. London: Macmillan.

Miller, Faye. 1987. "Acrolectal Jamaican English: Some aspects of phonological and morpho-syntactic variation." Unpublished M. Phil. thesis, University of the West Indies.

Morgan, Marcyliena (ed.). *Language and the social construction of identity in creole situations*. Los Angeles: Center for Afro-American Studies Publications.

Mufwene, Salikoko S. 1986. "Number delimitation in Gullah." *American Speech* 61(1): 33-60.

Mühlhäusler, Peter. 1986. *Pidgin and creole linguistics*. Oxford: Basil Blackwell Publishers.

Muysken, Pieter and Norval Smith. 1995. "The study of pidgin and creole languages." In J. Arends, P. Muysken and N. Smith (eds.) *Pidgins and creoles: An introduction*. Amsterdam/ Philadelphia: John Benjamins. 3-14.

Patrick, Peter L. 1988. "/a/ is for aspect: The grammaticalization of multifunctional particles in Jamaican Creole." New Ways of Analyzing Variation XVII, 30 October 1988, University of Montreal.

Patrick, Peter L. 1991. "Creoles at the Intersection of Variable Processes: *-t, -d* deletion and past-marking in the Jamaican mesolect." *Language Variation and Change* 3(2): 171-189.

Patrick, Peter L. 1992. "Linguistic variation in urban Jamaican Creole: A sociolinguistic study of Kingston, Jamaica." Unpublished Ph.D. dissertation, University of Pennsylvania.

Patrick, Peter L., Isolda Carranza, and Shari Kendall. 1993. "Number-Marking in the Speech of Jamaican Women." New Ways of Analyzing Variation XXII, October 1993, University of Ottawa, Ontario.

Patrick, Peter L. "Style and Register in Jamaican Patwa." To appear in Edgar Schneider (ed.), *Englishes around the world: A Festschrift for Manfred Görlach*. Amsterdam/Philadelphia: John Benjamins.

Poplack, Shana and Sali Tagliamonte. 1994. "*-S* or nothing: Marking the plural in the African-American diaspora." *American Speech* 69(3): 227–259.

Rickford, John R. 1979. "Variation in a creole continuum: Quantitative and implicational approaches." Unpublished Ph.D. dissertation, University of Pennsylvania.

Rickford, John R. 1983. "What happens in decreolization?" In Roger Andersen (ed.), *Pidginization and creolization as language acquisition*. Rowley, Massachusetts: Newbury House. 298–319.

Rickford, John R. 1987. *Dimensions of a creole continuum*. Stanford: Stanford University Press.

Rickford, John R. 1992. "The creole residue in Barbados." Society for Pidgin and Creole Linguistics Third Annual Meeting, 9–10 January 1992, Philadelphia, Pennsylvania.

Romaine, Suzanne. 1988. *Pidgin and creole languages*. London: Longman.

Roy, John D. 1986. "The structure of tense and aspect in Barbadian English Creole." In Manfred Görlach and John Holm (eds.), *Focus on the Caribbean*. Varieties of English around the World, General Series Volume 8. Amsterdam/Philadelphia: John Benjamins. 141–156.

Sankoff, David. 1988. "Variable rules." In Ulrich Ammon, Norbert Dittmar, and Klaus J. Mattheier (eds.), *Sociolinguistics: An international handbook of the science of language and society, Volume II*. Berlin: Walter de Gruyter. 984–997.

Santa Ana, Otto. 1991. "Phonetic simplification processes in the English of the Barrio: A cross-generational sociolinguistic study of the Chicanos of Los Angeles." Unpublished Ph.D. dissertation, University of Pennsylvania.

Shields, Kathryn. 1989. "Standard English in Jamaica: A case of competing models." *English World-wide* 10(1): 41–53.

Singler, John Victor. 1990. *Pidgin and creole tense-mood-aspect systems*. Amsterdam/Philadelphia: John Benjamins.

Stewart, William. 1962. "Creole languages in the Caribbean." In Frank A. Rice (ed.), *Study of the role of second languages in Asia, Africa and Latin America*. Washington, D.C.: Center for Applied Linguistics. 34–53.

Taylor, Douglas. 1963. "The origin of West Indian creole languages: Evidence from grammatical categories." *American Anthropologist* 65: 800–814.

Whinnom, Keith. 1971. "Linguistic hybridization and the 'special case' of pidgins and creoles." In D. Hymes (ed.), *Pidginization and creolization of languages*. Proceedings of a conference held at the University of the West Indies in Mona, Jamaica, April 1968. Cambridge, U.K.: Cambridge University Press. 91–115.

Winford, Donald. 1972. "A sociolinguistic description of two communities in Trinidad." Unpublished Ph.D. dissertation, University of York.

Winford, Donald. 1985. "The concept of 'diglossia' in Caribbean creole situations." *Language in Society* 14: 345–356.

Poisoning pidgins in the park: The study and status of Hawaiian Creole[1]

Theodore S. Rodgers
University of Hawaii/Bilkent University

This paper reviews several issues relating language to education in Hawaii. Consideration of the standard English, Hawaiian and foreign language school movements will provide context for remarks on educational responses to Hawaiian Pidgin/Creole. I discuss some linguistic treatments of Hawaiian Creole—more popularly, Hawaiian Pidgin—and some sociopolitical uses to which these descriptions have been put. I also consider various responses to Hawaiian Creole in the programs and policies adopted by the public schools of Hawaii. This includes demonstration of materials aimed both at elimination and elevation of creole. These remarks serve as background for some comments on the current and future linguistic and sociolinguistic status of Hawaiian Creole in Hawaii.

1. Background. The dialect that many locally born students in Hawaii bring with them to school is a creole that has English at its base. In various sources this dialect has been called Hawaii Creole, Islands Dialect, Hawaiian English, and, most popularly, Hawaiian Pidgin. A number of contemporary linguistic commentators have noted that, at present, no children bring with them to school anything like a true pidgin—as linguists define pidgin. The label persists, however, amongst advocates and attackers alike. I will use both Hawaiian Creole English (HCE) and Pidgin, depending on context, to refer to the same general phenomena.

In the past fifty years, Hawaiian English has spawned a number of linguistic analyses, both general and detailed, by both insiders and outsiders. (See Sato 1989 for references.) Writing in 1969, Tsusaki notes in his "Problems in the Study of Hawaiian English" that Hawaiian English is "synchronically a group of co-existent systems consisting of an English-based pidgin (immigrant classes), and English-based creole (lower and lower-middle classes) and a dialect of

[1]This paper is dedicated to the memory of Professor Charlene Sato—Creolist, Colleague, Comrade—who died on January 28, 1996. Charlie provided valuable help to me in the preparation of this paper and invaluable insights for us all in better understanding language and community.

English (upper middle class)" (1969: 120). And twenty years later another observer notes, Hawaiian English

> is a language in flux, encompassing a range of forms, a true speech continuum across time and social class. Therefore, a definitive description is not possible. Generally speaking, it differs from standard American English in pronunciation, and in grammar. Many bound morphemes are expressed syntactically, and free grammatical morphemes are deleted or their use is altered. The lexicon is based mainly on English, though there are differences in word usage between Hawaiian English and standard English. (Speidel 1987: 103).

The history of the development of HCE also ranges across a continuum. Hawaiian English Pidgin was born in the plantation fields where English-speaking "luna" bossed mixed language groups of immigrant plantation field hands. As plantation workers left the fields for the towns, they took with them their proto-English and passed it on to their children who, in succeeding generations, regularized early usages into Hawaiian Creole English.

In a book that was for a time the standard text for creolists, Todd posits six phases in the "process of development from pidgin to creole" (1974: 17). Phase One arises from "marginal contact between speakers of two (or more) languages giving rise to a marginal pidgin" and Phase Six is indicated "by complete coalescence with the standard language." Phase Five is marked at the "near standard end of the post-creole continua as in Hawaii" (1974: 17). Todd further notes that "as yet the complete circle from 1–6 has not been drawn" (1974: 18). One of the questions my paper addresses is, Is the complete circle (i.e. decreolization) being drawn in Hawaii and/or is it likely to be drawn in some foreseeable future?

A second issue which has considerable bearing on the answer to the first question concerns public, including media, attitudes towards HCE speech and speakers in Hawaii. As the Tsuzaki quote above indicates, points on the language continuum have been highly correlated with the ethnicity and family income of dialect speakers. Thus, comments about stage of standardization are often interpreted as comments about race and status. These, in turn, find their way into the articulation of public policy, especially educational policy. The second question at focus in this paper is, How are linguistic and popular attitudes towards Hawaiian pidgin reflected in official policies and educational programs in Hawaii?

2. Linguistic descriptions and linguistic attitudes. Several scholars in Hawaii have made English in Hawaii a major focus of their life work. These include Reinecke (1935/1969/1988), Carr (1972), Tsuzaki (1966,1968),

Bickerton (1977) and Sato (e.g., 1985). There is neither space nor the necessity to review their work here. I do wish to cite examples of how several analysts—linguists and language educators—have phrased their descriptions, and to consider what attitudinal perspectives appear to underlie these phrasings.

John Reinecke is probably the dean of Hawaiian English studies. His 1935 study was reprinted by the University of Hawaii Press in 1969 and again in 1988 with considerable fanfare. Reinecke was a school teacher and union organizer in the plantation town of Honokaa on the island of Hawaii, who was much beloved and warmly remembered by his students and co-workers. He was a student, speaker, admirer, and analyst of local English. Here is a sample of his writing on English dialect in Hawaii:

> The two predominant characteristics of Island syntax appear to be wholesale confusion of the verbal forms of tense, number, and person, and wholesale omission of particles and other words not absolutely necessary in a sentence ... There is a general confusion of grammatical forms which makes it difficult to formulate any generalizations; almost every "error" or peculiarity quoted can be matched in one or several sections of the United States, though not in the assembly of errors. (Reinecke 1935: 14)

"Wholesale confusion," "wholesale omission," "assembly of errors"? This certainly is not the language of contemporary sociolinguistic description. While it is unfair to fault writing of the 1930's for failing to observe the norms of sociolinguistic political correctness of the 1990's, Reineke's language has been quoted by pidgin poisoners in the 1990's to fault the community of creole speakers with which Reineke lived and worked.

Elizabeth Carr was for many years a Professor of Speech at the University of Hawaii and a specialist in the English of Hawaii. Her chef d'oeuvre was *Da Kine Talk* (Carr 1972). Here is a sample from her own writing on Hawaiian English:

> These speakers (of local English) are not all alike. Each should be represented with a separate colored pin, representing his own particular degree of progress in the drift of the whole group toward the mainstream of standard English. Some are near; some are a long way off. This group rightly deserves our concern. (Carr 1969: 113)

The language of description is attitudinally heavy-laden—including the implication that males are the primary language upgrading targets of "our concern."

Again, it is unfair to pose contemporary habits of politicolinguistic correctness as the appropriate critical standard for the work of other times and climes. However—again—it is just such language, taken out of its historical context, which fuels contemporary, irate, pidgin-poisoning letters to the editor in the *Honolulu Advertiser*. More recent professional commentary on pidgin is more positive in tone. A popular article written by linguists McKaughan and Forman contains the following:

> It is encouraging to note that children who learn Pidgin best also learn standard English best ... Pidgin does serve useful purposes in our community. It would not have survived and flourished to the extent it has, were this not so. (McKaughan and Forman 1982: 11)

We can sense the supportive attitude of the writers underlying this commentary. In fact, many Pidgin-positive comments in newspaper leads and stories repeat or paraphrase the language of this article. My point is that it is difficult for commentators, with professional language credentials and intentions of objectivity, to write about the local English situation without a heavy attitudinal overlay. We will note, not surprisingly, the same kind of attitudinal weighting in the language of school programs and policies.

In somewhat the same sense in which Todd posits six phases in the process of development from pidgin to creole, it is possible to speak of six attitudinal stances in respect to the acceptance or non-acceptance of HCE in Hawaii. I offer these organized into a kind of attitudinal scale on which one can weigh policies, programs and public statements in respect to use of HCE over time. Some samples of commentary, both informal and formal, demonstrate the scalar designations.

2.1 *Stance One: "Stamp out Pidgin."* Hawaiian pidgin represents a debased and incorrect deviation from standard English. Its use marks speakers as uneducated and impedes their possibilities for self-improvement and a better life.

2.1.1 SAMPLES: Hawaiian Pidgin is "a desecretion of the greatest language on earth, and an abomination in the sight of the Lord" (Letter to the Editor, *Honolulu Star Bulletin*, February 13, 1962).

"The writer, noting that English language textbooks in present use do not attack many of the errors made by Hawaiian children, developed some lessons which deal directly with specific errors associated with pidgin English" (Ching 1963: 133).

2.2 *Stance Two: "Pidgin for Parties."* Hawaiian pidgin is endemic to Hawaii and forms a social bond for those born here. There are informal occasions among peers when pidgin is okay, otherwise it should be suppressed.

2.2.1 SAMPLES: "Pidgin does not have a place in the classroom. It's a language for the home, for the outside, but not for education" (Recorded Readerline phone-in comment, *Honolulu Advertiser*, August 16, 1995).

"But why should anyone who has mastered the standard language deliberately choose to drop back? The best guess is that the dialect represents the warmth of relationship—delightful to return to for a few minutes of relaxation and fun between stretches of academic or business life" (Carr 1969: 58).

2.3 *Stance Three: "Required one-way bidialectalism."* Pidgin is a unique and appropriate language form for a range of occasions involving family and friends. Creole speakers should be encouraged to acquire a second, standard English dialect for vocational and out-of-Hawaii use. Bidialectalism is not required or encouraged for those who already speak standard English.

2.3.1 SAMPLES: "Despite the fact that there is still some proscription against the use of Island Dialect, current efforts are largely aimed at teaching SE as a second dialect to be used alongside ID, at teaching children to be bidialectal as the situation demands" (MacLeish 1969: 68)[2].

"Hawaii students fluent in both Pidgin and standard English will benefit from the cultural richness of Pidgin and the ability to communicate on an even playing field wherever they go after graduation from school" (Editorial in *Honolulu Advertiser*, August 15, 1995).

2.4 *Stance Four: "Whatevah works. You choose'm."* Schools should adopt whatever dialect best communicates and best teaches. Students should be exposed to the "dialect bias" facts of life and provided opportunities to acquire standard English (or whatevah) if and when they so choose.

2.4.1 SAMPLES: "Communication is the most important thing. It's getting the message across" (Farrington High School principal quoted in *Honolulu Advertiser*, May 15, 1995).

"What should be taught about language is choice ... Whether you want to use Pidgin or standard English with friends, or on a job interview or in front of an audience is up to you" (Recorded Readerline phone-in comment, *Honolulu Advertiser*, August 16, 1995).

"The new (Hawaii English Project) curriculum must allow for the greatest individual progress and freedom of choice" (Nunes 1975: 15).

---

[2]ID = Island Dialects; SE = Standard English.

2.5 *Stance Five: "Lucky you live Hawaii."* Hawaiian pidgin is the unique linguistic badge of those who are born and grow up in Hawaii. Nonpidgin speakers are marked and mocked in high school. Those living in Hawaii should be encouraged to acquire and use pidgin in all aspects of their daily lives.

2.5.1 SAMPLES: "Young immigrants to Hawaii from around the Pacific are becoming second language (pidgin) speakers by deliberate choice in the process of becoming acculturated ... it does not make much sense to teach an immigrant teenager to say 'Good Afternoon' without also suggesting that in some social situations it might be better to say 'Howzzit' (McKaughan and Forman 1982: 11).

"Anyone who knows anything about language, linguistics and any research done on this issue would know that research supports the use of Pidgin in the classroom" (Recorded Reader line phone-in comment, *Honolulu Advertiser*, August 16, 1995).

2.6 *Stance Six: "Pidgin mo bettah."* Hawaiian pidgin has a robustness and a capacity for poetic, dramatic and conversational use greater than that of bland standardized English. Pidgin use in formal and informal occasions should be joyfully encouraged.

2.6.1 SAMPLES: "Pidgin English is 'the heartspeak'—the communciation mode when voicing anger, personal hurt and humor" (Lois-Ann Yamanaka, Hawaiian writer, quoted in *Honolulu Advertiser*, May 14, 1995).

"Pidgin English, several experts say, also implies a set of values, including a relaxed and generous attitude and humility" (Esme Infante, Feature Writer, in *Honolulu Advertiser*, May 14, 1995).

There is another stance which, in a sense, bridges several of the above. It is a stance which represents a certain ambiguity and irresolution about HCE and its use. It is a stance we see often represented in local commentary about HCE.

2.7 *Stance Seven: "Hahd to say."* Bidialectalism in Hawaii is equivalent to biculturalism. Few live in two cultures equally successfully. This stance reflects the idea, "Damned if you do, damned if you don't."

2.7.1 SAMPLE: "Unfortunately, the rejection of SE that accompanied the affirmation of HCE often locked many HCE speakers into the vicious cycle of educational failure, socioeconomic stagnation, and political powerlessness. The alternative—switching more or less permanently to SE—effectively removed people from their primary social networks and often created tension within these networks. This, then, has been the dilemma confronting HCE speakers for the past three generations" (Sato 1985: 266).

3. Educational responses to Hawaiian English Creole. In this section, I review educational policies and programs bearing on the perceived role of English—HCE and Standard English—in schooling. There have been, in addition to the programs discussed below, a number of smaller, localized educational experiments in dialect modification as well as creole-based creative writing classes.

3.1 *Private schools.* Hawaii has one of the highest percentages (17%) of its young people in private schools of any state in the nation. The private school movement arose early in Hawaii as a way for haole (white American/European) parents to provide quality education for their children as well as to isolate them from the assumed deleterious effects of contact with Hawaiian and immigrant children. Pidgin English was the most evident of these potentially deleterious effects, and standard, educated Mainland American English was and is the private school model for teacher and student alike.

3.2 *English Standard schools.* A mainland team of investigators under the direction of the Federal Commission of Education visited Hawaii in 1920 and made an extensive set of recommendations for the improvement of Hawaii's public schooling. Two recommendations that attracted immediate attention were the proposals to eliminate the afternoon and Saturday foreign language schools in Hawaii and to group students on the basis of their ability to speak, read, and write English. The first proposal was only weakly responded to by setting up a state regulatory body for the foreign language schools. The foreign language schools, in fact, doubled their enrollment between 1920 and 1930.

The second proposal prompted more direct action. In 1924 the Department of Education established the first English Standard school, admission to which required evidence of being able to speak, read, and write standard English. These schools and their supporters were labelled "racist" by some, since the overwhelming proportion of students first admitted to these schools were haole students whose parents could not afford to send their children to private schools. A variety of standard English tutoring programs were established to prepare those applying for admittance to an English Standard school.

Over the years increasing numbers of non haole students were admitted to these schools, and by the time the English Standard system was abandoned in 1947, "the haole children, for whom the schools were designed, constituted less than a quarter of the student population" (Fuchs 1961: 277). Thus, these schools ultimately did integrate students of diverse ancestry whose parents held high expectations for their children's education and were willing to subscribe to the notion that standard English was the route to fulfilling these expectations.

Hawaii's best-known social historian notes that although only about 7% of the school-age population was enrolled in the English Standard schools at their peak of influence, "it was primarily these schools that proved to be Hawaii's crucibles of democracy" (Fuchs 1961: 279). Fuchs' view is not universally held. In reviewing the history of the English Standard schools, Sato concludes that the "major effect of this system was the further stratification of Hawaiian society along ethnic lines by means of discrimination along linguistic ones." (Sato 1985: 264).

3.3 *The Hilo Language Development Project.* In 1965 a team of local educators and Peace Corps trainers jointly applied for federal funds to support an experimental remedial English program for children speaking local English dialect. The methods were built around pattern practice excercises borrowed from the methodology of TESOL. The rationale of the program was stated by the management team as follows:

> The Project is designed to cover the first four years of school. It is felt that the earlier children learn to understand and produce standard classroom English the easier and more efficient it will be for them, and the sooner they will be able to participate more fully in other areas of the curriculum. Furthermore, the project staff feels that four years is ample time to present the children with all the major grammatical constructions and pronunciations they need to handle to function as speakers of standard classroom English. (Peterson 1967: 753)

Despite the assurance of the Project staff that "The staff has adopted the position that it is worse than useless to try to eradicate or stamp out the Hawaii Islands Dialect" (Peterson 1967: 754), friends and foes of the Project alike saw such dialect eradication among the Project population as possible and, perhaps, inevitable. The Project did not have a significant effect on the in-school language use of its target population and was not continued after its four years of federal funding expired.

3.4 *The Hawai'i English Program.* For fifteen years (1968–1983), I was Chief Planner for a large curriculum development and implementation project called the Hawaii English Program (HEP). In magnitude, subject breadth, budget and duration of development and implementation, HEP has been the most ambitious public or commercial language education program as yet undertaken in the U.S. The first of the original charges of the State of Hawaii to the development team was to develop a program to insure "that each individual's capacity for language (for utilitarian, aesthetic, and educational purposes) be enhanced to the fullest degree" while the fourth of these original responsibilities was to develop "a set of learning materials for students so designed that each child's individuality is respected to the highest degree possible" (Nunes 1975: 3). How were these charges interpreted in respect to HCE, the most conspicuous and controversial feature of language in Hawaii?

Treatment recommendations in respect to Hawaiian English were not explicit in any of the charges given to HEP. However, it was clear that underlying the charges was a concern with children's oral language development in regard to utilitarian and educational (SE) purposes (charge number 1) and, as well, a concern that the home language (HCE) of the child be respected (charge number 4). The program which ultimately emerged was a highly diverse, richly pluralistic, and intentionally reiterative one.

HEP is a program targeted for elementary schools. It is organized into three subprograms—Language Skills, Literature, and Language Systems. All three saw HCE as central to their individual educational concerns.

The perspective HEP assumed in respect to HCE might be seen as ambiguous, perhaps even schizophrenic. For example, the Language Skills Program comprises 65 developmentally organized self-instructional and pair study units. Twelve of these units focus specifically on characteristics of HCE. Some of these were clearly seen and used as "remedial" (e.g., Unit: Dialect Markers (DM) Materials: 15 audiocard booklets and 15 picture booklets, diagnostic audiocards and worksheets. Objectives: The child discriminates between and produces English sounds that are often confused by Island children.)

Some were seen as "consciousness-raising" (e.g., Unit: Negatives (Neg). Materials: 16 sets of audio cards. Objectives: The child discriminates between the Hawaiian dialect and standard English negation forms.)

Some were seen as "dialect elaborative" (e.g., Unit: Dialect Variations (DV). Materials: 29 sets of audio cards and 4 cassette tapes. Objectives: The child discriminates among and produces four English dialects.)

And some promoted the idea of "speaker choice" (e.g., Unit: Dialect Books. Materials: 3 sets of books, each with a pidgin and standard version of the same title. Objectives: The child reads stories either in Dialect or Standard English).

The Literature program was designed as a pre-reading, reading inducement program as well as an appreciation program for early readers. Some of the local stories are in a "literate creole" form. However, there were relatively few such local materials available in the late 1960's and early 1970's when the Literature program was being developed, so the HCE focus is less prominent in HEP Literature than in the other two programs. HCE selections are much more evident in the Secondary English Program (SEP), the high school program that followed HEP.

The Language Systems program comprises 15 elaborate kit-based study units exploring such topics as Advertising, Animal Communication, Dialects,

Gestures, International Languages, Names, Popular Songs, Propaganda, Secret Codes, Sign Language, Sounds, Symbols, and Writing Systems. HCE receives passing attention in several of these and is a key focus in the eight-week study unit called Dialects.

In the Teacher's Manual included with the Dialects kit, the rationale statement for the study of Dialects includes five justifications for the study of this unit. Excerpts from the first two of these are given below:

> (1) To overview Hawaii's unique language and dialect situation. Hawaii's history is richly reflected in the dialects spoken by today's inhabitants. Dialect study thus proves an interesting and insightful introduction to historical and cultural studies in Hawaii. Study of dialects in Hawaii supports other Hawaii area studies customarily undertaken in the social studies curriculum in upper elementary school.
>
> (2) To provide factual background information to equip students to understand the often heated discussions about Hawaiian English (especially Pidgin) in Hawaii. In Hawaii discussions about dialect are as heated and continuing as, perhaps, in any other place in the English-speaking world. Thus, it is important for all citizens of Hawaii to be well-grounded in some basic information about dialects and, particularly, the dialects of Hawaii. The Dialects Unit presents such basic factual information in an interesting and believable manner. (Rodgers 1975: 33–34)

Some twenty activities in the Dialects Unit focus on HCE. These activities encourage elementary school students to view HCE as a complete and legitimate language form, to undertake some simplified linguistic analyses of HCE, and to witness dialectal flexibility in local role models. In sum, it is fair to say that HCE received extensive consideration in HEP (and subsequent SEP). It is also fair to say that this consideration, while positive in intention, reflected the ambiguity of attitude of the general community towards HCE.

HEP completed its statewide implementation in Hawaii's elementary schools in 1976, and is still in use in many of the elementary schools of Hawaii and some school systems on the Pacific Rim. However, program revision, materials availability, and teacher inservice programs are no longer maintained by the state.

3.5 *Kamehameha Early Education Program (KEEP).* KEEP is (was) a program of the Kamehameha Schools, a richly endowed educational complex established in the nineteenth century to support the education of Hawaiian and part-Hawaiian children. KEEP was created in 1970 and had a specific charge:

"Find a way to teach Hawaiian children to read, a way that was economically realistic, and could be used in public schools" (Speidel 1987: 110).

Most of the children in the group served had several characteristics—other than their Hawaiianness—in common: They came from an at-risk community environment; they came from a group whose peers and siblings experienced difficulty in learning to read and succeeding in school generally, and they came from a family/community environment where HCE was the standard spoken norm. Early on, KEEP explored the relationship between oral language characteristics and reading mastery. They found, in keeping with other studies, that "the difficulties Hawaiian children experience in learning to read can be partly attributed to their unfamiliarity with the standard language ... Those children who are more familiar with standard English are the better readers" (Speidel et al. 1985).

KEEP then explored approaches that would simultaneously address the interrelated issues of learning to read and learning to use school (standard) English. The approach ultimately adopted was called the "conversational" (sometimes, "talk-story") approach. The unique characteristics of conversation—as opposed, say, to chalk/talk presentation—include constant turn-taking among the conversational partners; no long monologues or extended explanations; the conversational partners respond to each other's statements and build upon them; there is talk on the same topic for several turns" (Speidel 1987: 111). KEEP research found that learning to read among Hawaiian children was facilitated by this approach; in addition, "the students who participated in the conversational approach showed a greater advance on standardized production tests of standard English grammar than a group who did not have this experience" (Speidel 1987: 119).

Thus, KEEP, to some extent, built on Hawaiian English "talk-story" conversational patterns and then provided an alternative to Hawaiian English in the school setting. I think it fair to say that here lies some of the same ambiguity with respect to school treatment of HCE that we have noted elsewhere. Since KEEP has been largely disbanded by the Kamehameha Schools administration, the program's ultimate capacity to respond to its charge may now never be known.

3.6 *Board of Education policy: "In the classroom, Standard English only."* Hawaii's public education system is unique in that it is under the direction of a single board of education (BOE). In August of 1987 a subcommittee of the Hawaii BOE submitted a proposed policy statement to the BOE which read, in part, "Standard English will be the mode of oral communciation for students and staff in the classroom setting and all other school related settings except when the objectives cover native Hawaiian or foreign language instruction and practice" (Hawaii BOE 1987). The BOE had anticipated broad community support for or at least acquiescence to this policy. However, in a stormy four-hour public hearing, parents, teachers, academicians, Hawaiian rights activists, and mass media representatives delivered testimony largely in objection to the proposed policy. News reports support Sato's claim that "Never before in Hawaii's history had such a diversity of voices been raised, in a formal institutional setting, in defense of Hawai'i Creole English" (Sato 1991: 139). The BOE recanted and, after a long delay, adopted a statement which merely "encouraged" the modeling of standard English by teachers and staff members in the Department of Education.

The issue is by no means dead, however. In August 1995, the *Honolulu Advertiser* reported results of a poll indicating that two thirds of Hawaii's residents say standard English should be the only language used to teach in the classroom. In an editorial entitled "In the classroom Standard English must be used," the editor noted, "The official policy of the Board of Education is to encourage the use of standard English, not mandate it. It appears that the majority of Hawaii residents are a step ahead of the board in urging that only standard English be used" (*Honolulu Advertiser*, August 1995).

4. The Future of Hawaiian Creole English. The standard view of creole evolution is that decreolization is inevitable. (DeCamp 1971). In 1969 Tsusaki stated that "historically HE has been changing increasingly in the direction of so-called Standard (Hawaiian) English and that the rate of this change has been comparatively rapid" (Tsuzaki 1969: 119). Twenty two years later, Sato notes that "On the basis of the socioeconomic and linguistic evidence, one might reasonably expect to find most HCE speakers moving steadily toward the acrolect in Hawaii's creole continuum" (Sato 1991: 130). However, there are a variety of factors that affect, perhaps even inhibit, the process of decreolization in Hawaii. Some evidence that decreolization is being decelerated in Hawaii is offered by Sato (1991). She suggests, for example, that the BOE squabble over HCE discussed in the previous section was a milestone in the local language debate and served to support "solidarity idealogy" through "acts of identity" by HCE speakers. Let me briefly consider some current factors that might be expected to influence the acquisition, status, and evolution of HCE in the future.

4.1 *Ethnic identity and dialect maintenance.* Labov and his colleagues have noted in longitudinal studies of urban black English a recent conscious and intentional distancing of black English usage from the standard or "white" English usage of the larger community. Labov and Harris (1986) suggest that this distancing is promoted by influential members of the black community as "acts of identity" to support ethnic pride. In a similar vein, Sato has reviewed recent controversies regarding HCE and suggests how these "critical institutional events (may be) perceived by creole speakers as attacks on their personal and social identity (and) may actually serve to decelerate decreolization" (Sato 1991: 224).

I informally polled a number of senior local educators—primary, secondary and university—in an attempt to get a sense of their views of "decreolization." Their unanimous view was that HCE characteristics, number of speakers, and occasions for use had remained fairly constant over the last thirty years. Decreolization theory holds that each generation of speakers carries the creole closer to the standard. The informal evidence cited supports Sato's suggestion that decreolization has stabilized or, at least, decelerated.

4.2 *Foreign language instruction in Hawaii.* A number of commentators have noted that Hawaii's potential role in Asia and the Pacific is severely restricted by the lack of focus on Asian-Pacific languages at all levels of schooling in Hawaii. Editorials in the local newspapers observe that Hawaii cannot afford to be an English-only isolate in the Pacific. Suggestions have been made that energy devoted to acquiring standard English among HCE speakers could more profitably be spent in acquiring an Asian language.

Hawaiian high schools do, indeed, teach beginning Japanese to more students than schools in any other state in the U.S. And in 1988, the Board of Education in Hawaii made mandatory the teaching of foreign languages in the elementary schools of Hawaii, as well. However, details of timing and language selection were left to the schools. While elementary school data show dramatic growth in numbers of students studying foreign languages over the last five years, closer inspection indicates that such instruction is typically limited to an hour or less a week and is largely unsupported by materials or training for elementary school foreign language teachers.

Overall, it seems unlikely that learning of foreign languages is likely to have a significant impact on the next phases of HCE in Hawaii.

4.3 *Hawaiian and HCE.* In the last several years, two—as yet—unrelated movements have acquired a considerable following in Hawaii. Hawaiian sovereignty is one of these, and Hawaiian Language Immersion education is the other.

In November of 1993, the Hawaiian sovereignty movement was given dramatic impetus by the formal apology of the United States government acknowledging U.S. wrong-doing in the overthrow of the Hawaiian monarchy in 1893 and U.S. annexation of Hawaii in 1898. Several Hawaiian groups have used this apology as an acknowledgment of Hawaiian sovereignty, proposed models of sovereignty, and are working to see these realized. The Hawaiian Language Immersion program is nine years old and has grown to nearly 1,000 students. The first cohort of Hawaii Immersion students have completed their elementary schooling in Hawaiian and are proceeding to further schooling in Hawaiian-based secondary schooling.

One widespread reading of these movements is that some form of Hawaiian sovereignty—some kind of redirection of Hawaii resources to Hawaiian people—will come about in the next few years. A corollary is that there will be an increased interest in the revival of Hawaiian language and its role as a marker of sovereign identity. One might ask if the loyalty that many local residents presently display towards HCE as the community patois might be transferred to the Hawaiian language.

Public attitudes in respect to Hawaiian and Hawaiian Creole have similarities and dissimilarities. Among professionals, those who conduct sociolinguistic research on HCE and Hawaiian often come from the same academic departments, publish in some of the same journals, and generally have considered themselves allies in the nonstandard English periphery. As yet these alliances have not been threatened by funding competition or public favoritism. In the larger public arena, there are those who find fault with both the HCE and Hawaiian language movements on the grounds of their isolationism and inutility. And there are those who find glory in both on the grounds of their re-enforcement of island uniqueness and identity. It will be interesting to see how the likely growth of the Hawaiian sovereignty and the Hawaiian language movement affect attitudes, programs and literary arts rooted in Hawaiian Pidgin.

REFERENCES

Bickerton, Derek. 1976. *Change and variation in Hawaiian English: Final report on National Science Foundation grant no. GS-39748.*

Bickerton, Derek. 1983. "Creole languages: Pidgin English, Hawaii." *Scientific American* 249 (1): 116–122.

Carr, Elizabeth B. 1972. *Da kine talk; from pidgin to standard English in Hawaii.* Honolulu: University Press of Hawaii.

Ching, Doris C. 1963. "Effects of a six month remedial English program on oral, writing, and reading skills of third grade Hawaiian bilingual children." *Journal of Experimental Education* 32(2): 133–145.

DeCamp, David. 1971. "Toward a generative analysis of a post-creole speech continuum." In D. Hymes (ed.), *Pidginization and creolization of languages*. London: Cambridge University Press.

Fuchs, Lawrence. 1961. *Hawaii Pono: A social history*. N.Y.: Harcourt, Brace and World.

Hawaii Board of Education memorandum. Aug. 1987. *HEP Language Skills Teacher's Manual, Volume Two*. 1975. Honolulu: Hawaii English Program.

Honolulu Advertiser. 1995. Editorial. August 15, 1995.

Honolulu Advertiser. 1995. Farrington High School principal quote. May 15, 1995.

Honolulu Advertiser. 1995. Recorded Readerline phone-in comment. August 16, 1995.

Infante, Esme. 1995. Feature Article. *Honolulu Advertiser*, May 14, 1995.

Labov, William and Walter A. Harris. 1986. "De facto segregation of black and white vernaculars." In D. Sankoff (ed.), *Diversity and diachrony*. Amsterdam/Philadelphia: John Benjamins.

MacLeish, Andrew. 1969. "Teaching Standard English Vowels in Hawaii." *Pacific Speech* II(3): 59-68.

McKaughan, Howard P. and Michael L. Forman. 1982. "Pidgin in Hawaii." *Ampersand* 4(4): 11.

Meyerhoff, M. and N. Niedzielski. 1994. "Resistance to creolization: An interpersonal and intergroup account." *Language and Communication* 14(4): 313-318.

Nunes, Shiho. 1975. *Hawaii English Program. Report No. 1*. Honolulu: Hawaii English Program.

Peterson, Robert. 1967. "The Hilo Language Development Project." *Elementary English* XLIV(7): 753-755.

Reinecke, John E. 1988, c.1969, c.1935. *Language and Dialect in Hawai'i: A Sociolinguistic History to 1935*. Honolulu: University of Hawaii Press, Social Science Research Institute.

Rodgers, Theodore S. 1975. *Dialects Teacher's Manual*. Honolulu: Hawaii English Program.

Sato, Charlene. 1985. "Linguistic inequality in Hawaii: the post-Creole dilemma." In N. Wolfson and J. Manes (eds.), *Language of inequality*. Berlin: Mouton Publishers. 255-272.

Sato, Charlene. 1989a. "Language attitudes and sociolinguistic variation in Hawaii." *University of Hawaii working papers in ESL* 10(1): 127-147.

Sato, Charlene. 1989b. "A nonstandard approach to standard Engllish." *TESOL Quarterly* 23(2): 259-282.

Sato, Charlene. 1991a. "Language change in a creole continuum: Decreolization?" *University of Hawaii Working Papers in ESL* 8(1): 191-216.

Sato, Charlene. 1991b. "Sociolinguistic variation and language attitudes in Hawaii." In J. Cheshire (ed.), *English around the world: Sociolinguistic perspectives*. Cambridge, U.K.: Cambridge University Press.

Speidel, Gisella and Kathryn Au. 1976. "Hawaii creole speakers' listening comprehension abilities in Standard English and Hawaii Creole." *KEEP Technical Report* 53: 45-57.

Speidel, Gisella, Roland Tharp, and Lynn Kobayashi. 1985. "Is there a comprehension problem for children who speak nonstandard English? A study of children with Hawaiian-English backgrounds." *Applied Psycholinguisitcs* 6: 83-96.

Speidel, Gisella. 1987. "Conversation and language learning in the classroom." In K. E. Nelson and A. van Kleek (eds.), *Children's Language* 6. Hillsdale, N.J.: Lawrence Erlbaum. 99-135.

Todd, Loreto. 1974. *Pidgins and Creoles*. Language and Society Series No. 1. London and Boston: Routledge and Kegan Paul.

Tsai, Matthew. 1995. "Pondering Pidgin." *Honolulu Weekly*. 5(1): 4.

Tsuzaki, Stanley. 1966. "Hawaiian-English: pidgin, creole, or dialect?" *Pacific Speech* 1(2): 25-28.

Tsuzaki, Stanley. 1969. "Problems in the study of Hawaiian English." *Working Papers in Linguistics* 1(3): 117-133.

Yamanaka, Lois-Ann. 1995. Interview in *Honolulu Advertiser*. May 14, 1995: 16.

The problem of variation in SLA theory and research

Cristina Sanz
Georgetown University

Introduction. Within the concept of variation in interlanguage, we need to distinguish between inter-learner and intra-learner variation. Inter-learner variation is used to refer to differences in the production of x number of L2 learners considered to be at the same level of language proficiency. Intra-learner variation can be further subdivided into diachronic variation or changes in production found when comparing the L2 production of the same learner at different moments in her learning process; and synchronic variation, or differences found in the production of one single learner at one point in her learning process.

In this paper I concentrate on synchronic intra-learner variation. The first part of the paper discusses ways in which different perspectives in Second Language Acquisition (SLA) theory have approached variation, from those who place it at the heart of the SLA process, to those who consider it problematic and avoid it altogether. A special section is devoted to discussion of the way in which the psycholinguistic construct of attention has been used. The second part deals with issues related to L2 variation in research methodology and discusses results from an experimental study that attempted to proceduralize attention.

The problem of variation in SLA theory. Two terms are important in order to understand the way interlanguage variation has been approached: knowledge and access, or the mechanisms that put knowledge to use. In Chomskyan views of acquisition, there are two types of linguistic knowledge, explicit and implicit knowledge, and production varies according to the intensity of the interaction between them. In a variationist approach to language acquisition, variation is the manifestation of one variable source of knowledge. In processing approaches to SLA, variation is the effect not only of different types of memory, but also of different ways of accessing that knowledge.

Eckman (1994) presents a summary of the discussion between Tarone (1990), a variationist, and Gregg (1990), a Chomskyan, on a theoretical problem that centers around knowledge.

The variationist view. Variationists have adapted Labov's framework (1972) to SLA and consider variation essential to understanding acquisition (Adamson

1988; Preston 1989; Tarone 1988; Ellis 1990). For these researchers, variation in L2 production is not a consequence of intervening performance factors that mediate between the learner's competence and her production. In this framework, L2 production varies as a result of the use of different "versions" of one rule by the learner. What makes the learner use one rule or another? It is the amount of attention that the learner focuses on the form, rather than the content, of the utterance. This is a direct adaptation of the Labovian construct of attention to speech. The study of attention and its limitations falls within the realm of cognitive psychology. However, factors of a social nature have also been proposed, such as learners' age (Wode 1989), accommodation to the interlocutor (Beebe and Zuengler 1983), and emotional involvement in the topic (Eisenstein and Starbuck 1989).

Figure 1 represents the variationist explanation for variation in production. To avoid the confusion that results from using the term "interlanguage" both to refer to the language learner's system and her linguistic production, I do not use

Figure 1. The interaction of variable competence and attention to form in L2 production (Tarone 1985).

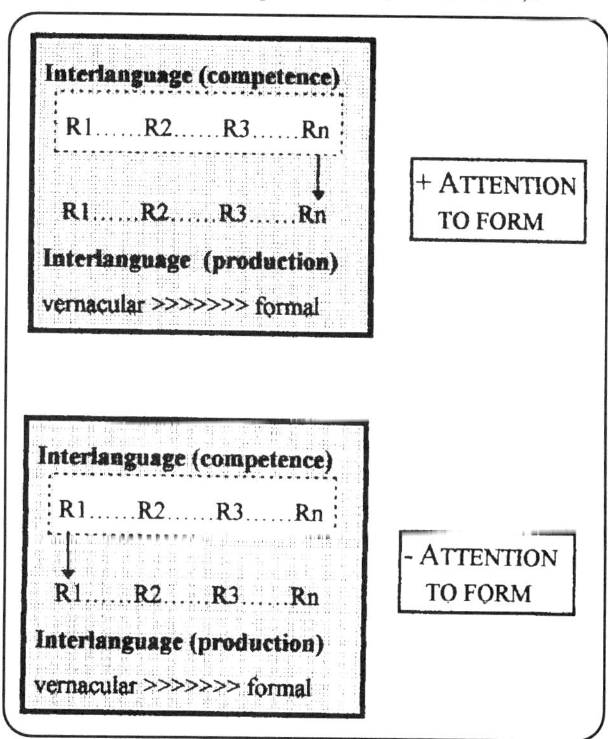

it in this paper.[1] However, I have left "interlanguage" in the figure with the equivalent "competence" or "production" indicated next to it.

The Chomskyan view. Figure 2 presents another explanation for variation based on knowledge. In this framework, variation is the result of the existence and use of two sources of knowledge: explicit and implicit. Explicit knowledge of the grammar is conscious, can be verbalized, and has all the conscious facts the learner knows about the language. Implicit knowledge of the grammar is not conscious and cannot be verbalized. Universal Grammar is identified with implicit, unconscious knowledge.

Krashen's Monitor Theory is compatible with this view of interlanguage variation. It was developed to capture both the constant order and variation found in the same morpheme studies (Krashen 1977). Whatever information is automatic and used spontaneously in language tasks is represented as implicit or acquired knowledge. Conscious explicit knowledge is used to modify and examine speech when the following three requirements are met: (a) The task allows for time; (b) the learner is focusing on form; and (c) the learner knows the rule.

Probably the best known example in L2 literature of a study that manipulates psycholinguistic processes in order to provide evidence for Krashen's Monitor is Hulstjin and Hulstjin (1984). These researchers separated a learner's linguistic awareness (knowledge) from her control over the processes in order to retrieve that knowledge. The hypothesis guiding Hulstjin and Hulstjin was that low-proficiency learners need extra time and attention when controlling speaking. If little time is given or the focus is placed on content, speech will be less accurate. Thirty-two adult learners of Dutch as an L2 were tested for their knowledge and use of two different word-order rules. The task consisted of a story retelling under four conditions: + time pressure; – time pressure; + focus on content; and + focus on form. Subsequently, the subjects were interviewed for explicit knowledge of the rule. The researchers found that production differed according to the instructions (i.e. that performance could be manipulated and that monitoring had a positive influence on L2 behavior). However, they did not find that the influence was due to a difference in explicit knowledge (i.e. whether the subjects could state the rule or not). Thus, Hulstjin and Hulstjin were unable to provide evidence for Krashen's Monitor (according to which, subjects control their speech by applying their explicit knowledge). This is so because they found no way to distinguish between self-correction on the basis of the acquired system from self-correction on the basis of the learned system (which Krashen named "monitor" vs. "Monitor," respectively).

---

[1]This confusion in the terminology has already been observed by Bialystok and Sharwood-Smith (1985).

Variation as competence or as performance: The debate over knowledge. More than just two different ways of explaining variation, what divides these two groups is a different view of what SLA theory should be about: whether the proper domain for a theory of SLA should be the abstract linguistic competence of the L2 learner or, alternatively, whether the domain should incorporate within-speaker variation (Eckman 1994).

For Tarone, variation is not a consequence of performance limitations, but the reflection of competence that is made up of variable rules. For variationists, the competence/performance distinction is not necessary. In native varieties, variation is central to the explanation of language change (Labov 1972). In non-native varieties, variation is also central, since it is at the heart of the acquisition process: First, forms appear spontaneously and are assigned to contexts, and then their use is extended from one context to others.

For Gregg, (1) the domain of a theory of SLA must be the linguistic competence of the learner; (2) the study of linguistic competence necessarily excludes the type of within-speaker variability that is important to variationist models; and (3) theories of SLA that attempt to account for this variability blur

Figure 2. The interaction of implicit and explicit knowledge and attention to form in L2 production (Krashen 1982; Schwartz 1993).

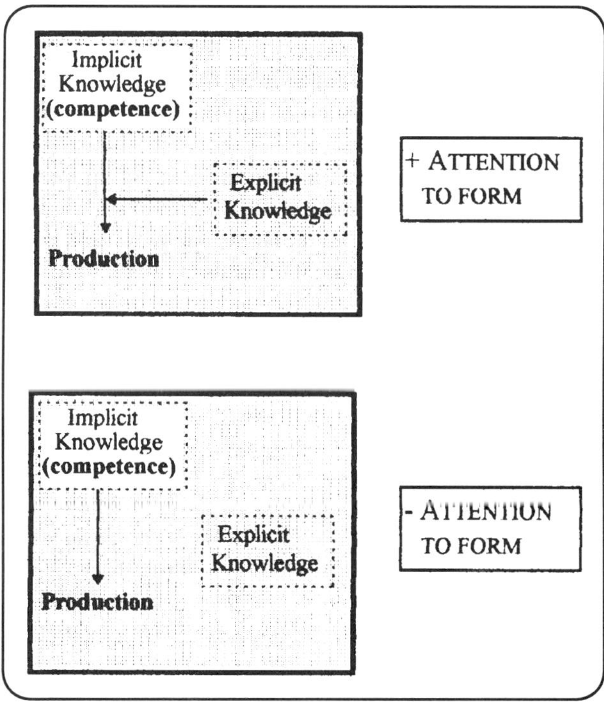

the competence/performance distinction. This, in turn, prevents such models from forming the basis for a successful theory of SLA. In other words, since the goal of a theory of SLA is to explain abstract, non-contextualized competence, researchers should avoid variable behavior and instead abstract from variable data, since contextual variation is a performance factor (Eckman 1994).

In conclusion, while in the Universal Grammar (UG) perspective variation is a problem that needs to be avoided, for variationists variation is a mechanism for language acquisition. Up to this point, the key term has been *knowledge*. There is a very different approach to language acquisition and variation in L2 production that considers both storage of knowledge and its access. Within this view of processing, four variables intervene, namely, short-term and long-term memory, and controlled and automatic processing of stored information. Variation in L2 production is determined by the interaction of these variables.

Processing approaches to L2 variation. Short-term memory is the subset of long-term memory in a current state of activation (Cowan 1993). It involves temporary activation of neural structures, is the site of controlled processes, is capacity-limited, and is the place where skill development begins and knowledge is encoded into and retrieved from long-term memory (Robinson 1995).

Long-term memory can be further divided into implicit and explicit memory. Implicit memory is inferred from faster and more accurate responses. Contrary to explicit memory, which is accessed by conscious retrieval, implicit memory is unconsciously accessed (Schacter 1989; Schacter, Chiue and Oschner 1993; Squire 1992; Squire and Cohen 1984). According to Paradis (1994), studies in neurophysiological structure of memory based on event potentials and MRIs (magnetic resonance images) indicate that there are concrete physiological distinctions between implicit and explicit memory. Specifically, explicit memory seems to be related to the hippocampal system (Squire, Maral and Press 1990). This evidence has been interpreted by Paradis (1994) as lending support to a modular approach to language learning and production (Shiffrin 1993), which proposes the existence of two sources of unconnected stores of knowledge; each corresponds to a different way of learning, as implied in Krashen's Monitor (1981, 1982).

I agree with Robinson, however, in that "claims of neurophysiological differentiation of two sorts of memory may be true, but do not imply that they are not interactive systems at the level of information processing. And that is what is of relevance here: not whether the store is separate or subparts of one big storage, but whether they interact" (1995: 30). To this I should add when, why, and how they interact. In addition, since explicit and implicit memory differ in the way their contents are accessed, it is also necessary to discuss access mechanisms.

Originally, controlled and automatic processes were conceived as a dichotomy (Shiffrin and Schneider 1977). However, they are better understood as two ends of a continuum (Robinson 1995). Automatic processing is fast and efficient, does not require effort, is not limited by short-term or attentional capacities, is not under subject control, and cannot be consciously accessed. In contrast, controlled processes are slow, inefficient, and require effort. They are accessible to introspection and can be controlled by the subject. Most importantly, they are limited by short-term memory capacity (Schmidt 1992). Within this view, L2 learning is parallel to automatization (Levelt 1977; McLaughlin et al. 1983).

Bley-Vroman and Chaudron (1994) assume that in the native speaker the language processor works automatically with little space taken up in short-term memory. Schmidt defines fluent speech as automatic and not requiring much attention or effort and as "the reflection of mechanisms of speech planning and speech production that function easily and effectively" (Schmidt 1990). However, for non-fluent L2 speakers who have not automatized language processes, processing places a load on short term, working memory, where controlled processes take place.

Speaking is an example of a hierarchical task structure, a complex activity that requires processing at many different levels more or less simultaneously (Levelt 1989). Levelt's monolingual model of speech production is applied in De Boot (1992) to bilingual production, thus providing a framework for conceptualizing the types of performance limitations that might be involved in L2 production. Levelt (1989) identified several stages in the processing chain, from intention to articulation. First, the message is generated by conceptualizing a preverbal message. Then, the message is processed by a formulator, which identifies lexical representations and uses these to initiate grammatical encoding and generate surface structure. An assumption the model makes is that in order for the speech production system to operate incrementally different processors must be able to operate automatically without sharing attentional resources. In this way, the output of the conceptualizer is processed online as it is generated. When the message is complex, however, the conceptualizer and the formulator interfere with each other because language learners—L1 and L2—have not yet automatized processing.

It is better to consider components of second-language production rather than the task as a whole as automatic or non-automatic. Each component of the structure requires more or less work depending on its degree of automatization. The more well-learned a subcomponent is, the less effort and processing time are required for its execution. Certain aspects of speaking may become automatic (phonological encoding) while others remain non-automatic (conceptual processing). Not everything that is learned shows up in performance. Situational demands and the cognitive demands of the task affect the likelihood that a new skill will be exhibited.

In lay terms, the better learned a grammatical rule is, the higher the likelihood of finding it stored in long-term, implicit memory, and the more automatized its processing will be. That the same rule used more or less accurately appears in a learner's production will depend on whether it is stored, where it is stored (implicit or explicit memory), and the degree to which its processing has been automatized.

Each of these approaches to language acquisition has developed its own methodologies. Therefore, when it comes to developing tasks to elicit language behavior, the Chomskyan and the variationist will approach the task in different ways. Chomskyans avoid the use of explicit knowledge, and design tasks with a focus on content, or avoid production altogether. Variationists manipulate attention. Both approaches, however, have their limitations.

The problem of variation in SLA research.

Research that manipulates the implicit/explicit distinction. In Chomskyan linguistics, "what is acquired is an implicit, unconscious mental grammar that is most clearly reflected in learners' intuitions about sentences, less directly in learner performance, and least directly in learners' conscious beliefs and statements about their use of language" (Schmidt 1990). There are two problems in applying this perspective to SLA research. One problem is that it is difficult to elicit syntactic structures (as opposed to examples of phonological variation). Another problem is that a parameter that is not violated in a speaker's production cannot be ascribed to a constraint in the learner's grammar. The interest of Chomskyan linguists lies in the determination of a context-independent set of abstract rules, i.e. underlying competence. For practical and theoretical reasons, then, performance data is not of interest to linguists working within this theory; they overwhelmingly prefer grammaticality judgments, followed by elicited imitations and act-out tasks.

The validity of grammaticality judgments has been challenged: Goss, Zhang and Lantolf (1994) suggest that learners rely on translation and pedagogical rules rather than on linguistic knowledge to determine the grammaticality of sentences in their L2. That something other than implicit underlying knowledge is used in grammaticality judgments has been suggested in Birdsong (1989), Christie and Lantolf (1992), Ellis 1989, Martohardjono (1993), and Nagata (1988). Gass (1994) suggests that learners' grammaticality judgments vary in a systematic way: Judgments become more reliable the higher one moves on the accessibility hierarchy (of relative sentences). And Sanz (in press) shows that results from grammaticality judgments are incompatible with results from performance data by the same learners.

As often happens in SLA, grammaticality judgments have been borrowed from research on native varieties. Native competence, at least for speakers of standard varieties, is quite stable, and their grammaticality judgments are reliable. SLA researchers do not have that recourse, since L2 grammaticality judgments are highly variable, as shown by Ellis (1991). Therefore, the choice, according to Bayley (1994), is not between studying a presumably invariant competence and variable performance, but between testing theories on variable grammaticality judgments and testing them on variable performance. Variation is unavoidable.

Schwartz (1993) also proposes the existence of two sources of knowledge: competence and Learned Linguistic Knowledge (LLK), either of which can be reflected in L2 performance. In the second case, performance is called Learned Linguistic Behavior (LLB). Schwartz (1993) is really about what type of information feeds the acquisitional system, and she proposes that only certain types of information feed competence. However, she necessarily relies on performance in order to investigate what is part of the acquired system. What needs to be emphasized is that at no point does Schwartz provide any criteria to differentiate between both types of linguistic behavior (true performance and LLB). Deciding what type of knowledge has been used is made in view of the results obtained. According to Schwartz, "true" performance reflects Universal Grammar (UG), while LLB transgresses UG rules, for example, when learners take "written tests that allow the L2ers time to 'think'" (1993: 15). This is an example of the post-hoc explanation for variability in production that has been commonly used. By relying on this solution, researchers fall into circular reasoning that is impossible to validate or invalidate.

This limitation is shared by those experimental studies that incorporate tasks designed to avoid the Monitor. In order to use the Monitor the learner needs to have time to focus on form and know the rule. However, in view of the problems encountered by studies that use rule explicitation, we should ask: What does it mean "to know the rule"? What is the independent measure of "focusing on form/focusing on content"? Moreover, it has been argued that a simple binary distinction, +/- Monitor, is inadequate to handle the complex, but systematic, variability found in the studies reviewed (Tarone 1985). The most significant problem with the Monitor Model for the development of reliable, informative elicitation tasks is that this approach leaves us only with post-hoc explanations to account for the variability we might encounter. It does not provide us with independent measures, criteria that we can preset and around which we can design our tasks.

Manipulation of variable competence. Variationists attribute variation to differences in task and discourse context. Variation studies (Larsen-Freeman 1975; Dickerson 1975, 1977; Tarone 1985, 1988, among many others) have used a multiplicity of tasks to elicit variable production and determine the contexts that constrain variation. In this research, the means of explaining variation is the manipulation of one variable in the task design, namely focus of attention, with emphasis either on form or content. For example, reading a list of words elicits a more careful style than talking about your most frightening experience. However, variationists have underestimated the problems of empirically operationalizing the concept of attention (Romaine 1984; Rampton 1987).

The role of attention as a key variable in production processes. The one construct that unifies Chomskyan, variationist, and processing approaches to SLA research methodology is attention. For Gregg (1990), Krashen (1981, 1982) and Schwartz (1993), when the learner focuses her attention on form rather than content, conscious access to explicit knowledge takes place, thus contaminating "true" performance. Variationists, rather than defending a dual +/- attention to form, view attention as a matter of degree that determines the use of a range of styles, from the most formal to the vernacular. That these studies all rely on attention to explain variation imposes the same limitations in all of them: We do not really know what the L2 learner monitors (i.e. pays attention to), since it is very hard to verify. In fact, how do we know that the subject is paying more attention to form in one task than in another? What is it in the task that causes the learner to vary the focus of attention? (Bialystok and Sharwood-Smith 1985).

The help needed from research in cognitive psychology is not readily available. Although a significant number of publications on the role of attention in input processing and learning have appeared recently (the 1994 issue of *AILA Review*; Robinson 1996; Schmidt 1995; Tomlin and Villa 1994), not much has been said about attention as it relates to output (except for important studies such as those in Dechert and Raupach 1980). We all agree that the concept of attention as it stands today is difficult to operationalize and needs a "fine-grained analysis" (Tomlin and Villa 1994).

It is fairly well accepted now that it is not just attention paid to form, but the attentional demands of other aspects of the task that must be taken into account, such as the amount of information that has to be stored in short-term memory (Sato 1985; Makoni 1992). A solution to the problem of variation in research methodology and the operationalization of the concept of attention in production is to manipulate processing demands. Within a processing approach, "the level of attentional awareness during retrieval is a function of task demands and automatic processes, which jointly determine access to a single long-term memory store" (Robinson 1995).

An experimental study that manipulates production processes. Although never tested, it has been claimed in SLA that the processing requirements made when producing in the oral mode are higher than in the written mode (Bialystok 1982) because of the difference in the amount of time needed for the processor to work. Moreover, the amount of production required by the task is proposed here as a way of manipulating the amount of space left in short-term memory and ultimately of operationalizing the continuum with the endpoints "automatic" and "control." As longer strings of language are produced and more information needs to be conveyed, the degree of control over speech gradually reduces. As short-term memory is occupied by the content that needs to be expressed, less space is left for use by controlled processes. Accuracy increases as the requirements in terms of amount of production decrease. Sanz (1994) investigates different cognitive demands placed on the processor by assessment production tasks.

Several assessment instruments were designed using the criteria of amount and mode of production manipulating L2 learners' processing demands. These criteria were chosen as a way of operationalizing the continuum between controlled and automatic processes in second language production.

A total of forty-four second-year learners of Spanish were divided into an experimental and a control group. The experimental group was exposed to two days of instructional treatment, the effects of which were measured using a pre-test/post-test design. Both the pre- and post-tests consisted of one interpretation task and three production tasks, which differed in the amount of production they required.

The first task was a sentence completion task, and its design is based on VanPatten and Cadierno (1993). It provides two consecutive figures as context that need to be described by two connected sentences. One sentence that describes the first picture is given, and the subject must produce a second sentence to describe the second picture. The second task is a Structured Interview Task, and it engages the subject in a dialogue that describes a story. The third task is named Video Narration and is a storytelling activity through which the subject is required to produce a series of connected utterances that describe a story previously watched on videotape.[2]

All subjects performed all tasks in both the written and oral modes. The written data were gathered in the classroom and the oral data in the Language Learning Laboratory, where the subjects were taken as a class, sitting at individual booths.

The research questions that motivated this study are:

1. Can the amount of production required by the task predict grammatical accuracy in the speech elicited? and
2. Can the mode in which a task is performed predict grammatical accuracy?

---

[2]Four video clips were filmed, each representing a short story. The stories and the instructions have special characteristics which were determined by the results of various pilot tests.

In a nutshell, the results show that the target item, in this case Object-Pronoun-Verb (OproV) sentences, was produced more accurately in the written mode by both the experimental and the control groups in all tests. Likewise, the main effect for Task indicates that all subjects in both the control and experimental groups produced OproV sentences more accurately when completing sentences than when retelling a story. These patterns were not altered after explicit classroom instruction.

These results show that by gradually increasing the amount of content that needs to be stored in short-term memory, there is less space available for the use of controlled processes. Thus, only knowledge that has been automatized can be used for production. Furthermore, they show that producing in the oral mode makes more demands on production processes. These results provide evidence supporting Skehan (1987), where production is seen as the result of a constant trade-off between competing demands on memory and control mechanisms. When memory space is taken up by planning operations, such as discourse content or organization, learners can only access those resources over which they have automatic control (Atkinson and Shiffrin 1968). The use of controlled and automatic processes in language production seems to depend at least on two factors: the time the processor is given and the amount of space there is left in short-term memory.

We need to return to Levelt's (1989) model of speech production. For Levelt, speaking is an example of a complex hierarchical task that requires processing at many different levels, more or less simultaneously. First, a preverbal message is conceptualized before being processed by a formulator, which identifies lexical representations and uses these to initiate grammatical encoding and generate surface structure. An assumption that the model makes is that the speech production system operates incrementally, so that the output of the conceptualizer is processed online as it is generated.

Bishop (1994) suggests that one reason why production varies is the slow pace of the system. Non-automatic, controlled processes are slower than automatic processes. Using the available message fragments, the grammatical encoder generates surface structures online. Because processing has not been automatized in language learners, the encoder works too slowly and finds it difficult to keep up with the incoming message fragments. By increasing the complexity of the message, we increase the amount of material the formulator has to process, making it lag behind. The result is an increase in the number of incomplete surface structures, with morphemes, rather than lexical items, missing. After all, lexical items have more communicative value (i.e. they carry more meaning) than grammatical morphemes (Brandsdorfer 1991). Moreover, as suggested by Lapointe (1985), inflected words, such as clitics, are harder to retrieve from the lexicon than stems. When the system is overloaded, the chance of an inflected form being deleted from the phonetic plan at the time of encoding is higher.

Conclusion. A theory of SLA is one about all the processes that intervene in the acquisition of a second language, from input processing, to rule formation, to processing rules for language use. Within this view, variation is more than just that annoying, unavoidable "thing" that stands between us and our goal. Variation is intrinsic to the acquisition of a language; it is the external sign of internal processes becoming automatized. In lay terms, variation occurs because the language is still being learned.

The issue of variation in research methodology is important. We have seen that production varies according to the cognitive requirements of a task. The type of task implemented in the design of an empirical study will determine the type of language elicited and, consequently, its results and conclusions. Because studies use different tasks, their authors arrive at different conclusions. This situation makes it difficult for scholars to draw generalizations on important issues in SLA, such as the effects of instruction (Larsen-Freeman and Long 1991).

It is also claimed here that the lack of criteria to differentiate among tasks and their demands on the learners' production abilities has led to the use of post-hoc explanations, and these have created theoretical and methodological problems. Tasks have traditionally been classified under the general heading of communicative and controlled, depending on the amount of attention required to perform them. But the concept of task and the terms that qualify it —communicative and controlled—hide a bundle of unanalyzed variables, such as the amount of time allowed to perform the task, the mode in which they are performed—oral or written—the amount of context provided, and the length of the utterance. Although all empirical studies use eliciting tasks, there is none that isolates any of the variables mentioned. The study reported here has attempted to do precisely that: isolate two variables—mode and amount of production—to see whether they could be used to manipulate the L2 speaker's processing capabilities and implement them as criteria along which to design elicitation tasks.

Interest in issues related to research methodology in SLA, and in particular the investigation of the role of elicitation tasks, has recently motivated other authors such as Shook (1994) and Leow (1993, 1994) to contribute studies in the field of L2 reading. Nevertheless, more research is needed. Crookes (1991) states that the study of second-language competence has received most of the attention in SLA to the detriment of research into the processing of that knowledge. And within the field, studies of second-language comprehension by far outnumber studies of L2 production. Interesting new approaches include learner introspection. Learners cannot introspect about the microstructure of automatic processes, but can say what the focus of their attention is while producing, and this can be assumed to be consciousness of a lack of choice points in the flow of action (Baars 1988). Pauses can also be used as data. L1 researchers agree that the alternation of pauses and speech reflect an alternation between phases in which hesitation is the result of preoccupation with macroplanning while stretches of fluent speech with little pausing reflect skilled microplanning that does not require much attention. Adapting these ideas to L2, Dechert and Raupach (1980) conclude that nonfluent learners' pauses, false starts, and other signs of hesitation reflect the need to focus attention on the lower levels of planning, whereas fluent learners act more like native speakers in exhibiting hesitation as result of macroplanning. These are just two of several interesting new venues for the study of L2 production which certainly deserve attention, since they can provide a solution to the "problem" of L2 variation.

References

Adamson, H.D. 1988. *Variation theory and second language acquisition.* Washington, D.C.: Georgetown University Press.

Atkinson, R. and Shiffrin, R.M. 1968. "Human memory: a proposed system and its control processes." In K. Spence (ed.), *The psychology of learning and motivation, Volume 2.* New York: Academic Press. 89–195.

Baars, B.J. 1988. *A cognitive theory of consciousness.* Cambridge: Cambridge University Press.

Bayley, R. 1994. "Interlanguage variation and the quantitative paradigm: Past-tense marking in Chinese-English." In E. Tarone, S. Gass, and A. Cohen (eds.), *Research methodology in second language acquisition.* Hillsdale, N.J.: Lawrence Erlbaum. 159–184.

Beebe, L.M. and J. Zuengler. 1983. "Accommodation theory: An explanation for style shifting in second language dialects." In N. Wolfson, E. Judd, and E. Hatch (eds.), *Sociolinguistics and language acquisition.* Rowley, Massachusetts: Newbury House. 195–213.

Bialystok, E. 1982. "On the relationship between knowing and using linguistic forms." *Applied Linguistics.* 3(3): 181–206.

Bialystok, E. and M.S. Smith. 1985. "Interlanguage is not a state of mind." *Applied Linguistics.* 6 (2): 101–117.

Birdsong, D. 1989. *Metalinguistic performance and interlanguage competence.* Berlin: Spinger Verlag.

Bishop, D.V.M. 1994. "Grammatical errors in specific language impairment: Competence or performance limitations?" *Applied Psycholinguistics* 15: 507–550.

Bley-Vroman, R. and Chaudron, C. 1994. "Elicited imitation as a measure of second-language competence." In E. Tarone, S. Gass, and A. Cohen (eds.), *Research methodology in second language acquisition.* Hillsdale, N.J.: Lawrence Erlbaum. 245–262.

Bransdorfer, R. 1991. "Communicative value and linguistic knowledge in second language oral input processing." Unpublished Doctoral Thesis, The University of Illinois at Urbana-Champaign.

Christie, K. and J.P. Lantolf. 1992. "The ontological status of learner grammaticality judgments in UG approaches to L2 acquisition." *Rassegna Italiana de Linguistica Applicata* 14(3): 31–52.

Cowan, N. 1993. "Activation, attention, and short-term memory." *Memory and Cognition* 21: 162–167.

Crookes, G. 1991. "Second language speech production research: A methodologically-oriented overview." *Studies in Second Language Acquisition* 13: 113–132.

De Bot, K. 1992. "A bilingual production model: Levelt's 'Speaking' model adapted." *Applied Linguistics* 13 (1): 1–24.

Dechert, H.W. and M. Raupach (eds.). 1980. *Towards a cross-linguistic assessment of speech production*. Frankfurt: Lang.

Dickerson, L. 1975. "The learner's interlanguage as a system of variable rules." *TESOL Quarterly* 9(4): 401-407.

Dickerson, L. and W. Dickerson. 1977. "Interlanguage phonology: Current research and future directions. The notions of simplification, interlanguages and pidgins." *Actes du 5ème Colloque de Linguistique Appliqué de Neufchatel*. Paris: AIMAD/Didier.

Eckman, F. 1994. "The competence-performance issue in SLA theory: A debate." In E. Tarone, S. Gass, and A. Cohen (eds.), *Research methodology in second language acquisition*. Hillsdale, N.J.: Lawrence Erlbaum. 3-16.

Eisenstein, M. and R. Starbuck. 1989. "The effect of emotional investment on L2 production." In S. Gass, C. Madden, D. Preston and L. Selinker (eds.), *Variation in SLA, Volume II*. Clevedon, U.K.: Multilingual Matters.

Ellis, R. 1989. "Sources of intra-learner variability in language use and their relationship to second language acquisition." In S. Gass, C. Madden, D.R. Preston, and L. Selinker (eds.), *Variation in SLA, Volume II*. Clevedon, U.K.: Multilingual Matters.

Ellis, R. 1990. "A response to Gregg." *Applied Linguistics* 6: 118-131.

Ellis, R. 1991. "Grammaticality judgments and second language acquisition." *Studies in Second Language Acquisition* 13: 161-186.

Gass, S. 1994. "The reliability of second-language grammaticality judgments." In E. Tarone, S. Gass, and A. Cohen (eds.), *Research methodology in second language acquisition*. Hillsdale, N.J.: Lawrence Erlbaum. 303-322.

Goss, N., Y. Zhang, and J.P. Lantolf. 1994. "Two heads may be better than one: Mental activity in second-language grammaticality judgments." In E. Tarone, S. Gass, and A. Cohen (eds.), *Research methodology in second language acquisition*. Hillsdale, N.J.: Lawrence Erlbaum. 263-282.

Gregg, K. 1990. The variable competence model of SLA and why it isn't. *Applied Linguistics* 11: 365-383.

Hulstjin, J.H. and W. Hulstjin. 1984. "Grammatical errors as a function of processing constraints and explicit knowledge." *Language Learning* 34(1): 23-43.

Krashen, S. 1981. *Second language acquisition and second language learning*. Oxford: Pergamon.

Krashen, S. 1982. *Principles and practice in second language acquisition*. Oxford: Pergamon.

Labov, W. 1972. *Sociolinguistic patterns*. Philadelphia: University of Pennsylvania Press.

Lapointe, S.G. 1985. "A theory of verb form use in the speech of agrammatic aphasics." *Brain and Language* 24: 100-155.

Larsen-Freeman, D. 1975. "The acquisition of grammatical morphemes by adult ESL students." *TESOL Quarterly* 9(4): 409-430.

Leow, R.P. 1993. "To simplify or not to simplify: A look at intake." *Studies in second language acquisition* 15(3): 336-356.

Leow, R.P. 1995. "Modality and intake in SLA." *Studies in Second Language Acquisition* 17(1): 79-89.

Levelt, W.J.M. 1977. "Skill theory and language teaching." *Studies in Second language Acquisition* 1: 53-70.

Levelt, W.J.M. 1989. *Speaking: From intention to articulation*. Cambridge, Massachusetts: The M.I.T. Press.

Makoni, S.B. 1992. "Conditions on transfer: A connectionist approach." *Issues in Applied Linguistics* 3(1): 69-90.

Martohardjono, G. 1993. "Movement constraints on the acquisition of Wh questions." Unpublished Doctoral Dissertation, Cornell University, Ithaca, N.Y.

McLaughlin, B., T. Rossman, and B. McLeod. 1983. "Second language learning: An information-processing perspective." *Language Learning* 33(2): 135-158.

Nagata, H. 1988. "The relativity of linguistic intuition: The effect of repetition on grammaticality judgments." *Journal of Psycholinguistic Research* 17: 205–214.

Paradis, M. 1994. "Neurolinguistic aspects of implicit and explicit memory: Implications for bilingualism and SLA." In N. Ellis (ed.), *Implicit and explicit learning of languages*. London: Academic Press. 393–419.

Preston, D.R. 1989. *Sociolinguistics and second language acquisition*. Oxford: Basil Blackwell.

Rampton, B. 1987. "Stylistic variability and not speaking normal English: Some post-Labovian approaches and their implications for the study of interlanguage." In R. Ellis (ed.), *Second language acquisition in context*. Englewood Ciffs, N.J.: Prentice Hall. 47–59.

Robinson, P. 1995. "Attention, memory and the 'Noticing' Hypothesis." *Language Learning* 45(2): 283–331.

Romaine, S. 1984. *The language of children and adolescents*. Oxford: Basil Blackwell.

Sanz, C. 1994. "Task, mode and the effects of input-based explicit instruction." Unpublished Doctoral Dissertation, University of Illinois at Urbana-Champaign.

Sanz, C. in press. "Issues in SLA research methodology: Production processes and variability". In W.R. Glass, and A.T. Pérez-Lerroux (eds), *L1 and L2 acquisition of Spanish*.

Sato, C. 1985. "Task variation in interlanguage phonology." In S. Gass (ed.), *Input in second language acquisition*. Rowley, Massachusetts: Newbury House. 181–196.

Schacter, D., P. Chiue, and K. Ochsner. 1993. "Implicit memory: A selective review." *Annual Review of Neuroscience* 16: 159–182.

Schacter, D. L. 1989. "On the relation between memory and consciousness: Dissociable interactions and conscious experience." In H.L. Roediger and F.I. Craik (eds.), *Varieties of memory and consciousness*. Hillsdale, N.J.: Lawrence Erlbaum. 355–389.

Schmidt, R. 1990. "The role of consciousness in second language learning." *Applied Linguistics* 11: 129–158.

Schmidt, R. 1992. "Psychological mechanisms underlying second language fluency." *Studies in Second Language Acquisition* 14: 357–386.

Schmidt, R. 1995. *Attention and Awareness in Foreign Language Learning. Technical Report # 9.* Honolulu: University of Hawai'i, Second Language Teaching and Curriculum Center.

Schwartz, B. 1993. "On explicit and negative evidence affecting and effecting competence and performance." *Studies in Second Language Acquisition* 15: 147–163.

Shiffrin, R.M. and W. Schneider. 1977. "Controlled and automatic human information processing II: Perceptual learning, automatic attending, and a general theory." *Psychological Review* 84: 127–190.

Shiffrin, R.M. 1993. "Short-term memory: A brief commentary." *Memory and Cognition* 21: 193–197.

Shook, D. 1994. "FL/L2 reading, grammatical information, and the input-to-intake phenomenon." *Applied Language Learning* 5(2): 57–95.

Squire, L. 1992. "Declarative and nondeclarative memory: Multiple brain systems supporting learning and memory." *Journal of Cognitive Neuroscience* 4: 232–243.

Squire, L., D. Amaral, and G. Press. 1990. "Magnetic resonance imaging measurements of hippocampal formation and mammillary nuclei distinguish medial temporal lobe and diencephalic amnesia." *Journal of Neuroscience* 10: 3106–3117.

Squire, L. and N. Cohen. 1984. "Human memory and amnesia." In J. McGaugh, G. Lynch, and N. Weinberger (eds.), *Proceedings of the conference on the neurobiology of learning and memory*. New York: Guildford Press. 3–64.

Tarone, E. 1985. "Variability in interlanguage use: A study of style-shifting in morphology and syntax." *Language Learning* 35: 373–404.

Tarone, E. 1988. *Variation in interlanguage*. Baltimore/London: Edward Arnold.

Tarone, E. 1990. "On variation in iterlanguage: A response to Gregg." *Applied Linguistics* 11: 392–399.

Tarone, E., S. Gass, and A. Cohen. *Research methodology in second language acquisition.* Hillsdale, N.J.: Lawrence Erlbaum.

Tomlin, R.S. and V. Villa. 1994. "Attention in cognitive science and second language acquisition." *Studies in Second Language Acquisition* 16: 183–203.

VanPatten, B. and T. Cadierno. 1993. "Explicit instruction and input processing." *Studies in Second Language Acquisition* 15: 225–244.

Wode, H. 1989. "Maturational changes of language acquisitional abilities." In S. Gass, C. Madden, D. Preston, and L. Selinker (eds.), *Variation in Second Language Acquisition. Volume II.* Clevedon, U.K.: Multilingual Matters. 176–186.

Endangered dialects: Sociolinguistic opportunity and obligation[1]

Walt Wolfram
North Carolina State University

1. Introduction. Recent symposia and collections of essays about the state of the world's languages (Dorian 1989; Hale et al. 1992; Robins and Uhlenbeck 1991) speak poignantly to the language endangerment epidemic. Ominous predictions of language death by linguists and demographers estimate that from 50 to 90 percent of the world's languages may become extinct within the next century. Understandably, linguists feel a compelling sense of urgency about the status of a majority of the world's languages.

At the same time, linguists rarely mention endangered dialects of a "safe" language—that is, particular varieties of a language whose unique status is threatened by other, encroaching varieties of the same language rather than other languages. Although the literature on language death includes examples of endangered varieties of safe languages (e.g. King 1989; Tsitsipis 1989), these cases invariably involve encroachment by different languages—not by different varieties of the same language. Operationally, language death and language endangerment seem to be defined by bilingual contact situations.

Many observers, including language scholars and lay people alike, may think that dialect death is not nearly as significant as the death of an entire language, but this is not necessarily the case. To say that dialect loss is not as important as language loss is like saying that we should be vitally concerned with the preservation of the general species *canis familiaris*, or dogs, but not worried about particular breeds of dogs. After all, dogs come in so many breeds and may be mixed in so many different ways that the preservation of a particular breed of dog is not very important. But suppose our options for dogs were reduced to Great Danes when our favorite dog—and the only kind of dog we had ever known in our home—was a miniature Pekinese?

---

[1] This analysis is based upon research supported by the National Science Foundation Grant No. SBR-93-19577, National Endowment for the Humanities Grant No. RO-22749, and the William C. Friday Endowment at North Carolina State University. Thanks to Natalie Schilling-Estes for the provision of data on performance style and for comments on an earlier draft of the manuscript. Thanks also to Dennis Preston for his assistance in conducting the trinomial analysis of VARBRUL reported here.

Arbitrary decisions about the inclusion and exclusion of language varieties in the endangerment canon do not seem appropriate given the significance of all types of linguistic diversity. On a scientific level, dialect diversity may be just as essential for examining the delicate balance between universality and diversity in language as the diversity found from language to language. Furthermore, dialects of a language are not detached objects devoid of social meaning. They can carry just as much social meaning as entire languages. So there is both a humanistic and a scientific basis for maintaining that dialect death in a bidialectal context should be a matter of concern—for linguists, dialectologists, and community residents who stand to lose an indigenous dialect.

In several recent articles, we (Wolfram and Schilling-Estes 1995, forthcoming), have argued that the exclusion of moribund dialects threatened by encroaching varieties of "healthy" or safe varieties of the same language have been unjustifiably excluded from the language endangerment canon. We maintain that this exclusion is based on a questionable set of assumptions about language variation, including the following:

(1) That the distinction between language and dialect is sufficiently well defined and discrete to make principled decisions about which varieties of language should and should not be included in the endangerment canon;
(2) That the death of a language variety in a bilingual context is a loss more significant than the death of a language variety in a bidialectal one;
(3) That intra-language variation is less significant than inter-language variation for understanding the interplay of diversity and universality in the organization of language;
(4) That intra-language dialect loss is less significant for developing models of language change and attrition than language loss in inter-language contexts; and
(5) That the loss of cultural identity and intellectual diversity involved in dialect loss is not nearly as significant as that involved in the loss of a language.

The empirical basis for our challenge to these assumptions comes from our research of post-insular dialect situations on the Outer Banks of North Carolina, particularly the eroding dialect found among the current generation of *ancestral islanders* (i.e. residents who have lived on the island for at least three generations) in Ocracoke. Ocracoke is a barrier island located off of the coast of North Carolina, approximately 14 miles long and less than a mile wide at its widest point. Most of the original settlers on Ocracoke in the early 1700's were from the Southwest and Southeast of England, with intermediate stops in the Maryland and Virginia colonies. Ocracokers were isolated from the mainland

South for a couple of centuries, not only geographically and economically but also socially.

Shortly after World War II, the longstanding isolation of Ocracoke Island came to an end as a state-run ferry service was instituted. Ocracoke now began to host ever-increasing numbers of tourists and new residents from the mainland. Today, Ocracoke is home to only about 200–250 ancestral islanders. This represents less than half the year-round population and less than one-tenth of the population on a typical day during the summer tourist season. In addition, the island economy has been converted from one largely independent of mainlanders to one almost wholly dependent on outsiders. With the breakdown of economic and geographic barriers separating Ocracoke from the mainland has come a corresponding breakdown in social barriers and an erosion of the traditional, once-distinct dialect. Today, we consider the traditional dialect moribund. That is, the current generation of ancestral islanders does not routinely acquire the traditional Ocracoke English variety, or "brogue" as it is referred to by islanders.

2. Sociolinguistic opportunity. As with any endangered dialect situation, we consider the documentation of the eroding Ocracoke brogue essential for the language history of English. Dialectology has typically been sensitive to the descriptive motivation for capturing obsolescing forms, as dialectologists realize that relic structures not found in mainstream standard varieties may be gone forever unless they are documented. Unlike the theoretical models which attempt to explain such forms, the descriptive documentation of language diversity has a timeless dimension to it. If we can broaden the observed pool of obsolescing structures, we can make a lasting contribution to the data base that must invariably feed the continuing development of linguistic science.

The need to document obsolescing structures and language varieties, however, goes beyond an observational-descriptive motivation. Such documentation also seems essential for both theoretical and applied concerns within linguistics. As we consider in Section 3 below, the examination of the end points of language change, as found in dialect attrition, can inform our models of language variation and change in important ways. Furthermore, given the interplay between universality and diversity in language, a full range of diverse structures in language needs to be chronicled in order to arrive at a valid account of the interaction of language principles and language parameters. The data from intra-language variation found in obsolescing forms may, in fact, prove valuable for examining templates of universal language. For example, Trudgill and Chambers (1991: 294), citing an empirical case of nonstandard syntax variation in Wessex English that challenges the universal Inflectional Phrase (IP) template (Ihalainen 1991), observe that familiarity with dialect variation "could potentially sharpen theoretical arguments as much as do imported 'exotica' from Kenyarwanda or Ponapean." Similarly, the current investigation of cross-clausal negative concord by Martin (1992, 1996)—a relatively rare and perhaps obsolescing process in some vernacular varieties of English—challenges the assumed configuration of the NegP and the nature of syntactic chains in universal grammar. So there is an essential theoretical rationale for examining the obsolescing forms of language as well.

But the motivation for examining moribund language varieties and obsolescing forms does not end with descriptive and theoretical opportunity. As language scholars, we are indebted to the communities and speakers who provide us the data for our research. Dying language varieties should provide us a unique opportunity to work with communities to document, preserve, and promote an appreciation for language history and heritage. To be quite honest, one of the dimensions of dialect study that has always made it a worthwhile endeavor for me is the fact that it offers the possibility of combining a commitment to the objective description of linguistic data with a concern for social and educational issues that attend language diversity. Happily, researchers have contributed substantively to our understanding of language variation while they have contributed in an important way to several significant social and socioeducational issues over the past several decades (e.g. Labov 1969; 1982; Wolfram 1993b). In the following sections, I hope to demonstrate how sociolinguistic opportunity and obligation go hand-in-hand in the consideration of endangered dialects.

3. Models of language change and moribund dialects. Obsolescing forms and the configurations of eroding structures in dying language varieties seem vital to our understanding of fundamental issues of language change and variation, as well as to the formulation of models describing and explaining such change. Conclusions reached in our study of Ocracoke English, for example, have led us to question some basic assumptions about language change and language variation. One is the model of change assumed in language attrition studies, in particular, the "widely shared intuition" (Hill 1989: 149) that the processes of change in language death differ from ordinary change processes primarily in the rapidity with which they occur. Another is the nature of stylistic variation as manifested by semi-speakers' use of a specialized register referred to as the "performance register." Schilling-Estes (forthcoming) shows how the production of an obsolescing vowel in "performance style" challenges our assumptions about the nature of stylistic variation in sociolinguistic inquiry. These insights seize upon the most widely recognized phonological variable of Ocracoke English, the unique Outer Banks production of /ay/ in words like *high* and *tide*. In fact, the production of this diphthong with a backed, raised nucleus which approximates the /oy/ vowel has become such an icon of Outer Banks speech that Outer Banks residents are often referred to as *hoi toiders*.

3.1. On the replacement of obsolescing structures. In many respects, the examination of /ay/ in Ocracoke brings into focus the linguistic complexity of dialect death, as well as the social embedding of phonological change and variation in dialect encroachment. Although the nucleus and glide of /ay/ show considerable phonetic range, there seem to be three competing, socially meaningful options for /ay/ on the Outer Banks of North Carolina. These are:

(1) A unique Outer Bank production with a backed, raised nucleus with a front upglide. It is represented here as [ɔy], but the phonetic quality is typically more like [ʌ ⊢ ᶦ]. This is the classic *hoi toider* variant that has become an emblem of the so-called Outer Banks brogue;
(2) A socially unmarked, low central variant with a front upglide—that is, [*a*ᶦ] (referred to henceforth simply as [*a*y]). This is the variant associated with non-Southern varieties and with standard English; and
(3) An unglided or glide-shortened variant ([a:]), typically occurring with a more fronted nucleus, the classic production associated with Southern varieties of English spoken in the contiguous mainland.

The [ɔy] variant, which is the older, relic form in Ocracoke (Wolfram and Schilling-Estes 1995), is at this point a highly variable production that is quite sensitive to internal linguistic and external social constraints. As a central part of our investigation of [ɔy] in Ocracoke, we conducted a quantitative study of the incidence of [ɔy] and the alternative variants [*a*y] and [a:]. Three different generations of speakers are included in our sample in order to represent an apparent time dimension: older (aged 59–81), middle-aged (aged 35–50), and younger (aged 10–22). This framework should allow us to observe the ways in which the traditional, relic form is receding in the face of external pressures. Both men and women are included for each age group, although in our statistical treatment we only distinguish by sex for middle-aged speakers. For middle-aged men, we distinguish two different groups, referred to here as "poker players" and "non-poker players." The designation "poker players" is a convenient label for members of an exclusive all-male islander group that meets several times a week to play poker. More importantly, this group shows relatively dense, multiplex networks (Milroy 1980) and shared cultural values. These men are typically involved in fishing or other marine-related industries (such as working on the ferry), and they socialize with each other on a regular basis. This group is well-known on the island and includes some of the indigenous leaders. It consists of middle-aged men, but younger initiates sometimes cluster around the fringes of the group. The members of the "poker game network" are united by their strong belief in the positive value of being true islanders, especially as contrasted with the tourists and new residents who increasingly threaten their traditional way of life. This belief is projected in a number of ways, including, as we shall see, the use of the [ɔy] dialect feature.

The relative incidence of the three socially meaningful variants of /ay/ was tabulated on the basis of four different kinds of following environments, using traditional procedures for tabulating linguistic variables in variation studies (Wolfram 1993a). These include (1) a following voiceless obstruent, as in *nice* or *light*; (2) a following voiced obstruent, as in *tide* or *dive*; (3) a following nasal, as in *time* or *nine*; and (4) a following lateral, as in *island* or *mile*.

In Table 1, a summary VARBRUL analysis is given for these three variants (for raw figures and percentages, see Wolfram and Schilling-Estes 1995) for a subgroup of 22 cross-generational speakers, taken from our more exhaustive interview sample of over 70 speakers. The figures are given for each linguistic environment, separated on the basis of different generational/social groups—that is, older speakers, middle-aged poker game network members, middle-aged non-poker-playing men, middle-aged women, and younger speakers. VARBRUL is a probabilistic-based multivariate statistical procedure that shows the relative contributions of different factors to the overall variability of fluctuating forms (Cedergren and Sankoff 1974; Sankoff and Labov 1979; Guy 1993). Factor groups may consist of independent linguistic constraints or external social ones. The weighting values range from 0 to 1. For a binomial application, a factor with a value greater than .5 favors the application of the process or rule whereas a value of less than .5 disfavors its application. The input probability, which is interpreted in the same way, is the likelihood of the rule application apart from the influence of the environmental factors (Fasold 1990: 280; Guy 1993). Since this analysis involved three primary variants, [ɔy], [a:], and [ay], a trinomial analysis was undertaken. In a trinomial analysis, a probability value greater than .333 favors the incidence of the variant, and a value of less than .333 disfavors it. This analysis permits us to examine the patterns of retention for the traditional Ocracoke variant, the encroaching Southern norm, and the non-Southern [*a*y] variant.

The overall figures clearly show that the traditional relic form [ɔy] is receding rapidly among the younger generation of speakers. However, there are also several important patterns that emerge from an examination of the figures in Table 1 indicating that this recession is not taking place unilaterally.

First, consider the constraint ordering for the variable incidence of [ɔy] with respect to the following phonological environment, as indicated by the VARBRUL analysis: *voiced obstruent* > *nasal* > *voiceless obstruent* > *lateral*. That is, a following voiced obstruent is the most favoring environment for the occurrence of [ɔy] as opposed to [*a*y] or [a:], followed by nasal, voiceless obstruent, and lateral.

Table 1. Trinomial VARBRUL Analysis for [ɔy], [a:], and [*a*y]

	VARBRUL Probabilities		
	[ɔy]	[a:]	[*a*y]
Social Factors			
Older	.474	.267	.259
Middle-Poker	.457	.319	.224
Middle-Non-Poker	.360	.271	.369
Middle-Women	.251	.355	.394
Younger	.176	.417	.407
Linguistic Factors			
VL Obstruents	.242	.240	.518
VD Obstruents	.600	.117	.283
Nasals	.344	.428	.229
Laterals	.150	.625	.225
Input Probability	.374	.082	.544

The ordering of constraints on the backing and raising of the nucleus of [ɔy] in Ocracoke is similar to that indicated for the ungliding of [a^{l}] to [a:] in the mainland South (e.g. Bernstein and Gregory 1994; Feagin 1994; Thomas and Bailey 1994), where we find that ungliding is more likely to occur before voiced segments than voiceless ones (e.g., *side* is more likely to unglide than *sight*). The typical constraint pattern for Southern ungliding is: *laterals* > *nasals* > *voiced obstruents* > *voiceless obstruents*. Both of these vowels qualify as peripheral vowels in Labov's (1994) essential distinction between peripheral and non-peripheral vowels, so it stands to reason that they would share constraint hierarchies in their systematic variability.

It is not surprising that Southern ungliding in Ocracoke is starting to make inroads, but the patterning of this encroaching norm is not what we might predict based on our knowledge of the structured variability of Southern ungliding. Table 1 shows a somewhat surprising constraint ordering for incipient ungliding in this variety. We would expect, as indicated in the data, that incipient ungliding is starting to make inroads before nasal and lateral segments, since these are favorable environments for ungliding. However, it is surprising that ungliding is more highly favored before voiceless obstruents than voiced obstruents. The ordering of constraints on the ungliding of [a:] in Ocracoke is: *lateral > nasal > voiceless obstruents > voiced obstruents*. We thus have an apparent linguistic anomaly in the orderly progression of change and replacement.

While Southern ungliding in Ocracoke is promoted before laterals and nasals, it is clearly being resisted where the [ɔy] associated with the traditional Ocracoke brogue is most strongly entrenched—before voiced obstruents. There is virtually no ungliding for any of our speakers before voiced obstruents. This constraint ordering—that is, the voiceless environment favoring ungliding over the voiced environment—does not make sense in terms of a natural sonorancy hierarchy and does not conform to our expectations regarding constraints which affect peripheral vowels like the unglided [a:].

There is a further irregularity which relates to the social distribution of these variants. We might expect that the incidence of the traditional Ocracoke [ɔy] will steadily decline with decreasing age, as islanders come into increasing contact with surrounding language varieties. However, the middle-aged poker-playing men and older speakers in our sample show no significant difference in the use of [ɔy], unlike the middle-aged non-poker-playing men and middle-aged women, who show a significant reduction in their [ɔy] usage. Does this indicate a reversal of—or at least resistance to—a change in progress on the island toward reduced [ɔy] usage? The incidence of [ɔy] among middle aged speakers who are not members of the poker game network, middle-aged women, and the youngest speakers shows that the maintained incidence of the [ɔy] variant by the poker players is not a true dialect reversal. The non-poker-playing age cohorts and younger speakers show reduced frequency levels for the traditional *hoi toider* variant compared with both older speakers and middle-aged poker players. In fact, if we restricted our tabulations to speakers aged 16 and under, we would find only vestiges of the [ɔy] production (less than 10% of all /ay/ tokens are realized with [ɔy]), showing how rapidly this form is fading.

The pattern of [ɔy] production by the middle-aged poker players suggests that the projection of the traditional vowel is a temporary maintenance of the traditional island variant, apparently taking place before giving way to external norms. This temporary revitalization in a declining variant is highly reminiscent of the situation Labov observed for centralized /ay/ and /aw/ in his classic study of Martha's Vineyard (1963). However, Labov reported that the dramatic rise in receding forms he observed among ancestral islanders who strongly identified with traditional island ways of life represented a permanent reversal of a change in progress. In the Ocracoke case, the maintenance of the traditional variant represents a sort of dialectal last gasp before the [ɔy] variant dies.

It is noteworthy that the traditional Outer Banks [ɔy] is maintained at a high level in the speech of Ocracoke poker players even as the Southern variant is added. The middle-aged poker players rank higher on the Southern [a:] index than both older speakers and their middle-aged non-poker-playing male cohorts, although middle-aged females and younger speakers outrank them in their use of [a:]. In a somewhat ironic way, these men are projecting island identity by mixing traditional vernacular variants with encroaching Southern vernacular variants. The selective, additive pattern uncovered with /ay/ seems to be confirmed by other emerging patterns we have observed in Ocracoke speech which show that speakers may add vernacular features from surrounding dialects to their speech, at the same time that they maintain a select group of some distinct island traits, in order to maximize the projection of island identity via vernacularity in speech (Schilling-Estes and Wolfram 1994). The adoption of selected features of external varieties is commonplace in threatened languages and is, according to Dorian (1994), one of the more viable strategies for preserving endangered languages, albeit in an altered form, in the face of external language encroachment.

The pattern of [ɔy] recession and the selective, additive pattern of [a:] expansion in Ocracoke suggest that obsolescing dialect forms do not simply represent "ordinary" language changes which proceed at an accelerated pace. We would expect linguistic variables associated with such "ordinary" changes to display a more orderly correlation with respect to external social factors such as age and internal linguistic factors such as following phonetic environment than the unexpected patterning we observe in the obsolescing Ocracoke [ɔy] and the incipient Southern American [a:]. Not only do the patterns we observe for [ɔy] and [a:] in Ocracoke inform our understanding of obsolescing forms in language death situations, but they also lead us to refine our notions regarding the structured nature of variability in language change. Thus, in Wolfram and Schilling-Estes (1995), we set forth the *principle of phonetic implausibility,* a set of conditions under which the apparent phonetic naturalness of constraint effects may be relaxed. The principle and its conditions are summarized as follows:

PRINCIPLE OF PHONETIC IMPLAUSIBILITY

Constraints on variability may be altered in ways that violate the apparent phonetic naturalness of constraint hierarchies if:

(i) There is a significant categorial shift in the status of the unit, such as a shift between peripheral and non-peripheral status for vowels;
(ii) The change is taking place at a beginning or end point in the *S*-slope change curve, thus involving incipient or obsolescing forms; and
(iii) The change involves competing socially significant norms at a conscious level.

If nothing else, our in-depth examination of Ocracoke /ay/ shows how simplistic models of language change and dialect mixture are inadequate if we hope to achieve a full understanding of how and why languages change. We cannot simply assume that obsolescing forms will recede in an orderly, linear fashion as has sometimes been assumed in the literature on language death. Processes of change in language death may very well differ from "ordinary" change processes in ways other than sheer rapidity of progress. Moribund dialects and dying forms thus provide an essential proving ground for developing and refining empirically based models of language change.

3.2. On the regularity of performance phrases by semi-speakers. As a stereotype of Outer Banks speech, the [ɔy] production has become the object of considerable attention, both by outsiders who imitate it when mimicking islanders and by islanders who sometimes display their dialect for outsiders. Among the present generation of ancestral islanders, we find an increasing core of islanders who qualify as "semi-speakers" in Dorian's (1981) classic definition—speakers who persist in using the dying language variety instead of the encroaching language despite the fact that they may possess only selective and incomplete mastery of the receding language. Such speakers may, in fact, be more proficient in the encroaching language variety than the moribund one. Because their creative ability in the dying language is diminished, semi-speakers may resort to formulaic utterances or confine their use of the dying language to ritualistic, performance-oriented speech events. This narrowing of contexts in which the dying variety can be used, referred to as "stylistic shrinkage" (e.g. Campbell and Muntzel 1989: 195), has been documented in dying language areas throughout the world.

Dialect semi-speakers in Ocracoke are quite aware of their speech as an object of curiosity and intrigue to outsiders, and they tend to exaggerate salient features of the brogue, especially the [ɔy] variant discussed above. Words like [sɔyd] *side* and [tɔyd] *tide* are an integral part of the phrases Ocracokers—and outsiders—use to highlight the speech differences between islanders and mainland Southerners. Performance phrases are not typically defined by their propositional content, but by the social situation and the discourse context which sets them up for linguistic showcasing. Performance utterances are characterized by special linguistic features, such as rhyme, special intonational contours, and special phonetic or grammatical features (Schilling-Estes forthcoming: 3). Not only are Ocracokers known throughout North Carolina as "hoi toiders," but they often display their dialect features to tourists with sayings such as "It's hoi toide on the sound soide." Exaggeration often occurs in stock performance phrases, such as that in the following passage. In this exchange, a 40-year-old fisherman and carpenter (S) is explaining our initial meeting to a fieldworker (FW) who had become his friend.

(3) S: I got him [Walt Wolfram] going with that "hoi toide on the sound soide."

FW: What did he say to that? Did he get all excited?
S: Oh my God, yeah. Came out there, said, "I'm studying speech." And I said, "Well, it's hoi toide on the sound soide. Last night the water fire; tonight the moon shine. No fish. What do you suppose the matter, Uncle Woods?" Well, he got a laugh out of that. He did.

This performance phrase is replete with the most marked phonetic features of the brogue, including the unique [ɔy] in words like *high*, *tide*, and *side*. Further, the phonetic distinctiveness of [ɔy] is noticeably exaggerated in performance phrases such as the above (Schilling-Estes forthcoming).

In studies of language variation, such performance phrases have often been dismissed because the focus of most language variation studies has been on the most spontaneous speech. It has further been assumed that conscious shifts toward more vernacular speech often end up being unsystematic and, therefore, not very useful for studies of the systematic nature of language variation. In fact, the presumed irregularity of such shifting caused Labov (1972: 111) to set forth the *principle of subordinate dialect shift*, in which he maintained that speakers of vernacular dialects will shift their language irregularly when asked direct questions about their language.

Schilling-Estes's (forthcoming) study of some of the performance phrases of an Ocracoke semi-speaker, however, has shown how the study of this performance register can inform the study of language variation, as well as our understanding of style and register. In her comparative acoustic analysis of the F1 and F2 values for the production of the nucleus of [ɔy] in performance and non-performance contexts, Schilling-Estes (forthcoming) shows that performance speech displays regular patterning which matches the constraint hierarchy found for non-performance speech. That is, exaggerated raising and backing of the vowel nucleus in performance phrases occurs more frequently before voiced obstruents, next most frequently before nasals, and least before voiceless obstruents. At the same time, the exaggerated raised and backed tokens of /ay/ in words like *tide* and *side* remain phonologically distinct from the /oy/ of words like *toy* and *soy*, unlike the merger of these vowels often found in the stereotypical mimicking of this vowel by outsiders. Schilling-Estes (forthcoming: 5) thus concludes that "self-conscious speech—including speech which is self-consciously shifted toward a more basilectal vernacular variety—does not necessarily display the irregularity of patterning traditionally ascribed to the 'subordinate dialect shifts' "(Labov 1972).

The acoustic analysis of performance speech by Schilling-Estes also provides insight into how speakers perceive dialect variants and how these perceptions relate to the production of these variants. In the performance-phrase productions of [ɔy] the F1 value for the nucleus, which typically correlates with vowel height, is more drastically altered than the F2 value. In fact, the mean F2 value of the nucleus in the crucial category of a following voiced obstruent is nearly identical to the non-performance mean F2 value in this context (F2=1037 for performance speech vs. F2=1041 for non-performance speech with the fieldworker), but the mean values of the F1 variants are significantly different in this context (F1=471 for performance speech vs. F1=632 for non-performance speech with the fieldworker). This finding supports the conclusion drawn from studies of vowel perception that height differences are more perceptually salient than fronting/backing differences (Flanagan 1955; DiPaolo 1992; Labov 1994). The exaggerated performance of the highly salient /ay/ production thus offers support from natural language usage patterns for the perceptual dichotomy between vowel height and backing.

These are just two of the ways in which the specialized performance register of semi-speakers informs our understanding of language change and variation. There are more. For example, Schilling-Estes' (forthcoming) analysis of the performance register challenges current reductionist definitions of style to "attention paid to speech" (Labov 1972) or "audience design" (Bell 1984). For our discussion here, it is adequate to recognize the linguistic and sociolinguistic insight that derives from the opportunity to examine moribund dialects.

4. Sociolinguistic obligation. The other dimension of sociolinguistic involvement with dying dialects and obsolescing dialect structures concerns the social responsibility that linguists and dialectologists should assume with respect to documenting and disseminating information about the state of moribund dialects. There are three principles of social involvement that may guide linguists, two articulated by Labov in his review of the Ann Arbor decision (1982) and one that I offered in a recent article in *Issues in Applied Linguistics* (Wolfram 1993b). I offered the PRINCIPLE OF LINGUISTIC GRATUITY because I felt that linguists should make a stronger, proactive social commitment to the language communities who provide them data rather than merely take a reactive role assumed in previous discussions of social obligation. This proactive role is particularly appropriate with respect to endangered dialects. These principles are summarized as follows:

PRINCIPLE OF ERROR CORRECTION

> A scientist who becomes aware of a widespread idea or social practice with important consequences that is invalidated by his own data is obligated to bring this error to the attention of the widest possible audience. (Labov 1982: 172)

PRINCIPLE OF DEBT INCURRED

An investigator who has obtained linguistic data from members of a speech community has an obligation to use the knowledge based on that data for the benefit of the community, when it has need of it. (Labov 1982: 173)

PRINCIPLE OF LINGUISTIC GRATUITY

Investigators who have obtained linguistic data from members of a speech community should actively pursue positive ways in which they can return linguistic favors to the community. (Wolfram 1993b: 227)

With respect to endangered dialects, there appear to be several ways that we can take a proactive role that is consonant with the principle of linguistic gratuity. Although we cannot necessarily revitalize a moribund dialect, we can work with community members (1) to ensure that the dialect is documented in a valid and reliable way; (2) to raise the level of consciousness within and outside the community about the traditional form of the dialect and its changing state; and (3) to engage representative community agents and agencies in an effort to understand the historic and current role of dialect in community life.

Our involvement with communities on the Outer Banks of North Carolina has attempted to exemplify this role by serving positive humanistic, scientific, and socio-historical purposes. Our involvement with the community includes institutions, agents, and curricular programs. A summary of some of products we have produced and the activities we have undertaken on the Outer Banks in implementing the gratuity principle is given below:

Products for a Community-Based Dialect Awareness Program:

- *Hoi Toide on the Outer Banks: The Story of the Ocracoke Brogue* (Wolfram and Schilling-Estes forthcoming, University of North Carolina Press). A popular book available at tourist sites on the Outer Banks, museums, and popular bookstores.
- *Ocracoke Dialect Vocabulary* (North Carolina Language and Life Project). A popular booklet for visitors to Ocracoke.
- *The Ocracoke Brogue: The Molding of a Dialect*. A student text used for an eighth grade social studies curriculum taught at the Ocracoke school.
- *Ocracoke Bites*. An archival tape of select community speech samples.
- *The Ocracoke Brogue*. A video documentary produced by Blanton and Waters 1995.
- *That Island Talk: The Harkers Island Dialect*. A video documentary produced by American Media Productions and the North Carolina Language and Life Project 1996.

- Presentations to the Ocracoke Preservation Society.
- Presentation of video to public audiences at Howard's Pub in Ocracoke.
- Design and distribution of "Save the Brogue" T-shirts distributed in the community, at local stores, and the Ocracoke museum operated by the Ocracoke Preservation Society.
- School newspaper articles dedicated to dialect awareness efforts, including articles and poems about the Ocracoke brogue.
- Seven different news articles on endangered dialects and dialect awareness distributed by the Associated Press.
- Three newspaper articles with accompanying sound bites for readers to call and listen to samples of the brogue.

As indicated in the list, our involvement has covered a broad range of products and activities. We have written a popular book, compiled archival tapes, developed a dialect awareness program for the school, and produced a couple of documentary videos on two Outer Banks sites where we have been collecting data. We even designed a commemorative T-shirt that we gave to our local participants and now sell through the Ocracoke Preservation Society.

Local institutions involved include the Ocracoke Preservation Society, the Ocracoke School, and various North Carolina museums. Key community members have also served as active participants in various phases of our program, including the president of the Ocracoke Preservation Society, community leaders, and students and teachers in the school.

The venues we use to disseminate information include both traditional and non-traditional agencies. For example, we have instituted experimental programs in the Ocracoke School and made presentations to the Ocracoke Historical Preservation Society. In fact, our dialect awareness materials are endorsed by the Society, and we will share royalties from the sales of our forthcoming book with them in the hopes that our programs and materials are considered as recognized preservation efforts. Along with these institutional activities, we have shown our documentary several times at the local bar and grill, Howard's Pub, where both local residents and tourists typically congregate for informal socializing. These showings have resulted in animated, positive discussions about the dialect by both ancestral islanders and tourists. The threatened status of the Ocracoke brogue has also been the subject of several local and regional television and radio news programs, and there were at least seven major feature articles in local and regional newspapers from 1993 to 1995 that focused on the state of the dialect and the threats to its survival. As noted above, several of these stories were accompanied by sound bites; readers were invited to call an advertised telephone number and listen to a recorded sample of the brogue for themselves. The *Virginian Pilot* newspaper reported that more readers called in to hear the brogue than any other sound bite they had yet made available to their readcrship.

We have attempted to engage students, teachers, and community members in collecting and documenting dialect data. For example, several of the local community members routinely make observations and take notes for us about lexical items; and one school teacher, following one of our school lessons, returned the following day with over two pages of lexical items and phrases elicited from her elderly relatives. On another occasion, she wrote a poem composed of many unique Outer Banks lexical items in celebration of the dialect, which I reproduce below. In the poem, the italicized words are particular lexical items which characterize the Ocracoke brogue.

The Ocracoke Brogue

Ocracoke Tradition, Heritage and Such—
For some *dingbatters* is really too much
What is a first cousin once-removed?
Does a trip *down below* have to be approved?

Mommuck, *doset*, and *miserable 'n in wind*
Is this *O'cock brogue* meant to offend?
When I see *wampus cat*, what do I see?
Hoi toid on the seund soid is Greek to me!

Hey, *puck* isn't used in the game of hockey.
Do *O'Cockers* "*hoid*" when playing *meehonkey*?
While on your *pizer*, do you sit for *a spell*?
If you go *down below*, do you got to ... well?

Been a *whit* since I took a *scud across the beach*.
Things get *catawampus* if they're hard to reach.
Every *whipstitch* the *creek* gets *slick cam*
If you're not confused, well *pucker dog*, I am!

If I'm *Down Point* or *Up Trent*, Where'll I be?
Well, *Bucky*, it's still *good-some* to me!
Some may get *quamish* from the attention,
but this Brogue's too unique not to mention.

by
Gail Hamilton, Middle School Teacher
Ocracoke Island, North Carolina
March, 1995

Perhaps the most significant aspect of Gail Hamilton's involvement is the fact that this language arts teacher has been converted from a person who once sought to stamp out the dialect in her classrooms to one who now understands and seeks to preserve the rich dialect heritage of her community. The teacher is, in fact, an ancestral islander who returned to the island after a couple of decades on the mainland. She now understands the significance of the dialect for islanders and has been a strong advocate for our dialect awareness program.

As linguists, of course, we may not be able to save this or any other variety of a language. But we can at least chronicle the dialect for the historical record—for community members, curious outsiders, and academicians. Dialects may die and we may be able to do nothing about it. But as Nancy Dorian (personal correspondence) put it, the least we can do in cases of dialect death is to give the variety a decent and celebrated funeral. That's the very least we can do as linguists who profit greatly from studying such varieties.

REFERENCES

Bell, Allan. 1984. "Language style as audience design." *Language in Society* 13(2): 145–204.

Bernstein, Cynthia and Elizabeth Gregory. 1994. "The social distribution of glide shortened /ai/ in LAGS." Paper presented at SECOL 50. Memphis, Tennessee. April, 1994.

Blanton, Phyllis and Karen Waters (producers). 1994. *The Ocracoke brogue: A video documentary.* Raleigh, N.C.: The North Carolina Language and Life Project.

Campbell, Lyle and Martha C. Muntzel. 1989. "The structural consequences of language death." In Nancy C. Dorian (ed.), *Investigating obsolescence: Studies in language contraction and obsolescence*. Cambridge, Massachusetts: Cambridge University Press. 181–196.

Cedergren, Henrietta and David Sankoff. 1974. "Variable rules: Performance as a statistical reflection of competence." *Language* 50(2): 333–355.

DiPaolo, Marianna. 1992. "Evidence for the instability of a low back vowel 'merger'." Paper presented at NWAVE 22, Ottawa, Canada. October, 1992.

Dorian, Nancy C. 1981. *Language death: The life cycle of a Scottish Gaelic dialect.* Philadelphia, Pennsylvania: University of Pennsylvania Press.

Dorian, Nancy C. (ed.). 1989. *Investigating obsolescence: Studies in language contraction and obsolescence*. Cambridge, Massachusetts: Cambridge University Press.

Dorian, Nancy C. 1994. "Purism vs compromise in language revitalization and language revival." *Language in Society* 23(4): 479–494.

Fasold, Ralph W. 1990. *The sociolinguistics of language*. Cambridge, Massachusetts: Basil Blackwell.

Feagin, Crawford. 1994. "'Long i' as a microcosm of Southern states speech." Paper presented at NWAVE 23. Stanford, California. October, 1994.

Flanagan, James L. 1955. "A difference limen for vowel formant frequency." *Journal of the Acoustical Society of America* 27(4): 613–647.

Guy, Gregory R. 1993. "The quantitative analysis of linguistic variation." In Dennis R. Preston (ed.), *American dialect research*. Philadelphia, Pennsylvania: John Benjamins. 223–249.

Hale, Ken, Michael Krauss, Lucille Watahomigie, Akira Yamamoto, Colette Craig, LaVerne Masayesva Jeanne, and Nora England. 1992. "Endangered languages." *Language* 68(1): 1–42.

Hill, Jane H. 1989. "The social functions of relativization in obsolescent and non-obsolescent languages." In Nancy C. Dorian (ed.), *Investigating obsolescence: Studies in language contraction and obsolescence*. Cambridge, Massachusetts: Cambridge University Press. 149–166.

Ihalainen, Ossi. 1991. "Periphrastic *do* in affirmative sentences in the dialect of East Somerset." In Peter Trudgill and J.K. Chambers (eds.), *Dialects of English: Studies in grammatical variation*. New York, N.Y.: Longman. 148–160.

King, Ruth. 1989. "On the social meaning of linguistic variability in language death situations: Variation in Newfoundland French." In Nancy C. Dorian (ed.), *Investigating obsolescence: Studies in language contraction and obsolescence*. Cambridge, Massachusetts: Cambridge University Press. 138–148.

Labov, William. 1963. "The social motivation of sound change." *Word* 19(3):273–307.

Labov, William. 1969. "The logic of nonstandard English." In James Alatis (ed.), *Georgetown monograph of language and linguistics 22*. Washington, D.C.: Georgetown University Press. 1–44.

Labov, William. 1972. "Some principles of linguistic methodology." *Language in Society* 1(1): 97–154.

Labov, William. 1982. "Objectivity and commitment in linguistic science." *Language in Society* 11(2): 165–201.

Labov, William. 1994. *Principles of linguistic change: Internal factors*. Cambridge, Massachusetts: Basil Blackwell.

Martin, Stefan. 1992. *Topics in the syntax of nonstandard English*. Unpublished Ph.D. Dissertation, University of Maryland, College Park.

Martin, Stefan. 1996. "Neg-criterion extensions: Negative concord across relative clause boundaries." Paper presented at Linguistic Society of American Annual Meeting. San Diego, California. January, 1996.

Milroy, Lesley. 1980. *Language and social networks*. Oxford, U.K.: Basil Blackwell.

Robins, Robert H. and Eugenius M. Uhlenbeck (eds.). 1991. *Endangered languages*. Oxford, U.K.: Berg.

Sankoff, David and William Labov. 1979. "On the uses of variable rules." *Language in Society* 8(2): 189–222.

Schilling-Estes, Natalie. Forthcoming. "Register shift as realignment strategy: Performance speech in Ocracoke English." *Language in Society*.

Schilling-Estes, Natalie and Walt Wolfram. 1994. "Convergent explanation and alternative regularization patterns: *were/weren't* leveling in a vernacular English variety." *Language Variation and Change* 6(3): 273–302.

Schmidt, Albert. 1985. *Young people's Dyirbal: An example of language death from Australia*. Cambridge, U.K.: Cambridge University Press.

Thomas, Erik and Guy Bailey. 1994. "The origins of monophthongal /ai/ in Southern speech." Paper presented at SECOL 50. Memphis, Tennessee. April, 1994.

Trudgill, Peter and J.K. Chambers (eds.). 1991. *Dialects of English: Studies in grammatical variation*. New York, NY: Longman.

Tsitsipis, Lukas D. 1989. "Skewed performance and full performance in language obsolescence: The case of an Albanian variety." In Nancy C. Dorian (ed.), *Investigating obsolescence: Studies in language contraction and obsolescence*. Cambridge, Massachusetts: Cambridge University Press. 139–148.

Wolfram, Walt. 1993a. "Identifying and interpreting variables." In Dennis R. Preston (ed.), *American dialect research*. Philadelphia, Pennsylvania: John Benjamins. 193–222.

Wolfram, Walt. 1993b. "Ethical considerations in language awareness programs." *Issues in Applied Linguistics* 4(2): 225–255.

Wolfram, Walt and Natalie Schilling-Estes. Forthcoming. *Hoi Toide on the Outer Banks: The story of the Ocracoke brogue.* Chapel Hill, N.C.: University of North Carolina Press.

Wolfram, Walt and Natalie Schilling-Estes. 1995. "Moribund dialects and the language endangerment canon." *Language* 71(4): 696–721.

Wolfram, Walt, Natalie Schilling-Estes, and Kirk Hazen. 1995. *Dialects and the Ocracoke brogue.* An eighth-grade curriculum. Raleigh, N.C.: The North Carolina Language and Life Project.

Beyond consciousness raising: Re-examining the role of linguistics in language teacher training

Andrea Tyler and Donna Lardiere
Georgetown University

Introduction. In recent years, established figures in language teaching—for example, Don Freeman, the former national president of TESOL, and Diane Larsen-Freeman, co-author of *The Grammar Book* and *An Introduction to Second Language Acquisition Research*—have argued that current linguistics has significantly less to offer language teaching than in the past. Based on this analysis, these writers have suggested that language-teacher-education programs should substantially de-emphasize linguistics. In this paper, we re-examine the claim (explicitly put forward in Larsen-Freeman 1995) that linguistics played an exclusively defining role in shaping the conception of language, language learning and language-teaching practices within the Audio-Lingual Method (ALM), and that since that time it has played a steadily more peripheral role.

We argue that an analysis which maximizes the relative role of linguistics in language teaching in the 1950's while marginalizing its role in the 1980's and 1990's is flawed. Examination of the relationship between language instruction and the disciplines which have informed it over the past sixty years reveals a consistent, complex interaction among many disciplines. This history is distorted by the misconception that an isomorphic relationship existed between theoretical linguistics as practiced by the American Structuralists and language teaching as practiced by adherents of the ALM. This misapprehension leads to the inaccurate conclusion that since the era of American Structuralism and Audio-Lingualism, other disciplines have supplanted the contribution of linguistics to our understanding of language, language learning, and, therefore, language teaching. Finally, we discuss how post-Structuralist linguistics, including "mainstream" linguistics—i.e. syntax, phonology, morphology and semantics—has continued to have substantial applications to language teaching right up to the present day. We conclude that the relationship between linguistic study and language pedagogy is alive and well and, thus, that linguistic study continues to be of central importance to language teachers.

There are three main parts to our argument:

1. A one-to-one relationship between the Audio-Lingual Method and theoretical linguistics as practiced by the American Structuralists never existed;
2. The disciplines of linguistics, psychology, philosophy, education, anthropology, and sociology have long had complex, mutually informing interrelations. Language teaching, in turn, has consistently drawn on the insights from these many disciplines throughout the last sixty years; and
3. Post-Structuralist linguistic theories have provided an overarching conceptualization of human language, language acquisition, language interpretation, and language use. All current major approaches to language teaching rest within this conceptual framework.

The analysis.

The relationship between American Structuralism and the Audio-Lingual method. Now we turn to a consideration of each of these arguments. Larsen-Freeman's representation of the history of language teaching for the past fifty years appears below in Table 1. Her representation asserts that a near isomorphism existed between American Structuralism and the ALM. This assumption is central to her argument as it lays the foundation for the perception that theoretical linguistics at one time was far more central to language teaching than in subsequent years.

Larsen-Freeman's argument involves two main elements—that the applications of American Structuralism to the ALM were "direct," and, moreover, that American Structuralism was the sole intellectual source of the ALM. In offering an explanation for why current linguistics is no longer as applicable to language teaching as in the past, Larsen-Freeman states, "[L]inguistic theories have become increasingly abstract ... a level removed from apparent classroom application ... The theories are often inaccessible without considerable expenditure of time and energy." (1995: 721). The unstated implication is that the work of American Structuralism was not abstract, was readily accessible, and consistently had direct, apparent classroom application. In addition, by Larsen-Freeman's account, American Structuralism is represented as the sole contributor to the ALM. As she states, "[O]nce there was a time linguistics was dominant in language teaching, defining language, language learning, and language-teaching practices" (1995: 719).

We argue this representation is inaccurate. In fact, most of the linguistic investigations of American Structuralists were far removed from the principles and practices evident in the ALM. Support for this position comes from a consideration of the articles published in *Language* from 1940 through 1960. A representative list of titles from *Language* for these years appears in Table 2. Table 3 represents a categorization of all articles according to their contents.

Table 1. Evolution of views on language, language learning, and language teaching for the past fifty years, and the disciplines which informed them.

DISCIPLINE	LANGUAGE	LANGUAGE LEARNING	LANGUAGE TEACHING
Linguistics: Descriptive/Structural	Patterns	Habit-formation	Audiolingualism: Repetition drills Pattern practice
Linguistics: (a) Transformational-generative	Rules	Rule-formation	Cognitive-code Approach: Inductive/Deductive exercises
(b) Government-binding	Principles/ Parameters	Resetting the Parameters	Grammatical consciousness-raising activities
Linguistics: Sociolinguistics	Functions	Interactionism	Communicative Approach: Role plays Information exchanges
Linguistics: Discourse/Functional Corpus	Texts	—	Authentic texts In context

Table 1 (continued).

DISCIPLINE	LANGUAGE	LANGUAGE LEARNING	LANGUAGE TEACHING
Education: General	Unanalyzed whole	Engagement	Whole Language Approach
		Developing learner autonomy	Learning-strategy instruction
	Medium of learning	Experiential	Content-based Approach Language across the curriculum Cooperative Learning Task-based Approach
L1 Acquisition Literary Criticism: Social Constructivism	Meaning-making activity	Co-construction	Process Approach
Education: Critical Pedagogy	Instrument of power	Empowerment	Participatory Approach

Table 2. A representative selection of titles from *Language* 1938–1960.

LOUNSBURY	"The Method of Descriptive Morphology"
BLOCH	"Phonemic Overlapping"
HOCKETT	"A System of Descriptive Phonology"
HARRIS	"Morpheme Alternates in Linguistic Analysis"
HOENIGSWALD	"Sound Change and Linguistic Structure"
MOULTON	"Juncture in Modern Standard German"
NIDA	"The Identification of Morphemes"
HALL	"The Reconstruction of Proto-Romance"
TWADDELL	"The Pre-historic German Short Syllables"
HOCKETT	"Two Models of Grammatical Description"

The central issues the American Structuralists addressed included the appropriate methodology for isolating phonemes and morphemes, the status of bi-uniqueness in linguistic representations, the number of levels of linguistic abstraction necessary for accurate analysis, and discovery techniques. Note that 95% of these investigations dealt with phonology and morphology.

As the titles suggest, the linguistics pursued by the American Structuralists was often abstract and far from readily accessible. We invite any reader who has doubts about this to read a few of the articles from these years. Moreover, few of these investigations have any readily apparent application to language teaching. The facts that, on one hand, only 5% of the articles considered language above the word level and, on the other hand, the ALM emphasized the memorization of sentences and even whole dialogues indicate how little overlap actually existed between linguistics as practiced by the American Structuralists and the ALM.

Table 3. A categorization of articles appearing in *Language* 1940–1960.

Level of Analysis	Number
Word/Etymology	45
Semantics	69
Syntax	21
Phonology	166
Morphology	55
Historical/ Origin of Language	19
Dialectology	2
Sociolinguistic	9
Translation	2
Philosophy of Language	12
Language Teaching	2
TOTAL	402

Furthermore, the theory of language espoused by the American Structuralists was a hybrid of linguistics, early behaviorist psychology, and philosophy as articulated by the Logical Positivists. Bloomfield (1933) clearly acknowledged the strong influence of behaviorist psychology and the philosophical school of Logical Positivism on his thinking. Bloomfield and the American Structuralists were particularly enamored with the Logical Positivists' conceptualization of "scientific rigor." The core of the argument was that "scientific" explanation must be based on observable factors and principles of logic and mathematics with no room for unobservable mental constructs such as "the mind" or "native speaker intuitions."

As part of the American Structuralists' rejection of mentalism, they asserted that all meaning of an utterance could be extracted from the speech stream. Important reflexes of this theoretical stance included an emphasis on studying the spoken language and considering only what native speakers actually say, rejecting any appeal to native speaker intuitions concerning their language, and rejecting the pronouncements of prescriptivist grammarians. Analogs of these tenets can be seen in the ALM with its emphasis on spoken language over written language, championing of descriptive language rather than prescriptive, and rejection of explicit study of grammar rules (which were seen as deductive generalizations representing someone's intuitions or prescriptions rather than those inductively extracted by the learner). Thus, we can certainly find important elements of the American Structuralist's particular interpretation of language in the ALM.

On the other hand, as we have seen, there is much of American Structuralism that was not applicable to the ALM. Moreover, there is much of the ALM which has no clear analog in American Structuralism. Although Larsen-Freeman asserts that American Structuralist linguistics "define[d] language learning and language-teaching practices" (1995: 720) in the ALM, she offers no evidence of how the use of repetition drills and pattern practice grew out of linguistic theory or linguistic analysis as practiced by the American Structuralists. In her discussion of the contribution of American Structuralism to the ALM, her primary evidence is the following statement by Charles Fries (1949, in Bowen et al. 1985: 36, cited in Larsen-Freeman 1995: 712): "The fundamental feature of this new approach [to language learning] consists in a scientific descriptive analysis as the basis upon which to build the teaching materials." In other words, Fries's claim is that the contribution of linguistics to language teaching was a more accurate description of language and a rationale for sequencing of materials. However, we would point out that even this fairly limited claim is suspect as there is little in the theoretical work of the American Structuralists that would inform language teaching at the sentence level. Although Fries (1949, 1960) claimed the selection and sequencing of sentence patterns was "scientific," he makes no reference to any experimental investigations showing that subjects learned one sequence of grammatical structures more readily than another, nor of any descriptive studies concerning either frequency of particular patterns or order in which L1 children learned the constructions. In fact, the sequencing appears to have been based on the intuitions of linguists writing the materials.

In terms of American Structuralism directly providing language-teaching methods, while the American Structuralists emphasized inductive methodology, this stance does not logically require use of pattern drills, memorization of dialogues without resort to understanding what they mean, and immediate error correction. Rather, the teaching practices found in ALM would seem to have their antecedents in early behaviorist psychology and earlier language-teaching practices as developed by Palmer and Jespersen, among others. According to Diller (1971), all the methods used in the ALM—with the possible exception of immediate error correction—were already being practiced by 1916, well before the rise of American Structuralism. Diller points out that the Structuralists, in their fervent belief about the correctness of their "new" scientific approach, ignored the fact that their language-teaching methods had been developed by earlier language teachers.

To summarize, the 1940's and 1950's were not a time when theoretical linguistics alone supplied language teaching with the conception of language, language learning, and language-teaching practices. The claim that the ALM grew directly out of theoretical linguistics as practiced by the American Structuralists simultaneously ignores the work the Structuralists were actually engaged in as well as the central influence of behaviorist psychology and previous second-language pedagogy on the ALM.

Multiple disciplinary sources of post-Audio-Lingual approaches. The complement of the analysis which inaccurately characterizes American Structuralism and the ALM as isomorphic is an analysis which characterizes post-Structuralist linguistics and recent language teaching as virtually disjunct. Post-ALM language teaching, like the ALM, has consistently drawn on insights from many disciplines, including linguistics. Failure to acknowledge these ongoing multiple influences on language pedagogy leads to the misperception that the centrality of linguistics to language teaching has recently been supplanted by other disciplines.

Reconsider Larsen-Freeman's characterization of the chronological influence of various disciplines on language teaching (reproduced in Table 1). This representation of the evolution of language teaching is flawed in two ways: (1) The chart appears to imply a chronological progression of approaches to language teaching, which is inaccurate. For instance, in this chronology, the communicative approach evolved sometime after grammatical consciousness raising; the communicative approach, in turn, appears to have been supplanted by the Whole Language Approach, content-based instruction, the process approach, etc. This "evolutionary" representation of the history of language teaching argues that in recent years fields such as education, L1 composition theory, and literary criticism, have supplanted linguistics; (2) Larsen-Freeman represents each of these language-teaching approaches as having a single disciplinary source.

Table 4 augments Larsen-Freeman's representation by providing dates of a few publications and conference presentations concerning post-Cognitive Code approaches.[1]

Note that most of the approaches characterized by Larsen-Freeman as most recent have been part of language teaching for some time. As one example, articles on the process approach by Taylor (1981) and Zamel (1982) appeared in *TESOL Quarterly* in the early 1980s. In fact, these "recent" approaches have been part of the language-teaching scene much longer than Focus-on-Form, which Larsen-Freeman represents as a pedagogical approach evolving well before the influence of the field of education was felt in language teaching. Our augmented chart shows that fields such as education and L1 composition theory, along with linguistics, have been simultaneously influencing language teaching throughout the past twenty-five years, just as was the case throughout the 1940's and 1950's. We see no reason to believe this will change in the foreseeable future.

In addition, note that, as with the ALM, Larsen-Freeman characterizes each of these approaches as having a single disciplinary source. For instance, content-based instruction is represented as growing out of general education with no influence from linguistics. In fact, Brinton et al. (1991) characterize their approach as growing out of the writing-across-the-curriculum movement in education as well as sociolinguistic insights concerning language in context and purposeful communicative functions of language.

Let's consider another multidisciplinary interweaving and its effects on language teaching—one which is not represented on Larsen-Freeman's chart. Explaining how humans use and interpret everyday conversation has been a central concern in philosophy, psychology and linguistics for the past thirty years. A few of the leading scholars in this general area include Grice, Austin, and Reddy from philosophy; Hymes, Chafe, Green, Gumperz, and Tannen in linguistics; and Bransford and Frank, Brewer, Kintsch, Abelson, and Shank in psychology. As a result of their combined work, the constructs of language in context, background knowledge, and constrained inferencing have emerged as necessary components of any explanation of how native speakers go about interpreting an utterance. The results of these endeavors pervade current L2 pedagogy. For instance, Bowen et al. (1985) argue that the influence of Hymes' discussion of communicative competence is so pervasive that virtually no language program in the U.S. has not incorporated aspects of language use into its curriculum. The process approach to writing characterizes writing as purposeful communication between a writer and a reader rather than writing as a forum for practicing particular grammar constructions. In L2 reading, attention

[1]These references are not meant to be definitive. They were chosen to give a sense of when examples of some of the earliest and most recent work in a particular area appeared.

Table 4. Augmentation of Larsen-Freeman's (1995) Table.

DISCIPLINE	LANGUAGE TEACHING
Linguistics: Structuralists	ALM
Linguistics: a. Transformational b. Government and Binding	*Cognitive Code* *Grammatical Consciousness Raising* (Sharwood-Smith 1981; Rutherford 1987) *Focus-on-Form* (Ellis 1990; Fotos 1994; Sharwood-Smith 1993; Long 1991, to appear)
Linguistics: Sociolinguistics (Functions)	*Communicative Approach* (Savignon 1972; Van Ek 1975; Canale and Swain 1980; Terrell 1980; Hoekje and Williams 1994)
Linguistics: Discourse	*Authentic Texts* (McCarthy 1992; Hatch 1994; McCarthy and Carter 1995)
Corpus	*Language in Context* (Little 1994; Ball 1995)
Education: General	*Whole Language Approach* (Hudelson 1984; Riggs 1986, 1991) *Learning-Strategies* (Rubin 1975; Oxford 1992) *Content-Based* (Brinton et al. 1991; ESP: Watts 1980) *Cooperative Learning* (Nunan 1988) *Task-Based* (Long 1983; Ur 1985; Dickens and Woods 1988)
L1 Composition Theory/Literary Criticism	*Process Approach* (Taylor 1981; Zamel 1982)
Education: Critical Pedagogy	*Participatory Approach* (Wallerstein 1982; Auerbach 1991)

to schema, top-down/bottom-up models of processing and inferencing is nearly universal. And in L2 oral communication, attention to varying language/culture specific enactments of speech events and politeness phenomena are assuming ever more importance.

In sum, we believe the evidence shows that language teaching has always been influenced by insights from multiple disciplines, one of which has consistently been linguistics. Furthermore, all major approaches to language teaching which have developed over the past sixty years have had multiple disciplinary sources. Just as representing the ALM as having its basis solely in linguistics masks the very real contributions of psychology and language pedagogy to its teaching practices, claiming that approaches like the Whole Language Approach or the Content-Based Approach grow solely out of education masks the very real contribution of linguistics to those teaching approaches.

The role of linguistics in post-ALM language teaching. At first glance, the Focus-on-Form movement, the Content-Based Approach, the Process Approach to writing, and the Participatory Approach may seem to involve very different conceptualizations of language learning. In delving beneath the surface of these post-ALM approaches, we find a fundamental core of assumptions about human communication and humans as language learners. These tenets appear below:

1. Language is more than just a collection of habits;
2. Humans bring more to the language-learning process than just the ability to memorize and mimic;
3. Humans are actively engaged in creating their own grammars. Simply mimicking and memorizing is not enough to create an operative language ability;
4. Many errors are likely to reflect the learner's emerging grammar;
5. Immediate correction of all errors, including pronunciation, in order to prevent bad language habits is often inappropriate and ineffective; and
6. The simple combination of lexical items plus the grammatical constructions in which they appear is insufficient for explaining the interpretations humans regularly assign to utterances in context:
   (a) Interpretation of language goes beyond what can simply be extracted from the speech stream;
   (b) Assessment of context is crucially involved in establishing an appropriate interpretation; and
   (c) Humans are actively engaged in creating interpretation.

These tenets suggest an overall conception of language, a theory of language learning, and certain language teaching practices.

The core tenets of generative linguistics—that experience and stimulus-response arcs cannot adequately account for complex human learning, that humans bring a great deal of cognitive machinery to the learning of language, and that humans actively engage in the construction of their internal grammar—clearly form the basis of the first five tenets. The last tenet reflects linguists' efforts to expand linguistics into the realm of language in society and language in use. It grows out of the investigations in sociolinguistics and pragmatics undertaken by language scholars such as Hymes, Gumperz, Green, Grice, Shuy, and Tannen. This tenet illustrates the expanding scope of linguistics over the past forty years. Thus to limit theoretical linguistics to the foci of linguistics as practiced in the 1950's and early 1960's, as Larsen-Freeman has done, represents a serious misconception of what contemporary linguistics is.

We believe that post-Structuralist linguistic theory has so permeated current understanding of human communication and language learning that its basic premises are taken for granted. In her discussion of the Whole Language Approach, Riggs points out that "the term whole language came from educators not linguists" (1991: 521). However, when she states that the Whole Language Approach emphasizes the "student as a member of a culture and as a creator of knowledge" (1991: 521), she is articulating core assumptions of linguistic theory developed over the past forty years. When she articulates the central premises of the Whole Language Approach as the beliefs that "[L]language is used purposefully..." (1991: 524) and she argues, "Language is social. It makes a difference who says what to whom, how and why. What is the social relationship of two people communicating? What are their purposes? What is the situation?" (1991: 525) she could be quoting from any basic writing on sociolinguistics and pragmatics. The fact that she does not cite Chomsky, Hymes, or Grice does not change the fact that they were instrumental in creating the intellectual framework upon which the approach is built.

Again reflecting on Larsen-Freeman's representation of the application of "mainstream" linguistic theory to pedagogy, we feel that representing that contribution as limited to "potentially providing as-yet-unarticulated guidance on grammatical consciousness-rasing activities" (1995: 716) seriously underrepresents the role of "mainstream" formal linguistics to current language pedagogy. For instance, many of the now standard ways of presenting grammar would seem to have their origins in specifics of post-Structuralist linguistic theory:

1. Presenting grammar explanations or rules. The linguistic analog is that human language learning is deductive as well as inductive;
2. Asking students to "transform" basic sentences, such as transforming declaratives into commands or active sentences into passive. The linguistic analog is that variations of sentence types are related;
3. Use of grammaticality judgments, such as exercises which ask students to find errors and suggest corrections. The linguistic analog is that speakers' competence is revealed through their ability to judge the grammaticality of sentences;
4. Overgeneralization as a standard explanation for many NNS errors. For instance, a typical explanation for the following NNS utterance, "I wonder how is the best way to get to the store" is that the student has overgeneralized the rule of subject-verb inversion; and

5. The acknowledgment of dual influence from L1 and L2, i.e. the emergent grammar of the learner's interlanguage, as the source of many errors.

Moreover, the crucial role played by L1 and L2 acquisition research in linking theory and pedagogy is curiously underplayed in Larsen-Freeman's account, despite the fact that much of what we do know about language acquisition not only informs pedagogical practice but also serves as a powerful constraint on formulating linguistic theory itself. In this section, we consider a few of the effects of advances in theory-based language acquisition research on language teaching and teacher preparation, and further illustrate the extent to which linguistic theoretic constructs continue to permeate more recent pedagogy and pedagogical research.

We find many attempts to apply the theoretical shift from "teaching" to "learning" to pedagogical (especially curricular) considerations, such as in the well-known "teachability" studies of Pienemann (1985), which focused on the extent to which the presumably "natural" order of acquisition processes could be manipulated by formal instruction.

Pienemann's research question was grounded in a generativist orientation to syntax and yet was also explicitly framed in pedagogical terms: He argued that it was "of immediate importance to discover in what way possible pedagogical options for L2 curricula are restricted by principles of language acquisition" (1985: 143). Such restrictions, he concluded, were necessarily imposed by consecutive stages of development in learner-centered processing capacities. The role of pedagogy, according to Pienemann, should therefore be based on determining "whether the speaker of a certain Interlanguage is prepared for the learning of a given structure or not" (1985: 162). The questions asked by Pienemann contributed enormously to the discourse of theories of language teaching, particularly his examination of the "crucial assumption" that language is even teachable (1985: 162), i.e. the Teachability Hypothesis. Thus, Pienemann's research directly reflects a fundamental question Chomsky has been raising for the past forty years. Although the Teachability Hypothesis rather negatively constrained the effect of formal instruction, Pienemann argued that giving up instruction in syntax altogether would likely result in fossilization of the interlanguage, a position whose echoes can be heard in the current focus-on-form trends.

Additionally, we might consider how the notion of "grammatical consciousness-raising," according to one of its original authors, Sharwood-Smith (1993), has more recently given way to "input enhancement." The latter term refers to a concretely pedagogical program which nonetheless acknowledges that teachers cannot directly manipulate learner attention. Again, simply framing a pedagogical problem in this manner involves implicit reference to learner-internal mental states and again reflects post-Structuralist linguistic thinking.

Other tenets of generative linguistic theory, such as Chomsky's competence/performance distinction, learnability, and modularity underlie the pedagogical issues addressed at recent conferences. At the 1991 Colloquium on the Role of Instruction in SLA, for example, SLA researchers (several of whom work within generative frameworks) discussed whether classroom instruction can bring about changes in underlying linguistic competence and what kinds of classroom input were necessary and/or sufficient to accomplish this successfully. Learnability considerations concerning the efficacy (or necessity) of negative feedback additionally provide theoretical underpinning for recent research on form-focused instruction in the language classroom conducted by, for example, Ellis (1990) and Long (1991, to appear). And even further motivation for form-focused instruction is provided by the theoretical insight of modularity, which can account for why, as noted by Carroll and Swain (1993: 359), feedback addressed solely to the conceptual content of an utterance will not necessarily affect the learning of grammatical distinctions mentally encoded as a representation in a distinct grammatical module.

To give some more concrete examples influenced by formal syntactic theory, consider Trahey and White's (1993) research into form-focused classroom instruction which was explicitly formulated in terms of parameter resetting and determining the effects of positive and negative evidence in the classroom. They demonstrated that an "input flood" of contextualized primary (positive) evidence used naturalistically in a classroom setting resulted in a dramatic increase in students' use of a correct target-language word order (one which was prohibited in their native language); however, in the absence of form-focused negative evidence, students still retained an L1 order prohibited by the L2, suggesting that negative evidence may in fact be required.

Furthermore, the question of what type of negative evidence might be most pedagogically effective was addressed in a study by Spada and Lightbown (1993), who reported the greatest learning success with context-embedded focus on form that incorporated implicit feedback over an extended time period. Again, the research was constructed to bear upon theoretical questions whose answers have rather direct application to classroom practices, i.e. what type of teacher response to errors in student language production is effective.

Specific applications of more recent linguistic theory to pedagogy are also discussed by Strozer, who argues that an up-to-date pedagogical grammar should "attend to the parametric differences between the target language and the native language of the acquirer, thus showing considerable factual overlap with the more technical ... grammar of the theoretical linguist" (1994: 179). Strozer provides, for Spanish L2 acquisition, detailed examples and data sets which might be included in such a pedagogical grammar, such as information about the properties of Spanish clitics not directly inducible from the input, and that *ser*/*estar* and the properties of individual and stage-level predicates are interrelated.

We can find pedagogical applications within other formal domains of linguistics as well. In phonology and phonetics, both Weinberger (1994) and Zsiga (1995) show how linguistic analysis of extralexical phonetic processes and timing patterns found in fast or casual speech processes can account for the fact that these are more likely than purely lexical processes to transfer from the native into the target language. This research suggests that these patterns are more likely to need direct instructional attention.

In the area of morphology, the development of recent theoretical models which draw a sharp distinction between abstract morphosyntactic functions versus the phonological forms which encode them not only can account for well-attested overregularization phenomena among language learners, but also have considerable implications for language pedagogy. Beard, for example, contends that there is a basic, probably universal set of grammatical functions which may be successfully utilized by learners of a wide range of languages (1995: 207). In other words, the morphology of a language should be conceived of and taught as ranging over sets of functions, rather than sets of particular affixes or morphemes, which, of course, vary enormously crosslinguistically. Focusing on, for example, crosslinguistic instantiations of definiteness between native and target languages rather than on a somewhat myopic view of, say, teaching articles in English would be a welcome application of linguistic theory to language teacher training.

A similar view could be taken with respect to features and functions in lexical semantics. To give a fairly detailed example, consider that L1 acquisition research in lexical semantics has shown that the acquisition of spatial words is closely tied to language-specific semantic organization. As pointed out by Choi and Bowerman (1991: 114), English "clearly and consistently" emphasizes PATH as an isolated component of motion events. The system of PATH particles "encourages learners to identify abstract notions of PATH" independently of considerations such as causativity or shape of the identity of the FIGURE undergoing the motion. In contrast, this independence of PATH is not found in Korean, where PATH as a semantic feature tends instead to be merged with other information about the shape or identity of FIGURE and GROUND objects. This finding provides valuable insights into problems the speakers of "non-PATH-prominent languages," such as Korean, are likely to have acquiring those notoriously difficult English prepositions and verbal particles that do express PATH in "relatively pure form." Moreover, the conceptual prominence of PATH is highlighted and exhaustively characterized in recent work by Brugman (1987) in her detailed case study of the characteristics of the English preposition *over*. Exploiting Brugman's description of *over* for pedagogical purposes would require only minimal tinkering by an imaginative English teacher. But of course, this adaptation requires knowledge that these studies exist, in other words, familiarity with recent linguistic literature. If language teachers are scarcely exposed to linguistic training, they will not be in a position to take the initiative actively in applying relevant linguistic research to their classroom practices. Therefore, we strongly advocate that language teachers be trained to look out for and draw crosslinguistic comparisons made possible by advances in linguistic theory, and to incorporate them into their pedagogical efforts whenever possible.

Conclusion. In the past forty years our understanding of human language and human communication has changed considerably from the Structuralist/ Behaviorist beliefs (represented in Skinner's 1958 *Verbal Behavior*) that all information necessary to account for language learning, language use, and language interpretation is present in the speech stream and can be adequately accounted for by viewing humans as passive receptacles who mindlessly respond to stimuli, much as pigeons respond to flashing lights. During this time, the discipline of linguistics has been evolving towards an ever more sophisticated understanding of language and the importance of examining language use and language in context. Moreover, as it has become clearer what theoretical syntax and morphology can and cannot account for, sociolinguistics, semantics, pragmatics, and discourse analysis have arisen to account for aspects of natural language that were formerly assigned to syntax and morphology. Discourse constructs (such as topic, focus, and speaker-hearer distinctions) have become solidly integrated into grammatical theory; for example, the definiteness effect in English existential *there*-sentences has recently been accounted for by Ward and Birner (1995) in terms of discourse-based principles. Several aspects of anaphoric interpretation, once the exclusive purview of Binding theory in the syntax, are increasingly seen as better accounted for within pragmatics, as demonstrated by, for example, Levinson (1978, 1991) and Ariel (1994).

Insights achieved by language scholars in the 1970's and early 1980's have pervaded virtually all current approaches to language teaching. In the late 1980's and 1990's, linguists and second-language acquisition researchers have continued to make important discoveries which have clear implications for language teaching, but have not yet been integrated into most language curricula. Despite the considerable insights we have gained over the past forty years, no serious linguistic scholar believes we now know all we need to or will know about human language, language learning, or language use. It is our firm belief that to encourage language-teaching-education programs to begin to de-emphasize linguistics at this time and instead focus teachers' attention primarily on how other teachers already teach will result in the stagnation of the profession. In following such a course, language teachers run the risk of being cut off from the conceptual frameworks which would allow them to develop an informed, evolving philosophy of teaching. Without such a conceptual framework, they may well end up with a bag of teaching tricks, but with no overall insight into why they are doing what they are doing, and what the next logical, consistent steps to improve their teaching should be. They are likely to be relegated to the role of passive consumers of whatever textbook writers and publishers deem appropriate. Rather, we agree with the stand taken by Nunan (1988) and others who advocate that classroom teachers be involved in research and innovation in teaching practices. In order to accomplish this, language teachers need a theoretical grounding in linguistics.

REFERENCES

Ariel, M. 1994. "Interpreting anaphoric expressions: A cognitive versus a pragmatic approach." *Journal of Linguistics* 30 (1): 3–42.

Auerbach, E. and L. McGrail. 1990. "Rosa's challenge: Connecting classroom and community contexts." In S. Benesch (ed.), *ESL in America: Myths and possibilities*. Portsmouth, N.H.: Heinemann, Boynton/Cook. 96–111.

Beard, R. 1995. *Lexeme-morpheme base morphology*. Albany, N.Y.: SUNY Press.

Bloomfield, L. 1933. *Language*. New York: Holt.

Bowen, J., H. Madson, and A. Hilferty. 1985. *TESOL Techniques and procedures*. Rowley, Massachusetts: Newbury House Publishers.

Brinton, D., M. Snow, and M. Wesche. 1991. *Content based second language instruction*. Rowley, Massachusetts: Newbury House Publishers.

Canale, M. and M. Swain. 1980. "Theoretical bases of communicative approaches to second language teaching and testing." *Applied Linguistics* 1: 1–47.

Carroll, S. and M. Swain. 1993. "Explicit and implicit negative feedback." *Studies in second Language Acquisition* 15: 357–386.

Chamot, A. U. This volume.

Choi, S. and M. Bowerman. 1992. "Learning to express motion events in English and Korean: The influence of language-specific lexicalization patterns." In B. Levin and S. Pinker (eds.), *Lexical and Conceptual semantics*. Cambridge, Massachusetts: Blackwell. 83–121.

Chomsky, N. 1959. "Review of verbal behavior." *Language* 35(1): 26–58.

Chomsky, N. 1986. *Knowledge of language: Its nature, origin, and use*. New York: Praeger.

Dickens, P. and E. Woods. 1988. "Some criteria for the development of communicative grammar tasks." *TESOL Quarterly* 22(4): 623–646.

Diller, K. 1971. *Generative grammar, structural linguistics, and language teaching*. Rowley, Massachusetts: Newbury House Publishers.

Ellis, R. 1990. *Instructed second language acquisition*. Cambridge, Massachusetts: Blackwell.

Fotos, S. 1993. "Consciousness raising and noticing through focus on form: Grammar task performance versus formal instruction." *Applied Linguistics* 14(4): 385–407.

Freeman, D. 1994. "Educational linguistics and the knowledge base of language teaching." In J. E. Alatis (ed.), *Georgetown University Round Table on Languages and Linguistics 1994*. Washington, D.C.: Georgetown University Press. 180–198.

Fries, C. 1962. *Teaching and learning English as a foreign language*. Ann Arbor, Michigan: The University of Michigan Press.

Hatch, E. 1992. *Discourse and language education*. Cambridge, Massachusetts: Cambridge University Press.

Hoekje, B. and J. Williams. 1994. "Communicative competence as a theoretical framework for international teaching assistants education." In C. Madden and C. Meyers (eds.), *Discourse performance of ITA's*. Alexandria, Virginia: TESOL. 11–26.

Hudelson, S. 1984. "Kan yu ret an rayt en ingles: Children becoming literate in English." *TESOL Quarterly* 18(2): 221–238.

Larsen-Freeman, D. 1995. "On the changing role of linguistics in the education of second language teachers: Past, present, and future." In J. E. Alatis et al. (eds.), *Georgetown University Round Table on Languages and Linguistics 1995*. Washington, D.C.: Georgetown University Press. 711–724.

Levinson, S. 1987. "Pragmatics and the grammar of anaphora: A partial pragmatic reduction of binding and control phenomena." *Journal of Linguistics* 23(2): 379–434.

Levinson, S. 1991. "Pragmatic reduction of the binding condition revisited." *Journal of Linguistics*, 27(1): 107–161.

Little, D. 1994. "Words and their properties: Arguments for a lexical approach to pedagogical grammar." In T. Odlin (ed.), *Perspectives on Pedagogical grammar*. Cambridge, Massachusetts: Cambridge University Press. 99–122.

Long, M. 1983. "Does second language instruction make a difference? A review of research." *TESOL Quarterly* 17(3): 359–382.

Long, M. 1991. "Focus on Form: A design feature in language teaching methodology." In K. de Bot, R. Ginsberg and C. Kramsch (eds.), *Foreign language research in cross-cultural perspective*. Amsterdam: John Benjamins. 39–52.

McCarthy, M. 1991. *Discourse analysis for language teachers*. Cambridge, Massachusetts: Cambridge University Press.

McCarthy, M. and R. Carter, R. 1995. *Language and discourse*. New York: Longman.

Nunan, D. 1988. *Understanding language classrooms: A guide for teacher-initiated action*. Cambridge, U.K.: Prentice Hall International.

Pienemann, M. 1985. "Learnability and syllabus construction." In K. Hyltenstam and M. Pienemann (eds.), *Modeling and assessing second language acquisition*. San Diego: College Hill Press. 23–75.

Rigg, P. 1986. "Reading in ESL: learning form kids." In P. Rigg and D. Enright (eds.), *Integrating perspectives: Children in ESL*. Washington, D.C.: TESOL. 55–92.

Rigg, P. 1991. "Whole language teaching in TESOL." *TESOL Quarterly* 25(3): 521–542.

Rubin, J. 1975. "What the good language learner can teach us." *TESOL Quarterly* 9(1): 41–51.

Rutherford, W. 1987. "The meaning of grammatical consciousness-raising." *World Englishes* 6(3): 209–216.

Savignon, S. 1972. *Communicative competence: An experiment in foreign language teaching*. Philadelphia: The Center for Curriculum Development.

Sharwood Smith, M. 1981. "Consciousness raising and second language learner." *Applied Linguistics* 2(2): 159–168.

Sharwood Smith, M. 1993. "Input enhancement in instructed SLA: Theoretical bases." *Studies in Second Language Acquisition* 15: 165–179.

Skinner, B. F. 1957. *Verbal behavior*. New York: Appleton Century-Crofts Inc.

Spada, N. and P. Lightbown. 1993. "Instruction and the development of question in L2 classroom." *Studies in Second Language Acquisition* 15: 205–224.

Strozer, J. 1994. *Language acquisition after puberty*. Washington, D.C.: Georgetown University Press.

Swain, M. 1985. "Communicative competence: Some roles for comprehensible input and comprehensible output in its development." In S. Gass and C. Madden (eds.), *Input in second language acquisition*. Rowley, Massachusetts: Newbury House. 235–253.

Taylor, B. 1981. "Content and written form: A two-way street." *TESOL Quarterly* 15(1): 5–13.

Terrell, T. 1982. "A natural approach." In R. Blair (ed.), *Innovative approaches to language teaching*. Rowley, Massachusetts: Newbury House. 160–173.

Trahey, M. and L. White. 1993. "Positive evidence and preemption in the second language classroom." *Studies in Second Language Acquisition* 15: 181–204.

Ur, P. 1981. *Discussions that work: Task-centered fluency practice*. Cambridge, Massachusetts: Cambridge University Press.

Van Ek, J. 1975. "System development in adult language learning." In C. Yaro, K. Perkins and J. Schachter (eds.), *On TESOL*. Washington, D. C.: TESOL. 322–329.

Wallerstein, N. 1983. *Language and culture in conflict: Problem-posing in the ESL classroom*. Reading, Massachusetts: Addison-Wesley.

Ward, G. and B. Birner. 1995. "Definiteness and the English existential." *Language* 71(4): 722–742.

Watts, R. 1980. "The future of science." In B. Fallis, Y. Wang and Z. Wu (eds.), *LASER: Laboratory in analysis and synthesis for efficient reading*. Guangzhou, China: Guangzahou English Language Center.

Weinberger, S. 1994. "The faster the better: On the L2 transfer of fast speech processes." A talk presented to the Washington linguistic Society, Georgetown University, December, 1994.

Zamel, V. 1982. "Writing: The process of discovering meaning." *TESOL Quarterly* 16(2): 195–209.

Zsiga, E. 1995. "Phonology and phonetics in the education of second language teachers." In J. E. Alatis et al. (eds.), *Georgetown University Round Table on Languages and Linguistics 1995*. Washington, D.C.: Georgetown University Press. 575–587.